Easy French
STEP-BY-STEP

Master High-Frequency Grammar for French Proficiency—*FAST!*

Myrna Bell Rochester

Original Series Author: Barbara Bregstein

New York   Chicago   San Francisco   Athens   London   Madrid
Mexico City   Milan   New Delhi   Singapore   Sydney   Toronto

21 22 23 24 25   LCR   21 20 19 18

ISBN   978-0-07-145387-5
MHID   0-07-145387-3

e-ISBN   978-0-07-164221-7
e-MHID   0-07-164221-8

Library of Congress Control Number 2008928672

McGraw-Hill Education products are available at special quantity discounts to use as
premiums and sales promotions or for use in corporate training programs. To contact a
representative, please visit the Contact Us pages at www.mhprofessional.com.

This book is printed on acid-free paper.

Contents

5 Regular *-re* Verbs in the Present Tense and *-er* Verbs with Spelling Changes 87

6 Expressing the Future with *aller*, Prepositions, and the Verb *faire* 109

Preface

Easy French Step-by-Step will help you learn the basics of French—for speaking, reading, and writing—as quickly and as thoroughly as possible. Prepared for beginners and advanced beginners, this book teaches French grammar and natural, everyday speech in logical order to enable you to develop and build on your language skills.

To take full advantage of the grammatical progression of this book, you'll need to learn each chapter or step—and the sequence within each chapter—one after another. We advise you not to skip around. Each step you take will lead you to the next. Chapters consist of clear grammar explanations, numerous reinforcement activities (with a complete Answer Key), vocabulary study, and short practice readings in French. Try to learn every concept before you undertake the next one.

Chapter 1 teaches the basics of French nouns, their articles, and the descriptive adjectives that modify them. Chapters 2 and 3 present the fundamentals of verb conjugation and verb use in the present tense (to express declarative statements, negation, *yes/no* questions, and information questions). We start with the most common French verbs, **être** (*to be*) and **avoir** (*to have*), and the largest group of verbs (those with infinitives ending in **-er**). Complete model verb conjugations allow you to practice all the forms as you learn their meanings. Chapters 4 through 9 present the rest of the regular and irregular verb system, step-by-step, alongside other topics. Vocabulary was selected based on frequency and thematic usefulness. The vocabulary lists will help expand your communicative skills and allow you to function in various settings.

A variety of exercises and activities follow each grammar step and vocabulary list. You may use them to check your understanding and progress. There is a complete Answer Key in the back of the book, which also includes sample answers to all personalized questions. We suggest that you also keep a journal or diary, jotting down your own vocabulary lists, questions, and statements so you can practice them aloud. If you take control of your own learning, you'll never be bored!

Original, author-written readings are included in every chapter (starting in Chapter 2). They become more challenging in form and content as the book progresses. Use these Reading Comprehension sections to learn additional vocabulary (a list of new words follows each reading), to practice reading aloud, and to gain confidence in reading other materials. Try to answer the follow-up questions in complete sentences.

Easy French Step-by-Step is divided into three parts. The first part gives you the elements of French, using the present tense. You'll notice that the word order of English and French is essentially the same. This makes learning in the early stages very quick. The second part explains the use of object nouns and pronouns, pronominal (or reflexive) verbs, the present participle (equivalent to the English *-ing*), and the imperative (or command form). You will find some of these structures different from English in syntax (word order). The third part of *Easy French Step-by-Step* expands your competence into the past and future tenses, and the conditional and subjunctive moods, with usage specific to French.

English speakers often say that French is easy enough to read—there are an extraordinary number of cognate (similar) words in the two languages—but that it is difficult to pronounce. French does have several sounds that do not exist in English; you'll need to learn those. Most French sounds, however, both consonants and vowels, are quite similar to English. Be sure to use the upcoming Guide to Pronunciation section for study, review, and reference. Return to it whenever you wish to check something. Practice the sounds and examples out loud. If possible, try to practice with a native or near-native French speaker. Throughout the book, remember to read all the French examples and activities aloud to help develop your pronunciation.

Once you have some experience with the sounds and the letter combinations, you will see that they are limited and consistent, which, believe it or not, will make French easy for you to understand and to spell. If you can spell in English, which is notoriously difficult, you will be able to pronounce and spell in French. Supplement your study by listening to French radio and online broadcasts, CDs, movies, videos, and television programs. With modern media, these opportunities are increasingly easy to come by.

This book was prepared with a logical approach that makes it accessible, whether you are a self-study learner—starting out, reviewing, or brushing up on your own—or studying in an organized program. With *Easy French Step-by-Step*, you will see your skills fall quickly into place. In just a few weeks, you will be communicating, reading, and writing in French.

If you learn the French in this book, you'll be well on your way to being able to get along in France and Francophone regions such as Belgium, Luxembourg, French Switzerland, countries in North and West Africa, the province of Quebec, Haiti, Martinique, Guadeloupe, and French Polynesia . . . not to mention exploring their rich cultural and artistic heritages. We hope you enjoy learning and using your French wherever you need it.

Abbreviations

adj.	adjective	*m. pl.*	masculine plural
f. or *fem.*	feminine	*pl.*	plural
fam.	familiar, colloquial	*pol.*	polite
inf.	infinitive	*s.* or *sing.*	singular
inv.	invariable	*s.o./qqun*	someone/**quelqu'un**
m. or *masc.*	masculine	*s.th./qqch*	something/**quelque chose**
f. pl.	feminine plural		

Acknowledgments

Warm thanks to my editors Garret Lemoi and Christopher Brown, as well as to Jenn Tust, Debbie Anderson, Maki Wiering, and Pamela Juárez at McGraw-Hill Professional, and to Barbara Bregstein, who initiated the *Easy* series. To Leon, I'm more grateful than I can express, for your patient support and tech help.

Guide to Pronunciation

Easy French Step-by-Step occasionally includes guides to help you pronounce certain word combinations. When you read them out loud, pronounce them as you would words and syllables in English.

French has several sounds not found in English. They are what make French sound like French! You will see the symbols that represent these special sounds in the Pronunciation columns below, in brackets. Some are printed in capital letters, which will help you spot them easily.

Vowels

Vowels are shown here both with and without accent marks, an important part of French spelling.

The sounds of French vowels are clear and short, generally placed forward in the mouth. With few exceptions, *final* consonants of French words are *silent*.

Letters and Combinations	Pronunciation	Examples and Tips
a, **à**, **â**	[ah]	**sa**, **là**, **pâte**
ai	[ay]	**j'ai**, **mais**
eau, **au**, **aux**	[oh]	**eau**, **auto**, **jaune**, **aux**, **bateaux**
é, **er**, **ez**, **es**, **et** (closed **e**)	[ay]	**pré**, **parler**, **parlez**, **mes**, **et**
è, **ê**, **e** followed by double consonants, *and* final -**et** (open **e**)	[eh]	**chèvre**, **tête**, **belle**, **appelle**, **effet**
e in one-syllable words, *and* in **eu**, **œu** (*cf.* **œufs**)	[uh]	**le**, **que**, **de**, **peu**, **œufs**, **bleu**
		To say the sound [uh], hold your tongue as if to make the [ay] sound and round your lips as if to make the [oh] sound.
eur, **œu**, **œur**	[ERR]	**chanteur**, **leur**, **sœur**, **œuf**, **œuvre**, **heure**
		When followed by **r** or another sounded consonant, this is a more "open" version of the sound [uh].
i, **î**, and **y** as a pronoun	[ee]	**cri**, **fil**, **ils**, **île**, **il y a**
ill (with double **ll**)	[eel]	Pronounced [eel] only in **ville**, **village**, **mille**, **million**, and **tranquille**. Otherwise the **ill** combination contains a *semi-vowel* (see below).
Final **o**, **o** before **s**, and **ô** (closed **o**)	[oh]	**vélo**, **zoo**, **roses**, **hôtel**, **môme**
o before consonants (not **s**) (open **o**)	[uh]	**bonne**, **monnaie**, **homme**
ou, **où**, **oû**	[oo]	**sou**, **où**, **goûtez**, **foule**

or	[uhR]	**port, accord, sorbet, ordre**
u (single **u**), **û**	[U]	**tu, rue, jupe, flûte**
		To pronounce [U], hold your tongue as if to make the [ee] sound, and round your lips as if to make the [oh] sound.

Semi-Vowels

Semi-vowels are written vowel combinations that are pronounced in a single syllable.

Letters and Combinations	Pronunciation	Examples and Tips
ill, ail, eil	[eey], [ahy], [ayy]	**fille, famille, travail, Marseille**
ie, i, *and* **y** (not final)	[y]	**bien, science, voyage, nation, croyez**
oi, ua	[wah]	**moi, quoi, revoir, fois, guano**
oui	[wee]	**oui**
ui, ue, ua	[Uee], [Uay], [Uah]	**huit, fruit, muet, suave** This semi-vowel contains the single **u** sound [U]. (See Vowels section for pronunciation of [U].)

Nasal Vowels

French has several "nasalized" vowels, spelled with the letter combinations **a, e, i, y, o** plus the letters **n** or **m** (examples: **fin, manteau, mon, symbole**).

The nasalized combinations appear at the end of a syllable or a word, or are followed by a silent or sounded consonant (examples: **flan, montagne, lent**).

Pronounce the nasal vowels as a single sound through your mouth and nose at the same time.

The letters **n** or **m** are *not* pronounced in a nasal combination. But they are pronounced when immediately followed by a vowel (examples: **fine, guano**) or when the **n** or **m** is doubled (examples: **homme, bonne**).

Letters and Combinations	Pronunciation	Examples and Tips
an, am, en, em	[A^n]	dans, lampe, trente, exemple
en, in, un, ym, im, yn, ain, aim, ein	[I^n]	bien, matin, vingt, un, sympathique, train, faim, plein
on, om	[O^n]	bonbon, son, combien, fondation

Consonants

Many French consonant sounds (for example: **b, c, d, f, k, l, m, n, p, t, v, z**) closely resemble their English counterparts.

Pronounce the consonants forward in your mouth, and always try to avoid making plosive sounds (puffs of air), particularly with **b, p,** and **t**.

Here are several consonant sounds specific to French. Some variants are the same as in English (for example, "hard" **c** [k], "hard" **g** [g], and **qu** [k]. Sounds not listed here are pronounced nearly like English.

Letters and Combinations	Pronunciation	Examples and Tips
c, cc before a, o, u, or a consonant	[k]	court, chacun, accord, classe
c before i, e, y, and the letter ç	[s]	merci, cercle, cyclisme, François
ch	[sh]	chose, machine
g before a, o, u, or a consonant	[g]	glace, gare
g before e, i, y	[zh]	Georges, gigot
j	[zh]	bonjour, joli, jardin
gn	[ny]	montagne, peigner
h	—	The letter **h** is always silent in French. Some words starting with **h** don't elide articles or pronouns (examples: **le héros, le hasard**).
qu, q	[k]	quelquefois, cinq
r, rr	[R]	riche, bizarre, original The French **r** (as in **bonjour, Robert**) is normally pronounced at the back of the throat, with a slight gargling sound.

s, initial or double s, t in -tion, final x	[s]	**salut**, **fausse**, **nation**, **six**, **dix**
s between two vowels or in -sion	[z]	**mademoiselle**, **excursion**
th	[t]	**Thomas**, **thé** The English "lisp" **th** does not exist in French.
x before a consonant	[ehks]	**excellent**, **expression**
x before a vowel	[ehg]	**examen**, **exemple**

Pronunciation Tips

- When you speak, remember to keep vowel sounds and all syllables short and clear.

- Syllables in French are considered part of an utterance, not part of a word. Syllables start with a consonant: **les idées** [lay-zee-day], **vous allez** [voo-zah-lay]. Words in a phrase and successive words in a sentence are usually linked.

- French sounds, except for the "gargled" sound of **r** [R], are farther forward in the mouth than English.

- There is a slight "fall" or descending intonation on the last word of a sentence or syllable of a word.

- In *yes/no* questions, intonation rises slightly (**Tu arrives?**). It tends to fall slightly at the end of information questions (**Comment allez-vous?**).

Greetings

Bonjour, Mademoiselle. (Madame/Monsieur)	*Hello,/Good morning, Miss.* *(Madam, Ma'am/Sir)*
Salut, ça va?	*Hi!/Hi there! How's it going? (fam.)*
Ça va bien./Ça va mal.	*It's going well./It's going badly.*
Comment allez-vous?	*How are you? (pol.)*
Comment vas-tu?	*How are you? (fam.)*
Très bien, merci, et vous (et toi)?	*Fine, thanks. And you?*
Pas mal, merci, et vous (et toi)?	*Not bad, thanks. And you?*
Comme ci, comme ça.	*So-so.*
Bonsoir.	*Good evening.*
Bonne nuit.	*Good night. (when departing)*

Je m'appelle Suzanne.	*My name is Suzanne.*
Comment vous appelez-vous?	*What's your name?*
Je m'appelle David.	*My name is David.*
Enchanté(e).	*Pleased to meet you.*
Merci beaucoup.	*Thank you very much.*
De rien.	*You're welcome.*
Au revoir.	*Good-bye.*
À bientôt.	*See you soon.*

I

First Elements of French

1

Nouns, Articles, and Descriptive Adjectives

Gender and Number of Nouns and Articles

A noun is a person, place, or thing. In French, all nouns are *masculine* or *feminine* (gender) and *singular* or *plural* (number). The French definite article is used more frequently than *the* is used in English.

The Definite Article

The French *definite article* agrees with the noun in gender and number.

	Singular	Plural
Masculine	le	les
Feminine	la	les
Masculine and feminine before a vowel sound or mute **h**	l'	les

Masculine Nouns

Masculine singular nouns take the definite article **le**. The genders of French nouns are hard to guess. You will learn them as you go along. Pronounce the following nouns with their article. Refer to the Guide to Pronunciation as needed.

le chat (*the cat*)	le frère (*the brother*)
le chien (*the dog*)	le garçon (*the boy*)
le cinéma (*the cinema, film, movies*)	le livre (*the book*)
le cours (*the course, class*)	le téléphone (*the telephone*)
le football (*soccer*)	le vin (*the wine*)

Feminine Nouns

Feminine singular nouns take the definite article **la**.

la banque *(the bank)*	la lampe *(the lamp)*
la boutique *(the store, shop)*	la langue *(the language)*
la chemise *(the shirt)*	la sœur *(the sister)*
la femme *(the woman, wife)*	la table *(the table)*
la jeune fille *(the girl)*	la voiture *(the car)*

Many feminine nouns end in **-e**, but please don't consider this a general rule. The nouns in the following list do not end in **-e**; however, they are all feminine.

Most final consonants are silent in French. In the list below, only the final **-r** is sounded.

la chaleur *(heat, warmth)*	la forêt *(the forest)*
la croix *(the cross)*	la fourmi *(the ant)*
la distraction *(the amusement)*	la main *(the hand)*
la fleur *(the flower)*	la nuit *(the night)*
la fois *(the time [occasion])*	la radio *(the radio)*

Masculine and Feminine Articles Before a Vowel Sound or Mute *h*

The definite article **l'** is used before all singular nouns, maculine and feminine, starting with a vowel or a mute (non-aspirate) **h**. The **-e** or **-a** of the definite article is dropped (elided). When the noun starts with **h**, pronounce the vowel that follows the **h**.

Learn the gender (*m.* or *f.*) in parentheses for each noun. When you begin to attach adjectives to nouns, it will be easier to remember their gender.

l'ami (*m.*) *the friend (m.)*	l'histoire (*f.*) *the story, history*
l'amie (*f.*) *the friend (f.)*	l'homme (*m.*) *the man*
l'anglais (*m.*) *English (language)*	l'hôtel (*m.*) *the hotel*
l'architecte (*m.* or *f.*) *the architect*	l'île (*f.*) *the island*
l'emploi (*m.*) *the job*	l'orange (*f.*) *the orange (fruit)*
l'énergie (*f.*) *energy*	l'université (*f.*) *the university*
l'enfant (*m.* or *f.*) *the child (m. or f.)*	l'usine (*f.*) *the factory*

Singular Nouns and the Definite Article

The definite article indicates a specific person, place, thing, or idea. It also precedes nouns that are used in a general sense.

C'est *l'amie* de ma mère.	*That's (She's) my mother's friend.*
Les Français adorent *le* **football** et *le* **cyclisme**.	*The French love soccer and cycling.*

Le, la, and l'

Remember: **Le** is used with masculine singular nouns beginning with a *consonant*; **la** is used with feminine singular nouns beginning with a *consonant*; and **l'** is used with both masculine and feminine singular nouns beginning with a *vowel* and for most nouns beginning with the letter **h**.

The Initial Letter *h*

The letter **h** is always silent in French. Words starting with the letter **h**—**l'homme**, for example—are pronounced beginning with the first vowel sound. This is called a *mute* **h**.

However, in front of some French words starting with **h**, for historical reasons, the article does *not* elide the **-e** or **-a**. For example:

la *harpe	*the harp*	la *honte	*shame*
le *héros	*the hero*	le *hors-d'œuvre	*the appetizer*

This is called an *aspirate* **h**. This **h** is also a silent letter; it is not pronounced. French dictionaries show the aspirate **h** with a diacritical mark. In this book, words beginning with an aspirate **h** are indicated by an asterisk (*).

Learning the Gender of Nouns

Gender is linked to the noun *word*, rarely to the physical thing or the person. Always learn the gender of a noun with its article: **le livre** (*the book*), **la fenêtre** (*the window*). Genders of nouns starting with a vowel need to be memorized separately: **l'âge** (*m.*) (*the age*), **l'hôtel** (*m.*) (*the hotel*), **l'horloge** (*f.*) (*the clock*).

Several rules can help you guess if a French noun is masculine or feminine:

- Nouns that refer to males are usually masculine; nouns that refer to females are usually feminine: **l'homme** (*m.*) (*the man*); **la femme** (*the woman*).

- The *ending* of a noun can be a clue to its gender. Here are some common masculine and feminine endings. Be aware of *cognate* nouns, which are close to English in spelling and meaning.

Masculine		Feminine	
-eau	le bureau, le château	**-ence**	la différence, l'existence
-isme	le tourisme, l'idéalisme	**-ie**	la tragédie, la compagnie
-ment	le moment, le département	**-ion**	la nation, la fonction
		-té	l'université, la diversité
		-ude	l'attitude, la solitude
		-ure	la littérature, l'ouverture

Watch out for exceptions: **l'eau** (*f.*) (*water*), **la peau** (*skin*), **le silence** (*silence*).

- Nouns adopted from other languages are usually masculine: **le jogging**, **le tennis**, **le jazz**, **le basket-ball**. Exception: **la pizza**.

- Some nouns referring to people indicate gender by their ending. The feminine form often ends in **-e**.

l'Alleman**d**	*the German* (*m.*)	l'Alleman**de**	*the German* (*f.*)
l'Américai**n**	*the American* (*m.*)	l'Américai**ne**	*the American* (*f.*)
l'am**i**	*the friend* (*m.*)	l'am**ie**	*the friend* (*f.*)
l'étudian**t**	*the student* (*m.*)	l'étudian**te**	*the student* (*f.*)
le Françai**s**	*the Frenchman*	la Françai**se**	*the Frenchwoman*

Note that final **d**, **n**, **s**, and **t** are silent in the masculine form, as in the examples above. When followed by **-e** in the feminine form, **d**, **n**, **s**, and **t** are *pronounced*.

- Some nouns that end in **-e** and the names of some professions have only one singular form, used to refer to both males and females. In this case, the article remains the same whether the actual person is male or female.

l'auteur (*m.*)	(***the** author*)	la personne	(***the** person*)
l'écrivain (*m.*)	(***the** writer*)	le professeur	(***the** teacher, professor*)
l'ingénieur (*m.*)	(***the** engineer*)	la sentinelle	(***the** guard, watchman*)
le médecin	(***the** physician*)	la victime	(***the** victim*)

Evolving Style

In contemporary Canadian French and among some other French speakers, you may also see or read a feminine form for a few traditional professions (**la professeure**, **l'écrivaine**, **l'auteure**).

For learners, however, it's best to continue using the masculine forms of these nouns to refer to both males and females.

- For certain nouns referring to people, the gender of the individual is sometimes indicated by the article alone. Such nouns most often end in **-e**; the spelling of the noun does not change when the gender changes.

le journaliste/**la** journaliste	***the*** *journalist*
le secrétaire/**la** secrétaire	***the*** *secretary*
le touriste/**la** touriste	***the*** *tourist*

Exercise 1.1

Write the appropriate singular definite article for each of the nouns. Pronounce each word in French as you write the answer, making sure you know its meaning.

1. _____ ami
2. _____ homme
3. _____ lampe
4. _____ fenêtre
5. _____ hôtel
6. _____ réalisme
7. _____ ingénieur

8. _____ publicité
9. _____ comédie
10. _____ différence
11. _____ médecin
12. _____ sculpture
13. _____ prononciation
14. _____ gâteau

The Indefinite Article

The singular indefinite article in French, corresponding to *a* (*an*) in English, is **un** for masculine nouns and **une** for feminine nouns. The plural of both forms is **des**, roughly equivalent to *some* (though it's usually not translated as *some*). Depending on the context, **un/une** can also mean the number *one*.

	Singular	Plural
Masculine	un	des
Feminine	une	des

Masculine Nouns

Pronounce the examples, learning the gender of each noun along with its article. The indefinite article is the same for nouns beginning with a consonant or a vowel.

un ami	*a friend (m.)*	un hôtel	*an hotel*
un autobus	*a bus*	un jardin	*a garden*
un billet	*a ticket*	un musée	*a museum*
un dictionnaire	*a dictionary*	un pianiste	*a pianist (m.)*
un fauteuil	*an easy chair*	un salon	*a living room*

Feminine Nouns

Pronounce the following examples and learn the meaning of words new to you. A practical way to learn the gender of a noun is to link it with **un** or **une**.

une amie	*a friend (f.)*	une librairie	*a bookstore*
une bibliothèque	*a library*	une mère	*a mother*
une héroïne	*a heroine*	une page	*a (book) page*
une *Hollandaise	*a Dutchwoman*	une valise	*a suitcase*
une leçon	*a lesson*	une ville	*a city*

Note that **l'héroïne** (*f.*) (unlike **le *héros**) is pronounced with a *mute* **h** and elides its definite article. The **h** of **le *héros** is an *aspirate* **h** (no elision).

Plural Nouns

The plural definite article of all nouns is **les**; the plural indefinite article is **des**. Most French nouns are made plural by adding an **-s** to the singular. In addition, note the following plural endings:

- Nouns that end in **-s**, **-x**, or **-z** in the singular stay the same in the plural.

un choi**x**	**des** choi**x**	*a choice, (some) choices*
le cour**s**	**les** cour**s**	*the course, the courses*
le ne**z**	**les** ne**z**	*the nose, the noses*

- Some plural noun endings are irregular.

le bur**eau**	**les** bur**eaux**	*the desk* (or *office*), *the desks* (or *offices*)
un hôpit**al**	**des** hôpit**aux**	*a hospital, (some) hospitals*
le l**ieu**	**les** l**ieux**	*the place, the places*
le trav**ail**	**les** trav**aux**	(*the*) *work, the tasks* (or *jobs*)

- The masculine form is always used to refer to a group (two or more people) that includes at least one male.

un étudian**t** et six étudian**tes**	des étudian**ts**	*students*
un Françai**s** et une Français**e**	des Françai**s**	*French (people)*

Pronouncing the Plural

The final **-s** is usually not pronounced in French:

les touristes [lay too-Reest]

Spoken French distinguishes most singular and plural nouns by the pronunciation of the definite article:

le **touriste** [luh too-Reest] versus *les* **touristes** [lay too-Reest]

When the **-s** of a plural article (**les** or **des**) is followed by a vowel sound, it is pronounced [z] and begins the following syllable; this is called a **liaison**:

les_exercices (*m.*) [lay-zehg-zehR-sees]; **des_hommes** (*m.*) [day-zuhm]

There is no **liaison** with the *aspirate* **h**. Pronounce the nasal vowel **un** [Iⁿ] before **un *héros** [Iⁿ ay-Roh], and do not make the **liaison** with **-s** in **les *héros** [lay ay-Roh]. Pronounce the following out loud:

des_artistes [day-zahr-teest]   les_hommes [lay-zuhm]
les cafés [lay kah-fay]   des *hors-d'œuvre [day
                                       uhr-dERR-vR]
des_étudiants   les restaurants [lay Rehs-toh-RA^n]
    [day-zay-tU-dyA^n]

NOTE: The word **les** (or **des**) ***hors-d'œuvre** is *invariable* in the plural; it has
      no final **-s**.

Exercise 1.2

Write the plural form of each singular noun. Make sure you know its meaning.

1. une artiste _____

2. un *hors-d'œuvre _____

3. le milieu _____

4. l'étudiante _____

5. un Français _____

6. un café _____

7. le chapeau (*hat*) _____

8. l'eau _____

9. la fenêtre _____

10. un choix _____

11. une préférence _____

12. le travail _____

13. le nez _____

14. un cours _____

Exercise 1.3

Pronounce the nouns with their articles, then write the English equivalent. If the gender is not clear from the spelling, show it by writing m. or f.

1. la fenêtre _____

2. le cyclisme _____

3. les hôpitaux _____

4. une sentinelle _____

5. les écrivains _____

6. les amies _____

7. des chapeaux _____

8. le travail _____

9. des choix _____

10. un cours _____

11. des *hors-d'œuvre _____

12. des hommes _____

13. la peau _____

14. l'Allemande _____

15. les livres _____

16. un lieu _____

17. des histoires _____

18. une horloge _____

19. des gâteaux _____

20. la femme _____

Descriptive Adjectives

Descriptive adjectives are used to describe nouns. In French, descriptive adjectives usually *follow* the nouns they modify. Descriptive adjectives may also follow forms of the verb **être** (*to be*): **il/elle est...** (*he/she/it is . . .*); **ils/elles sont...** (*they are . . .*). See Chapter 2 for the conjugation of the verb **être**.

un professeur **intéressant**	*an **interesting** teacher*
un ami **sincère**	*a **sincere** friend*
Il est **pratique**.	*He/It is **practical**.*
Elle est **sportive**.	*She is **athletic**.*

Agreement of Adjectives in Gender and Number

In French, adjectives agree in both gender and number with the nouns they modify. The feminine form of adjectives usually ends in **-e**. The regular plural adds an **s**.

	Singular	Plural
Masculine	un ami intelligent	des amis intelligent**s**
Feminine	une amie intelligent**e**	des amies intelligent**es**

- If the masculine singular form of the adjective ends in an unaccented or silent **-e**, the ending remains the same in the feminine singular.

C'est un homme **extraordinaire**.	*He's an **extraordinary** man.*
C'est une femme **extraordinaire**.	*She's an **extraordinary** woman.*
Paul est **optimiste**.	*Paul is **optimistic**.*
Mais Claire est **pessimiste**.	*But Claire is **pessimistic**.*

- If the singular form of an adjective ends in **-s** or **-x**, the plural ending remains the same.

Bradley est **anglais**; les amis de Bradley sont aussi **anglais**.	*Bradley is **English**; Bradley's friends are also **English**.*
M. Blin est **généreux**; ses (*his*) enfants sont aussi **généreux**.	*Mr. Blin is **generous**; his children are also **generous**.*

- If a plural subject or group contains one or more masculine items or people, the plural adjective is masculine.

Suzanne et Georges sont intelligent**s**.	***Suzanne and Georges** are intelligent.*
Suzanne et Amélie sont intelligent**es**.	***Suzanne and Amélie** are intelligent.*

- Invariable adjectives or adjectival phrases do not change in gender or number.

Ce sont des chaussures **chic** et **bon marché**.	*These are **stylish** and **inexpensive** shoes.*

- Some descriptive adjectives have irregular forms.

Singular

MASCULINE	FEMININE	ENGLISH
conserva**teur**	conserva**trice**	*conservative*
courag**eux**	courag**euse**	*courageous*
fi**er**	fi**ère**	*proud*
gent**il**	gent**ille**	*nice*
natur**el**	natur**elle**	*natural*
paris**ien**	paris**ienne**	*Parisian*
sport**if**	sport**ive**	*athletic*
travaill**eur**	travaill**euse**	*hardworking*

Plural

MASCULINE	FEMININE	ENGLISH
conserva**teurs**	conserva**trices**	*conservative*
courag**eux**	courag**euses**	*courageous*
fi**ers**	fi**ères**	*proud*
gent**ils**	gent**illes**	*nice*
natur**els**	natur**elles**	*natural*
paris**iens**	paris**iennes**	*Parisian*
sport**ifs**	sport**ives**	*athletic*
travaill**eurs**	travaill**euses**	*hardworking*

Other descriptive adjectives with irregular forms include the following examples:

canadien (canadienne)	*Canadian*
cher (chère)	*expensive; dear*
conspirateur (conspiratrice)	*conspiratorial*
ennuyeux (ennuyeuse)	*boring*
naïf (naïve)	*naïve*
paresseux (paresseuse)	*lazy*
sérieux (sérieuse)	*serious*

Adjectives of Color

Adjectives of color normally follow the noun and agree with it in gender and in number.

une chemise **bleue**	*a **blue** shirt*
des livres **gris**	***gray** books*
des chaussures **vertes**	***green** shoes*

- Two adjectives of color, **blanc** and **violet**, have irregular feminine forms.

un crayon **blanc**	*a **white** pencil*
une chemise **blanche**	*a **white** shirt*
des cahiers **violets**	***purple** notebooks*
des voitures **violettes**	***purple** cars*

- Adjectives of color ending in silent **-e** are spelled the same in both masculine and feminine.

des cahiers (*m. pl.*) **jaunes**	***yellow** notebooks*
des fleurs (*f. pl.*) **jaunes**	***yellow** flowers*
une chaise **rouge**	*a **red** chair*
un manteau **rouge**	*a **red** coat*
des pull-overs (*m. pl.*) **roses**	***pink** sweaters*
des chaussettes (*f. pl.*) **roses**	***pink** socks*

- Two adjectives of color, **marron** and **orange**, are **invariable** in gender and number.

des chaussures **marron** (*f. pl.*)	***brown** shoes*
des sacs **orange** (*m. pl.*)	***orange** handbags*

- The names of colors are masculine when used as nouns.

J'aime **le rose** et **le bleu**.	*I love **pink** and **blue**.*

Adjectives That Precede the Noun

Most descriptive adjectives follow the noun, but these adjectives usually *precede* it:

autre	*other*	joli(e)	*pretty*
beau (*m. s.*)	*beautiful, handsome*	mauvais(e)	*bad*
bon(ne)	*good*	même	*same*

grand(e)	*big, tall; great*	nouveau (*m. s.*)	*new*
gros(se)	*fat, big*	petit(e)	*small; short*
jeune	*young*	vieux (*m. s.*)	*old*

- The adjectives **beau** (*beautiful, handsome*), **nouveau** (*new*), and **vieux** (*old*) are irregular. In addition, each has a second masculine singular form that is used before a vowel sound or mute **h**.

	Singular		**Plural**	
Masculine	**beau**		**beaux**	
	un **nouveau** } livre		de **nouveaux** } livres	
	vieux		**vieux**	
Masculine	**bel**		**beaux**	
Before Vowel	un **nouvel** } objet		de **nouveaux** } objets	
Sound	**vieil**		**vieux**	
Feminine	**belle**		**belles**	
	une **nouvelle** } auto		de **nouvelles** } autos	
	vieille		**vieilles**	

Pronounce the examples below, and practice by substituting other nouns for **maison** and **homme**. What changes do you need to make in the articles and adjectives?

C'est **une belle** maison.	*It's **a pretty** house.*
C'est **un vieil** homme.	*He's **an old** man.*
C'est **le nouveau** professeur.	*That's **the new** teacher.*

- When a plural adjective precedes a plural noun, the indefinite article **des** usually shortens to **de/d'**, as you may have noticed in the previous chart.

de grandes autos	(**some**) **big** *cars*
de nouvelles idées	(**some**) **new** *ideas*
d'autres amis	(**some**) **other** *friends*

However, colloquial French often retains **des** before the plural.

| Ce sont **des bons** copains! | *They're **good** pals!* |

- A few adjectives that usually precede nouns can also follow them. This change of position causes a change in meaning. For example:

un **ancien** professeur	(*a **former** teacher*)
une maison **ancienne**	(*an **ancient** [**very old**] house*)
le **dernier** exercice	(*the **final** exercise*)

l'année **dernière** (*f.*)   (***last*** *year*)
un **pauvre** garçon   (*an **unfortunate** boy*)
un garçon **pauvre**   (*a **poor** [not rich] boy*)
une **chère** amie   (*a **dear** friend*)
un repas **cher**   (*an **expensive** meal*)

 ## Key Vocabulary

Learn these common adjectives to answer the question: **Comment est... ?**
(*What is . . . like?*) when you want to describe something or someone. Answer
with **Il est.../Elle est...** (*He/She/It is . . .*).

Les adjectifs descriptifs (Descriptive Adjectives)

agréable   (*pleasant*)
avare   (*stingy*)
beau (bel, belle)   (*beautiful/handsome*)
bon (bonne)   (*good*)
bon marché (*inv.*)   (*inexpensive*)
cher (chère)   (*expensive; dear*)
chic (*inv.*)   (*stylish, chic*)
content(e)   (*happy, pleased*)
costaud(e)   (*sturdy [person]*)
dernier (-ière)   (*last, final*)
désolé(e)   (*sorry*)
difficile   (*difficult*)
drôle   (*funny*)
excellent(e)   (*excellent*)
facile   (*easy*)
fantastique   (*wonderful*)
fatigué(e)   (*tired*)
formidable   (*fabulous*)
fort(e)   (*strong*)
grand(e)   (*big, tall; great*)
gros(se)   (*fat*)

heureux (-euse)   (*happy*)
idéaliste   (*idealistic*)
intelligent(e)   (*intelligent*)
intéressant(e)   (*interesting*)
jeune   (*young*)
joli(e)   (*pretty*)
laid(e)   (*ugly*)
mauvais(e)   (*bad*)
mince   (*thin*)
nouveau/nouvel/nouvelle (*new*)
pauvre   (*poor*)
petit(e)   (*small; short*)
premier (-ière)   (*first*)
riche   (*rich*)
sincère   (*sincere*)
sociable   (*friendly*)
sympathique   (*nice*)
timide   (*shy, timid*)
triste   (*sad*)
typique   (*typical*)
vieux/vieil/vieille   (*old*)

Les couleurs (Colors)

blanc(he)   (*white*)
bleu(e)   (*blue*)

blond(e)   (*blond[e]*)
brun(e)   (*dark-haired*)

gris(e) (*gray*)   rose   (*pink*)
jaune (*yellow*)   rouge   (*red*)
marron (*inv.*) (*brown*)   vert(e) (*green*)
noir(e) (*black*)   violet(te) (*purple*)
orange (*inv.*) (*orange*)

Exercise 1.4

Write the feminine singular form of the adjectives given.

1. intéressant _____   11. cher _____

2. naïf _____   12. conservateur _____

3. agréable _____   13. beau _____

4. sérieux _____   14. gros _____

5. jaune _____   15. actif _____

6. marron _____   16. gentil _____

7. bleu _____   17. travailleur _____

8. costaud _____   18. drôle _____

9. fier _____   19. vieux _____

10. chic _____   20. heureux _____

Exercise 1.5

Complete the phrases with the correct adjective that agrees in gender and number.

1. le _____ (*old*) homme

2. la situation _____ (*difficult*)

3. la _____ (*beautiful*) maison

4. la personne _____ (*nice*)

5. les fleurs _____ (*yellow*)

6. des amis _____ (*sincere*)

7. un _____ (*great*) homme

8. une voiture _____ (*ancient*)

9. d' _____ (*former*) professeurs

10. des appartements _____ (*inexpensive*)

11. une comédie _____ (*funny*)

12. un livre _____ (*interesting*)

Key Vocabulary

In French, names of all languages are *masculine*. They often correspond to
the masculine singular form of the noun of nationality: **l'anglais** (*m.*) (*the
English language*); **l'Anglaise** (*the Englishwoman*). Adjectives of nationality
and languages are *not* capitalized, but nouns are.

Les nationalités (Nationalities)

ADJECTIFS	PERSONNES	LANGUES
allemand(e) (*German*)	un(e) Allemand(e)	l'allemand
américain(e)	un(e) Américain(e)	l'anglais
anglais(e) (*English*)	un(e) Anglais(e)	l'anglais
belge (*Belgian*)	un(e) Belge	le français, le flamand
canadien(ne)	un(e) Canadien(ne)	l'anglais, le français
chinois(e)	un(e) Chinois(e)	le chinois
espagnol(e) (*Spanish*)	un(e) Espagnol(e)	l'espagnol
français(e) (*French*)	un(e) Français(e)	le français
haïtien(ne)	un(e) Haïtien(ne)	le français, le créole
israélien(ne)	un(e) Israélien(ne)	l'hébreu
italien(ne)	un(e) Italien(ne)	l'italien
japonais(e)	un(e) Japonais(e)	le japonais
libanais(e) (*Lebanese*)	un(e) Libanais(e)	l'arabe
marocain(e) (*Moroccan*)	un(e) Marocain(e)	l'arabe, le français
mexicain(e)	un(e) Mexicain(e)	l'espagnol
russe (*Russian*)	un(e) Russe	le russe
sénégalais(e)	un(e) Sénégalais(e)	le français, le wolof
suisse	un(e) Suisse	l'allemand, le français, l'italien, le romanche
vietnamien(ne)	un(e) Vietnamien(ne)	le vietnamien, le français

Exercise 1.6

Write the plural form of each of the noun-adjective phrases.

1. une lampe bleue _____

2. un ami sérieux _____

3. le chat gris _____

4. une Suisse sympathique _____

5. une personne costaude _____

6. le bel appartement _____

7. un jeune garçon _____

8. un examen difficile _____

9. le dernier train _____

10. le quartier ancien _____

 Exercise 1.7

Translate the phrases into French.

1. the dark-haired men _____

2. the kind woman _____

3. (some) red shoes _____

4. the old hotels _____

5. the beautiful apartments _____

6. the interesting courses _____

7. the courageous heroes _____

8. the rich appetizers _____

9. (some) expensive cars _____

10. (some) idealistic Americans _____

11. the great universities _____

12. (some) new books _____

13. the orange hats _____

14. (some) sad tragedies _____

15. the hardworking teachers _____

16. (some) proud people (persons) _____

2

The Verbs *être* and *avoir,* Subject Pronouns, and Negation

The Verb

The *verb* in French is the most important element of a statement or question, since it conveys so much information: the person, the action or state, and the time of the action.

An *infinitive* is the unconjugated form of the verb. For example, *to be* is an English infinitive. French infinitives are single words; they do not contain the element *to*.

Conjugations are the verb forms that belong to particular subjects. *I am* and *he is* are conjugations of the English infinitive *to be*.

The Verbs *être* (to be) and *avoir* (to have)

Être (*to be*) and **avoir** (*to have*) are the most common French verbs. It makes sense to learn them first. You will find **être** and **avoir** everywhere: in descriptions, in idiomatic expressions, as linking verbs, and as helping (auxiliary) verbs in compound tenses.

Like many common French verbs, **être** and **avoir** are *irregular*—with special conjugation patterns. You will begin to learn *regular* verbs in Chapter 3.

Je **suis** américain.	*I **am** American.*
Nous **avons** deux enfants.	*We **have** two children.*

Être and Subject Pronouns

All verb conjugations in French have six "persons." Three are singular, corresponding to: *I, you (familiar),* and *he/she/it/one.* Three are plural, corresponding to: *we, you (pol. singular, and fam. or pol. plural),* and *they.* The verb **être** has six different conjugated forms:

Present Tense of être   *(to be)*

		SINGULAR
1st Person	je **suis**	*I am*
2nd Person	tu **es**	*you are (fam.)*
3rd Person	il **est**	*he/it is*
	elle **est**	*she/it is*
	on **est**	*one is, we/they are*
		PLURAL
1st Person	nous **sommes**	*we are*
2nd Person	vous **êtes**	*you are (pol. s.; fam./pol. pl.)*
3rd Person	ils **sont**	*they (m. pl.) are*
	elles **sont**	*they (f. pl.) are*

Subject Pronouns

As in English, conjugated forms of French verbs are preceded by one of the following:

- A *common noun* (a person, animal, place, thing, or idea)

- A *proper noun* (a name)

- Or a *subject pronoun* (a word used in place of a noun)

Subject Pronouns

PERSON	SINGULAR		PLURAL	
1st	je/j'	*I*	nous	*we*
2nd	tu	*you (fam.)*	vous	*you (pol. s.; fam./pol. pl.)*
3rd	il	*he/it (m.)*	ils	*they (m. pl. or mixed)*
	elle	*she/it (f.)*	elles	*they (f. pl.)*
	on	*one/we/they*		

Gender and Number

Remember that all French nouns have gender and number: Every noun is either masculine or feminine (**le livre**, **la table**), and either singular or plural (**l'hôtel** [*m.*], **les hôtels**).

The subject pronoun of a conjugated verb corresponds to the gender and number of the noun (a person or thing) that it replaces.

La table est dans le salon.	***The table is*** *in the living room.*
Elle (La table) **est** dans le salon.	***It is*** *in the living room.*

Context will help you determine the person or object the subject pronoun refers to.

Uses of Subject Pronouns

Conjugated verb forms in French are always preceded by a noun or a subject pronoun.

Verb Forms Without Subjects

Verb infinitives, commands (or imperatives; covered in Chapter 11), and present participles (Chapter 12) do *not* include a noun subject or a subject pronoun.

- To avoid repetition, the subject pronoun often replaces a noun.

Richard est en ville.	***Richard is*** *downtown.*
Il est au cinéma.	***He is*** *at the movies.*
Mes sœurs sont en voyage.	***My sisters are*** *on a trip.*
Elles sont à Lille.	***They're*** *in Lille.*

- **Je** (*I*). In French, **je** is capitalized only when it begins a sentence. Like the definite articles **le** and **la**, **je** drops (elides) the letter **-e** before a vowel sound. It is replaced by an apostrophe and closed up to the conjugated verb.

Je suis content; **j'ai** un nouveau travail.	***I am*** *happy;* ***I have*** *a new job.*

- **Tu** and **vous** (*you*). **Tu** (with its verb form) is always singular. It is used to speak to one person who is a friend or relative, to a child, or to a pet. **Vous** is used to speak to someone you don't know well or to anyone with whom you have a relationship of respect, for example, strangers, new acquaintances, salespeople, or professionals. The plural of both **tu** and **vous** is **vous** (with its conjugated verb form).

Sylvie, **tu es** étudiante?	*Sylvie, **are you** a student?*
Pardon, Madame, **vous êtes** la mère de Sylvie?	*Excuse me, Ma'am, **are you** Sylvie's mother?*
Attention les enfants! **Vous êtes** prêts?	*Children! **Are you** ready?*

Do as the Natives Do

As you get to know a native speaker of French, a good rule of thumb for the nonnative is to wait until your new friend addresses you with **tu**, before starting to use **tu** with him or her.

- **Il** and **ils**; **elle** and **elles**. The English subject pronouns *he, she, it* (singular), and *they* (plural) are expressed by **il** or **ils** (for masculine nouns) and **elle** or **elles** (for feminine nouns).

Elles sont formidables!	***They*** *(fem. persons or things) **are** fantastic!*
Il est drôle.	***He/It*** *(**The puppy**[?]) **is** funny.*

The plural **ils** (*they, m. pl.*) refers to any group that includes at least one masculine noun.

Voilà Marie, Anne et Patrick. —**Ils sont** en retard!	*There's Marie, Anne, and Patrick.* —***They're*** *late!*

- **On**. The subject pronoun **on** (third-person singular) is used in French to convey the English indefinite subjects *one, we, people,* and *they.*

Alors, **on est d'accord**?	*O.K., so **we agree**?*
Le matin, **on est en bonne forme**.	*In the morning, **they** (**we, people**) **feel good**.*

Modern speech often replaces **nous** (*we*) by **on**. The adjective can be spelled in the singular or the plural.

Vous êtes fatigués? —Oui, **on est** très fatigué(s)! (—Oui, **nous sommes** très fatigué[e]s!)	*You're tired?* —*Yes, **we're all** (**everybody's**) very tired!*

Exercise 2.1

Complete the sentences, translating the subject pronouns that precede the forms of
être. *Make sure you understand the meaning of each sentence.*

EXAMPLE: (We) _____*Nous*_____ sommes fatigués.

1. (*You, pl.*) _____ êtes en ville?

2. (*I*) _____ suis à la maison.

3. (*They, f.*) _____ sont au travail.

4. (*We*) _____ sommes très sympathiques!

5. (*You, sing.*) _____ es architecte?

6. (*I*) _____ suis grand et beau.

7. (*They, m.*) _____ sont français.

8. Les Américains sont en voyage. (*They*) _____ sont dans le train.

9. (*Georges and Marilyn, you*) _____ êtes drôles!

10. Le prof est absent. (*He*) _____ est en vacances.

 Exercise 2.2

Complete each of the sentences with the correct form of **être**. *Focus on meaning.*

EXAMPLE: L'homme ___*est*___ beau. La femme ___*est*___ belle aussi.

1. Le parfum _____ de France.

2. Ils _____ médecins. Elle _____ dentiste.

3. Les touristes _____ du Portugal?

4. Les frères de Paul _____ riches!

5. Le vieil hôtel _____ excellent.

6. Nous _____ les amis de Robert.

7. Les chaussures _____ en cuir (*leather*).

8. La dame et le monsieur _____ suédois.

9. Je _____ de Lyon. Vous aussi, vous _____ de France?

10. L'appartement des étudiants _____ bien situé.

Uses of *être*

As you know, **être** is the equivalent of *to be* in English.

Nous sommes français.	*We're French.*
Tu es au restaurant?	*You're (**Are you**) at the restaurant?*

- **Être** is often followed by an expression of location (using a preposition) or a descriptive adjective.

Marianne **est à la campagne**.	*Marianne **is in the country**.*
Nous **sommes en voiture**.	*We **are in the car**.*

- When a form of **être** is followed by an adjective, the adjective agrees with the subject of the sentence in gender and number.

Les roses rouges **sont belles**.	*Red roses **are beautiful**.*
Mon appartement **est** assez **grand**.	*My apartment **is** rather **large**.*

- The French definite article (**le/la/les**) or indefinite article (**un/une/des**) is *omitted* after forms of **être** for simple (unmodified) identification of nationality, religion, or profession.

Je suis **dentiste**.	*I'm **a dentist**.*
Elles sont **protestantes**?	*Are they (f.) **Protestant**?*
Chantal est **sénégalaise**.	*Chantal is **Senegalese**.*

Adjectives of religion, such as **protestant(e)(s)**, and nationality, for example, **sénégalais(e)**, are *not* capitalized in French.

- With nouns that are *modified* (accompanied by an adjective or other descriptor), use the indefinite subject pronoun **ce** (**c'est.../ce sont...**). With **c'est** and **ce sont**, articles or possessive adjectives (Chapter 10) are always used before a noun. At times, the context will identify the person.

C'est un professeur **d'histoire**.	*He's/She's a history teacher.*
Ce sont mes amies **françaises**.	*These/Those are my French friends.*
C'est le médecin **de mon fils**.	*He's/She's/That's my son's doctor.*

- When you use **c'est** or **ce sont** to describe nationalities, be sure to include the article and capitalize the noun of nationality.

Voici Bill. **C'est un Américain**.	*Here's Bill. **He's an American**.*
Ce sont des Suisses, de Lausanne.	*They're Swiss, from Lausanne.*

Exercise 2.3

Translate these sentences into French.

1. I am in the garden.

    _____.

2. The red flowers are beautiful.

    _____.

3. They (*f.*) are on (**sur**) the table.

    _____.

4. We are in front of (**devant**) the library.

    _____.

5. Charles is a teacher. He's young and intelligent.

    _____.

6. You're (*m., fam.*) sad and tired? I'm (*f.*) sorry!

    _____!

7. Marie-Laure is in the car. She's late!

    _____!

8. You're (*pol.*) from (**du**) Canada?

    _____?

9. People (**On**) are nice in this neighborhood (**ce quartier**).

    _____.

10. Sara and Patrick are on a trip. They are in (**à**) Montreal.

    _____.

Exercise 2.4

Complete the paragraph, choosing among: **il/elle est, ils/elles sont, c'est,** *or* **ce sont.** *Remember:* **C'est/ce sont** *is used when a noun is modified (either with an article, or an article and an adjective).*

EXAMPLES: Alain est médecin. ____*C'est*____ un jeune médecin travailleur.

Michelle est une voisine (neighbor). ____*Elle*____ ____*est*____

sociable.

1. Jeanne est architecte. _____ _____ travailleuse.

2. Mes parents sont canadiens. _____ _____ des Québécois fiers.

3. Loïc est de Bretagne. _____ _____ breton.

4. Mon voisin est gentil. _____ un voisin super sympathique.

5. Nommez une ville américaine d'origine française. _____ La Nouvelle-Orléans.

6. Comment est Claude? Eh bien, _____ _____ très intelligent, mais un peu arrogant.

 Exercise 2.5

Complete each sentence using the conjugated forms of **être,** *the subject pronoun +* **être,** *or* **c'est/ce sont.**

1. Voyons, Michel! Nous _____ très en retard! Les amis _____ sûrs que tu _____ toujours ponctuel. Mais, _____ _____ des amis très tolérants!

2. Odette, tu _____ américaine? —Non, je _____ martiniquaise, de Fort-de-France.

3. Rosa et Mario, vous _____ mexicains? —Non, _____ _____ italiens, mais Jorge _____ mexicain.

4. Robert _____ ingénieur. _____ un ingénieur très créatif. Nous _____ fiers de lui (of him).

5. Khaled, _____ (pol.) _____ chrétien ou musulman? —_____ _____ musulman, mais une partie de la famille _____ chrétienne. _____ _____ des coptes (Coptic).

Reread the previous sentences in the exercise, and correct these statements using subject pronouns.

6. Michel est généralement à l'heure. Non, _____.

7. Odette est américaine. Non, _____.

8. Rosa et Mario sont mexicains. Non, _____.

9. Robert est biologiste. Non, _____.

10. Dans la famille de Khaled, les chrétiens sont catholiques.

    Non, _____.

Expressions with *être*

Numerous fixed expressions use the verb **être**.

> être à l'heure/en retard/en avance   (*to be on time/late/early*)
> être d'accord (avec)   (*to agree [with]*)
> être de retour   (*to be back [from a trip or outing]*)
> être en coton/en cuir/en briques...   (*to be made of cotton/leather/brick . . .*)
> être en train de/d' + *inf.*   (*to be [in the midst of] doing [s.th.]*)
> être en vacances   (*to be on vacation*)
> être prêt(e) (à + *inf.*)   (*to be ready [to do s.th.]*)
> être sur le point de/d' + *inf.*   (*to be about to [do s.th.]*)

Nous **sommes en train de** travailler.	We **are** (**in the midst of**) working.
Je **suis** tout à fait **d'accord**!	I **agree** completely! (**I couldn't agree** more!)
Les chaussures **sont en cuir**.	The shoes **are** (**made of**) **leather**.
Vous **êtes en vacances** en août?	**Are** you **on vacation** in August?
Attention, Annie! Tu **es** déjà **en retard**!	Careful, Annie! You **are** already **late**!

Quelle heure est-il?

Learn **Quelle heure est-il?** (*What time is it?*) as a fixed expression.

Quelle heure est-il?	What time is it?
—Il est deux heures.	—It's two o'clock.

You will learn more about question forms in Chapter 3 and about telling time in Chapter 4.

Exercise 2.6

Complete the sentences with expressions chosen from the list. Use each expression once with the correct form of **être**.

> être sur le point de   être de retour
> être d'accord   être en coton
> être en train de   être prêt(e)
> être en vacances

1. Claudine et moi voyageons maintenant (*now*) en Italie.
   Nous _____.

2. Les enfants sont très occupés. Ils _____ jouer (*play*)
   au volley.

3. Ma sœur rentre (*is coming home*) de vacances. Elle _____
   aujourd'hui.

4. O.K., on _____? C'est de la pizza ce soir (*this
   evening*)?

5. Mon T-shirt rose? Il _____.

6. Tu (*m.*) _____? Il est tard. Le film commence
   bientôt (*soon*). Nous _____ quitter la maison.

Key Vocabulary

These common words (adverbs and conjunctions) help link ideas and enliven adjectives, nouns, and verbs. Their placement in a sentence closely resembles that of their English equivalents.

Conjonctions, qualificatifs, et adverbes (**Conjunctions, Qualifiers, and Adverbs**)

assez (*fairly, rather*)	et (*and*)
assez de (*enough*)	ici (*here*)
aujourd'hui (*today*)	là-bas (*over there*)
aussi (*also*)	maintenant (*now*)
beaucoup (de) (*much, many, a lot*)	mais (*but*)
bien (*very, well*)	ou (*or*)
donc (*therefore, so*)	parfois (*sometimes*)

peu (*hardly*, *not very*)	souvent (*often*)
plutôt (*rather*)	toujours (*always*)
quelquefois (*sometimes*)	très (*very*)
rarement (*rarely*)	trop (de) (*too, too much* [*many*])
si (*if*)	un peu (de) (*a little*)

Je suis de Bruxelles, **mais** Sylvie
    est de Paris.

*I'm from Brussels, **but** Sylvie is*
    from Paris.

Claude est professeur, **donc** il
    est en vacances.

*Claude is a teacher, **so** he's on*
    vacation.

Nous sommes **parfois** mécontents.

*We are **sometimes** unhappy.*

Tu es **un peu** fatiguée?

*Are you **a little** tired?*

Les repas sont **trop** chers **ici**.

*The meals are **too** expensive **here**.*

 Exercise 2.7

Translate the words in parentheses to complete the sentences.

1. (*sometimes, very*) Je suis _____ _____ heureuse.

2. (*here, today*) Il est _____ _____?

3. (*now*) Tu es au travail _____?

4. (*today, a little*) _____, nous sommes _____ en retard.

5. (*rather*) Les livres sont _____ chers dans cette librairie.

6. (*often*) Elles sont _____ au café.

7. (*always*) Nous sommes _____ à l'heure.

8. (*but, very*) Sylvie est petite, _____ Sylvain est _____ grand.

9. (*very*) Vous êtes _____ belles ce soir!

10. (*much, too*) Le dessert est _____ _____ riche.

11. (*a little*) Les enfants sont _____ fatigués.

12. (*over there*) Marc est _____, devant la pharmacie.

Negation with *ne... pas*

To make a sentence negative in French, **ne** is placed before a conjugated verb and **pas** after the verb. **Ne** becomes **n'** before a vowel or vowel sound.

Je **ne suis pas** français.	*I **am not** French.*
Elle **n'est pas** à l'université.	*She **isn't** at the university.*
Nous **ne sommes pas** catholiques.	*We **aren't** Catholic.*

 ## Exercise 2.8

*Answer each of the questions using a complete sentence with the negative of **être**. Remember, **ne** becomes **n'** before a vowel sound.*

1. Arlette est vieille? Non, _____.

2. Vous êtes acteur (actrice)? _____.

3. Nous sommes en retard? _____.

4. Tu es à la maison? _____.

5. Léon et Chantal sont de retour? _____.

6. Tes sœurs sont d'accord? _____.

7. Georges est en train de danser? _____.

8. Je suis trop fière? _____.

The Verb *avoir* (to have)

Avoir most often expresses ownership or possession.

Present Tense of avoir *(to have)*

SINGULAR

1st	j'**ai**	*I **have***
2nd	tu **as**	*you **have** (fam.)*
3rd	il/elle/on **a**	*he/she/it/one **has**, we **have***

PLURAL

1st	nous **avons**	*we **have***
2nd	vous **avez**	*you **have** (pol. s.; fam./pol. pl.)*
3rd	ils/elles **ont**	*they **have***

Tu **as** un chat?	*Do you **have** a cat?*
—Non, mais j'**ai** un perroquet.	*—No, but I **have** a parrot.*
Nous **avons** de bons amis.	*We **have** good friends.*
Nos amis **ont** du temps aujourd'hui.	*Our friends **have** time today.*

Ne... *pas de*... with *avoir*

In negative sentences with **avoir** and also with most other verbs, the indefinite article **un/une/des** becomes **de/d'** after the negation **ne... pas**. The form **d'** is used before vowel sounds. The noun that follows **de/d'** can be singular or plural.

Michel **a une** bicyclette.	*Michel **has a** bicycle.*
Marlène **n'a pas de** bicyclette et je **n'ai pas de** voiture.	*Marlène **doesn't have** a bicycle, and I **don't have** a car.*
Nous **n'avons pas de** bagages.	*We **have no** luggage.*
Vous **n'avez pas d'**amis?	*You **don't have** (**any**) friends?*

More About Definite and Indefinite Articles with *ne... pas*

The *definite* article **le/la/les** is always retained after **ne... pas**.

Je **n'ai pas *les*** bonnes adresses.	*I **don't have the** right addresses.*
Tu **n'as pas *le*** livre d'Antoine?	***Don't* you *have** Antoine's book?*

The *indefinite* article **un/une/des** is never dropped after the negation of the verb **être**.

Ce **n'est pas *un*** vin rouge. Il est blanc.	*This **isn't a** red wine. It's white.*
Ce **ne sont pas *des*** touristes.	*Those **aren't** tourists.*

Il y a... (There is . . . , There are . . .)

The expression **il y a** (*there is, there are*) points out people, ideas, or objects. **Il y a** is invariable (does not change) in the plural.

Il y a des problèmes dans ce document.	***There are** problems in this document.*
Il y a un médecin dans la salle?	***Is there a** doctor in the room (hall)?*

Il y a une touriste devant le musée.	**There's a** tourist in front of the museum.
Il y a des arbres dans le parc.	**There are** trees in the park.

The negative of **il y a** is **il n'y a pas de/d'**, followed by a singular or plural noun.

Il n'y a pas d'arbres dans mon jardin.	**There aren't any** trees in my garden (yard).
Il n'y a pas de restaurant ouvert?	**Isn't there an** open restaurant (a restaurant that's open)?

Exercise 2.9

Translate each sentence into French using a form of the verb **avoir**.

1. I have a red bicycle (**vélo**, *m.*). _____.

2. Arthur has a new friend (*f.*). _____.

3. You (*fam.*) have a lot of homework (**devoirs**)?

   _____?

4. They (*f.*) don't have a garden. _____.

5. I don't have friends here. _____.

6. Simon and Annie have an old car. _____.

7. We don't have bicycles. _____.

8. There are too many tourists in town. _____.

9. There's a difficult problem in class. _____.

10. There aren't enough restaurants at the university.

    _____.

Exercise 2.10

Make these statements negative (if affirmative) or affirmative (if negative).

1. Il y a beaucoup de devoirs ce soir.

   _____.

2. Nous n'avons pas de rendez-vous (*m.*) aujourd'hui.

_____.

3. Il y a une voiture devant la maison.

_____.

4. Je n'ai pas de dictionnaire (*m.*).

_____.

5. Ils sont en classe ce matin (*this morning*).

_____.

6. Mes parents ont un nouvel appartement.

_____.

7. Je suis souvent à la montagne le week-end.

_____.

8. Elles n'ont pas d'idées concrètes.

_____.

9. Tu n'as pas de copains (*close friends*) ici?

_____?

10. Il n'y a pas assez de livres pour les étudiants.

_____.

Expressions with *avoir*

The verb **avoir** occurs in numerous idiomatic expressions. Many ideas conveyed with expressions using **avoir** relate to feelings or sensations. They often have English equivalents that use the verb *to be*.

avoir... ans   (*to be . . . years old*)
avoir chaud   (*to be warm, hot*)
avoir froid   (*to be cold*)
avoir faim   (*to be hungry*)
avoir soif   (*to be thirsty*)
avoir sommeil   (*to be sleepy*)
avoir envie de   (*to feel like*)
avoir besoin de   (*to need [to]*)
avoir peur (de)   (*to be afraid [of]*)

avoir honte (de) *(to be ashamed [of])*
avoir mal (à) *(to have a pain, a[n] -ache [in])*
avoir raison *(to be right)*
avoir tort *(to be wrong)*
avoir l'air (de) *(to seem)*
avoir l'habitude de *(to be accustomed, used to)*
avoir de la chance *(to be lucky)*
avoir lieu *(to take place [an event])*

J'ai vingt ans.	*I am twenty years old.*
J'ai faim et j'**ai mal à la tête.**	*I am hungry, and I have a headache.*
Nous **avons de la chance!** Les jeux Olympiques **ont lieu** ici.	*We are lucky! The Olympic games are taking place here.*
Elle **a tort**; je **n'ai pas sommeil.**	*She is wrong; I am not sleepy.*
Nous **n'avons pas envie de** danser.	*We don't feel like dancing.*

Avoir... ans: Asking Someone's Age

Learn **Quel âge avez-vous?** or **Quel âge as-tu?** (*How old are you?*) as a fixed expression. You will learn more about question forms in Chapter 3.

Quel âge avez-vous?	*How old are you?*
—**J'ai** vingt-neuf ans.	—*I'm twenty-nine.*

Exercise 2.11

Translate the sentences into French, using idiomatic expressions with **avoir**.

1. I'm cold, and I'm sleepy.

 _____.

2. He's twenty-five (**vingt-cinq**) years old.

 _____.

3. We need a new apartment.

 _____.

4. She's lucky in (**à**) Las Vegas!

 _____!

5. We're hungry! We feel like having lunch (**déjeuner**).

   _____.

6. Are you (*fam.*) ashamed of your (**tes**) bad grades (**notes**, *f.*)?

   _____?

7. The children are thirsty.

   _____.

8. The meeting (**La réunion**) takes place this evening.

   _____.

9. She doesn't have a headache today.

   _____.

10. They (*m.*) aren't accustomed to dining late (**dîner tard**).

   _____.

 Exercise 2.12

*Answer the personal questions in complete French sentences, using idiomatic expressions with **avoir**. Then repeat the answers aloud.*

1. Quel âge avez-vous?

   _____.

2. Vous avez froid en hiver (*winter*) ici?

   _____.

3. Vous avez raison ou tort dans les discussions politiques?

   _____.

4. Les fêtes ont lieu ce week-end?

   _____.

5. Vous avez mal à la tête quand (*when*) vous avez faim?

   _____.

6. Votre chien a l'air intelligent?

   _____.

7. Vous avez envie de danser ce soir (*this evening*)?

   _____.

8. Les étudiants ont sommeil en classe? Et le professeur?

   _____.

9. Le professeur a toujours raison?

   _____.

10. Les petits enfants ont souvent peur des clowns?

    _____.

 # Key Vocabulary

Your home or apartment and its furnishings make up your most familiar surroundings.

La maison (The House)

- **Noms** (*Nouns*)

Make sure to learn the gender (masculine or feminine) of each of these nouns.

la bibliothèque (*library, study*)	la glace (*mirror*)
le bois (*wood*)	le jardin (*garden, yard*)
le cahier (*notebook*)	la lampe (*lamp, light*)
le canapé (*sofa*)	le lit (*bed*)
la chaise (*chair*)	la maison (*house*)
la chambre (*bedroom*)	le mur (*wall*)
la cheminée (*fireplace; chimney*)	l'ordinateur (*m.*) (*computer*)
la clé (*key*)	le piano (*piano*)
le crayon (*pencil*)	le placard (*cupboard; closet*)
la cuisine (*kitchen*)	le plafond (*ceiling*)
la cuisinière (*stove*)	le plancher (*floor*)
le fauteuil (*armchair, easy chair*)	la porte (*door*)
la fenêtre (*window*)	le réveil (*alarm clock*)
le four (*oven*)	les rideaux (*m.*) (*curtains*)
le foyer (*entryway, hearth*)	la salle à manger (*dining room*)
le frigo (*refrigerator*)	la salle de bains (*bathroom*)

le salon   (*living room*)   le tapis   (*rug, carpet*)
le stylo   (*pen*)   la terrasse   (*patio, terrace*)
le tableau   (*picture, painting*)   la vidéo (le DVD)   (*video [DVD]*)

- **Adjectifs** *(Adjectives)*

In the following list, the feminine forms of adjectives are shown only if the adjective changes.

agréable   (*pleasant*)   joli(e)   (*pretty*)
ancien(ne)   (*old; former*)   long(ue)   (*long*)
bleu marine   (*navy blue*)   ma, mon, mes   (*my*)
confortable   (*comfortable*)   privé(e)   (*private*)
extérieur(e)   (*outside*)   propre   (*clean*)
fin(e)   (*fine, delicate*)   simple   (*simple*)
gris(e)   (*gray*)   spacieux (-euse)   (*spacious*)
intérieur(e)   (*inside, interior*)

- **Adverbes** *(Adverbs)*

assez (de)   (*rather; enough*)   en général   (*generally*)
aussi   (*also*)   toujours   (*always*)
beaucoup de   (*a lot of*)   très   (*very*)
encore   (*still, yet*)

- **Prépositions** *(Prepositions)*

avec   (*with*)   devant   (*in front of*)
dans   (*in*)

Exercise 2.13

Translate the phrases into French.

1. a modern kitchen _____

2. a pleasant apartment _____

3. some roomy closets _____

4. a navy blue armchair _____

5. in front of the big window _____

6. an old mirror _____

7. a clean oven _____

8. a new computer _____

9. a private bathroom _____

10. some long curtains _____

11. the interior walls _____

12. a big living room _____

13. a very beautiful piano _____

14. a table with six chairs _____

15. a white refrigerator _____

 # Reading Comprehension

La maison de Jean-Pierre

Ma maison est grande et assez vieille, avec beaucoup de fenêtres. Les rideaux devant les fenêtres sont longs et **épais**. Les murs intérieurs sont **peints en blanc**; l'extérieur de la maison est gris. La terrasse est jolie; il y a encore des fleurs. Dans le foyer, il y a une glace ancienne et une table **en bois**. La salle à manger est simple, avec une table et **six** chaises; le tapis est rouge et bleu marin. **Notre** cuisine est spacieuse; **ses** murs sont jaunes et ses placards sont blancs.

Le frigo est assez grand; la cuisinière et le four sont toujours propres. Dans le salon, il y a des fauteuils confortables et un piano. **Moi**, je n'ai pas de salle de bains privée, mais ma chambre est très agréable; elle est bleue et blanche et **ensoleillée**. En général, **mon** ordinateur, **mes** livres, mes cahiers, mes crayons, mes stylos, etc., sont dans la bibliothèque **à côté**.

épais(se)	*thick*	ses	*its*
peint(e) en (blanc)	*painted (white)*	moi	*me, myself*
en bois	*wooden*	ensoleillé(e)	*sunny, bright*
six	*six*	mon, mes	*my*
notre	*our*	à côté	*next door*

Questions

After you read the selection, answer the questions in French.

1. La maison est vieille ou moderne?

   _____.

2. La cuisine est petite ou grande?

   _____.

3. Où (*Where*) est le piano?

   _____.

4. Jean-Pierre a une salle de bains privée?

   _____.

5. Il a une chambre obscure (*dark*)?

   _____.

6. Où est l'ordinateur de Jean-Pierre?

   _____.

3

Days and Months, Regular -*er* Verbs in the Present Tense, and Interrogatives

Days of the Week, Months, and Seasons

In French, days of the week, months, and seasons are not capitalized. With some exceptions, they are used *without* the definite article (**le/la/l'/les**). The week begins on Monday.

Some example sentences in this section use verbs you will learn later. Many are cognates; their meaning should be clear from the translations.

Les jours de la semaine (Days of the Week)

lundi	*Monday*	vendredi	*Friday*
mardi	*Tuesday*	samedi	*Saturday*
mercredi	*Wednesday*	dimanche	*Sunday*
jeudi	*Thursday*		

Quel jour sommes-nous aujourd'hui?	*What day is it today?*
(C'est quel jour aujourd'hui?)	
—Nous sommes **jeudi**.	—*It's **Thursday**.*
(C'est **jeudi**.)	
Maman arrive **samedi**, et Sylvie, **dimanche**.	*Mom arrives **Saturday**, and Sylvie, on **Sunday**.*
Demain, c'est **vendredi**.	*Tomorrow's **Friday**.*

To say that you do the same activity regularly *every Monday, each Saturday, on Sundays*, etc., use the masculine singular definite article **le** before the day. The day also remains in the singular.

42

Le lundi, je suis au gymnase.	**On Mondays**, I'm at the gym.
Les amis dînent ensemble **le vendredi**.	*The friends have dinner together **every Friday**.*
Le mercredi, il y a un examen.	***Each Wednesday**, there's an exam.*
Où est-ce que tu es **le dimanche**?	*Where are you **on Sundays**?*

Les mois de l'année (Months of the Year)

janvier	*January*	juillet	*July*
février	*February*	août	*August*
mars	*March*	septembre	*September*
avril	*April*	octobre	*October*
mai	*May*	novembre	*November*
juin	*June*	décembre	*December*

The preposition **en** (*in*) is used in sentences before the names of the months. The phrase **au mois de/d'** can also be used.

Quel mois sommes-nous?	*What month is it?*
—Nous sommes **en janvier**. (C'est janvier.)	*—It's **January**.*
Noël est **en décembre**.	*Christmas is **in December**.*
On a des vacances **en août**.	*We have vacation **in August**.*
Les cours commencent **en septembre**.	*Classes begin **in September**.*
Ils skient encore **au mois d'avril**.	*They're still skiing **in April**.*

Les saisons (Seasons)

l'été (*m.*)	*summer*	l'hiver (*m.*)	*winter*
l'automne (*m.*)	*autumn, fall*	le printemps	*spring*

Names of the seasons are used with the definite article, the preposition **en**, or with **au** (only with **au printemps**).

L'hiver, c'est la saison froide.	***Winter** is the cold season.*
Arielle adore **l'automne**.	*Arielle loves **autumn**.*
Moi, je passe **l'été** à la plage.	*Me, I'm spending **the summer** at the beach.*

En été nous ne portons pas de manteau.	**In** (**the**) **summer** *we don't wear coats.*
Il est très occupé **en automne**.	*He's very busy **in the fall**.*
Au printemps, je porte toujours un chapeau.	**In** (**the**) **spring**, *I always wear a hat.*
Tu es à Montréal **en hiver**?	*Are you in Montreal **in** (**the**) **winter**?*

Les parties du jour (Parts of the Day)

le matin	*morning*	le soir	*evening*
l'après-midi (*m.*)	*afternoon*	la nuit	*night*

Parts of the day are used with the definite article for regular activities or are used with words like **demain** (*tomorrow*), **hier** (*yesterday*), or with **ce/cet/cette** (*this*). **Cette nuit** means *last night*.

Le soir, nous regardons la télé.	**In the evenings**, *we watch TV.*
Demain matin, je retourne au travail.	**Tomorrow morning**, *I return to work.*
Cet après-midi, on déjeune avec les parents.	**This afternoon**, *we're having lunch with the folks.*
La nuit, les animaux sont dans leur lit.	**At night**, *the animals are in their beds.*

Exercise 3.1

Respond to the sentences in French. Complete sentences are not necessary.

1. What days of the week do you work?

   _____

2. What days of the week do you like to do your hobbies?

   _____

3. When (days or parts of the day) do you study French?

   _____

4. Quel jour sommes-nous? Quel mois?

   _____

5. Quelle est votre saison préférée?

_____

6. Quels sont les mois de l'hiver? et de l'été?

_____

7. Name the months that feature the following holidays. If a holiday moves around, name a typical month or months: Thanksgiving (**le jour de l'Action de grâces**) U.S.? _____, Canada? _____; Christmas (**Noël**) _____; Easter (**Pâques**) _____; the "Fourth" (**la Fête nationale**) _____; Canada Day (**la Fête du Canada**) _____; **le jour de la Bastille** _____; **Ramadan** _____; Hanukkah (**Hanoukka**) _____; Victoria Day (Canada) (**la Fête de la Reine**) _____; Veteran's or Remembrance Day (**le jour du Souvenir**) _____.

Regular Verbs in the Present Tense

French has three groups of verbs with regular conjugations. They are usually identified by their infinitive endings: **-er** (**parler**, *to speak, talk*), **-ir** (**choisir**, *to choose*), or **-re** (**attendre**, *to wait for*).

Regular French verbs are conjugated in person and number by adding six regular endings to the verb root or stem—the infinitive minus the ending: **parl-**, **chois-**, and **attend-**. Learning the model verb for each group will allow you to conjugate most French verbs.

Conjugating Regular -er Verbs

A majority of French verbs have infinitives that end in **-er**: **parler** (*to speak, talk*), **aimer** (*to like, love*). When new verbs are coined, they are most often regular **-er** verbs (**cliquer sur**, *to click on*; **mondialiser**, *to globalize*).

All **-er** verbs (except for **aller**, *to go*) are *regular*. The present tense endings for regular **-er** verbs are: **-e**, **-es**, **-e**, **-ons**, **-ez**, and **-ent**. Conjugated verbs always include a subject noun or pronoun. The regular conjugations of verbs ending in **-ir** and **-re** are presented in Chapters 4 and 5.

Present Tense of parler (*to speak, talk*); Stem: parl-

SINGULAR FORMS

je	parl**e**	*I speak, I do speak, I am speaking*
tu	parl**es** (*fam.*)	*you speak, you do speak, you are speaking*
vous	parl**ez** (*pol.*)	*you speak, you do speak, you are speaking*
il	parl**e**	*he speaks, he does speak, he is speaking*
elle	parl**e**	*she speaks, she does speak, she is speaking*
on	parl**e**	*one speaks, we speak, they speak*

PLURAL FORMS

nous	parl**ons**	*we speak, we do speak, we are speaking*
vous	parl**ez** (*fam./pol.*)	*you speak, you do speak, you are speaking*
ils	parl**ent**	*they* (m.) *speak, they do speak, they are speaking*
elles	parl**ent**	*they* (f.) *speak, they do speak, they are speaking*

Vous parlez français?	***Do you speak*** *French?*
—Bien sûr, et **je parle** aussi italien.	—*Of course, and **I** also **speak** Italian.*
En Iran, **on parle** farsi.	***They speak*** *Farsi in Iran.*

Here are two more **-er** verbs, conjugated in the present tense.

aimer (*to like, love*); Stem: **aim-**		**écouter** (*to listen to*); Stem: **écout-**	
j'aim**e**	nous aim**ons**	j'écout**e**	nous écout**ons**
tu aim**es**	vous aim**ez**	tu écout**es**	vous écout**ez**
il/elle/on aim**e**	ils/elles aim**ent**	il/elle/on écout**e**	ils/elles écout**ent**

As with forms of **avoir**, the **-e** of **je** elides to **j'** before a vowel sound. It is replaced by an apostrophe and closed up to the verb: **j'**aime, **j'**écoute.

Nous parlons avec les voisins.	***We're speaking*** *with the neighbors.*
J'aime beaucoup ce quartier.	***I like*** *this neighborhood a lot.*
Ton ami et toi, **vous écoutez** la radio?	***Are you and your friend listening*** *to the radio?*

Pronunciation of -er Verb Forms

The final **-s** of a conjugated verb is silent (**tu parles**), as are the final **-z** (**vous parlez**) and the ending **-ent** (**ils/elles aiment**). Thus, in the spoken language, an **-er** verb has three sounded forms: [pahRl] (**je parle, tu parles, il/elle/on parle, ils/elles parlent**), [pahR-lOⁿ] (**nous parlons**), and [pahR-lay] (**vous parlez**).

The final **-s** of a subject pronoun (**nous, vous, ils, elles**) is pronounced [z] when it immediately precedes a verb form starting with a vowel sound. This is called **liaison**.

ils_aiment [eel-zehm]	vous_êtes [voo-zeht]
nous_habitons [noo-zah-bee-tOⁿ]	elles_étudient [ehl-zay-tU-dee]

Here are several more regular **-er** verbs:

adorer	*to love, to adore*	habiter	*to live*
aimer mieux	*to prefer, to like better*	jouer	*to play*
arriver	*to arrive*	louer	*to rent*
chercher	*to look for*	regarder	*to look at, to watch*
danser	*to dance*	rêver (de)	*to dream (about)*
détester	*to hate, to detest*	travailler	*to work*
étudier	*to study*	trouver	*to find*
expliquer	*to explain*	utiliser	*to use*
fermer	*to close*	visiter	*to visit (a place)*

Exercise 3.2

Translate the verb forms into French.

1. we speak _____

2. she listens _____

3. I like _____

4. they (*f.*) rent _____

5. you (*pol.*) use _____

6. we live _____

7. I arrive _____

8. he hates _____

9. you (*fam.*) dream _____

10. she finds _____

 ## Exercise 3.3

Change the verb forms from singular to plural, or from plural to singular. **Je** *becomes* **nous**, il/elle *becomes* **ils/elles**, **tu** *becomes* **vous**, *and vice versa. Focus on meaning.*

1. j'adore _____

2. nous dansons _____

3. vous regardez _____

4. tu expliques _____

5. il cherche _____

6. elles ferment _____

7. vous parlez _____

8. nous expliquons _____

9. elle utilise _____

10. tu détestes _____

Uses of the Present Tense

The present tense in French has three equivalents in English.

Je **parle** français.   *I **speak** French; I **am speaking** French; I **do speak** French.*

- The present tense often conveys the meaning of a near future.

Elles **arrivent** vers six heures ce soir.   *They **will arrive** around six this evening.*

Tu **cherches** un emploi cet été?   ***Will** you **be looking** for a job this summer?*

- When two verbs are used consecutively, the first is conjugated and the second is an infinitive. The infinitive directly follows some verbs (such as **aimer**, **aimer mieux**, **détester**, **préférer**), with no intervening preposition.

Vous **détestez regarder** la télé?	*You **hate to watch** TV?*
Pas vrai!	*You're kidding!*
—Oui, j'**aime mieux travailler**.	*—Yes, I **prefer working**.*

Other verb + verb constructions require **à** or **de** before the infinitive. Chapter 7 contains lists of common verbs in their verb + verb construction.

Je commence **à** travailler.	*I begin to work.*
On refuse **de** continuer.	*They refuse to continue.*

- The simple negation of verbs (in all tenses) is made with **ne... pas**.

Nous fermons la porte.	*We close the door.*
Nous **ne** fermons **pas** la porte.	*We **don't** close the door.*

Ne becomes **n'** (i.e., it elides) before a vowel sound or a mute **h**.

Jacqueline habite ici.	*Jacqueline lives here.*
Jérôme **n'**habite **pas** ici.	*Jérôme **doesn't** live here.*
Elle écoute la radio.	*She listens to the radio.*
Il **n'**écoute **pas** la radio.	*He **doesn't** listen to the radio.*

If a verb is followed by an infinitive, **ne/n'** and **pas** usually surround the conjugated verb form.

Nous aimons discuter.	*We like to discuss (issues).*
Vous **n'**aimez **pas** discuter.	*You **don't** like to discuss (issues).*

When the infinitive is negated, the combination **ne pas** precedes the infinitive.

Je demande au professeur de **ne pas donner** d'examen.	*I ask the teacher **not to give** a test.*
Ils aiment mieux **ne pas danser** samedi soir.	*They prefer **not to dance** Saturday night.*

- As with **avoir**, in negative sentences (except for those with **être**), the indefinite article (**un/une/des**) changes to **de/d'** after **ne... pas**. The noun following **de/d'** can be singular or plural.

Le dimanche, on visite **un** musée.	*On Sundays, we visit **a** museum.*
Le dimanche, on **ne** visite **pas de** musée.	*On Sundays, we **don't** visit a (**any**) museum(s).*

Je **cherche des** oranges.
—Tu **ne trouves pas** d'oranges?

*I'm **looking for** oranges.*
*—**Aren't** you **finding** (**any**)*
oranges?

Verbs Without Prepositions

Some English verbs require a preposition where their French equivalents do not. They include **chercher** (*to look **for***), **écouter** (*to listen **to***), and **regarder** (*to look **at***).

Don't be tempted to add a preposition when you speak or write these verbs in French. With these French verbs the direct object comes immediately after the verb.

Je **cherche** mon ami.

*I **am looking for** my friend.*

Nous **écoutons** une bonne émission.

*We **are listening to** a good program.*

Tu **regardes** les cartes de France?

*Are you **looking at** the maps of France?*

Exercise 3.4

Answer each question in the negative, forming a complete sentence.

1. Tu chantes bien?

   Non, je _____.

2. Mireille travaille à la banque?

   Non, elle _____.

3. André écoute souvent la radio?

   Non, il _____.

4. Vous rêvez en classe?

   Non, nous _____.

5. Tu aimes mieux le jogging?

   Non, je _____.

6. Tes parents cherchent une nouvelle maison?

   Non, ils _____.

Exercise 3.5

Complete each sentence with the correct form of the appropriate verb. Choose from the verbs listed below, using each verb once.

adorer, aimer, aimer mieux, danser, écouter, étudier, louer, parler, refuser, regarder, trouver, utiliser

EXAMPLE: Les étudiants _____*louent*_____ un bel appartement. (rent)

1. Je/J' _____ la radio le matin. (*listen to*)

2. Nous _____ après les cours. (*study*)

3. On _____ travailler le samedi. (*don't like*)

4. Vous _____ un ordinateur tous les jours? (*use*)

5. Tu _____ au prof dans son bureau. (*talk*)

6. Mes parents _____ de prêter (*to lend*) la voiture. (*refuse*)

7. Marc et Josiane _____ _____ la télé le soir. (*adore watching*)

8. Tu _____ le vendredi soir? (*don't dance*)

9. Nous _____ regarder un film. (*prefer*)

10. Amélie _____ de bonnes carottes au marché. (*finds*)

Exercise 3.6

Read each indirect statement in English and write the direct statement in French.

1. My friend says he hates to work.

   « Je _____. »

2. He says that Robert is looking for a job (**un emploi**).

   « Robert _____. »

3. Also, he says that Robert doesn't like to travel (**voyager**).

   « Robert _____. »

4. Marguerite says she talks to the (**au**) teacher after class.

   « Je _____. »

5. The other students say they don't study much.

   « Nous _____. »

Exercise 3.7

Complete each blank with a verb chosen from the list; verbs may be used more than once. Make sure the present tense verb forms are correct.

arriver, avoir, chanter, écouter, être, étudier, habiter, jouer, louer, parler, regarder

1. Richard _____ son iPod dans le parc.

2. Simone _____ beaucoup; les leçons de français _____ difficiles!

3. Nous _____ toujours à la maison à six heures du soir.

4. Pendant la fête les enfants _____ des chansons et _____ de la guitare.

5. Dans les conversations, qui _____ le plus, les hommes ou les femmes?

6. Dans mon expérience, les hommes et les femmes _____ les uns aussi souvent que (*as often as*) les autres, mais ils _____ des intérêts différents.

7. Le week-end, nous _____ libres de _____ la télévision.

8. Je ne/n' _____ pas besoin de _____ un appart; je/j' _____ chez mes parents!

Interrogatives and Interrogative Words

Most questions (or interrogatives) in French contain a verb. Interrogatives either ask for a *yes/no* answer or for information or facts. There are four types of *yes/no* questions: three are largely conversational; the fourth is used in writing and sometimes in conversation. Questions that ask for *information* or *facts* usually begin with interrogative words such as **Qui... ?** (*Who . . . ?*), **Que... ?/ Qu'est-ce que... ?** (*What . . . ?*), or **Quand... ?** (*When . . . ?*).

Yes/No Questions

Like English, French has several types of *yes/no* questions.

Yes/No Questions with No Change in Word Order

• *Questions with rising intonation*

In this type of question, the pitch of the voice rises at the end of a sentence to create a vocal question mark. The subject-verb order remains unchanged.

Vous êtes d'ici?	*Are you from around here?*
On a du temps pour un café?	*Do we have time for a coffee?*

• *Tag questions*

Here, the invariable tag **n'est-ce pas?** is added to the end of a sentence. The speaker generally expects agreement or confirmation. The subject-verb order does not change.

Tu es allemand, **n'est-ce pas?**	*You're German, **aren't you?***
En été on a des vacances, **n'est-ce pas?**	*We'll have vacation in the summer, **won't we?***

The English equivalent of a tag question varies according to the subject of the question (*aren't you? won't we? do we? isn't it?* etc.), while the French **n'est-ce pas?** remains the same.

• *Questions starting with* est-ce que...

In this form the entire statement is preceded by **est-ce que**. The subject-verb order of the sentence does not change. **Est-ce que** is pronounced as a single two-syllable word [ehs-kuh]. Before a vowel, **est-ce que** becomes **est-ce qu'**: **Est-ce qu'il(s)... /Est-ce qu'elle(s)...** [ehs-keel/ehs-kehl].

Est-ce que nous sommes déjà en ville?	*Are we already in the city?*
Est-ce qu'elle a une opinion?	*Does she have an opinion?*

Exercise 3.8

Ask a yes/no question based on each of the statements, as though you had just asked the speaker. Use a variety of question forms. Suggested answers are in the Answer Key.

EXAMPLE: Fatima est française. *Fatima est française, n'est-ce pas?*

1. Je suis étudiante.

   _____?

2. Léonard et Claudine détestent le cinéma.

   _____?

3. Les voisins ont un gros chien.

   _____?

4. Nous avons des opinions politiques.

   _____?

5. Micheline aime mieux jouer au tennis.

   _____?

6. Je travaille dans une boulangerie.

   _____?

7. Raoul joue de la trompette.

   _____?

8. Nous regardons des vidéos vendredi soir.

   _____?

Yes/No Questions with a Change in Word Order

In French, questions with a change in the subject-verb order (inversion) are often used in written or formal spoken language. Short questions with inversion are often used in colloquial speech.

- In questions with pronoun subjects, the subject pronoun and verb are inverted. A hyphen connects the subject pronoun to the verb.

   Êtes-vous déjà en retard? **Are you** *already late?*
   Avons-nous assez d'argent? **Do we have** *enough money?*
   Sont-elles au travail?   **Are they** *at work?*

- In negative questions with inversion, **ne/n'** precedes the conjugated verb and **pas** follows the inverted subject pronoun.

N'as-tu pas envie de manger?	***Don't you*** *want to eat?*
Ne sommes-nous pas à la gare?	***Aren't we*** *at the train station?*
N'ont-ils pas soif?	***Aren't they*** *thirsty?*

- The subject pronoun **je** is almost never inverted with the verb. Use **Est-ce que... ?** instead.

Est-ce que je suis à l'heure?	***Am I*** *on time?*

  However, several irregular verbs may invert the first-person singular **je**: (verb: **être**) **Suis-je... ?** (*Am I . . . ?*), (verb: **pouvoir**) **Puis-je... ?** (*May I . . . ?*), and (verb: **devoir**) **Dois-je... ?** (*Must I . . . ?*). These three forms are found only in rather formal speech.

- In an inverted question, when a third-person singular (**il/elle/on**) verb form ends in a vowel, the letter **-t-**, surrounded by hyphens, is inserted between the verb and the pronoun to aid in pronunciation.

A-t-on l'adresse de Marianne?	***Do we have*** *Marianne's address?*
[ah-tO^n]	

  Note especially the inverted question form of the expression **il y a** (*there is, there are*). In the affirmative, it goes like this:

Y a-t-il... ?	***Is there*** *. . . ?* ***Are there*** *. . . ?*
Y a-t-il des devoirs?	***Is there*** *any homework?*

  Des becomes **de/d'** in the negative form of the question.

N'y a-t-il pas de... ?	***Isn't there*** *. . . ?* ***Aren't there*** *. . . ?*
N'y a-t-il pas de bons films?	***Aren't there any*** *good movies?*
N'y a-t-il pas d'eau?	***Isn't there any*** *water?*

  Everyday language, however, asks questions such as **Il y a des devoirs?** and **Il n'y a pas d'eau?** with no inversion.

  The added **-t-** between vowels in a third-person singular inverted question is found in all present-tense verbs (see Chapters 5 and 6).

Parle-**t**-il?	[pahR-luh-teel]	*Is he speaking?*
Discute-**t**-elle?	[dees-kU-tuh-tehl]	*Does she argue?*
Ne va-**t**-elle pas habiter à Paris?	[vah-tehl]	*Isn't she going to live in Paris?*

Questions with Noun Subjects

When an inverted question has a noun subject, *both* the noun subject and the inverted pronoun are used.

Ce monsieur est-**il** français?   *Is that man French?*
Simon a-t-**il** une moto?   *Does Simon have a motorcycle?*
Annick et Chantal n'ont-**elles**   *Don't Annick and Chantal have*
   pas de logement?   *a place?*

This table recaps how to ask questions with subject-verb inversion in French.

Summary of Subject-Verb Inversion in Questions

	PRONOUN SUBJECT	NOUN SUBJECT
Statement	Elle est professeur. *She is a teacher.*	Renée est professeur. *Renée is a teacher.*
Question	**Est-elle** professeur? *Is she a teacher?*	**Renée est-elle** professeur? *Is Renée a teacher?*
Negative Question	**N'est-elle pas** professeur? *Isn't she a teacher?*	**Renée n'est-elle pas** professeur? *Isn't Renée a teacher?*

Exercise 3.9

Translate the English questions into yes/no French questions, using inversion.

1. Do you (*fam.*) have a cat?

   _____?

2. Does Sylvie play the (**du**) piano?

   _____?

3. Are you (*pol.*) American (*m.*)?

   _____?

4. Do you (*fam.*) like tennis or golf better?

   _____?

5. Are we playing (**au**) Scrabble this evening?

   _____?

6. Are the children hungry?

_____?

7. Isn't Jacques a teacher?

_____?

8. Don't you (*fam.*) work in a bookstore?

_____?

 Exercise 3.10

Create eight yes/no questions in French that you might ask your seat partner on an airplane flight.

1. _____?
2. _____?
3. _____?
4. _____?
5. _____?
6. _____?
7. _____?
8. _____?

Information Questions

Information questions begin with an interrogative word or expression such as **Qu'est-ce que... ?** (*What . . . ?*); **Quel(le)(s)... ?** (*Which . . . ?*); and **Comment... ?** (*How . . . ?*).

Information questions may be expressed with the interrogative expression + subject-verb inversion and also with **est-ce que**, with no change in word order. Some of the following examples use verbs you will learn to conjugate later.

Interrogative *Subject* of the Verb

In the sentences *She sees the dog* and *Sam buys a car*, the words *She* and *Sam* are both *subjects* of the sentence. Questions corresponding to those sentences would be: **Who** *sees the dog?* and **Who** *is buying a car?*

A *thing* can also be the subject of a question: **What's** *happening?* **What** *makes that noise?* In French, there is no short form for asking about *things* as subject of the question. Study the following French forms and their English equivalents.

Persons: Subject Long Form
Qui est-ce qui (as subject) + verb   *Who* . . . *?*

Qui est-ce qui arrive?	**Who's** *arriving?*

Persons: Subject Short Form (Most Common)
Qui (as subject) + verb   *Who* . . . *?*

Qui arrive?   **Who's** *arriving?*
Qui parle?   **Who's** *speaking?*

Things: Subject Long Form
Qu'est-ce qui (as subject) + verb   *What* . . . *?*

Qu'est-ce qui arrive?	**What's** *happening?*
Qu'est-ce qui est dans la rue?	**What's** *(down there) in the street?*

Interrogative Object of the Verb

In the English sentences *I see Richard* and *I see the car*, *Richard* and *the car* are both *objects* of the verb *see*. Corresponding English questions would be: **Who(m)** *do you see?* and **What** *do you see?* Study the following French forms and their English equivalents.

Persons: Object Long Form
Qui est-ce que/qu' + subject + verb   *Who(m)* . . . *?*

Qui est-ce que tu invites?	**Who(m)** *are you inviting?*
Qui est-ce que vous attendez?	**Who(m)** *are you waiting for?*
Qui est-ce qu'elle aime?	**Who(m)** *does she love?*

Persons: Object Short Form
Qui (as object) + inverted verb/subject   *Who(m)* . . . *?*

Qui invitez-vous?	**Who(m)** *are you inviting?*
Qui est-ce?	**Who** *is it?*/**Who's** *that?*
Qui aime-t-elle?	**Who(m)** *does she love?*

Things: Object Long Form

Qu'est-ce que/qu' + subject + verb   *What . . . ?*

Qu'est-ce que tu as?	**What** *do you have?*/**What**'s *the matter with you?*
Qu'est-ce que vous pensez?	**What** *do you think?*

Things: Object Short Form

Que/Qu' + inverted verb/pronoun subject   *What . . . ?*

Qu'a-t-il?	**What** *does he have?*/ **What**'s *the matter with him?*
Que cherchez-vous?	**What** *are you looking for?*

Que/Qu' + verb + inverted noun subject   *What . . . ?*

Que regarde Iris?	**What**'s *Iris looking at?*
Que cherche le prof?	**What**'s *the teacher looking for?*

Exercise 3.11

Translate the questions into English.

1. Qui arrive samedi? _____?

2. Que cherchent les enfants? _____?

3. Qui est-ce que tu invites? _____?

4. Qu'est-ce qu'elle regarde? _____?

5. Qu'aimes-tu? _____?

Now, translate these questions into French.

6. Who is it? _____?

7. What's happening? _____?

8. What do you (*fam.*) have? _____?

9. Who(m) is she listening to? _____?

10. What are you (*pol.*) looking at? _____?

Interrogative Words (with Word Inversion or with *est-ce que/qu'*)

Questions asking information other than *What . . . ?* or *Who . . . ?* (as subject or object) use specific question words.

Comment... ?   *How . . . ? What . . . ?*

Comment vas-tu?	***How*** *are you?*
Comment est-il?	***What's*** *he like?*

Combien (de/d')... ?   *How much/many . . . ?*

Combien coûte-t-il?	***How much*** *does it cost?*
Combien est-ce que ça coûte?	
Combien d'heures travaillez-vous?	***How many*** *hours are you working?*

Où... ?   *Where . . . ?*

Où vas-tu?/**Où est-ce que** tu vas?	***Where*** *are you going?*

Quand... ?   *When . . . ?*

Quand arrive-t-elle?/**Quand est-ce qu'**elle arrive?	***When*** *does she arrive?*

Quel(le)(s) (as adjective) + noun + verb   *What (Which) . . . ?*

Quel(le)(s) is an adjective that always agrees with its noun.

Quelle heure est-il?	***What*** *time is it?*

Quel(le)(s) + être + noun

Quel est ton film préféré?	***What is*** *your favorite movie?*

Pourquoi... ?   *Why . . . ?*

Pourquoi Gérard arrive-t-il si tard?	***Why*** *is Gérard arriving so late?*
Pourquoi est-ce que Gérard arrive si tard?	

The conversational answer to a **pourquoi** (*why*) question often begins with **parce que** (*because*).

Comment vas-tu?	***How*** *are you?* (*fam.*)
Comment est-elle?	***What's*** *she like?*

Combien d'argent as-tu?	***How much*** *money do you have?*
Où allons-nous?	***Where*** *are we going?*
Quand est-ce qu'on dîne?	***When*** *are we (people) having dinner?*
Quand dîne-t-on?	***When*** *are we (people) having dinner?*
Quel livre aimes-tu?	***Which*** *book do you like?*
Quelle est son adresse?	***What is*** *his/her address?*
Quelles sont vos opinions?	***What are*** *your opinions?*
Pourquoi es-tu en retard?	***Why*** *are you late?*

Exercise 3.12

Translate the questions from French to English.

1. Quel restaurant aimes-tu? _____?

2. Quand arrivons-nous au cinéma? _____?

3. Pourquoi Marie-Laure est-elle contente? _____?

4. Comment vas-tu? _____?

5. Comment est le professeur de maths? _____?

Now, translate the questions from English to French.

6. How are you (*pol.*)? _____?

7. Why do students love music? _____?

8. Where is the bookstore? _____?

9. Which are the best (**meilleurs**) courses? _____?

10. When do you (*fam.*) study? _____?

Exercise 3.13

Read the questions aloud, answer them aloud, and then answer them in writing.

1. Comment allez-vous?

   _____.

2. Où est votre famille? Ma... (*My . . .*)

   _____.

3. D'où êtes-vous?

_____.

4. Avez-vous une voiture? Quelle sorte de voiture?

_____.

5. Où est votre maison ou votre appartement? Elle est… /Il est…

_____.

6. Comment est la maison ou l'appartement où vous habitez?

_____.

 ## Key Vocabulary

In the following lists, you will see that the nouns are divided into masculine and feminine.

Noms masculins (Masculine Nouns)

l'an (*year*)
l'anniversaire (*birthday; anniversary*)
l'arbre (*tree*)
l'argent (*money*)
l'ascenseur (*elevator*)
l'autobus (*bus*)
l'avion (*airplane*)
les bagages (*luggage*)
le bâtiment (*building*)
le bruit (*noise*)
les cheveux (*hair*)
le crayon (*pencil*)
les devoirs (*homework*)
l'enfant (*child*)
l'escalier (*stairway*)
l'étage (*floor [building]*)
le feutre (*felt-tip pen*)
le foyer (*fireplace; hearth*)
les gens (*people*)
le jardin (*garden, yard*)

le jour (*day*)
le journal (*newspaper*)
le lieu (*place*)
le magasin (*store*)
le mail (*e-mail*)
le médicament (*medicine*)
le message (*message*)
le mois (*month*)
le mot (*word*)
le mur (*wall*)
le musée (*museum*)
le papier (*paper*)
le parc (*park*)
le pays (*country*)
le prix (*price*)
le rêve (*dream*)
le stylo (*ballpoint pen*)
le théâtre (*theater*)
le thème (*theme*)
le voyage (*trip*)

Noms féminins (Feminine Nouns)

l'addition   (*check, bill*)
l'avenue   (*avenue*)
la bibliothèque   (*library*)
la campagne   (*country*)
la carte postale   (*postcard*)
la chambre   (*bedroom*)
la chemise   (*shirt*)
la clé   (*key*)
la cuisine   (*kitchen; cooking*)
la douche   (*shower, bath*)
l'école   (*school*)
l'église   (*church*)
l'entrée   (*entry; first course*)
la fête   (*party; holiday*)
la feuille   (*leaf; sheet* [*paper*])
la guerre   (*war*)
la lettre   (*letter*)

la librairie   (*bookstore*)
la maison   (*house, home*)
la musique   (*music*)
la page   (*page*)
la phrase   (*sentence*)
la pièce   (*room; play* [*theater*])
la plage   (*beach*)
la porte   (*door*)
la question   (*question*)
la rue   (*street*)
la salle de classe   (*classroom*)
la santé   (*health*)
la semaine   (*week*)
la soirée   (*evening; party*)
la sortie   (*exit*)
la ville   (*city*)
la voiture   (*car*)

Adjectifs (Adjectives)

affectueux (-euse)   (*affectionate*)
aimable   (*nice, kind*)
amical(e)   (*friendly*)
aveugle   (*blind*)
bas(se)   (*low, short*)
beau/bel/belle   (*beautiful*)
court(e)   (*short* [*in length*])
curieux (-euse)   (*curious; odd*)
dangereux (-euse)   (*dangerous*)
difficile   (*difficult*)
doux (-ce)   (*sweet; mild; soft*)
drôle   (*funny*)
dur(e)   (*hard*)
élégant(e)   (*elegant*)
étrange   (*strange*)
étroit(e)   (*narrow*)
facile   (*easy*)
faible   (*weak*)
fidèle   (*faithful*)

fier (-ère)   (*proud*)
gentil(le)   (*kind*)
grand(e)   (*tall*)
large   (*wide*)
lent(e)   (*slow*)
libre   (*free*)
long(ue)   (*long*)
lourd(e)   (*heavy*)
nouveau/nouvel/nouvelle   (*new*)
paresseux (-euse)   (*lazy*)
particulier (-ière)   (*special*)
passionnant(e)   (*exciting*)
petit(e)   (*short* [*height*])
profond(e)   (*deep*)
rapide   (*fast*)
sourd(e)   (*deaf*)
spécial(e)   (*special*)
timide   (*shy*)
tranquille   (*calme*)

Conjonctions (Conjunctions)

Conjunctions link ideas and parts of a sentence. You learned several in Chapter 2.

donc (*therefore, so*)	parce que/qu' (*because*)
et (*and*)	pendant que/qu' (*during*)
mais (*but*)	puisque/puisqu' (*since [reason]*)
ou (*or*)	si (*if*)

Exercise 3.14

Translate the phrases into French using the new vocabulary you learned.

1. a special birthday _____
2. a dangerous trip _____
3. an elegant party _____
4. a strange noise _____
5. some exciting dreams _____
6. a faithful friend (f.) _____
7. a blind child _____
8. a narrow staircase _____
9. some difficult sentences _____
10. some heavy keys _____

Reading Comprehension

Une petite ville en province

Avec des amis canadiens, je suis en France — à Évreux, une petite ville ancienne de Normandie, **entre** Paris et Rouen. Nous sommes ici en juillet avec les parents de Laure. Laure et moi, nous étudions le français. **La mère de Laure** est archéologue et **son père** est législateur au Canada.

À Évreux, il y a une école d'été qui offre des cours de langue, d'art, d'histoire et de musique. C'est l'été, le climat est merveilleux et nos nouveaux amis français sont très sympathiques. Le week-end, les jeunes organisent souvent des fêtes. De lundi à vendredi, nous avons nos cours, et nous sommes des étudiantes sérieuses.

    La mère de Laure est très contente parce qu'il y a **dans les environs** des ruines des villages du **cinquième siècle**. Le père de Laure est content parce que ce sont des vacances tranquilles et **reposantes**. Et moi, je suis heureuse dans la maison normande que nous louons. J'ai **mes copains**, de la bonne conversation, des cours intéressants et les bons **repas** normands!

entre (*between*)	cinquième siècle (*fifth century*)
la mère de Laure (*Laure's mother*)	reposant(e)(s) (*restful*)
son père (*her father*)	mes copains (*my friends, pals* [*fam.*])
dans les environs (*in the vicinity*)	le repas (*meal*)

Questions

1. Où est la narratrice?

    _____

2. Est-elle seule (*alone*) en vacances?

    _____

3. Quels cours offre l'école d'été?

    _____

4. Qu'est-ce que les deux jeunes filles étudient?

    _____

5. Pourquoi la mère de Laure est-elle contente?

    _____

6. Le père de Laure travaille-t-il pendant les vacances?

    _____

4

Numbers, Dates, and Time and Regular *-ir* Verbs in the Present Tense

Cardinal Numbers

A *cardinal* number is any number expressing an amount, such as *one*, *two*, or *three*.

Numbers from 0 to 99

Here are the French cardinal numbers from 0 to 99:

0	zéro	18	dix-huit
1	un	19	dix-neuf
2	deux	20	vingt
3	trois	**21**	**vingt** et **un**
4	quatre	22	vingt-deux
5	cinq	23	vingt-trois
6	six	24	vingt-quatre
7	sept	25	vingt-cinq
8	huit	26	vingt-six
9	neuf	27	vingt-sept
10	dix	28	vingt-huit
11	onze	29	vingt-neuf
12	douze	30	trente
13	treize	31	trente **et** un
14	quatorze	32	trente-deux
15	quinze	33	trente-trois
16	seize	34	trente-quatre
17	dix-sept	35	trente-cinq

36 trente-six	76	soixante-seize
37 trente-sept	77	soixante-dix-sept
38 trente-huit	78	soixante-dix-huit
39 trente-neuf	79	soixante-dix-neuf
40 quarante	80	**quatre-vingts**
50 cinquante	81	**quatre-vingt-un**
60 soixante	82	quatre-vingt-deux
70 **soixante-dix**	83	quatre-vingt-trois
71 **soixante et onze**	90	**quatre-vingt-dix**
72 soixante-douze	91	**quatre-vingt-onze**
73 soixante-treize	92	quatre-vingt-douze
74 soixante-quatorze	93	quatre-vingt-treize
75 soixante-quinze	99	quatre-vingt-dix-neuf

Pronouncing Numbers

The final consonant of the numbers **cinq**, **six**, and **dix** is *silent* before a word that begins with a consonant: **cinq** [sɪⁿ] **livres**, **six** [see] **femmes**, **dix** [dee] **petits chats**. The sound **x** [s] becomes [z] before a vowel: **six** [seez] **oranges**. The final consonant of **deux**, **cinq**, **six**, **dix**, and **vingt** is *pronounced* at the beginning of a word that begins with a vowel: **deux** [duhz] **étudiants**, **cinq** [sɪⁿk] **images**, **dix** [deez] **hommes**, **vingt** [vɪⁿt] **articles**.

- Numbers from **17** (**dix-sept**) to **19** (**dix-neuf**) are formed by combining numbers.

- Seventy (**soixante-dix**) is literally "sixty-ten," seventy-one (**soixante et onze**) is "sixty *and* eleven," and so on. Eighty (**quatre-vingts**), "four-twenties," starts a new series that ends in *ninety-nine* (**quatre-vingt-dix-neuf**).

- Eighty (**quatre-vingts**) takes an **-s**, but numbers based on it do not: **quatre-vingt-un**.

- In Belgium and French Switzerland, **70** is **septante** (**septante et un, septante-deux...**); **90** is **nonante** (**nonante et un, nonante-deux...**). In Belgium, **80** is **huitante** (**huitante et un, huitante-deux...**); while French Switzerland uses **quatre-vingts**, etc.

- When a feminine noun follows the numbers **un**, **vingt et un**, **trente et un**, etc., an **-e** is added to **un**: *une* **table**, **vingt et** *une* **étudiantes**, **trente et** *une* **voitures**.

Doing Arithmetic in French

+	plus *or* et	quatorze **plus** (**et**) quinze **font** (**égalent**) vingt-neuf
−	moins	vingt **moins** douze **font** (**égalent**) huit
×	fois	six **fois** dix **font** (**égalent**) soixante
÷	divisé par	trente-six **divisé par** douze **font** (**égalent**) trois
=	font *or* égalent	

Exercise 4.1

Continue each series with three more digits, writing out the numbers in French.

1. un, deux, trois,

_____

2. deux, quatre, six,

_____

3. vingt, trente, quarante,

_____

4. sept, quatorze, vingt et un,

_____

5. soixante-sept, soixante-huit, soixante-neuf,

_____

6. quatre-vingt-huit, soixante-dix-sept, soixante-six,

_____

Exercise 4.2

Solve these arithmetic problems, and write out the answers in French.

1. quatre-vingts ÷ quatre = _____.
2. quarante-cinq + quarante-cinq = _____.
3. vingt et un × trois = _____.
4. soixante et onze − vingt-six = _____.

5. quatre-vingt-huit − trente-quatre = _____.

6. quarante-huit × deux = _____.

Numbers from 100

Here are the numbers starting with 100:

100	cent	700	sept cents
101	cent un	800	huit cents
102	cent deux	900	neuf cents
200	deux cents	970	neuf cent soixante-dix
201	deux cent un	980	neuf cent quatre-vingts
222	deux cent vingt-deux	999	neuf cent quatre-vingt-dix-neuf
300	trois cents	1 000	mille
400	quatre cents	1 001	mille un
500	cinq cents	2 000	deux mille
600	six cents	3 750	trois mille sept cent cinquante

999 999	neuf cent quatre-vingt-dix-neuf mille neuf cent quatre-vingt-dix-neuf
1 000 000	un million
1 000 000 000	un milliard

Knowing Your Numbers

Numbers are some of the most important vocabulary words you'll need: to ask for and to say prices, schedules, directions, addresses, telephone numbers, etc. Practice them aloud regularly.

- The **-s** of **cents** (**trois cents**) is dropped when followed by any other number: **201** (**deux cent un**), **735** (**sept cent trente-cinq**).

- Like **cent**, **mille** (*one thousand*) has no article. The word **mille** never ends in **-s**: **1 004** (**mille quatre**), **7 000** (**sept mille**), **9 999** (**neuf mille neuf cent quatre-vingt-dix-neuf**).

- European Union currency (now used by sixteen EU countries, including France, and six non-EU countries) is **l'euro** (*m.*) (€); it is divided into 100 **centimes** (*m.*).

- To express thousands in figures, French uses a space or a period where English uses a comma: **2 695/2.695**. In decimal numbers, such as prices, French uses a comma where English uses a period: **77,50€/15,90€**.

- The nouns **million** (*million*) and **milliard** (*billion*) take **-s** in the plural: **2 300 000€** (**deux millions trois cent mille euros**). The preposition **de/d'** is used between **million(s)** or **milliard(s)** and a noun: **un milliard d'euros**, **trois millions d'habitants**.

Exercise 4.3

Read the prices in euros out loud. Next, write them out as if on a bank check.

1. deux litres de lait: 2€ 50 centimes _____

2. un kilo d'oranges: 4€ 75 centimes _____

3. un dîner à deux: 44€ _____

4. une paire de chaussures: 110€ _____

5. une nuit dans un hôtel parisien: 188€ _____

6. une voiture Smart: 9.450€ _____

Ordinal Numbers

Ordinal numbers express position in a series, such as *first*, *second*, *third*, *fourth*, and *fifth*.

In French, ordinal numbers, with the exception of **le premier/la première** (*the first*), are formed by adding **-ième** to cardinal numbers. Except for **le premier/la première**, only the article (**le/la/les**) changes to agree with the noun.

le premier/la première	le/la onzième	le/la vingt et unième
le/la deuxième	le/la douzième	le/la vingt-deuxième
le/la troisième	le/la treizième	le/la trentième
le/la quatrième	le/la quatorzième	le/la quatre-vingtième
le/la cinquième	le/la quinzième	le/la quatre-vingt-dixième
le/la sixième	le/la seizième	le/la centième
le/la septième	le/la dix-septième	
le/la huitième	le/la dix-huitième	

le/la **neuvième**   le/la **dix-neuvième**
le/la **dixième**   le/la **vingtième**

le **premier** homme	*the **first** man*
la **première** classe	*the **first** class*
le **quatrième** étage	*the **fourth** floor*
le **sixième** mois	*the **sixth** month*
la **trente-neuvième** marche	*the **thirty-ninth** step*

Où est le **dix-huitième**   *Where's the **eighteenth***
   arrondissement?   *arrondissement (Paris district)?*

C'est ton **cinquième** repas   *Is that your **fifth** meal of the day?*
   du jour?

Le **dixième** chapitre est   *The **tenth** chapter is interesting.*
   intéressant.

Le cabinet du médecin est   *The doctor's office is on the **sixth***
   au **sixième** étage.   *floor.*

- Note the irregular spelling of **cinquième** and **neuvième**, and the forms **vingt et unième**, **trente et unième**, etc.

- **Le** and **la** do not elide before **huitième** and **onzième**: **le huitième étudiant** (*the eighth student*), **la onzième cliente** (*the eleventh customer*).

- The abbreviation **e**, sometimes printed in superscript, indicates that a number should be read as an ordinal, as does the suffix **-ième**: **5** = **cinq**; **5e** and **5ième** = **le/la cinquième**.

- In many countries, including France, **le premier étage** refers to the second level of a building (called the *second floor* in the United States). The *ground floor* in French is **le rez-de-chaussée**. Take this difference into account when renting a hotel room.

 ## Exercise 4.4

Translate the sentences into French.

1. In (**À**) Paris, the sixteenth arrondissement (*m.*) is quite (**très**) elegant.

   _____.

2. The Sorbonne (*f.*) is in the fifth arrondissement.

   _____.

3. Alain's apartment is on the (**au**) fourth floor.

_____.

4. It's (This is) the first time (**fois**, _f._) (that) I'm visiting Paris.

_____.

5. This is the twentieth time (that) he's watching the first _Harry Potter_!

_____.

The Date and the Year

French uses the definite article **le** and the cardinal numbers 2 to 31 to indicate the days of the month.

French uses an ordinal number (**le premier**) to indicate _the first of the month_ only.

Quelle est la date d'aujourd'hui?	_What's today's date?_
—Aujourd'hui, c'est **le premier** août.	—_Today's **the first** of August._
C'est **le premier** janvier, le Nouvel An.	_It's **the first** of January, New Year's Day._
Demain, c'est **le deux** août.	_Tomorrow's **the second** of August._
Aujourd'hui, c'est **le cinq** juillet.	_Today's **the fifth** of July (July **5**)._
—Demain, c'est **le six** juillet.	—_Tomorrow's **the sixth** of July (July **6**)._
C'est lundi, **le vingt-huit** février.	_It's Monday, **the twenty-eighth** of February._
C'est dimanche, **le trente et un** octobre.	_It's Sunday, **the thirty-first** of October._

- _Years are expressed with a multiple of_ **cent** _or with_ **mille.**

1789	**dix-sept cent quatre-vingt-neuf** _or_ **mille sept cent quatre-vingt-neuf**
1956	**dix-neuf cent cinquante-six** _or_ **mille neuf cent cinquante-six**
1984	**dix-neuf cent quatre-vingt-quatre** _or_ **mille neuf cent quatre-vingt-quatre**
2010	**deux mille dix**
2013	**deux mille treize**

- *The day of the month comes before the month in French.*
The following are examples of some dates written out:

2.9.2009   le **deux** septembre deux mille neuf
13.11.1993   le **treize** novembre dix-neuf cent quatre-vingt-treize
31.12.2005   le **trente et un** décembre deux mille cinq

- **En** *is used to say the year in a complete sentence.*

Il est né *en* **1974** (**mille neuf**   *He was born in 1974.*
   cent soixante-quatorze).
Nous sommes *en* **2010**   *It's 2010.*
   (**deux mille dix**).

- **Les années cinquante/soixante/soixante-dix/quatre-vingts...** *(the fifties, the sixties, the seventies, the eighties . . .) is used to refer to a decade or era.*

Exercise 4.5

Match the dates below with the significant events that occurred on that date. Then write out a sentence with the full date and the event, as you see in the example.

   11.09.2001, 7.12.1941, 22.11.1963, 29.3.1973, 24.10.1929, 1.01.1863,
   14.07.1789, 18.06.1940, 10.11.1989

EXAMPLE: *la prise de la Bastille à Paris*

   Le quatorze juillet dix-sept cent (ou mille sept cent) quatre-vingt-dix-neuf, c'est la prise de la Bastille à Paris.

1. l'appel du général de Gaulle vers la France libre

   _____.

2. le Krach de Wall Street, jeudi noir

   _____.

3. l'attaque japonaise de Pearl Harbor

   _____.

4. la fin de la guerre (américaine) du Viêt-Nam

   _____.

5. les attentats contre le World Trade Center à New York

   _____.

6. la destruction du mur de Berlin

   _____.

7. la proclamation de l'émancipation des esclaves américains

   _____.

8. l'assassinat de John F. Kennedy

   _____.

 ## Exercise 4.6

Answer the questions in French by writing out the dates and the year as necessary.

1. Quelle est la date d'aujourd'hui?

   _____

2. Donnez les dates (jour et mois) suivantes:

   a. le Nouvel An _____

   b. la fête nationale des États-Unis _____

   c. la fête nationale française _____

   d. la fête nationale canadienne (1.07) _____

   e. Noël _____

   f. l'Halloween _____

   g. le Poisson d'avril (1.04) _____

3. Quelle est la date de votre anniversaire?

   _____

4. En quelle année êtes-vous né(e)? Je suis né(e) en...

   _____

5. Si vous êtes marié(e), quelle est votre date d'anniversaire? Et l'anniversaire de vos parents? _____

Telling Time

To express *time* in the sense of telling time, French uses **l'heure**. To ask the time, say:

Excusez-moi, **quelle heure est-il**? *Excuse me, **what time is it**?*

- French expressions for telling time always use the third-person singular form of **être**, preceded by the impersonal **il** (**Il est...**). Start by learning the expressions for telling time on the hour, from one o'clock to eleven o'clock. From two o'clock on, **heures** is plural.

Il est **une heure**. (*It's **one** o'clock*.)	Il est **quatre heures**. (*It's **four** o'clock*.)
Il est **deux heures**. (*It's **two** o'clock*.)	Il est **dix heures**. (*It's **ten** o'clock*.)
Il est **trois heures**. (*It's **three** o'clock*.)	Il est **onze heures**. (*It's **eleven** o'clock*.)

- Twelve o'clock *noon* and *midnight* are expressed in French with **midi** and **minuit**.

Il est **midi**.   (*It's **noon**.*)   Il est **minuit**.   (*It's **midnight**.*)

- To ask *at what time* something happens, use **à quelle heure** in the question, as follows. The answer is expressed with **à** + the time of day.

À quelle heure commence le cours?	(***At***) ***What time*** *does the class start?*
—**À** dix heures.	—**At** *ten (o'clock).*
À quelle heure déjeunes-tu?	***What time*** (***When***) *are you having lunch?*
—**À** midi.	—**At** *noon (twelve o'clock).*

- To indicate A.M. and P.M., use **du matin** (*in the morning*), **de l'après-midi** (*in the afternoon*), and **du soir** (*in the evening*).

Il est huit heures **du matin**.	*It's eight* A.M.
Il est trois heures **de l'après-midi**.	*It's three* P.M.
Il est dix heures **du soir**.	*It's ten* P.M.

The 24-Hour Clock

The 24-hour clock (or "military" time) is very often used in French for transportation and entertainment schedules, and for making appointments, to avoid ambiguity.

Note the abbreviation **h** for **heures** when the time is given in figures.

	24-Hour Clock	12-Hour Clock
7 h	**sept** heures	**sept** heures (du matin)
11 h	**onze** heures	**onze** heures (du matin)
14 h	**quatorze** heures	**deux** heures (de l'après-midi)
17 h	**dix-sept** heures	**cinq** heures (de l'après midi)
20 h	**vingt** heures	**huit** heures (**du soir**)
23 h	**vingt-trois** heures	**onze** heures (**du soir**)

- To express time *after* the hour, state the hour + the number of minutes.

Il est une heure **vingt**.	*It's 1:**20** (twenty minutes past one).*
Il est cinq heures **dix**.	*It's 5:**10** (ten minutes past five).*
Il est deux heures **cinq**.	*It's 2:**05** (five minutes past two).*
Il est huit heures **quarante-cinq**.	*It's 8:**45** (eight forty-five).*

When it is a *quarter* after the hour, use **quinze** (*fifteen*) or **et quart** (*and a quarter*).

| Il est trois heures **quinze**. | *It's 3:**15**.* |
| Il est six heures **et quart**. | *It's 6:**15**.* |

When it is *half* past the hour, use **trente** (*thirty*) or **et demi(e)** (*and a half*). **Demie** is feminine (with a final **-e**) when it qualifies **heure(s)**; it is spelled **demi** (masculine) when it qualifies **midi** (*noon*) and **minuit** (*midnight*).

Il est neuf heures **trente**.	*It's 9:**30**.*
Il est huit heures **et demie**.	*It's 8:**30**.*
Il est dix heures **et demie**.	*It's 10:**30**.*
Il est **midi et demi**.	*It's **12:30** (P.M.).*
Il est **minuit et demi**.	*It's **12:30** (A.M.).*

- To express a time *before* the hour, state the hour + **moins** (*minus*) + the number of minutes. For *fifteen* minutes to (before) the hour, use **moins le quart**.

Il est trois heures **moins dix**.   *It's 2:50 (**ten minutes to** three).*
Il est onze heures **moins cinq**.   *It's 10:55 (**five minutes to** eleven).*
Il est neuf heures **moins le quart**.   *It's 8:45 (**a quarter to** nine).*
Il est midi **moins le quart**.   *It's 11:45 (**a quarter to** twelve [noon]).*

As in English, you can *add* minutes to the previous hour to express time before the hour.

Il est quatre heures **trente-cinq**.   *It's 4:35 (twenty-five minutes to five).*

Exercise 4.7

You have a friend who usually arrives late. Add one-half hour to each of the times of day, and write out the new time using a complete sentence.

1. Il est cinq heures et quart. _____.

2. Il est huit heures dix. _____.

3. Il est midi. _____.

4. Il est une heure et demie. _____.

5. Il est trois heures moins le quart. _____.

6. Il est neuf heures vingt. _____.

Exercise 4.8

Answer the personal questions in writing.

1. C'est jeudi. Vous déjeunez. Quelle heure est-il?

   _____.

2. Vous êtes en train de travailler. Quelle heure est-il?

   _____.

3. Vous êtes dans le métro, dans le bus ou dans la voiture. Quelle heure est-il?

   _____.

4. Vous dînez au restaurant. Quelle heure est-il?

_____.

5. Vous regardez un film. Quelle heure est-il?

_____.

Expressions Used for Time of Day

Learn the following expressions that go with telling time. The first two use the *impersonal* **il** with the verb **être**.

Il est **tard**!   (*It's **late**!*)   Il est **tôt**!   (*It's **early**!*)

With the following expressions, the sentence has a personal subject pronoun or noun.

de bonne heure	*early (in the morning)*
être en avance	*to be early, arrive early*
être à l'heure	*to be on time*
être en retard	*to be late*

Nous quittons la maison **de bonne heure**.	*We leave the house **early in the morning**.*
Amélie **est en retard** ce matin!	*Amélie **is late** this morning!*
On arrive **en avance** pour avoir une place.	*We arrive **early** to get a seat.*
Il n'est pas toujours facile d'**être à l'heure**.	*It isn't always easy **to be on time**.*

Regular -*ir* Verbs in the Present Tense

Here is the conjugation of regular French verbs with infinitives ending in **-ir**.

Present Tense of choisir   (*to choose, to select*)

je chois**is**	nous chois**issons**
tu chois**is**	vous chois**issez**
il/elle/on chois**it**	ils/elles chois**issent**

Elles **choisissent** toujours des cours difficiles.

They always **pick** difficult classes.

—Tu **ne choisis pas** les mêmes?

—Don't you **choose** the same ones?

Vous **choisissez** vos amis avec soin.

You **select** your friends carefully.

Plural Forms of Regular -*ir* Verbs

Note the pronunciation and spelling of the plural forms of regular -**ir** verbs, in which -**iss**- [ees] is added between the verb stem (**chois-**) and the personal endings. Thus, regular -**ir** verbs have four different spoken forms.

je/tu/il/elle/on choisis/choisit   [shwah-zee]

nous chois**iss**ons   [shwah-zee-sO^n]

vous chois**iss**ez   [shwah-zee-say]

ils/elles chois**iss**ent   [shwah-zees]

- Other regular -**ir** verbs include:

agir   *to act*
finir (de), finir par (+ *inf.*)   *to finish; to end up (by doing)*
réfléchir (à)   *to reflect (on), to consider*
remplir   *to fill (up); to fill out*
réussir (à)   *to succeed (in); to manage (to)*

Ma mère **agit** toujours raisonnablement.

My mother always **acts** reasonably.

Ils **remplissent** les formulaires.

They **fill out** the forms.

Tu **réussis à** contacter notre prof?

Are you **managing to** contact our professor?

Vous **finissez** bientôt?

Will you **be finished** soon?

- The verb **réfléchir** (*to reflect on, contemplate*) requires **à** before a noun.

Nous **réfléchissons aux** questions.

We **are thinking about the** questions.

—Moi, je **réfléchis à** l'avenir.

—Me, I **am contemplating the** future.

À contracts with the definite articles **le** and **les** to form **au** and **aux**. **La** and **l'** do not contract with **à**.

- The verb **réussir** is used with **à** before an infinitive and before a noun in the expression **réussir à un examen** (*to pass an exam*).

Je **réussis à terminer** mon projet.	*I **am managing to finish** my project.*
D'habitude, ils **réussissent à leurs examens**.	*Usually, they **pass their exams**.*

- **Finir** is followed by the preposition **de** before an infinitive. **Finir par** + infinitive means *to end up (by) doing something*.

Tu **finis de travailler** à trois heures?	*Do you **finish work**(**ing**) at three o'clock?*
Nous **finissons** souvent **par parler** avec le patron.	*We often **end up talking** with the boss.*

- Many verbs that describe physical change or transformation are regular **-ir** verbs.

blanchir	(*to bleach, whiten*)	pâlir	(*to grow pale*)
brunir	(*to tan; to brown*)	ralentir	(*to slow down*)
élargir	(*to widen, broaden*)	rétrécir	(*to shrink, grow smaller*)
grandir	(*to grow up*)	rougir	(*to blush, grow red*)
grossir	(*to gain weight*)	salir	(*to get dirty*)
jaunir	(*to yellow*)	vieillir	(*to grow old, age*)
maigrir	(*to lose weight*)		

Nous **ralentissons** devant l'école.	*We **slow down** in front of the school.*
Roméo **rougit** en présence de Juliette.	*Romeo **blushes** when he's with Juliette.*
Les enfants **grandissent** vite!	*Children **grow up** fast!*
Je **vieillis** dans ce boulot!	*I **am growing old** in this job!*

Several groups of *irregular* **-ir** verbs will be presented in Chapters 7 and 8.

Exercise 4.9

Translate the sentences into French.

1. We choose. _____.

2. You (*fam.*) act (behave) well. _____.

3. They (*f.*) blush. _____.

4. I'm succeeding. _____.

5. The children grow. _____.

6. They (**On**) widen the street. _____.

7. You're (*pol.*) losing weight. _____.

8. I slow down at night (**la nuit**). _____.

9. The leaves (**Les feuilles**) are turning yellow. _____.

10. We finish (**de**) working. _____.

Exercise 4.10

Complete the sentences with the appropriate verb in the correct form. Consider using the infinitive. Choose among the suggested verbs.

blanchir, choisir, finir, grandir, grossir, pâlir, remplir, réussir, rougir

1. Éric, vous avez peur de quelque chose? Vous _____.

2. Nous _____ un grand verre d'eau pour vous.

3. Est-ce que tu _____ bien tes cours? Il y a énormément de choix ici!

4. Les jeunes chiens _____ très vite.

5. Vendredi après-midi, les employés _____ rapidement le travail.

6. _____-vous toujours aux examens?

7. Trop de gâteaux, ça fait _____!

8. Georges est amoureux de Marie. En présence d'elle, il _____ toujours.

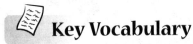

Key Vocabulary

Food and clothing are some of our basic shopping needs. Cities and towns in Francophone regions often have popular small stores, in addition to supermarkets and department stores.

Les magasins et les commerces (Stores and Businesses)

l'agence de voyages (f.)   (travel agency)
la blanchisserie   (laundry)
la boucherie   (butcher, butcher shop)
la boulangerie   (bakery)
la charcuterie   (delicatessen; pork products)
le/la coiffeur (-euse)   (hairdresser)
la confiserie   (candy store)
le cordonnier   (shoemaker)
la droguerie   (paint store, cleaning products)
l'épicerie (f.)   (grocer's, grocery)
le/la fleuriste   (florist's shop)
le grand magasin   (department store)
l'hypermarché (m.)   ("big box" store)
la librairie   (bookstore)
le magasin de chaussures   (shoe store)
le magasin de fruits et légumes   (produce market)
le magasin d'informatique   (computers and software)
le magasin de vêtements   (clothing store)
le marchand de vins   (wine merchant)
l'opticien (m.)   (optician)
la papeterie   (stationery store)
la pâtisserie   (pastry shop)
la pharmacie   (drugstore, pharmacy)
la poste   (post office)
un rabais   (a discount)
la quincaillerie   (hardware store)
des soldes (m. pl.)   (a sale)
le supermarché   (supermarket)
le tailleur   (tailor)
la teinturerie   (dry cleaner's)

Exercise 4.11

Where can you find these products? Write the name of the store or business next to the product or service given. Use **à la/au/à l'** *for places and* **chez le/la/l'** *for people.*

1. de la salade et des fruits _____

2. des bonbons _____

3. des livres _____

4. du papier et des cahiers _____

5. des fleurs _____

6. un billet d'avion _____

7. des médicaments _____

8. des lentilles de contact _____

Key Vocabulary

Les repas et les provisions (Meals and Groceries)

l'abricot (*m.*) (*apricot*)
l'addition (*f.*) (*bill, check*)
l'ananas (*m.*) (*pineapple*)
l'apéritif (*m.*) (*before-dinner drink*)
l'assiette (*f.*) (*plate; bowl*)
la baguette (*baguette*)
la banane (*banana*)
le beurre (*butter*)
la bière (*beer*)
le bifteck (*steak*)
le bœuf (*beef*)
la boisson (*drink*)
la bouteille (*bottle*)
le café (*coffee; café*)
la carotte (*carrot*)
la carte (*menu*)
le céleri (*celery*)

les céréales (*f.*) (*cereal*)
les cerises (*f.*) (*cherries*)
les champignons (*m.*) (*mushrooms*)
le chocolat (*chocolate*)
le/la client(e) (*customer*)
la confiture (*jam, preserves*)
le couteau (*knife*)
la crème (*cream*)
les crevettes (*f.*) (*shrimp*)
le croissant (*croissant*)
la cuillère (*spoon*)
le déjeuner (*lunch*)
le dessert (*dessert*)
le dîner (*dinner*)
l'eau (minérale) (*f.*) (*[mineral] water*)
l'entrée (*f.*) (*first course*)

les épices (*f.*) (*spices*)
la farine (*flour*)
la fourchette (*fork*)
les fraises (*f.*) (*strawberries*)
les framboises (*f.*) (*raspberries*)
les frites (*f.*) (*French fries*)
le fromage (*cheese*)
le fruit (*fruit*)
le gâteau (*cake; cookie*)
la glace (*ice cream*)
le goûter (*afternoon snack*)
les °haricots verts (*m.*) (*green beans*)
les herbes (*f.*) (*herbs*)
le °homard (*lobster*)
les °hors-d'œuvre (*m.*) (*appetizers*)
l'huile d'olive (*f.*) (*olive oil*)
le jambon (*ham*)
le lait (*milk*)
le lard (*bacon*)
le légume (*vegetable*)
la limonade (*carbonated soft drink*)
le melon (*melon*)
le menu du jour (*daily special*)
la moutarde (*mustard*)
la noix (*nut, walnut*)
l'œuf (*m.*) (*egg*)
les olives (*f.*) (*olives*)
l'orange (*f.*) (*orange*)
le pain (*bread*)
le pain au chocolat (*chocolate croissant*)
le pamplemousse (*grapefruit*)
la pêche (*peach*)
la petite cuillère (*teaspoon*)

le petit déjeuner (*breakfast*)
les petits pains (*m.*) (*rolls*)
les petits pois (*m.*) (*peas*)
le plat (*dish; course*)
le plat principal (*main course*)
la poire (*pear*)
le poisson (*fish*)
le poivre (*pepper*)
le poivron (*green pepper*)
la pomme (*apple*)
la pomme de terre (*potato*)
le porc (*pork*)
le potage (*vegetable soup*)
le poulet (*chicken*)
le pourboire (*tip*)
le raisin (*grapes*)
le riz (*rice*)
la salade (*salad; lettuce*)
le sandwich (*sandwich*)
les saucisses (*f. pl.*) (*sausages*)
le sel (*salt*)
le/la serveur (-euse) (*server*)
service compris (*tip included*)
la serviette (*napkin; towel*)
la soupe (*soup*)
le sucre (*sugar*)
la tartine (*buttered bread*)
la tasse (*cup*)
la tarte (*tart, pie*)
le thé (*tea*)
la tomate (*tomato*)
le veau (*veal*)
le verre (*glass*)
la viande (*meat*)
le vin (*wine*)
le yaourt (*yogurt*)

Exercise 4.12

*List some typical ingredients you'll need for the recipes. Use the phrase **j'ai besoin de/d'...** or **on a besoin de/d'...** (without an article).*

1. une omelette: _____

2. un gâteau au chocolat: _____

3. une salade de fruits: _____

4. un potage aux légumes: _____

Exercise 4.13

Complete the sentences with the appropriate noun or nouns from the previous vocabulary lists.

1. Avant le dîner, nous posons sur la table _____.

2. Au restaurant, le serveur apporte d'abord _____.

3. Au petit déjeuner, j'aime _____.

4. Je n'aime pas beaucoup le café, s'il n'a pas beaucoup de _____ et trois cuillérées de _____.

5. Au déjeuner, je suis toujours pressé(e), donc je préfère

   _____.

6. Les végétariens refusent généralement _____; ils aiment mieux _____.

Reading Comprehension

Au restaurant

Il est une heure de l'après-midi et le restaurant français est **plein**. C'est **une brasserie du quartier** économique et **très fréquentée**. Elle a dix-huit tables et cinq serveurs excellents. Il y a quatre ou cinq clients à **chaque** table. L'ambiance est **chaleureuse**. Les gens sont **détendus** parce que c'est **un jour de fête**, le premier mai, **le jour du travail**.

L'établissement a deux étages; au **rez-de-chaussée** il y a des boissons, des sandwichs et des salades; au **premier étage**, il y a le menu complet. Sur la carte, il y a un menu du jour au **prix fixe** et d'autres plats: du poulet, de la viande et du poisson. Le menu du jour propose une soupe, du **saumon poché**, des pommes de terre, des légumes, de la salade, un dessert et une boisson — du café ou du thé. Tout est délicieux aujourd'hui!

plein(e)	*full*
une brasserie	*bistro*
du quartier	*neighborhood*
très fréquenté(e)	*very popular*
chaque	*each, every*
chaleureux (-euse)	*warm, friendly*
détendu(e)	*relaxed*
jour de fête	*holiday*
le jour du Travail	*Labor Day*
l'établissement (*m.*)	*place, business*
le rez-de-chaussée	*ground floor*
premier étage	*second floor (level)*
prix fixe	*fixed-price menu*
du saumon poché	*poached salmon*

Questions

After reading the selection, answer the questions in French.

1. À quelle heure est-ce que les amis déjeunent?

   _____.

2. Où déjeunent-ils? _____.

   _____.

3. Est-ce que le restaurant est vide (*empty*)? _____.

   _____.

4. Si non, pourquoi n'est-il pas vide? _____.

   _____.

5. Quel étage choisissent-ils? Pourquoi? _____.

   _____.

6. Imaginez le repas du narrateur. _____.

   _____.

5

Regular -re Verbs in the Present Tense and -er Verbs with Spelling Changes

Regular -re Verbs in the Present Tense

Regular verbs with infinitives ending in **-re** are conjugated in the present tense as follows:

Present Tense of attendre (to wait, wait for)	
j'attend**s**	nous attend**ons**
tu attend**s**	vous attend**ez**
il/elle/on attend	ils/elles attend**ent**

Elle **attend** l'autobus, et nous **attendons** la conférence.	*She **is waiting for** the bus, and we **are waiting for** the the lecture.*
Mes amis **attendent** les vacances.	*My friends **are waiting for** the holidays.*

Be aware of these details regarding regular **-re** verbs:

- The third-person singular form (**il/elle/on attend**) of regular **-re** verbs has no ending. To conjugate it, remove the infinitive ending (**-re**); the stem of the verb is the conjugated form. In this form, the letter **-d** is silent (not pronounced), and the word ends with the nasal vowel:

  elle attend [ah-tA^n], **il vend** [vA^n]

- The English verb *to wait* always uses the preposition *for* before a noun. In French, **attendre** is followed directly by the noun.

J'**attends** mon ami.	*I **am waiting for** my friend.*

87

- In French, **attendre** does not mean *to attend*. *To attend* (*a lecture, a concert*, etc.) is expressed by **assister à** (**une conférence, un concert, etc.**).

    Other regular **-re** verbs include:

défendre	*to defend; to forbid*
descendre	*to go down; to get off*
entendre	*to hear*
perdre	*to lose*
perdre du temps	*to waste time*
rendre	*to give (back), to return*
répondre (à)	*to answer*
rendre visite à	*to visit (a person)*
tendre	*to stretch (out) (s.th.); to offer*
vendre	*to sell*

Michel **vend** sa vieille voiture.	*Michel **is selling** his old car.*
Nous **rendons visite aux** voisins dimanche.	*We **are visiting the** neighbors on Sunday.*
Tu **entends**? C'est ton portable.	***Do** you **hear**? That's your cell phone.*
—Je **réponds**!	*—I **am answering**!*
Les enfants **perdent** souvent les clés.	*Children often **lose** the keys.*
Où est-ce qu'on **descend** de l'autobus?	*Where **do** we **get off** the bus?*

- **Rendre visite** and **répondre** both require the preposition **à** before a noun.

Ils **répondent** toujours *à* mes questions.	*They always **answer** my questions.*
Tu **rends visite** *aux* voisins?	***Are** you **visiting** the neighbors?*

    Use the verb **visiter** + noun to express a visit to a city, building, museum, natural site, etc. Use **rendre visite à** for visits to people.

    Irregular verbs with infinitives ending in **-re** are presented in Chapters 7 to 9.

Inverted Question Forms and *liaison*

In the *inverted question form*, the **-d** of regular third-person singular **-re** verbs is pronounced [t]. It links with the vowel in **-il**, **-elle**, or **-on**.

Vend-on... ?	[vAⁿ-tOⁿ]	*Do they sell . . . ?*
Attend-il?	[ah-tAⁿ-teel]	*Is he waiting?*
Perd-elle... ?	[pehR-tehl]	*Does she lose . . . ?*

The **liaison** with the letter **t** [t] is also pronounced in the third-person singular or plural, linking with the following subject pronoun that starts with a vowel. This applies to verbs of all groups.

Vendent-elles... ?	[vAⁿ-d(uh)-tehl]	*Do they sell . . . ?*
Aiment-ils... ?	[ehm-teel]	*Do they love . . . ?*
Choisit-on... ?	[shwah-zee-tOⁿ]	*Are we choosing . . . ?*

Exercise 5.1

Say and write these sentences in French. Use the present tense of regular verbs ending in **-re**.

1. Are you (*fam.*) coming down? _____?

2. I'm losing. _____.

3. We're answering. _____.

4. Xavier is selling a truck (**un camion**). _____.

5. They (*f.*) visit Grandfather. _____.

6. You (*pol.*) don't answer. _____.

7. We're waiting for Charles. _____.

8. They (*m.*) defend their clients. _____.

9. The student (*m.*) isn't wasting time. _____.

10. Do you (*pol.*) hear? _____?

11. Is she returning the book? _____?

12. I'm answering the phone. _____.

Key Vocabulary

How often do you do things? The following adverbs are used after verbs to tell how often or how much you do something. You have already been using some of them.

Expressions de temps (Expressions of Frequency and Time)

beaucoup (*a lot; often*)	toujours (*always*)
quelquefois, parfois (*sometimes*)	très peu (*rarely, hardly ever*)
rarement (*rarely*)	un peu (*a little*)
souvent (*often*)	

J'étudie **toujours** à la maison.	*I **always** study at home.*
Gaspard réussit **rarement**.	*Gaspard **rarely** succeeds.*
Ils ne répondent pas **beaucoup**.	*They don't answer **much**.*

The expressions below also help situate the action. They can all be used with the present tense, sometimes with the meaning of the near future.

actuellement	*presently, currently, nowadays*
bientôt	*soon*
en ce moment	*right now*
maintenant	*now*
(un peu) plus tard	*(a little) later*
prochain(e)	*next (adj.)*
tout à l'heure	*in a little while*

Où est-ce que tu travailles **actuellement**?	*Where are you working **nowadays**?*
Attends! Je descends **bientôt**.	*Wait! I'm coming down **soon**.*
On rend visite à Sylvie **tout à l'heure**.	*We're visiting Sylvie **in a little while**.*
Paul quitte son boulot **la semaine prochaine**.	*Paul is leaving his job **next week**.*

Exercise 5.2

Complete each sentence with the correct form of one of the verbs listed, and translate the time and frequency expressions in parentheses into French. Some of the verbs given will be used more than once.

attendre, défendre, descendre, entendre, perdre, rendre, répondre, vendre

1. Le samedi et le dimanche, on _____ (*often*)
   _____ du temps; on adore le week-end!

2. Tu _____ (*rarely*) _____ des amis qui
   trichent (*cheat*).

3. Attends-moi! Je _____ (*presently*) _____
   au téléphone.

4. À l'épicerie, les employés _____ (*always*)
   _____ la monnaie en espèces (*in cash*).

5. (*Right now*) _____ je/j' _____ les
   résultats de l'examen.

6. _____-vous (*now*) _____ le bruit des
   avions?

7. Nous _____ (*soon*) _____ la vieille auto
   de Papa à un étudiant pauvre.

8. La semaine (*next*) _____, c'est promis: on
   _____ à tous les courriels de la semaine passée,
   n'est-ce pas?

9. Margot _____ (*sometimes*) _____ visite à
   des amis à Montréal.

10. Est-ce que tu _____ (*later*) _____ en ville
    retrouver tes amis?

11. Les gens très organisés _____ (*hardly ever*)
    _____ leurs affaires (*their belongings*).

Depuis Versus *Since*

The word **depuis**, meaning *for* or *since* (in time) follows verbs in the present tense. It precedes either a period of time (**deux ans, cinq minutes...**) or a beginning point in time (**le 15 août, midi, cinq heures, 2003, mon enfance, le début de l'année...**).

J'étudie le français **depuis** **un an**.	*I've been studying French for a year.*
Nous attendons le bus **depuis quelque temps**.	*We've been waiting for the bus for a while.*
Mon frère habite à Paris **depuis mars**.	*My brother has been living in Paris since March.*
Ils sont membres de ce groupe **depuis 2002**.	*They've been members of this group since 2002.*

- In English the verbs in sentences with *for* or *since* are in the present perfect, with *have* + past participle or *has been* + a present participle (the *-ing* form of the verb): *They've been members . . . , I've been studying . . ., My brother has been living . . . .*

  French always uses the *present tense* with **depuis** (**Ils sont...** , **J'étudie...** , **Mon frère habite...**), if the action is current and ongoing.

- To ask the question *Since when . . . ?* with a *point in time*, say **Depuis quand... ?**

Depuis quand voyagez-vous?	*Since when have you been traveling?*
—Nous voyageons **depuis le 25 janvier**.	*—We have been traveling since January 25.*

To ask the question *For how long . . . ?* or *How long . . . ?* with a *span of time* say **Depuis combien de temps... ?**

Depuis combien de temps habites-tu ici?	*How long have you been living (lived) here?*
—J'habite ici **depuis six ans**.	*—I've lived here for six years.*

Other French Expressions for *Since*

When used with the present tense, the expressions (**il y a... que...** , **voilà... que...** , and **ça fait... que...**) have the same meaning as **depuis** (*since, for*).

These expressions—each one includes the time elapsed—precede the main verb.

J'habite à Paris **depuis deux ans**.

Il y a deux ans que j'habite à Paris.

Voilà deux ans que j'habite à Paris.

Ça fait deux ans que j'habite à Paris.

I've lived (been living) in Paris ***for two years***.

Exercise 5.3

Answer the personal questions using **depuis** *and the present tense. Here, the answer to* **votre...** *(your) is* **mon/ma/mes...** *(my), before a noun.*

1. Depuis combien de temps étudiez-vous le français?

   _____.

2. Depuis quand êtes-vous étudiant(e)?

   _____.

3. Parlez-vous une autre langue? Depuis quand?

   _____.

4. Depuis quand habitez-vous votre maison?

   _____.

5. Depuis combien de temps travaillez-vous? et dans ce lieu (*place*) de travail?

   _____.

6. Depuis quand passez-vous du temps avec votre meilleur(e) ami(e)?

   _____.

-er Verbs with Spelling Changes

The conjugations of several groups of regular **-er** verbs have slight spelling irregularities.

There are six major patterns of spelling changes. Learn the following models, and you will know the others in each group.

Verbs like *commencer* (to begin)

To keep the soft [s] sound, verbs with infinitives ending in **-cer** change **-c-** to **-ç-** (**c** cedilla) when **-c-** occurs before **-a-** or **-o-**.

In the present tense, this change occurs in the **nous** form only (**nous commençons**).

Present Tense of *commencer* and *lancer*

commencer (*to begin*)

je commence	nous commen**ç**ons
tu commences	vous commencez
il/elle/on commence	ils/elles commencent

lancer (*to throw, launch*)

je lance	nous lançons
tu lances	vous lancez
il/elle/on lance	ils/elles lancent

The spelling change in **-cer** verbs is also found in forms of the imperfect past tense (Chapter 14) and the present participle (Chapter 12). Other verbs like **commencer** include the following:

annoncer	*to announce*	percer	*to pierce*
avancer	*to advance*	placer	*to place*
dénoncer	*to denounce*	prononcer	*to pronounce*
divorcer	*to divorce*	remplacer	*to replace*
forcer (à)	*to force*	tracer	*to trace (out)*
menacer	*to threaten*		

Tu **lances** ta boîte cette année?	*Are you opening your business this year?*
Nous **prononçons** bien le nouveau vocabulaire!	*We pronounce the new vocabulary well!*
Mes voisins sont en train de **divorcer**.	*My neighbors are divorcing.*
—Quel dommage! C'est un beau couple.	*—What a pity! They're a lovely couple.*
Vous **remplacez** ce cours par un autre?	*Are you replacing this class with another one?*

Verbs like *manger* (to eat)

To keep the soft **g** sound [j], verbs with infinitives ending in **-ger** introduce the letter **e** (a mute **e**) before an **-a-** or an **-o-** at the start of the conjugated verb ending. In the present tense this spelling change occurs in the **nous** form only (**nous mangeons**).

Present Tense of *manger* and *exiger*

manger (*to eat*)	**exiger** (*to demand*)
je mange	j'exige
tu manges	tu exiges
il/elle/on mange	il/elle/on exige
nous mang**e**ons	nous exi**ge**ons

vous mangez   vous exigez
ils/elles mangent   ils/elles exigent

The spelling change for **-ger** verbs is also seen in the imperfect (Chapter 14) and the present participle (Chapter 12). Other verbs like **manger** include the following:

arranger (*to arrange*)	loger (*to live [somewhere]*;
bouger (*to move*)	*to house*)
changer (*to change*)	mélanger (*to mix*)
corriger (*to correct*)	nager (*to swim*)
dégager (*to free, release*)	neiger (*to snow*)
diriger (*to direct*)	obliger (à) (*to oblige; to force*)
échanger (*to exchange*)	partager (*to share*)
engager (*to hire*)	songer (à) (*to dream; to think of,*
interroger (*to question*)	*about*)
juger (*to judge*)	voyager (*to travel*)

Nous **mélangeons** le sucre et les fruits.	*We **mix** the sugar and the fruit.*
Mes parents **voyagent** beaucoup.	*My parents **travel** a lot.*
Le patron **engage** deux ingénieurs.	*The boss **is hiring** two engineers.*
Nous **logeons** chez tante Lucie cet été?	***Are** we **staying** with Aunt Lucie this summer?*
Tu **nages** bien?	***Do** you **swim** well?*

Il neige (*it snows, it is snowing*) is used only in the third-person singular (impersonal).

Exercise 5.4

*Translate the sentences into French, using verbs conjugated like **commencer** and* **manger**.

1. We share the sandwich. _____.

2. They (*m.*) eat well. _____.

3. When do we begin to talk? _____?

4. You (*fam.*) pronounce the sentence (**la phrase**). _____.

5. The neighbors are housing two students. _____.

6. Are you (*pol.*) launching the new business (**l'entreprise** [*f.*])?

   _____?

7. Charlotte is mixing the ingredients (**les ingrédients**).

   _____.

8. Are we announcing the party? _____?

9. Do you (*pol.*) exchange books? _____?

10. Aren't you (*fam.*) dreaming about vacation? _____?

11. The professor demands the homework. _____.

12. We oblige the children to eat vegetables. _____.

13. Are you (*fam.*) tracing out the plan (**le projet**)? _____?

14. The boss isn't hiring (any) new employees (**employés**, *m.*).

    _____.

15. Pronouns (**pronoms**) replace nouns (**noms**). _____.

Verbs like *acheter* (to buy)

Verbs with a mute **e** in the syllable before the **-er** infinitive ending (**acheter**, **lever**) change the mute **e** to **è** (adding a grave accent) in forms that have a mute **e** in the verb *ending*. This means that the rule does *not* apply to **nous** and **vous** forms.

Present Tense of *acheter* and *lever*

acheter (*to buy*)	**lever** (*to raise, lift*)
j'ach**è**te	je l**è**ve
tu ach**è**tes	tu l**è**ves
il/elle/on ach**è**te	il/elle/on l**è**ve
nous achetons	nous levons
vous achetez	vous levez
ils/elles ach**è**tent	ils/elles l**è**vent

Other verbs like **acheter** include:

achever (de)	*to finish*
amener	*to bring (s.o.)*
élever	*to erect; to raise*
emmener	*to lead away*

enlever	*to remove*
geler	*to freeze*
se lever	*to get up, stand up*
mener	*to lead, guide*
peser	*to weigh*
promener	*to walk* (e.g., *the dog*)
se promener	*to take a walk, a drive*
soulever	*to lift* (*up*)

The pronoun **se** (or **s'**), when listed with an infinitive (**se lever**, **se promener**), indicates that the verb is reflexive or pronominal. Reflexive and pronominal verbs are presented in Chapter 12.

Je **pèse** les légumes?	***Shall I weigh*** *the vegetables?*
Nous **amenons** nos amis ce soir.	*We **will bring** our friends this evening.*
Guy et sa copine **promènent** le chien?	***Are*** *Guy and his girlfriend **walking** the dog?*
Tu **n'achèves pas** le travail?	***Aren't** you **finishing** the job?*

Exercise 5.5

*Translate the sentences into French, using verbs conjugated like **acheter** and **lever**.*

1. We finish the work. _____.

2. Marthe weighs the onions (**les oignons**). _____.

3. Are you (*fam.*) walking the dog? _____?

4. They (*m.*) lead away the horse (**le cheval**). _____.

5. Léon removes the books. _____.

6. I'm not bringing Christine this evening. _____.

7. Nicolas and Lise are raising the children well. _____.

8. What are you (*fam.*) buying? _____?

9. Pierre lifts up the big cartons (**les gros cartons**). _____.

10. The guide leads the tourists to the hotel. _____.

11. Don't you (*pol.*) buy eggs? _____?

12. We raise our hands (**la main**) in class. _____.

13. Does Émile raise rabbits (**des lapins**)? _____?

14. They (*f.*) finish speaking. _____.

15. I'm not buying the groceries (**les provisions**). _____.

Verbs like *préférer* (to prefer)

Verbs with an **-é-** (acute accent) in the syllable before the **-er** infinitive ending (**préférer**, **céder**) change the **-é-** to **-è-** (with a grave accent) in forms where it occurs in the final sounded syllable.

The verb ending after **-è-** is *unsounded*. Therefore, this spelling change does not apply to **nous** or **vous** forms, or to the infinitive.

Present Tense of *préférer* and *céder*

préférer (*to prefer*)	**céder** (*to yield, give in*)
je préfère	je cède
tu préfères	tu cèdes
il/elle/on préfère	il/elle/on cède
nous préférons	nous cédons
vous préférez	vous cédez
ils/elles préfèrent	ils/elles cèdent

Verbs like **préférer** *retain* the acute accent (**-é-**) in all forms of the future and the conditional (**je préférerai** *I will prefer*; **elle préférerait** *she would prefer*) (Chapter 15). Other verbs like **préférer** include:

célébrer	to celebrate
compléter	to complete
considérer	to consider
espérer	to hope to
exagérer	to exaggerate
(s')inquiéter	to worry
pénétrer	to penetrate
posséder	to own, possess
répéter	to repeat
révéler	to show, reveal
suggérer	to suggest

Qu'est-ce que vous **préférez**?

J'**espère** que tu **considères**
le résultat.

Ils **suggèrent** que je mange
moins de sucre.

Tu **exagères**!
—Non, je **n'exagère pas**!
Elle t'aime bien.

*What **do** you **prefer**?*

*I **hope** you **are thinking** about
the result.*

*They **suggest** I eat less sugar.*

*You **are exaggerating**!
—No, I **am not exaggerating**!
She likes you a lot.*

 Exercise 5.6

Translate the sentences into French using verbs conjugated like **préférer** *and* **céder.**

1. We hope to succeed. _____.

2. Are they (*f.*) celebrating the birthday? _____?

3. I hope to travel in the summer. _____.

4. The professor repeats the question. _____.

5. She doesn't own a car. _____.

6. He's exaggerating. _____.

7. The article reveals the truth (**la vérité**). _____.

8. Are you (*fam.*) considering the facts (**les faits**)?

    _____?

9. Aren't you (*pol.*) repeating the course? _____?

10. You're (*fam.*) worrying your (**tes**) parents! _____!

11. We suggest a good movie. _____.

12. Aren't you (*fam.*) completing the assignment (**le devoir**)?

    _____?

13. Do you (*pol.*) prefer coffee or tea? _____?

14. She's yielding the lane (**la voie**) to the other car.

    _____.

15. Christophe prefers green beans. _____.

Verbs like *appeler* (to call; to name) and *jeter* (to throw [away])

Present tense forms of verbs with infinitives ending with **-eler** or **-eter** double the consonant (**l** or **t**) when the conjugated verb ending contains a mute **e**. This change does not occur in the present tense **nous** and **vous** forms of **appeler** and **jeter**.

Present Tense of *appeler* and *jeter*

appeler *(to call; to name)*	**jeter** *(to throw [away])*
j'appe**ll**e	je je**tt**e
tu appe**ll**es	tu je**tt**es
il/elle/on appe**ll**e	il/elle/on je**tt**e
nous appelons	nous jetons
vous appelez	vous jetez
ils/elles appe**ll**ent	ils/elles je**tt**ent

The spelling change to a double consonant for verbs like **appeler** and **jeter** also occurs in all forms of the future and the conditional (Chapter 15). Other verbs like **appeler** and **jeter** include:

s'appeler	*to be named, be called* (see Chapter 12)
épeler	*to spell*
projeter	*to plan; to project*
rappeler	*to recall; to call again; to remind*
se rappeler	*to remember* (see Chapter 12)
rejeter	*to reject; to throw back*
renouveler	*to renew; to renovate*

Je vous **rappelle** que nous sommes en retard.	*I **am reminding** you that we're late.*
Vous **jetez** déjà les journaux?	*Are you **throwing out** the newspapers already?*
On **projette** le film lundi prochain.	*They **are showing** the film next Monday.*
Elles **appellent** leurs amis le soir.	*They **phone** their friends in the evenings.*

Exercise 5.7

Translate the sentences into French using verbs conjugated like **appeler** *and* **jeter**.

1. What's your (*pol.*) name? _____?

2. My name is Rachelle. _____.

3. Are you (*fam.*) calling Marc? _____?

4. I don't throw away the magazines. _____.

5. How does one (**on**) spell the name? _____?

6. We're planning a vacation. _____.

7. I call Mom on Saturdays. _____.

8. She's calling Zoé again this evening (**ce soir**). _____.

9. He doesn't throw the ball (**le ballon**). _____.

10. We're renovating the bathroom. _____.

11. She rejects the idea. _____.

12. Are you (*pol.*) tossing out the old newspapers? _____?

13. I'm renewing the passport. _____.

14. When are they (**on**) showing the movie? _____?

15. What are they (*m.*) planning? _____?

Verbs like *envoyer* (to send) and *essayer* (to try)

Verbs with infinitives ending in **-yer** change **-y-** into **-i-** before a mute **e** in a conjugated verb ending. This spelling change does not occur in the **nous** and **vous** forms.

Present Tense of *envoyer* and *essayer*

envoyer (*to send*)	**essayer** (*to try*)
j'envoie	j'essaie
tu envoies	tu essaies
il/elle/on envoie	il/elle/on essaie
nous envoyons	nous essayons
vous envoyez	vous essayez
ils/elles envoient	ils/elles essaient

The spelling change for verbs like **envoyer** also occurs in the future and the conditional (Chapter 15).

Some writers in French do not make the spelling change for verbs ending in **-ayer** (**essayer** and **payer**), retaining the **-y-** before a mute **e** (**j'essaye**, **elles essayent**). Pronunciation remains the same: [jeh-say, ehl-zeh-say]. Other verbs like **envoyer** and **essayer** include:

aboyer	*to bark (dog)*
appuyer (sur)	*to lean on; to support; to press on*
employer	*to use*
ennuyer	*to bore; to annoy*
essuyer	*to wipe; to undergo, suffer*
nettoyer	*to clean*
s'ennuyer	*to be/get bored* (see Chapter 12)
payer	*to pay, to pay for*

Elles **envoient** des cartes au Nouvel An.	*They **send** cards at New Year's.*
Le samedi nous **nettoyons** la salle de bains.	*We **clean** the bathroom on Saturday.*
Je t'assure. Ce chien **aboie** toute la nuit.	*Believe me. That dog **barks** all night.*
Vous **payez** les factures à la fin du mois?	***Do** you **pay** the bills at the end of the month?*

The French verb **payer** (*to pay for*) is followed immediately by a direct object; there is no equivalent of the English *for*: **Je paie mon repas en espèces**. (*I pay for my meal in cash.*)

Exercise 5.8

Translate the sentences into French using verbs conjugated like **envoyer** *and* **essayer**.

1. I send postcards. _____.

2. You (*fam.*) don't try to succeed. _____.

3. The little dog barks. _____.

4. She tries to be patient. _____.

5. He supports my application (**ma demande**). _____.

6. Don't you (*pol.*) use a computer? _____?

7. We use dictionaries. _____.

8. I wipe the stove. _____.

9. You (*fam.*) pay for lunch. _____.

10. Évelyne cleans the kitchen. _____.

11. Does she bore the students? _____?

12. I press (on) the keys (**les touches**). _____.

13. We're paying their salary (**leur salaire**). _____.

14. Are you (*pol.*) using the money (**l'argent**) well? _____?

15. They (*m.*) send the books. _____.

Exercise 5.9

Using the suggested verbs, complete the sentences, possibly using the infinitive. Each verb will only be used once.

acheter, annoncer, appeler, commencer, envoyer, essayer, jeter, lever, manger, partager, payer, préférer, projeter, prononcer, répéter, voyager

1. _____-tu les provisions à l'épicerie?

2. Marc et Sophie n'aiment pas la cuisine vietnamienne; ils _____ la cuisine thaïlandaise.

3. On _____ le film à vingt-deux heures.

4. Marie est à la poste; elle _____ un gros paquet.

5. Le repas dans ce restaurant est trop copieux; donc, nous _____ le plat.

6. Je trouve les exercices difficiles, pourtant je/j' _____ de finir les devoirs.

7. Il est déjà tard. Quand _____-nous à dîner?

8. Finalement, nous _____ bien les voyelles et les consonnes françaises.

9. Le mardi soir, je/j' _____ toujours les vieux journaux.

10. Le professeur _____ un examen pour demain.

11. Monique _____ toujours la main, pour répondre à une question.

12. Les enfants adorent _____ des bonbons.

13. Mes parents sont libres maintenant; ils _____ beaucoup en Europe.

14. Tu _____ les factures (*bills*) à la fin du mois?

15. Vous êtes aussi dans cette classe? Comment vous _____- vous?

16. En classe, le prof _____-t-il les phrases (*sentences*) plusieurs fois?

 ## Key Vocabulary

When we travel, we often want to replace items, purchase new clothes, or shop for souvenirs.

Les vêtements et les accessoires (Clothing and Accessories)

un appareil-photo (*camera*)	un maillot de bain (*swimsuit*)
des bas (*m.*) (*stockings*)	un manteau (*coat, overcoat*)
des boucles d'oreille (*f.*) (*earrings*)	une montre (*wristwatch*)
un bracelet (*bracelet*)	un pantalon (*pants, trousers*)
un caleçon (*men's briefs*)	des pantoufles (*f.*) (*slippers*)
une ceinture (*belt*)	un parapluie (*umbrella*)
un chapeau (*hat*)	un portable (*cell phone*)
des chaussettes (*f.*) (*socks*)	un portefeuille (*wallet*)
des chaussures (*f.*) (*shoes*)	un pull (*sweater*)
une chemise (*shirt*)	un pyjama (*pyjamas*)
un chemisier (*blouse*)	une robe (*dress*)
un collier (*necklace*)	une robe de nuit (*nightgown*)
une écharpe (*scarf* [*knit*])	un sac (à main) (*handbag*)
un foulard (*scarf* [*silk*])	des sandales (*f.*) (*sandals*)
des gants (*m.*) (*gloves*)	un short ([*pair of*] *shorts*)
un gilet (*vest*)	un slip (*underpants* [*f.*])
un jean (*jeans*)	un sweat-shirt (*sweatshirt*)
une jupe (*skirt*)	un T-shirt (*T-shirt*)
des lunettes (de soleil) (*f.*) ([*sun*]*glasses*)	un soutien-gorge (*bra*)
	une veste (*jacket*)

Articles de toilette (Toiletries)

une brosse à cheveux	*hairbrush*
une brosse à dents	*toothbrush*
des couches (jetables) (*f.*)	*disposable diapers*
une crème démaquillante	*cleansing cream, cold cream*
une crème solaire	*sunscreen*
du démêlant (*m.*)	*(hair) conditioner*
du dentifrice (*m.*)	*toothpaste*
du déodorant (*m.*)	*deodorant*
une éponge	*sponge*
du fil et une aiguille	*thread and a needle*
une lotion (après-rasage)	*(after-shave) lotion*
du maquillage (*m.*)	*makeup*
un miroir	*mirror*
des mouchoirs (*m.*)	*tissues*
une lime à ongles	*nail file*
du vernis à ongles (*m.*)	*nail polish*
du papier hygiénique (*m.*)	*toilet paper*
du parfum (*m.*)	*perfume*
un peigne	*comb*
des lames de rasoir (*f.*)	*razor blades*
un rouge à lèvres	*lipstick*
un rasoir (électrique)	*(electric) razor*
un savon	*(cake of) soap*
un sèche-cheveux	*hair dryer*
des serviettes hygiéniques (*f.*)	*sanitary napkins*
du shampooing (*m.*)	*shampoo*
des tampons périodiques (*m.*)	*tampons*

Exercise 5.10

Write the names of the items in French.

1. a lipstick _____

2. men's briefs _____

3. razor blades _____

4. earrings _____

5. a belt _____

6. a wristwatch _____

7. a pair of jeans _____

8. a swimsuit _____

9. a handbag _____

10. tissues _____

11. a hair dryer _____

12. a jacket _____

13. sunglasses _____

14. an umbrella _____

15. a wallet _____

16. a skirt _____

17. sunblock _____

18. a comb _____

19. slippers _____

20. toothpaste _____

Exercise 5.11

You're packing for a summer trip. Write in French the items requested below.

1. Vous organisez votre trousse de toilette (*toiletry kit*). De quoi avez-vous besoin?

   _____.

2. Vous partez pour la Martinique. Qu'est-ce que vous placez dans la valise?

   _____.

3. Avant le voyage, achetez-vous certaines choses? Qu'achetez-vous?

   _____.

Reading Comprehension

En ville

Le samedi matin vers onze heures, j'adore **retrouver** mes amies pour visiter les magasins et **les boutiques** de **notre centre-ville**. On réfléchit bien **avant de** choisir **les courses**: parfois, on a besoin de provisions pour le dîner de samedi soir. Ou bien, c'est bientôt **les Fêtes** et nous avons le plaisir de choisir **des cadeaux** pour **nos proches**, et naturellement pour **nous-mêmes**! Les grands magasins et les hypermarchés sont bien, mais nous préférons fréquenter les petits commerces qui sont encore **tenus** par une **seule** famille: pour les aliments, il y a la boulangerie, le marchand de fruits et légumes et la boucherie, et pour **les autres achats**, il y a par exemple: la librairie-papeterie, la cordonnerie, la droguerie, etc. **En fin de matinée** nous passons à l'agence de voyages pour **feuilleter** des brochures et rêver de nos prochaines vacances.

À midi et demi, dans notre restaurant favori, le serveur nous demande: « Vous **êtes prêtes à commander**? » Et nous **lui** demandons de recommander **quelque chose de bon**. Nous choisissons **une bisque de homard**, une salade verte, et comme dessert, **une bombe glacée** à **partager**.

retrouver	*to get together*
les boutiques (*f. pl.*)	*shops*
avant de	*before*
notre centre-ville (*m.*)	*our downtown*
les courses (*f. pl.*)	*errands*
les Fêtes (*f. pl.*)	*the holidays*
des cadeaux (*m. pl.*)	*gifts*
nos proches (*m. pl.*)	*our loved ones*
nous-mêmes	*ourselves*
tenu(e)(s)	*maintained, managed*
seul(e)	*one, single*
les autres achats (*m. pl.*)	*other purchases*
en fin de matinée	*in the late morning*
feuilleter	*to leaf through*
être prêt(e)(s) à	*to be ready to*
commander	*to order*
lui	*him*
quelque chose de bon	*something good*
une bisque de homard	*lobster bisque*
une bombe glacée	*ice-cream dessert*
partager	*to share*

Questions

After reading the selection, answer the questions in French.

1. Quelles sont les activités de la narratrice et de ses (*her*) amies? Quelles courses choisissent-elles?

   _____.

2. Quels commerces préfèrent-elles?

   _____.

3. Que regardent-elles à l'agence de voyages? Pourquoi?

   _____.

4. Qu'est-ce qu'elles commandent comme repas au restaurant?

   _____.

6

Expressing the Future with *aller*, Prepositions, and the Verb *faire*

The Verb *aller* (to go)

The verb **aller** is irregular in the present tense. It expresses direction, movement, or intention.

You will notice that the conjugations of **aller** and **faire** (*to do; to make*), are similar in some forms, but it is best to learn them separately.

Present Tense of aller (*to go*)

je **vais**	nous **allons**
tu **vas**	vous **allez**
il/elle/on **va**	ils/elles **vont**

Nous **allons** au resto, mais Richard **va** au cinéma.	We **are going** to the restaurant, but Richard **is going** to the movies.
Mes sœurs **vont** bientôt à Paris.	My sisters **are going** to Paris soon.
Vous **n'allez pas** en Europe?	**Aren't** you **going** to Europe?

You've already learned forms of the verb **aller** in several expressions of greeting.

Comment **allez**-vous?	How are you? (*pol.*) (Literally: How **are** you **going**?)
(Comment **vas**-tu?)	(How are you? [*fam.*])
—Je **vais bien**, merci.	—I am well, thank you.
Salut, ça **va**?	Hi, how **is** it **going**? (*fam.*)

109

—Ça **va** bien, merci.

(Ça **ne va pas** très bien.)

—*Fine, thanks.* (*It **is going** well, thanks.*)

(*It **is not going** very well.*)

 ## Exercise 6.1

Complete the sentences with the correct forms of the verb **aller**.

1. Tu _____ en Suisse cet été?

2. Philippe _____ bientôt au travail.

3. Nous _____ au théâtre samedi soir.

4. Régine _____-t-elle à La Nouvelle-Orléans?

5. Comment _____-vous?

6. Comment _____ les enfants?

Expressing the Future with *aller*

Aller + infinitive (called **le futur proche**) is often used to express a future event, usually something that will happen in the near future.

Aller + infinitive may also refer to more distant future plans, events, or intentions.

On **va appeler** Simone.	*We **are going to call** Simone.*
Elles **vont quitter** Genève ce soir.	*They **are going to leave** Geneva this evening.*
Tu **vas porter** un jean?	*You **are going to wear** jeans?*
Nous **allons décider** plus tard.	*We **are going to decide** later.*

Questions with **aller** + infinitive are formed with intonation or **est-ce que** in the usual way. Inversion, if used, is made with the conjugated form of **aller**, before the infinitive.

With a Pronoun Subject

Tu vas porter un jean?
Est-ce que tu vas porter un jean?   } *Are you going to wear jeans?*
Vas-tu porter un jean?

With a Noun Subject

Jean-Claude **va** porter un jean? ⎫
Est-ce que Jean-Claude **va** porter un jean? ⎬ *Is Jean-Claude*
Jean-Claude **va-t-il** porter un jean? ⎭ *going to wear jeans?*

As with other verbs, the *negative* **ne... pas** construction surrounds the conjugated forms of **aller**. In **aller** + infinitive, **pas** precedes the infinitive.

Elle **ne va pas** arriver avant midi.   *She **won't/isn't going** to arrive before noon.*

Vous **n'allez pas** passer à la poste?   ***Aren't** you **going** to stop at the post office?*

Key Vocabulary

The following expressions are often used with the construction **aller** + infinitive. They can follow the verb or be placed at the beginning or end of a sentence.

Alors, quand vas-tu... ? **(So, when are you going to . . . ?)**	
l'année prochaine	*next year*
après-demain	*the day after tomorrow*
cet après-midi	*this afternoon*
bientôt	*soon*
demain	*tomorrow*
dans huit/quinze jours	*in a week/two weeks*
ce matin	*this morning*
la semaine prochaine	*next week*
ce soir	*this evening, tonight*
tout à l'heure	*in a little while, soon*
tout de suite	*right away, immediately*
(un peu) plus tard	*(a little) later*
ce week-end	*this weekend*

Je vais dîner **tout à l'heure**.   *I'm going to have dinner **in a little while**.*

Demain, nous allons retrouver nos copains.   ***Tomorrow**, we'll meet our friends.*

Où est-ce que tu vas loger **ce soir**?   *Where are you going to stay **tonight**?*

Exercise 6.2

Create and write a question using the elements given, and then answer it in French.

1. où/aller/vous/étudier/cet après-midi?

   _____?

   _____.

2. quand/les étudiants/aller/quitter/le campus?

   _____?

   _____.

3. combien de/argent/aller/vous/gagner (*to earn*)/cet été?

   _____?

   _____.

4. quel/aliments/aller/elle/acheter?

   _____?

   _____.

5. que/aller/tu/nettoyer/ce week-end?

   _____?

   _____.

Exercise 6.3

Read the English indirect *sentence, and then write the original* direct *sentence in French.*

1. Simone says she's going to arrive this afternoon.

   « Je _____. »

2. Mom says the children are going to visit the museum (**le musée**) next week.

   « Les enfants _____. »

3. Pierre says he and Josette are going to travel next year.

   « Nous _____. »

4. My good friend Diane asks me if I'm going to work this weekend.

« _____ ? »

5. Dad asks the children where they are going to go.

« Où _____ ? »

À, *de*, and Other Prepositions

A *preposition* shows the relationship of a noun or a pronoun to another word in a sentence, clause, or phrase. In general, prepositions are followed by verb infinitives, nouns, or pronouns.

- A few of the most commonly used prepositions are:

à   (*at; to; in*)   en   (*in; on*)
avec (*with*)   pour (*for; to, in order to*)
de (*of; from; about*)   sans (*without*)

Bruno arrive **avec** Éliane.	*Bruno is coming **with** Éliane.*
Roger va dîner **avec** nous.	*Roger is going to have dinner **with** us.*
Marceline parle souvent **sans** écouter.	*Marceline often speaks **without** listening.*
Est-ce que tu travailles **pour** gagner ta vie?	*Do you work **in order to** earn a living?*
J'aime voyager seul, **sans** compagnons.	*I like to travel alone, **without** companions.*

- **En** is often used in fixed expressions of space and time. It's best to learn each expression as a whole.

Nous sommes **en classe** ce matin.	*We're **in class** this morning.*
Elle est **en retard/en avance**.	*She's **late/early**.*
Michel préfère voyager **en avion**.	*Michel prefers to travel **by plane**.*
On skie **en hiver**.	*We ski **in (the) winter**.*

Exercise 6.4

Read the sentences, inserting the French translation of the missing elements.

1. Ariane arrive (*without Nicolas*) _____.

2. Est-ce que tu étudies (*in order to succeed*) _____?

3. Les élèves sont (*in class*) _____ toute la semaine.

4. Je préfère entrer chez le dentiste (*without waiting*) _____.

5. Est-ce que Roger travaille (*in order to pay*) _____ le loyer (*the rent*)?

6. Nous aimons aller à la plage (*in summer*) _____.

The Prepositions *à* and *de*

The prepositions **à** and **de** are so common in French that they are hardly noticed, except when the wrong one is used!

À

The preposition **à** is used in a number of constructions.

- ***To indicate** location **or** destination (at, in, or to), and with the names of most cities*

J'habite **à Bruxelles**.	*I live **in Brussels**.*
Elles vont **à la banque**.	*They're going **to the bank**.*
Est-ce que Pierre est **à la maison**?	*Is Pierre **at home**?*

- ***Meaning** to or for, before an indirect object noun (usually a person or a pet)*

Tu donnes le pull **à Jacques**.	*You give the sweater **to Jacques**.*
Il demande le numéro **à Chantal**.	*He asks **Chantal** for the number.*
Attends! Nous donnons à manger **à Fido**!	*Wait up! We're feeding **Fido**!*

The following French verbs *always* require **à** before the indirect object noun.

demander à (*to ask [for]*)	parler à (*to speak to*)
donner à (*to give to*)	répondre à (*to answer [to]*)
montrer à (*to show to*)	téléphoner à (*to phone, to call*)

Le prof **montre** la leçon à l'étudiant.	*The professor **shows** the lesson to the student.*
Patrick, tu **ne vas pas répondre** à Maman?	*Patrick, **aren't** you **going to answer** Mom?*

De/d'

The preposition **de/d'** is used in four different ways:

- *To indicate where someone or something comes from*

Est-ce que Salim est **de Marseille**?	*Is Salim **from Marseille**?*
Nous arrivons **d'Orléans**.	*We're coming **from Orléans**.*

- *To express **possession** and the concept of **belonging to** or **being a part of something***

There is no possessive *'s* (apostrophe *s*) in French.

Voici la valise **de Mme Leblanc**.	*Here's **Mme Leblanc's** suitcase.*
Tu travailles à la librairie **de l'université**?	*Do you work at the **university** bookstore?*

- *When used with the verb **parler** to mean **about***

De quoi parlez-vous?	***What** are you talking **about**?*
—On parle **de** la nouvelle épicerie.	*—We're talking **about** the new grocery store.*

- *When used as a descriptive phrase before a noun*

This type of phrase is the equivalent of an adjective in English.

le professeur **de chimie**	*the **chemistry** professor*
la vie **d'étudiant**	***student** life*
le livre **de chinois**	*the **Chinese** book*
l'agent **de voyages**	*the **travel** agent*

Though English nouns can be used as adjectives (*the history book*), French always uses **de/d'** + noun in these cases (**le livre d'histoire**).

Contractions of *à* and *de* with the Definite Articles *le* and *les*

The prepositions **à** and **de** must combine with the definite articles **le** and **les** (both *m.* and *f.* plural), forming the contractions below. **La** and **l'** (both *m.* and *f.*) *do not* combine with **à** and **de**.

- *à + la = à la*

  Camille va **à la** boulangerie.   *Camille is going **to the** bakery.*

- *à + l' = à l'*

  Elle arrive **à l'**école.   *She arrives **at** school.*

- *à + le = au*

  Elle va **au** cinéma.   *She's going **to the** movies.*

- *à + les = aux*

  Elle téléphone **aux** amis de Nicole. *She's phoning Nicole's friends.*

- *de + la = de la*

  Bernard arrive **de la** banque.   *Bernard is coming **from the** bank.*

- *de + l' = de l'*

  Il rentre **de l'**université.   *He comes back **from the** university.*

- *de + le = du*

  Il rentre **du** travail.   *He comes home **from** work.*

- *de + les = des*

  Il rentre **des** champs.   *He comes in **from** the fields.*

There is a **liaison**—linking with the sound [z]—when **aux** and **des** precede a noun starting with a vowel: **aux_hommes** [oh-zuhm], **des_amis** [day-zah-mee].

Exercise 6.5

Read the questions and answer each one three times using the nouns provided.

1. Annick répond à la dame? —Non, elle... (élèves, serveur, femme du prof)

   _____.

   _____.

   _____.

2. De quoi parlez-vous? de l'art africain? —Non, nous... (livre de sociologie, musique des Beatles, sports américains)

   _____.

   _____.

   _____.

3. Khaled va arriver de Rabat? —Non, il... (librairie, cours [*sing.*] d'anglais, Paris)

   _____.

   _____.

   _____.

Exercise 6.6

Translate the phrases into French.

1. Michelle's class _____
2. the restaurant's menu _____
3. the professor's handbag _____
4. Monsieur Dupont's house _____
5. the children's books _____
6. the pharmacy's bill (**la facture**) _____
7. the neighbor's (*m.*) jacket _____
8. the child's toothbrush _____

Prepositions of Location

Here are some common prepositions of location, place, or position. Several sets are opposites and can be learned in pairs.

Some prepositions are compound, i.e., made up of more than one word. The **de** of a compound preposition changes to **d'** before a vowel, and to **du** and **des** combined with the articles **le** and **les** respectively: **à côté *du* mur** (*next* **to the** *wall*); **loin *des* grandes villes** (*far* **from the** *large cities*).

à côté de   (*beside, next to*)
à droite de ≠ à gauche de   (*to the right [left] of*)
entre   (*between*)
à l'est de ≠ à l'ouest de   (*to the east [west] of*)
loin de ≠ près de   (*far from ≠ near*)
en face de   (*facing, opposite*)
au nord de ≠ au sud de   (*to the north [south] of*)
par   (*by; through*)
dans ≠ hors de   (*in, inside [outside] of*)
par terre   (*on the floor/ground*)
derrière ≠ devant   (*behind ≠ in front of*)
sous ≠ sur   (*under ≠ on top of*)

Marielle est **dans** la cuisine.	*Marielle is **in** the kitchen.*
Elle est **devant** le frigo.	*She is **in front of** the fridge.*
Le frigo est **en face de** la fenêtre.	*The fridge is **opposite** the window.*
Dans le frigo, le lait est **derrière** les œufs.	*In the fridge, the milk is **behind** the eggs.*
Les gâteaux sont **entre** le lait et les pommes.	*The cookies are **between** the milk and the apples.*
Le chat est **par terre**, **à droite de** Marielle.	*The cat is **on the floor**, on Marielle's **right**.*
La boîte est **à côté du** lait, **près de la** porte.	*The can is **next to the** milk, **near the** door.*

 ## Exercise 6.7

Read the descriptions, and sketch what is described on a separate sheet of paper.

1. Il y a un livre à côté d'un crayon.

2. Il y a une pomme entre une banane et un sandwich.

3. Il y a un portefeuille dans le sac d'Anne-Marie.

4. Il y a une fenêtre à gauche du bureau du professeur.

 Exercise 6.8

Read the questions and answer each question with the opposite preposition.

1. Frédéric est **dans** la maison?

   Non, il _____.

2. Marthe travaille-t-elle **près de** chez elle?

   Non, elle _____.

3. Passons-nous **à gauche de** l'église?

   Non, nous _____.

4. La voiture est-elle **devant** le cinéma?

   Non, elle _____.

5. Est-ce que l'Allemagne est **à l'ouest de** la France?

   Non, elle _____.

6. Les assiettes sont-elles **sous** la table?

   Non, elles _____.

Prepositions of Time and Sequence

Prepositions that deal with time and sequence can be hard to distinguish from one another. The following example sentences and explanations will help.

après + noun *after*	
Je vais en ville *après* (**le**) déjeuner.	*I'm going into town **after lunch**.*

avant de/d' + infinitive *before (in time)*	
Nous dînons *avant de* regarder le film.	*We have dinner **before watching** the movie.*

dans + time period   *in (the time that will elapse until something occurs)*

Chantal arrive **dans dix jours**.	*Chantal arrives **in ten days** (ten days from now).*

depuis + point in time or length of time   *since, for (action still going on in the present)*

J'étudie le français **depuis** deux ans.	*I've been studying French **for two years**.*
J'étudie le français **depuis** janvier 2007.	*I've been studying French **since January 2007**.*

en + time period   *in (the length of time it takes to accomplish something)*

Il est possible de préparer un repas **en une heure**.	*It's possible to prepare a meal **in an hour**.*

jusqu'à + point in time   *until*

Laurence reste ici **jusqu'à mercredi**.	*Laurence is staying here **until Wednesday**.*

pendant + time period   *during; for (duration of an action)*

***Pendant** l'année scolaire*, René travaille dur.	***During** the school year*, René works hard.
En été, je vais à Grenoble ***pendant** deux semaines*.	*Every summer, I go to Grenoble **for two weeks**.*

Pendant can very often be *omitted* before the expression of duration.

Je travaille **quatre heures** aujourd'hui.	*I'm working (**for**) **four hours** today.*
Il regarde la télé **toute la journée**!	*He watches TV **all day long**!*

pour   *for (before a time expression, used only in making future plans)*

Nous projetons d'aller au Brésil ***pour** un mois*.	*We're planning to go to Brazil **for a month**.*

Do not confuse **pendant** + duration with **pour** + duration. **Pendant** (*for*) is the preposition used to express *length of time or duration*, while **pour** (*for*) is used only to express *future plans*.

How Do We Travel?

En is used with the means of transportation that one may *enter*.

en autobus (en bus)	*by bus*
en autocar	*by (intercity) bus*
en avion	*by plane*
en bateau	*by boat (ship)*
en camion	*by truck*
en métro	*by subway*
en train	*by train*
en voiture	*by car*

À is used with the means of transportation that one *mounts or rides on*.

à bicyclette (à vélo)	*by bicycle (bike)*
à cheval	*on horseback*
à mobylette	*by (on a) moped*
à motocyclette (à moto)	*by (on a) motorcycle*
à scooter	*by (on a) scooter*

À is also used in the expression **à pied** (*on foot, by walking*).

On va **à pied** au cinéma?	*Shall we walk to the movies?*

Exercise 6.9

Translate the sentences into French.

1. After breakfast, we'll wait for Marceline.

   _____.

2. I think she'll be ready (**prête**) in two hours.

   _____.

3. I'm finishing the assignment in an hour and a half.

   _____.

4. Shall we walk to the supermarket?

_____?

5. Joseph and Christine are going to Switzerland (**en Suisse**) for three weeks.

_____.

Interrogatives with Prepositions

To ask about people and things, question words are sometimes combined with prepositions.

Qui and *quoi* in a Question After Prepositions

After a preposition, **qui** is used to refer to *people*, and **quoi** (*not* **que**) is used to refer to *things*. Use either **est-ce que** or inversion.

Study the examples below, with and without prepositions. The verb determines the preposition to be used, if any.

Qui appelles-tu?	**Whom** *are you calling?*
À qui est-ce que tu téléphones?	**Whom** *are you phoning?*
Avec qui est-ce qu'il travaille?	**With whom** *does he work?*
Qu'est-ce que tu regardes?	**What** *are you watching?*
À quoi est-ce que le prof réfléchit?	**What** *is the professor thinking **about**?*
De quoi parlez-vous?	**What** *are you talking **about**?*

The Interrogative Pronoun *lequel*

Lequel, **laquelle**, **lesquels**, and **lesquelles** (*which one[s]?*) refer to, and agree with, one or more persons or things already mentioned in a sentence or conversation. Interrogatives using **lequel** are often single-word questions.

On va regarder le film ce soir?	*Are we going to watch the movie this evening?*
—**Lequel**?	—**Which one**?
Voici des actrices françaises.	*Here are some French actresses.*
Laquelle est-ce que tu préfères?	**Which one** *do you prefer?*
Je choisis trois romans dans cette liste.	*I'm picking three novels from this list.*
—**Lesquels** (choisis-tu)?	—**Which ones** *(are you choosing)?*

In questions, **lequel** follows a preposition when the verb or the following noun calls for one.

De and **à** contract with the syllables **le** and **les** to make **duquel**, **desquel(le)s**, **auquel**, and **auxquel(le)s**. **Laquelle** does not contract (*de laquelle*, *à laquelle*).

Éric joue **dans** une pièce de théâtre.	*Éric is acting **in** a play.*
—**Dans laquelle** joue-t-il?	*—**Which** (**one**) is he acting in?*
Dans mon article, je parle **de** plusieurs sujets.	*In my article, I talk **about** several subjects.*
—**Desquels** (parlez-vous)?	*—**Which ones** (are you talking about)?*
Marianne et Guy vont **à** plusieurs conférences.	*Marianne and Guy are going **to** a few lectures.*
—**Auxquelles** (vont-ils)?	*—**Which ones** (are they going to)?*

Exercise 6.10

Answer the questions using the nouns provided.

1. À qui téléphones-tu? (professeur) _____.

2. Qu'est-ce que tu jettes? (vieux journaux) _____.

3. À quoi penses-tu? (vacances d'été) _____.

4. De qui parles-tu? (vedettes [*stars*] de cinéma) _____.

5. De quoi as-tu besoin maintenant? (verre de limonade) _____.

*Now, complete each of the questions with a form of **lequel**. Antecedents are in italics.*

6. Jeanne-Marie parle *plusieurs langues* (*f.*). —_____ est-ce qu'elle parle?

7. Marc entre *dans une boutique*. —_____ entre-t-il?

8. Je parle *de mes bons amis*. —_____ parles-tu?

9. Nous pensons *aux romans policiers* (*m. pl.*). —_____ pensez-vous?

10. Je préfère *un roman d'Alexandre Dumas*.—_____ préfères-tu?

Key Vocabulary

See Chapter 1 for a list of nouns and adjectives of nationality.

Des pays du monde (Some Nations of the World)

l'Afghanistan (*m.*) (*Afghanistan*)	Israël (*m.*) (*Israel*)
l'Algérie (*f.*) (*Algeria*)	l'Italie (*f.*) (*Italy*)
l'Allemagne (*f.*) (*Germany*)	le Japon (*Japan*)
l'Angleterre (*f.*) (*England*)	la Jordanie (*Jordan*)
l'Arabie saoudite (*f.*) (*Saudi Arabia*)	le Liban (*Lebanon*)
l'Autriche (*f.*) (*Austria*)	la Libye (*Libya*)
la Belgique (*Belgium*)	le Maroc (*Morocco*)
le Cameroun (*Cameroon*)	le Mexique (*Mexico*)
le Canada (*Canada*)	le Pakistan (*Pakistan*)
la Chine (*China*)	la Pologne (*Poland*)
la Côte-d'Ivoire (*Ivory Coast*)	la République slovaque
l'Écosse (*f.*) (*Scotland*)	(*Slovakia*)
l'Égypte (*f.*) (*Egypt*)	la République tchèque
l'Espagne (*f.*) (*Spain*)	(*the Czech Republic*)
les États-Unis (*m.*)	la Russie (*Russia*)
(*the United States*)	le Sénégal (*Senegal*)
la France (*France*)	la Suisse (*Switzerland*)
la Grèce (*Greece*)	la Syrie (*Syria*)
l'Haïti (*m.*) (*Haiti*)	la Thaïlande (*Thailand*)
l'Indonésie (*f.*) (*Indonesia*)	la Tunisie (*Tunisia*)
l'Irak (*m.*) (*Iraq*)	la Turquie (*Turkey*)
l'Iran (*m.*) (*Iran*)	le Viêt-Nam (*Vietnam*)
l'Irlande (*f.*) (*Ireland*)	

Exercise 6.11

Choose three or more countries from the list above to complete the statements. Use the definite article (except for **Israël***).*

1. _____ sont en Europe.

2. _____ sont en Afrique du Nord.

3. _____ sont dans le Moyen-Orient.

4. _____ sont en Asie.

Prepositions with Geographical Names

The prepositions **à**, **en**, **au**, **de/d'**, **du**, and **dans** are used with geographical names in French.

Gender of Geographical Names

In a sentence, names of continents, countries, provinces, and states are generally preceded by a masculine or feminine definite article.

La France est un beau pays.	*France is a beautiful country.*
Le Canada et **le Mexique** participent à l'ALÉNA.	*Canada and Mexico belong to NAFTA.*

- Place names ending in **-e** are usually *feminine*: **l'Italie** (*f.*). There are exceptions: **le Mexique**.

- Place names *not* ending in **-e** are usually *masculine*: **le Canada**. See examples in the previous list.

- The names of most continents are *feminine*.

l'Afrique (*f.*) (*Africa*)	l'Arctique (*m.*) (*the Arctic*)
l'Amérique (*f.*) du Nord (*North America*)	l'Asie (*f.*) (*Asia*)
	l'Australie (*f.*) (*Australia*)
l'Amérique (*f.*) du Sud (*South America*)	l'Europe (*f.*) (*Europe*)
l'Antarctique (*m.*) (*Antarctica*)	
l'Océanie (*f.*) (*Oceania or South Sea Islands*; may include *Australia* and *New Zealand*)	

- The names of most states in the United States are *masculine*: **le Kentucky**, **le Connecticut**. However, the names of nine U.S. states are *feminine*:

la Californie	*California*	la Louisiane	*Louisiana*
la Caroline du Nord	*North Carolina*	la Pennsylvanie	*Pennsylvania*

la Caroline du Sud	*South Carolina*	la Virginie	*Virginia*
la Floride	*Florida*	la Virginie	*West Virginia*
la Géorgie	*Georgia*	occidentale	

Canada

Here are the French and English names and genders of the Canadian provinces and territories. The capital or principal city is in parentheses after the English name.

l'Alberta (*m.*)	*Alberta (Edmonton)*
la Colombie-Britannique	*British Columbia (Victoria)*
l'Île-du-Prince-Édouard (*f.*)	*Prince Edward Island (Charlottetown)*
le Manitoba	*Manitoba (Winnipeg)*
le Nouveau-Brunswick	*New Brunswick (Fredericton)*
la Nouvelle-Écosse	*Nova Scotia (Halifax)*
le Nunavut	*Nunavut Territory (Iqaluit)*
l'Ontario (*m.*)	*Ontario (Toronto)*
le Québec	*Quebec (Quebec)*
la Saskatchewan	*Saskatchewan (Regina)*
la Terre-Neuve-et-Labrador	*Newfoundland and Labrador*
les Territoires du Nord-Ouest (*m.*)	*the Northwest Territories (Yellowknife)*
le Yukon	*the Yukon (territory) (Whitehorse)*

To, *in,* and *from* with Geographical Names

Cities, states, islands, countries, and continents are used with different prepositions.

- With the names of *cities* and many *islands*, use **à** to express *to* or *in* and **de/d'** to express *from*.

Nous habitons **à Genève**.	*We live **in Geneva**.*
Aujourd'hui, nous rentrons **de Paris**.	*Today, we're coming home **from Paris**.*

A few cities—such as **La Nouvelle-Orléans** (*New Orleans*), **La Havane** (*Havana*), **Le Havre**, and **Le Caire** (*Cairo*)—are always expressed with a definite article. **Le** forms the usual contractions with **à** and **de**.

Les Hébert arrivent **de La Nouvelle-Orléans**.	*The Héberts are coming **from New Orleans**.*
Ils voyagent **au Caire**.	*They are traveling **to Cairo**.*

À and **de/d'** are also used with states or countries located on islands or groups of islands.

Les étudiants vont **à Hawaï**.	*The students are going **to Hawaii**.*
Cette famille arrive **d'Haïti**.	*This family is coming **from Haiti**.*
Je vais **à la Martinique** et **à la Guadeloupe**.	*I'm going **to Martinique** and **Guadeloupe**.*

En can also be used to express *to* with **Martinique** and **Guadeloupe**.

- With *masculine* countries, states, and provinces, use **au** (**aux** for plural) to express *to* or *in*, and **du** (**des** for plural) to express *from*.

Mes voisins retournent **au Japon**.	*My neighbors are returning **to Japan**.*
Ils voyagent aussi **aux États-Unis**.	*They're also traveling **in the United States**.*
On parle français **au Québec**.	*French is spoken **in Quebec**.*
Nous rentrons **du Mexique** et **du Texas**.	*We're coming back **from Mexico** and **from Texas**.*
Cet avion arrive **des États-Unis**.	*That plane's arriving **from the United States**.*
Sylvie est originaire **du Québec** et Roland, **du Nouveau-Brunswick**.	*Sylvie is from (**the province of**) Quebec, and Roland is **from New Brunswick**.*

With masculine states and provinces, you may sometimes see **dans le/l'** for *to* or *in* and **du/de l'** for *from*.

New Haven est **dans le Connecticut**.	*New Haven is **in Connecticut**.*
Carole rentre **de l'Ontario**.	*Carole's coming home **from Ontario**.*

- With names of continents and feminine countries, states, and provinces, **en** expresses *to* or *in* and **de/d'**—without the article—expresses *from*.

Les Métayer habitent **en Louisiane**.	*The Métayers live **in Louisiana**.*
Je vais **en Afrique** au mois de mars.	*I'm going **to Africa** in March.*
Il a une maison **en France**.	*He has a house **in France**.*
Son vol arrive **d'Italie**.	*Her flight is arriving **from Italy**.*
Georges est originaire **de Pologne**.	*Georges is **from Poland**.*
Voici un bon vin **de Californie**.	*Here's a good wine **from California**.*
Nous voyageons **en Bretagne** et **en Normandie**.	*We're traveling **in Brittany** and **in Normandy**.*

- Masculine countries that start with a *vowel* sound (**Israël**, **l'Irak**, **l'Iran**) also use **en** for *to* and *in* and **d'** for *from*.

Ce diplomate travaille **en Israël**.	*That diplomat works **in Israel**.*
Ses parents sont originaires **d'Iran**.	*His parents are **from Iran**.*
Voici des nouvelles **d'Irak**.	*Here's some news **from Iraq**.*

The country of **Israël** is never expressed with a definite article: **Israël est au Moyen-Orient**. (*Israel is in the Middle East.*)

Exercise 6.12

Insert the correct French preposition or the preposition and the country name.

To, in:

1. Nous allons _____ Bretagne cet été. —Moi, je préfère aller _____ Paris.

2. Les Dubois projettent de voyager _____ Turquie et _____ Grèce.

3. Vas-tu _____ Hawaï?

4. J'aime mieux passer les vacances _____ Mexique.

5. Robert va travailler _____ Afrique pour six mois.

6. _____ Québec (*province*), tout le monde parle français.

7. Bangkok est _____.

8. Kaboul est _____.

From:

9. Ils arrivent _____ Canada.

10. Mes parents sont originaires _____ France.

11. Les soldats sont de retour _____ Irak.

12. Ce sont des oranges _____ Afrique du Nord.

13. Cet avion arrive _____ États-Unis.

14. La touriste téléphone _____ La Havane.

The Verb *faire* (to do; to make)

The irregular verb **faire** is used in numerous expressions and contexts.

Present Tense of faire *(to do; to make)*

je **fais**	nous **faisons**
tu **fais**	vous **faites**
il/elle/on **fait**	ils/elles **font**

Qu'est-ce qu'on **fait** ce soir?	*What **are** we **doing** this evening?*
—Nous **faisons** nos devoirs.	*—We **are doing** our homework.*
—Robert et Ginette **font** des courses.	*—Robert and Ginette **are doing** errands.*

Fais/fait [feh] and **faites** [feht] are pronounced with an open vowel sound [eh], but **faisons** [fuh-zOⁿ] is pronounced with a mute **e** sound [uh].

Je **fais** [feh] ma valise.	*I'm packing my bag.*
Vous **faites** [feht] du sport?	*Do you do any sports?*
Nous **faisons** [fuh-zOⁿ] le ménage aujourd'hui.	*We're cleaning house today.*

The Weather, Day, and Night

Use **faire** to describe the weather and to point out the change from day to night, and vice versa. The singular impersonal form **Il fait** is used in all such expressions.

Il fait beau.	*It's nice out.*	Il fait frais.	*It's cool.*
Il fait chaud.	*It's hot (warm).*	Il fait froid.	*It's cold.*

Il fait du brouillard.   *It's foggy.*
Il fait du soleil.   *It's sunny.*
Il fait du vent.   *It's windy.*

Il fait jour.   *It's daylight (dawn).*
Il fait mauvais.   *It's bad weather.*
Il fait noir (nuit).   *It's dark (night).*

Demain, s'**il fait beau**, nous allons faire une promenade; s'**il fait mauvais**, on va faire une partie de Scrabble.

*Tomorrow, if **the weather's nice**, we'll go for a walk; if **the weather's bad**, we'll play a game of Scrabble.*

En janvier, à Paris, **il fait jour** assez tard, et **il ne fait pas chaud**!

*In January, in Paris, **the sun rises** rather late, and **it's not warm out**!*

Other Weather Expressions

The impersonal expressions **il pleut** (*it's raining*), from **pleuvoir**, and **il neige** (*it's snowing*), from **neiger**, do not use the verb **faire**.

N'oublie pas ton parapluie, **il pleut**!

*Don't forget your umbrella, **it's raining**!*

À Chicago, **il neige** parfois en avril.

*In Chicago, **it** sometimes **snows** in April.*

Idioms with the Verb *faire*

Faire is used in expressions to describe many activities: studies, sports, the arts, hobbies, and household chores. Many expressions of emotion and relationships also use **faire**. The following lists group these idioms roughly according to activity.

Des activités quotidiennes (Everyday Activities)

faire des achats   (*to shop, go shopping*)
faire des courses   (*to do errands*)
faire la cuisine   (*to cook*)
faire des économies   (*to save money*)
faire la lessive   (*to do the laundry*)
faire le lit   (*to make the bed*)
faire le marché   (*to shop for groceries*)
faire le ménage   (*to clean house*)
faire le plein   (*to fill up with gasoline*)

faire une promenade   *(to go for a walk/outing)*
faire la sieste   *(to take a nap)*
faire sa toilette   *(to wash up, get ready)*
faire la vaisselle   *(to do the dishes)*
faire les valises   *(to pack one's bags)*
faire de la vitesse   *(to speed while driving)*
faire un voyage   *(to take a trip)*

Le samedi matin, Charles et Arielle **font le ménage, la lessive** et **le marché**. L'après-midi, ils **font la cuisine** ou bien, ils **font une sieste**.	*Saturday morning, Charles and Arielle **do the housework, the laundry**, and **the shopping**. In the afternoon, they **cook** or they **nap**.*

Le sport et l'exercice physique (Sports and Exercise)

faire de l'aérobic   *(to do aerobics)*
faire du bateau (de la voile)   *(to go boating [sailing])*
faire de la bicyclette (du cyclisme, du vélo)   *(to bike, go cycling)*
faire du camping   *(to go camping)*
faire de l'équitation (du cheval)   *(to ride horseback)*
faire de l'exercice   *(to exercise)*
faire du golf   *(to golf)*
faire du jogging   *(to jog, go jogging)*
faire de la motocyclette (de la moto)   *(to ride a motorcycle)*
faire de la planche à voile   *(to go windsurfing)*
faire du ski   *(to ski, go skiing)*
faire du sport   *(to do/engage in sports)*
faire une partie de (tennis, football, etc.)   *(to play a game of [tennis, golf, etc.])*

Tu **fais du sport**?	*Do you do (any) sports?*
—Je préfère **faire du camping**, mais ici, je **fais du jogging** et **du golf**.	*—I prefer to go camping, but here, I jog and I play golf.*
On **fait du vélo** samedi matin?	*Shall we go biking Saturday morning?*

The Verb *jouer* + Preposition

Jouer à (*to play*) + article + noun is also used to talk about *sports and games*.

When needed, make the contractions **à + le = au** and **à + les = aux**.

Tu **joues au golf**?	*Do you **play golf**?*
Ils **jouent aux cartes** le dimanche.	*They **play cards** every Sunday.*

To talk about playing a *musical instrument* with **jouer**, use **jouer de** + article + noun.

Be sure to use the contraction **de + le = du**, when necessary.

Elles **jouent de la flûte**.	*They **play the flute**.*
Vous **jouez du piano**?	*Do you **play the piano**?*

Expressions with **faire** can also be used with musical instruments.

Elles **font de la** flûte.	*They **play the flute**.*
Vous **faites du** piano?	*Do you **play the piano**?*

Les études (School and University Studies)

faire de la biologie (de la physique, de la chimie, etc.)   (*to study biology [physics, chemistry, etc.]*)
faire ses devoirs   (*to do one's homework*)
faire son droit   (*to study law*)
faire des (ses) études   (*to study; to be in school*)
faire des langues modernes   (*to study modern languages*)
faire de la littérature   (*to study literature*)
faire de la médecine   (*to study medicine*)

Monique **fait son droit**; son petit ami **fait** aussi **ses études**. Il **fait de la chimie**. Le soir, ils **font** ensemble **leurs devoirs**.	*Monique **is studying law**; her boyfriend **is also in school**. He **studies chemistry**. In the evenings, they **do their homework** together.*

Les arts et les passe-temps (Arts and Hobbies)

faire du bricolage   (*to tinker; to do household projects*)
faire de la couture   (*to sew; to make clothing*)
faire de la guitare   (*to play/learn the guitar*)
faire de la musique   (*to do/play music*)
faire de la peinture   (*to paint*)
faire de la photographie   (*to do photography*)
faire du piano   (*to play/learn the piano*)
faire de la poésie   (*to write poetry*)
faire de la poterie   (*to do pottery*)
faire du théâtre   (*to act*)

J'adore **faire de la poterie**, mais maintenant que j'ai une maison, nous **faisons du bricolage**.

*I love **doing pottery**, but now that I have a house, we **do do-it-yourself projects**.*

Les émotions et les rapports humains (Emotions and Relationships)

faire attention (à)   (*to pay attention [to]*)
faire du bien (à)   (*to do good; to be good for*)
faire la connaissance de   (*to meet [for the first time], get acquainted with*)
faire du mal (à)   (*to hurt [s.o.]*)
faire de son mieux   (*to do one's best*)
faire partie de   (*to belong to, be a part of*)
faire de la peine à   (*to hurt [emotionally]*)
faire peur (à)   (*to frighten, scare*)
faire plaisir (à)   (*to please [s.o.]*)

Faites attention! Vous **faites peur** aux enfants avec les masques.

Careful! You are scaring the kids with the masks.

Je **fais partie d**'un orchestre. Je **fais du saxo.** Je suis débutante, mais je **fais de mon mieux**.

I belong to a band. I play the saxophone. I'm a beginner, but I do my best.

Exercise 6.13

*Translate the sentences into French. Use the verb **faire** or an expression with **faire**.*

1. I love to do photography.

   _____.

2. Today, the weather is good, but it's cool.

   _____.

3. Marguerite does the cooking and the children do the dishes.

   _____.

4. I fill up (the car with gas) on Fridays.

   _____.

5. The clowns (**Les clowns**) scare the children.

   _____.

6. He's meeting the professor (*for the first time*).

   _____.

7. Before (**Avant de**) going on a trip, when do you (*pol.*) pack the bags?

   _____?

8. At school, I do my best.

   _____.

9. Marie-Christine is studying medicine.

   _____.

10. We belong to a sports club (**une association sportive**).

    _____.

 ## Exercise 6.14

Answer the personal questions.

1. Quand préférez-vous faire les devoirs? _____.
2. Faites-vous de la musique? Depuis quand? _____.
3. Quel temps fait-il aujourd'hui? _____.

4. Quels vêtements portez-vous quand il fait chaud? _____.

5. Chez vous, qui fait le ménage? _____.

6. Quelles tâches (*chores*) faites-vous? _____.

Key Vocabulary

When planning a trip and while traveling, you will be particularly aware of the weather and the natural features that surround you. See the expressions listed in the previous section in "The Weather, Day, and Night."

Le temps et l'environnement (Weather and the Environment)

l'atmosphère (*f.*) (*atmosphere*)	la neige (*snow*)
l'aube (*f.*) (*dawn*)	les nuages (*m.*) (*clouds*)
la baie (*bay*)	l'océan (*m.*) (*ocean*)
le brouillard (*fog*)	l'orage (*m.*) (*storm*)
la brume (*mist*)	l'ouragan (*m.*) (*hurricane*)
le canyon (*canyon*)	la plage (*beach*)
le ciel (*sky*)	la plaine (*plain*)
la colline (*hill*)	la pluie (*rain*)
la comète (*comet*)	la pollution (*pollution*)
le continent (*continent*)	la poussière (*dust*)
la côte (*coast*)	le réchauffement de la planète
le coucher du soleil (*sunset*)	(*global warming*)
le désert (*desert*)	la rivière (*river* [*tributary*])
la dune (*sand dune*)	la roche (*rock*)
l'étoile (*f.*) (*star*)	le ruisseau (*stream*)
la falaise (*cliff*)	le sable (*sand*)
le fleuve (*river*)	le soleil (*sun*)
la foudre (*lightning*)	la tempête (*storm*)
la grotte (*cave*)	la terre (*the Earth; soil, land*)
l'incendie (*m.*) (*accidental fire*)	le tonnerre (*thunder*)
l'inondation (*f.*) (*flood*)	le tremblement de terre
le lac (*lake*)	(*earthquake*)
le lever du soleil (*sunrise*)	la vague (*ocean wave*)
la lune (*moon*)	la vallée (*valley*)
le marais (*swamp, marsh*)	le vent (*wind*)
la mer (*sea*)	le volcan (*volcano*)
la montagne (*mountain*)	

Exercise 6.15

Using the previous vocabulary list, create a list of words that you associate with each cue word.

1. la pluie: _____

2. la lune: _____

3. la montagne: _____

4. l'océan: _____

5. une catastrophe: _____

Reading Comprehension

Des projets de vacances

J'habite une petite ville en Bretagne. Cet après-midi j'attends **l'arrivée** de mon ami Christian. Il arrive de Belgique en autobus, et nous projetons de voyager **ensemble** pour une semaine, car ce sont les vacances de fin d'année. Il fait assez froid, et il va **peut-être pleuvoir** ou faire du brouillard. Donc, une randonnée à bicyclette, le moyen de transport que nous préférons, n'est pas pratique. Quoi faire?

Alors, comme **tout le monde** en cette saison, on va partir en voiture. **D'abord**, nous faisons **tous les deux** une petite valise et un sac à dos. Nous n'avons pas beaucoup d'argent, donc, on demande à une copine, Mireille, de nous accompagner, pour la compagnie, bien sûr, et... pour partager **les frais**. Mireille et moi nous habitons la Bretagne depuis toujours, mais c'est la première visite de Christian. Notre route va **nous amener** à Quimper. Nous espérons visiter plusieurs musées et églises, et puis, nous allons au parc naturel régional de l'Armorique. Il y a 40.000 habitants dans cette région, **pourtant** elle a un air tout sauvage. Nous avons l'intention de **voir** les estuaires, **les presqu'îles** et les archipels, **leurs** plages et leurs **oiseaux**. Après, si nous avons encore du temps, nous allons continuer **vers** Saint-Malo et finalement vers le Mont-Saint-Michel, un des monuments les plus importants de France.

l'arrivée (*f.*) (*the arrival*)	tout le monde (*everyone*)
ensemble (*together*)	d'abord (*first*)
peut-être (*maybe, perhaps*)	tous les deux (*both [of us]*)
pleuvoir (*to rain*)	les frais (*m.*) (*the cost[s]*)

nous amener   (*to take us*)   les presqu'îles (*f.*)   (*peninsulas*)
pourtant   (*however*)   leurs   (*their*)
voir   (*to see*) vers   (*toward*)   les oiseaux (*m.*)   (*birds*)

Questions

After reading the selection, answer the questions in French.

1. Qu'est-ce que les deux amis vont faire? Qu'est-ce qu'ils préfèrent faire?

   _____.

2. Quel temps fait-il en Bretagne? Quel temps fait-il chez vous en hiver?

   _____.

3. Qui va accompagner les deux amis? Pourquoi? Et vous, aimez-vous voyager seul(e) ou avec des amis?

   _____.

4. Qu'est-ce que vous allez faire ce week-end? Et pendant les vacances, que faites-vous?

   _____.

7

Irregular Verbs I and Verb + Verb Constructions

Learning Irregular Verbs

As in other languages, irregular verbs in French are the most common. It is useful to learn them by groups or "families," usually identifiable by the spelling of the infinitive.

Conjugated forms in these groups are not always identical to each other, but their similarities will help you memorize the forms.

Verbs like *partir* (to leave, depart)

Verbs conjugated in the same way as **partir** are sometimes called irregular **-ir** verbs.

Present Tense of partir (*to leave, depart*)

je **pars**	nous **partons**
tu **pars**	vous **partez**
il/elle/on **part**	ils/elles **partent**

Note that in the present tense, the *plural* forms of verbs like **partir** have the same endings as **-er** verbs. Other verbs like **partir** include:

dormir	*to sleep*
mentir	*to lie, tell a lie*
sentir	*to smell; to feel; to sense*
servir	*to serve*
sortir	*to go out; to exit*

Nous **partons** tout de suite après le cours?	*Are we **leaving** right after class?*
Tu **pars** en vacances cet été?	*Are you **leaving** on vacation this summer?*
Nous **ne sortons pas** sans Jeanne.	*We **won't go out** without Jeanne.*
Ah, je **sens** quelque chose de délicieux!	*Ah, I **smell** something delicious!*
Il **ment** comme il respire!	*He's a natural-born liar! (Literally: He **lies** like he breathes!)*
Ne parle pas, les enfants **dorment**.	*Don't talk, the children **are sleeping**.*

Partir, sortir, and quitter

The verbs **partir**, **sortir**, and **quitter** all mean *to leave*, but they are used differently.

- **Partir** is either used alone or followed by a preposition, usually **de/d'** (*from*) or **pour** (*for; in the direction of*).

Quand **pars**-tu?	*When **are** you **leaving?***
—Je **pars** tout à l'heure.	*—I **am leaving** shortly.*
Dominique **part de** (**pour**) Paris.	*Dominique **is leaving from** (**for**) Paris.*

- **Sortir** can also mean *to leave*. It is used either alone or with a preposition, to describe *leaving (going out of) an enclosed space*, such as a room or building.

  Sortir also means *to go out for the evening (with a friend or friends)*.

La maîtresse **sort** quand la cloche sonne.	*The teacher **goes out** when the bell rings.*
Les élèves **sortent** aussi **de** la salle.	*The pupils also **leave** the classroom.*
Tu **sors** vendredi soir avec Luc?	*Are you **going out** Friday night with Luc?*

- The **-er** verb **quitter** always requires a direct object, either a place or a person.

Nous **quittons New York** en mai.	We **are leaving New York** in May.
Elle **quitte ses amis** à midi.	She **is leaving her friends** at noon.
Je vais bientôt **quitter cette réunion**.	I **will leave this meeting** soon.

Exercise 7.1

Translate the sentences into French, using verbs conjugated like **partir**.

1. I serve the coffee. _____.

2. The cats sleep a lot. _____.

3. You're (*pól.*) not leaving soon? _____?

4. Éliane is leaving for New York. _____.

5. Are you (*fam.*) sleeping? _____?

6. We're going out Friday. _____.

7. Dad serves dinner. _____.

8. Is the witness (**le témoin**) lying? _____?

9. I sense some difficulties here. _____.

10. Do you (*pol.*) smell the soup? _____?

Verbs like *venir* (to come; to arrive)

Verbs like **venir**, another group of irregular **-ir** verbs, have a stem change (from **-e-** to **-ie**) in all forms *except* **nous** and **vous**. (Note that a number of other irregular verbs have an "*except* **nous** and **vous**" stem change.)

Present Tense of venir (*to come; to arrive*)

je **viens**	nous **venons**
tu **viens**	vous **venez**
il/elle/on **vient**	ils/elles **viennent**

Tu **viens** voir le jardin de ma mère?	**Are** you **coming** to see my mother's garden?
Tes sœurs **viennent**-elles à la plage?	**Are** your sisters **coming** to the beach?
Nous **venons** aussi.	We **are coming**, too.
On **vient** chercher Myriam après le déjeuner.	We **will come** pick up Myriam after lunch.

Other verbs like **venir** include:

devenir	*to become*
intervenir	*to intervene, interrupt*
obtenir	*to obtain, get*
parvenir (à)	*to succeed (in), manage to*
revenir	*to come back*
tenir	*to hold, have, keep*

Les valeurs montent; les riches **deviennent** plus riches!	*Stock prices are climbing; the rich **are getting** richer!*
Un instant. Je **reviens** tout de suite.	*Wait a sec. I **will be back** soon.*
Je tiens les billets pour ce soir.	*I **am holding** the tickets for this evening.*
Nous **tenons** toujours le chien en laisse.	*We always **keep** the dog on leash.*
Tu **interviens** quand tes amis sont tristes?	***Do** you **intervene** when your friends are sad?*

Special Uses of *venir* and *tenir*

Some constructions with **venir** and **tenir** have idiomatic meanings.

- **Venir de/d'** + infinitive means *to have just done something*. It is called **le passé récent**. However, this expression uses the *present* tense of **venir**.

Je **viens de terminer** ce travail.	*I **have just finished** this job.*
Nous **venons de rendre visite** à Jean-Paul.	*We **have just visited** Jean-Paul.*

Using **venir de** + infinitive offers a way to speak about the past. It can be seen as the past equivalent of the near future construction **aller** + infinitive (*to be going to* + infinitive).

Je **vais** bientôt **terminer** ce travail.	*I **will** soon **finish** this job.*
Nous **allons rendre visite** à Jean-Paul.	*We **are going to visit** Jean-Paul.*

- **Venir chercher** means *to come get/pick up someone or something.* **Aller chercher** means *to go get* or *to pick up someone or something.*

Tu **viens chercher** Papa?	***Are you coming to pick up** Dad?*
Je **vais chercher** le journal.	*I **will go get** the newspaper.*

- **Tenir à** + a person means *to be attached to.* **Tenir à** + infinitive means *to be determined to do, to be bent on doing something.*

Cet enfant **tient** beaucoup **à son frère**.	*That child **is** very **attached to his brother**.*
Je **tiens à visiter** Paris.	*I **am determined to visit** Paris.*

- **Tenir compte de** + a person or thing means *to take into account, pay attention to.*

Tu tiens compte des besoins de tes amis?	***Do** you **attend to** your friends' needs?*

Exercise 7.2

*Say and write the sentences in French, using verbs conjugated like **venir** and **tenir**. Use the expression **venir de/d'** + infinitive (to have just . . .), where needed.*

1. He comes back at two o'clock. _____.

2. We're holding the packages (**les colis**). _____.

3. They're (*f.*) coming later. _____.

4. I just had lunch. _____.

5. Did you (*fam.*) just arrive? _____?

6. Renée and Yves are not coming now. _____.

7. I'm very (**beaucoup**) fond of my (**mes**) friends. _____.

8. Are we becoming rich? _____?

9. Are you (*fam.*) taking the others into account? _____?

10. I'm getting the books for you (**toi**). _____.

Dire (to say, tell), lire (to read), and écrire (to write)

The verbs **dire**, **lire**, and **écrire** are all verbs of communication. Their conjugations have similar patterns, except for the **vous** form.

Present Tense of *dire* and *lire*

dire (*to say, tell*)		**lire** (*to read*)	
je **dis**	nous **disons**	je **lis**	nous **lisons**
tu **dis**	vous ***dites***	tu **lis**	vous ***lisez***
il/elle/on **dit**	ils/elles **disent**	il/elle/on **lit**	ils/elles **lisent**

Note the spelling of **dire** and **lire** in the **vous** forms: **vous dites**, **vous lisez**.

On **dit** toujours bonjour aux personnes âgées.	*We always **say** hello to elderly people.*
Elles **disent** qu'elles vont être en retard.	*They **say** they'll be late.*
Nous **lisons** le journal tous les matins.	*We **read** the paper every morning.*
—Vous **lisez** aussi *Le Monde*?	*—**Do** you also **read** Le Monde?*

Other verbs like **dire** include:

contredire   (*to contradict* [vous contre**disez**])
interdire (à qqun de faire qqch)   (*to forbid, prohibit* [*s.o. from doing s.th.*] [vous inter**disez**])
redire   (*to say again, repeat*)

Note the spelling (-**isez**) in the **vous** form of **contredire** and **interdire**.

Ces recherches **contredisent** ce qu'on dit.	*That research **contradicts** what is said.*

Another verb like **lire** is **élire** (*to elect*).

Nous **élisons** toujours de bons candidats.	*We always **elect** good candidates.*

Present Tense of écrire *(to write)*

j'**écris**	nous **écrivons**
tu **écris**	vous **écrivez**
il/elle/on **écrit**	ils/elles **écrivent**

Tu **n'écris pas** à ta mère?	***Aren't*** *you **writing** to your mother?*
Mon amie **écrit** son deuxième roman.	*My friend **is writing** her second novel.*
D'abord vous écoutez, puis vous **écrivez**.	*First you listen, then you **write**.*
Qu'**écrivent** ces étudiants?	*What **are** those students **writing**?*

Other verbs like **écrire** include:

décrire	*to describe*
inscrire	*to write, inscribe (on a register)*
transcrire	*to transcribe*

Vous **inscrivez** votre nom sur cette liste.	*You **write** your name on this list.*
On **transcrit** le discours de l'avocat.	*They **transcribe** the lawyer's statement.*
Ces étudiants **décrivent** les difficultés.	*Those students **describe** the problems.*

Exercise 7.3

*Say and write the sentences in French, using verbs like **dire**, **lire**, and **écrire**.*

1. I read in the evening. _____.
2. Are you (*pol.*) writing the homework? _____?
3. We don't always say good-bye. _____.
4. When do they (*m.*) write e-mails (**des mails**)? _____?
5. You (*pol.*) always tell the truth (**la vérité**). _____.
6. What is he saying? _____?
7. She's writing a letter. _____.

8. Is the teacher describing the problem? _____?

9. Students don't read enough (**assez**). _____.

10. To whom do you (*fam.*) say hello? _____?

Verbs like *mettre* (to put [on], place)

Mettre and verbs in its group are irregular verbs whose infinitive ends in **-re**.

Present Tense of mettre (*to put [on]*, *place*)

---

je **mets**	nous **mettons**
tu **mets**	vous **mettez**
il/elle/on **met**	ils/elles **mettent**

Il pleut, je **mets** mon imperméable.	*It's raining, I **am putting on** my raincoat.*
Vous **mettez** ces livres sur la table?	*You **are putting** those books on the table?*
On **ne met pas** les bananes dans le frigo.	*You **don't put** bananas in the fridge.*

Other verbs like **mettre** include:

permettre (à qqun de faire qqch) *to permit, allow (s.o. to do something)*
promettre (à qqun de faire qqch) *to promise (s.o. to do something)*
remettre   *to postpone; to give back; to turn in*
soumettre   *to submit; to subject*

Il est tard; on **remet** la séance?	*It's late; **shall** we **postpone** the session?*
Elles **soumettent** leur proposition.	*They **are submitting** their proposal.*
La chaise est libre? Vous **permettez**?	*Is the chair free? **May I** (take it)?*

In constructions with **permettre** and **promettre**, the preposition **à** precedes the indirect object noun (usually a person) and the preposition **de/d'** precedes the infinitive.

Je ne **permets** pas à Sophie   *I am not **letting** Sophie buy a*
   d'acheter un scooter.   *   scooter.*
Vous **promettez de** dire la vérité?   ***Do you promise** to tell the truth?*

The present tense of the verbs **battre** (*to hit; to beat; to win*) and **combattre** (*to fight, combat*) resemble **mettre**.

Present Tense of battre (*to hit; to beat; to win*)

je **bats**	nous **battons**
tu **bats**	vous **battez**
il/elle/on **bat**	ils/elles **battent**

Cette équipe **bat** des records   *This team **breaks** records every*
   tous les ans.   *   year.*
Ces groupes **combattent** la faim.   *Those groups **fight** hunger.*

Exercise 7.4

*Say and write the sentences in French, using verbs conjugated like **mettre**.*

1. I put the plate on the table. _____.

2. The table is free? Do you (*pol.*) mind? _____?

3. Are you (*fam.*) beating the rug (**le tapis**)?

   _____?

4. What do you (*pol.*) put on when it rains?

   _____?

5. The player (**Le joueur**) is breaking records. _____.

6. They (**On**) don't park the car on the street. _____.

7. Do you (*pol.*) promise to arrive on time?

   _____?

8. We don't put shoes on in the house. _____.

9. She's postponing the appointment (**le rendez-vous**).

   _____.

10. I turn in my (**mon**) homework. _____.

Pouvoir (to be able to) and vouloir (to want to, wish to)

The **nous** and **vous** forms of **pouvoir** and **vouloir** also have a distinctive stem (**nous pouvons, vous voulez**). The third-person plural form (**elles veulent, ils peuvent**) resembles the forms of the singular.

Present Tense of pouvoir and vouloir

pouvoir (to be able to)		vouloir (to want to, wish to)	
je **peux**	nous **pouvons**	je **veux**	nous **voulons**
tu **peux**	vous **pouvez**	tu **veux**	vous **voulez**
il/elle/on **peut**	ils/elles **peuvent**	il/elle/on **veut**	ils/elles **veulent**

Je peux has an alternate form: **je puis**. It is used in the formal inverted question form: **Puis-je... : Puis-je avoir une tasse de thé?** *May I have a cup of tea?*

Pouvez-vous **arriver** avant midi?	*Can you get here before noon?*
—Non, mais je **veux déjeuner** quand même.	*—No, but I would like to have lunch anyway.*
Qu'est-ce qu'on **peut manger** au resto-U?	*What can we eat at the cafeteria?*
—Nous **pouvons partager** une pizza.	*—We can share a pizza.*

• **Pouvoir** and **vouloir** most often precede an infinitive (verb + verb construction). The infinitive directly follows these verbs, with no intervening preposition (whether or not the preposition *to* appears in the English equivalent).

Je **peux marcher**.	*I can (am able to) walk.*
Elle **veut dîner**.	*She wants to have dinner.*

• In a verb + verb construction, the negative elements **ne... pas** surround the conjugated verb form. **Ne pas** (joined) can also precede the infinitive, if the infinitive is negated.

Nous **ne voulons pas travailler** le dimanche.	*We don't want to work on Sundays.*
Ne peuvent-ils **pas venir?**	*Can't they come?*
Je peux aussi **ne pas partir**.	*I could also not leave.*

- **Vouloir bien** + infinitive means *to be willing* or *glad to do something*.

Je **veux bien accompagner** le groupe.	*I **would be happy to come along** with the group.*
Voulez-vous **bien passer** par là.	***Please go** that way.*
Qui veut aller au cinéma?	*Who wants to go to the movies?*
—Moi, je **veux bien**!	*—Me, I **would be glad to**!* *(Me, I **am willing**!)*

- **Vouloir dire** expresses *to mean* or *to signify*.

Que **veut dire** « amuse-bouche »?	*What does* amuse-bouche ***mean**?*
—C'est un petit plat à manger avant le dîner.	*—It's a small dish you eat before dinner.*
Les prénoms Simon et Simone **veulent dire** « celui qui entend ».	*The first names Simon and Simone **mean** "the one who hears."*

The Verb *devoir* (to have to; to owe)

The verb **devoir** has several meanings, all of which indicate obligation or necessity. Like **pouvoir** and **vouloir**, **devoir** is normally used in a verb + infinitive construction, with no intervening preposition: **Je dois partir**. *I must leave.*

Present Tense of devoir *(to have to; to owe)*

je **dois**	nous **devons**
tu **dois**	vous **devez**
il/elle/on **doit**	ils/elles **doivent**

Qu'est-ce que tu **dois faire** aujourd'hui?	*What **do you have to do** today?*
Doivent-elles **téléphoner** à Marie-Josée?	***Do they need to call** Marie-Josée?*
Vous **devez terminer** le devoir ce soir.	*You **must finish** the homework this evening.*
Nous **devons faire le plein** avant de partir.	*We **have got to fill the tank** before we leave.*

- The present tense of **devoir** in the affirmative or negative conveys *obligation* or *necessity*.

Je **dois finir** ce travail.	*I **must finish** this job.*
Nous **ne devons pas boire** de café le soir.	*We **mustn't drink** coffee in the evening.*

Falloir also expresses obligation or necessity. It is used only in the third-person singular form: **il faut** + infinitive (*one/you must . . . , we have to . . . , it is necessary to . . .*).

Il **faut faire** de l'exercice tous les jours.	*It **is necessary** to exercise every day.*
Il **ne faut pas** trop **manger** au dîner.	*One **must not eat** too much at dinner.*

- **Devoir** + infinitive can also express *supposition* or *probability*; the English equivalent often uses *must*.

Paul est absent; il **doit être** malade.	*Paul is absent; he **must be** ill.*
Il fait gris ce matin; il **doit pleuvoir**.	*It's gray out this morning; it **will probably** rain.*
Attendons un peu, ils **doivent** bientôt **arriver**.	*Let's wait a little longer, they **are sure to be here** soon.*
Quel beau bracelet! Il **doit coûter** cher.	*What a beautiful bracelet! It **must be** expensive.*

- When **devoir** is not followed by an infinitive, it means *to owe* (e.g., *a sum of money*). The person or entity to whom the amount or thing is owed is expressed by an indirect object, beginning with **à** or **pour**.

Nous **devons** trois cents euros **à Papa**.	*We **owe Dad** three hundred euros.*
Je **dois** un service **à mon voisin**.	*I **owe my neighbor** a favor.*
Les élèves **doivent** des devoirs **au prof**.	*The pupils **owe the teacher** some homework.*

Le devoir and les devoirs

The noun **le devoir** means *duty* or *obligation*. **Les devoirs** are *school assignments*.

> Je ne fais que **mon devoir**.   *I'm only doing **my duty**.*

Faire ses devoirs means *to do one's schoolwork* or *homework*.

Roger **fait ses devoirs** l'après-midi.	*Roger **does his homework** in the afternoon.*
Nous **faisons nos devoirs** le week-end.	*We **do our homework** on the weekend.*

Verbs like *recevoir* (to receive; to have guests)

The present tense forms of **recevoir** (*to receive*) resemble the present tense of **devoir**. Note the **-ç-** (**c** cedilla) in all forms of **recevoir**, except for **nous** and **vous**. The **ç** retains the soft sound of [s].

Present Tense of recevoir (*to receive; to have guests*)

je **reçois**	nous **recevons**
tu **reçois**	vous **recevez**
il/elle/on **reçoit**	ils/elles **reçoivent**

Nous **recevons** des cadeaux tous les ans.	*We **receive** gifts every year.*
Reçoivent-elles le samedi soir?	***Do** they **entertain** on Saturday night?*
Vous **recevez** un salaire suffisant?	***Do** you **get** an adequate salary?*

Other verbs like **recevoir** include:

apercevoir	*to perceive; to glimpse*
s'apercevoir de	*to notice* (Chapter 12)
décevoir	*to disappoint; to deceive*

Tiens! J'**aperçois** quelque chose.	*Hang on! I **see** something.*
Les prédictions économiques **déçoivent**.	*The economic forecast **is disappointing**.*

Exercise 7.5

Complete each of the sentences with the suggested verb.

1. Je/J' _____ bientôt chercher un nouvel emploi. (devoir)

2. Nous _____ venir à l'heure aujourd'hui. (pouvoir)

3. Tu ne _____ pas accompagner Papa? (vouloir)

4. Iris et Marie-Jo _____ voyager avec vous. (pouvoir)

5. Je/J'_____ quelqu'un au loin. (apercevoir)

6. Les notes (*grades*) de Monique _____. (décevoir)

7. Les jeunes élèves _____ rentrer tout de suite. (devoir)

8. Arnaud ne _____ pas payer son déjeuner. (pouvoir)

9. _____-tu de l'argent à tes amis? (devoir)

10. _____-vous mettre votre nom ici? (vouloir)

Exercise 7.6

Say and write the sentences in French, choosing from **pouvoir**, **vouloir**, **devoir**, *and from among the verbs like* **recevoir**.

1. Can you (*pol.*) read this (**ceci**)? _____?

2. I don't want to say good-bye. _____.

3. He owes Claudine two hundred euros. _____.

4. You (*fam.*) must not lie. _____.

5. What a beautiful painting! It must be very old. _____.

6. We can't come this evening. _____.

7. Anne isn't here; she must be sick (**malade**). _____.

8. We want to elect a good president (**président**). _____.

9. Do you (*fam.*) receive e-mails from Yvonne?

   _____?

10. They (*m.*) want to buy a house. _____.

11. Can I have two cups of coffee? _____?

12. We must do the homework. _____.

13. She cannot leave on time. _____.

14. They (*f.*) must have dinner before leaving. _____.

15. Don't you (*pol.*) want to watch the movie? _____?

16. I glimpse two cars in the distance (**au loin**). _____.

 ## Exercise 7.7

Answer the personal questions in French.

1. Pensez à votre week-end ou à vos vacances. Qu'est-ce que vous voulez faire?

   _____.

2. Quelles activités sont possibles ce week-end? Qu'est-ce que vous pouvez faire?

   _____.

3. Avez-vous des obligations particulières? Que devez-vous faire?

   _____.

4. Normalement, qu'est-ce qu'il faut faire tous les jours en semaine?

   _____.

5. D'habitude, combien de coups de téléphone recevez-vous chaque (*every*) jour? Combien de mails? Combien de lettres?

   _____.

Verb + Verb Constructions

In a verb + verb construction, the conjugated verb is directly followed by an infinitive (with no intervening preposition), by **à** + infinitive, or by **de/d'** + infinitive. You have already learned several of these constructions:

Je **vais faire** du ski en février.	*I **am going to go** skiing in February.*
Ginette **réussit à contacter** son ami.	*Ginette **manages to contact** her friend.*
Tu **décides d'accompagner** les élèves?	*Are you **deciding to go with** the students?*

Verbs with No Intervening Preposition

These verbs are directly followed by an infinitive (no preposition is necessary):

aimer *(to love to)*	falloir (il faut) *(to have to, be necessary to)*
aller *(to be going to)*	pouvoir *(to be able to, can)*
désirer *(to want to)*	préférer *(to prefer to)*
détester *(to hate to)*	savoir* *(to know how to)*
devoir *(to have to)*	venir *(to come to [do s.th.])*
espérer *(to hope to)*	vouloir *(to want, wish to)*

*NOTE: You will learn the conjugation of **savoir** *(to know)* and its uses in Chapter 8.

Martin **déteste dîner** au restaurant; il **préfère faire la cuisine**.	*Martin **hates eating** out; he **prefers to cook**.*
Non, nous **ne pouvons pas sortir**.	*No, we **can't go out**.*
On **doit terminer** la dissertation.	*We **have to finish** the term paper.*

- In the negative form of a verb + verb construction, **ne... pas** surrounds the first (conjugated) verb, followed by the infinitive. (The joined **ne pas** construction precedes a negative infinitive.)

Je **n'aime pas faire** les devoirs le vendredi.	*I **don't like to do** homework on Friday.*
Nous **préférons ne pas sortir**.	*We **prefer not to go out**.*

- **Penser** + infinitive means *to count on* or *plan on* doing something.

Odette **pense faire** des études de médecine.	*Odette **is planning to** study medecine.*
Ils **pensent passer** chez nous.	*They **intend to drop by** our place.*

Verbs Requiring *à* Before the Infinitive

Verbs that require **à** before an infinitive include:

aider qqun à *(to help s.o. to)*	hésiter à *(to hesitate to)*
arriver à *(to manage to)*	inviter qqun à *(to invite s.o. to)*
chercher à *(to try to)*	réussir à *(to succeed in)*
commencer à *(to begin to)*	servir à *(to serve to)*
continuer à *(to continue to)*	tenir à *(to be eager to)*
enseigner à qqun à *(to teach s.o. to)*	

Je **tiens à acheter** cet appareil photo.	*I **am anxious to buy** that camera.*
Patrick **cherche à gagner** assez d'argent.	*Patrick **is trying to earn** enough money.*
Nous **invitons** nos amis **à partir** avec nous.	*We **invite** our friends **to leave** with us.*

- Several verbs that take **à** before the infinitive may also have a *direct object* or an *indirect object* (preceded by **à**).

J'**aide** les élèves **à faire** leurs devoirs.	*I **am helping** the pupils **do** their homework.*
Michel **enseigne** à sa fille **à écrire**.	*Michel **teaches** his daughter **to write**.*

Verbs Requiring *de/d'* Before the Infinitive

Verbs and verbal expressions that require **de/d'** before an infinitive include:

accepter de	*to accept, agree to*
avoir peur de	*to be afraid of*
choisir de	*to choose to*
conseiller de	*to advise to*
décider de	*to decide to*
demander de	*to ask to*
dire de	*to tell to*
empêcher qqun de	*to prevent s.o. from*
essayer de	*to try to*
éviter de	*to avoid*
finir de	*to finish (doing s.th.)*
oublier de	*to forget*
permettre à qqun de	*to allow s.o. to*
promettre à qqun de	*to promise s.o. that*
refuser de	*to refuse to*
regretter de	*to regret (doing)*
rêver de	*to dream about*
venir de	*to have just (done s.th.)*

- Some verbs that take **de/d'** before the infinitive may also have a direct object or an indirect object (preceded by **à**).

Le bruit **empêche** les enfants **de dormir**.	*The noise **keeps** the children **from sleeping**.*
Je **permets à** mon frère **d'utiliser** l'ordinateur.	*I **allow** my brother **to use** the computer.*

- A sentence may have more than one infinitive.

J'essaie d'éviter de faire des fautes.	*I **try to avoid making** mistakes.*
Nous **avons peur d'oublier de fermer** à clé.	*We **are afraid we'll forget to lock** up.*

Exercise 7.8

Complete the sentences by inserting the correct prepositions when needed.

1. Nous invitons André _____ déjeuner.

2. Vous commencez _____ mettre la chambre en ordre.

3. Tu veux _____ faire une promenade avec nous?

4. J'aide le prof _____ corriger les copies.

5. Mireille continue _____ bien manger.

6. La bicyclette sert _____ amener Patrick à la faculté.

7. Nous détestons _____ travailler tard.

8. Hésites-tu parfois _____ dire la vérité?

9. Oubliez-vous quelquefois _____ fermer la porte?

10. Paul cherche _____ retrouver ses copains.

11. Est-ce que vous choisissez _____ changer de carrière?

12. Mes amis essaient _____ quitter la ville pendant le week-end.

13. Caroline doit _____ ranger sa chambre aujourd'hui.

14. Réussissent-ils _____ gagner leur (*their*) vie?

15. L'instituteur empêche les enfants _____ jouer dans l'école.

16. Il ne faut pas _____ dormir en classe.

17. Nicolas finit _____ parler au téléphone.

18. Je regrette _____ ne pas pouvoir venir.

 ## Exercise 7.9

*Translate the sentences into French. Be aware of the verb + verb constructions: those with no prepositions, with the preposition **à**, and with the preposition **de/d'**.*

1. I like to dance. _____.

2. We prefer to go on foot. _____.

3. They (*f.*) can play golf today. _____.

4. Do you (*fam.*) have to leave? _____?

5. He doesn't want to have lunch. _____.

6. We're coming to help (**aider**) Guy. _____.

7. Are you (*pol.*) hoping to study law? _____?

8. I'm helping my (**mon**) friend finish his homework.

   _____.

9. We're succeeding in winning (**gagner**). _____.

10. Are you (*fam.*) inviting Madeleine to eat with us?

    _____?

11. Do I start working at ten? _____?

12. I teach the pupil (**à l'élève**) to write. _____.

13. We refuse to answer. _____.

14. They (*m.*) allow the neighbor (**au voisin**) to use the mower (**la tondeuse**).

    _____.

15. You're (*fam.*) forgetting to buy the bread. _____.

16. She promises Mom to do the errands. _____.

17. I prevent the students from making mistakes (**des fautes**).

    _____.

18. He regrets coming so late. _____.

Key Vocabulary

We all interact with the written word every day. Here is a list of the appropriate vocabulary.

Lire et écrire (Reading and Writing)

l'article (*m.*)   (*article*)
l'auteur (*m.*)   (*author*)
la bibliothèque   (*library; shelf*)
la biographie   (*biography*)
le bloc-notes   (*notepad*)
le cahier   (*notebook*)
la carte   (*map; menu*)
la carte postale   (*postcard*)
le chapitre   (*chapter*)
le clavier   (*keyboard*)
le compte rendu   (*review*)
le conte (de fées)   (*story [fairy tale]*)
le crayon   (*pencil*)
le/la critique   (*critic*)
le dictionnaire   (*dictionary*)
la dissertation   (*term paper*)
l'écran (*m.*)   (*screen*)
les écrits (*m.*)   (*writings*)
l'écrivain (*m.*)   (*writer*)
l'éditeur (*m.*)   (*publisher*)
l'édition (*f.*)   (*publishing*)
l'encyclopédie (*f.*)   (*encyclopedia*)
l'enveloppe (*f.*)   (*envelope*)
l'essai (*m.*)   (*nonfiction*)
l'étude (*f.*)   (*[research] study*)
l'examen (*m.*)   (*exam, test*)
une feuille de papier
   (*a sheet of paper*)
le fichier   (*computer file*)
hebdomadaire   (*weekly*)
imprimer   (*to print [out]*)
l'imprimante (*f.*)   (*printer*)
sur Internet (*m.*)   (*on the Internet*)
le journal   (*newspaper*)

la librairie   (*bookstore*)
la littérature   (*literature*)
le lien   (*link, Web link*)
le livre (d'histoire)   (*[history] book*)
le logiciel   (*software*)
le magazine   (*magazine*)
le manuel   (*textbook*)
mensuel(le)   (*monthly*)
le mot   (*word*)
le moteur de recherche
   (*search engine*)
la nouvelle   (*novella; news*)
l'ordinateur (*m.*)   (*computer*)
du papier (*m.*)   (*paper*)
les paroles (*f.*)   (*words
   [poem, song]*)
le paragraphe   (*paragraph*)
les petites annonces (*f.*)
   (*classified ads*)
la phrase   (*sentence*)
la pièce (de théâtre)   (*play*)
le poème   (*poem*)
la poésie   (*poetry*)
le portable   (*laptop; cell phone*)
le programme   (*program*)
la publicité (la pub)   (*advertising*)
les recherches (*f.*)   (*research*)
le/la rédacteur (-trice)
   (*copyeditor*)
la revue   (*journal, review*)
le roman   (*novel*)
le roman policier   (*mystery*)
le site Web   (*website*)
la souris   (*mouse*)

le stylo (*pen*)	le traitement de texte
la thèse (*thesis*)	(*word processing*)
le timbre (*postage stamp*)	les touches (*f.*) (*keys* [*keyboard*])
le/la journaliste (*journalist*)	le/la traducteur (-trice)
le kiosque (*newsstand*)	(*translator*)
le lecteur (la lectrice) (*reader*)	la traduction (*translation*)
la lettre (*letter*)	

Exercise 7.10

Complete each of the sentences with logical words or expressions from the previous list.

1. Quand j'ai envie de lire pour le plaisir, je lis...

   _____

2. Quand on utilise un ordinateur, normalement on utilise aussi...

   _____

3. Pour écrire aux amis quand nous sommes sans Internet, nous avons besoin de/d'...

   _____

4. Quand je deviens écrivain professionnel, je vais devoir tenir compte de/du/des...

   _____

Reading Comprehension

Mes décisions

Je m'appelle Clarice. J'ai vingt-quatre ans et je fais des études d'**hôtellerie** à Lyon. Je viens de parler avec mon **directeur d'études**. On me dit que c'est le moment de choisir définitivement une carrière. Quoi faire? **À l'avenir**, je veux tenir **une auberge haut de gamme**, dans un village **voisin** peut-être, avec **mon copain** Guillaume. Mais cette année j'ai d'autres décisions importantes à faire.

J'écoute **les conseils** de mes profs et je lis régulièrement les petites annonces de **la faculté** de mon école. J'ai plusieurs options: je peux **rester** à

Lyon **faire un stage** dans un des **célèbres** restaurants de la ville. **Ou bien** je peux essayer de trouver un emploi **à l'étranger** — à Montréal, à New York, à San Francisco, ou même à La Nouvelle-Orléans. Mais je dois aussi penser à ma famille. Mes parents me disent de faire **ce que** je veux, qu'ils me **soutiennent** dans toutes mes décisions. Mais si je pars en Amérique du Nord, **ils vont me manquer** terriblement, **ainsi que** mon frère et ma petite sœur. **En revanche**, il y a Internet, nous pouvons **nous écrire** des mails, ils peuvent visiter l'Amérique et il y a toujours le téléphone. Et bien sûr, le temps passe **vite**!

l'hôtellerie (*f.*)	*hotel management*
le directeur d'études	*(academic) advisor*
à l'avenir	*in the future*
une auberge	*an inn, a small hotel*
haut de gamme	*upscale, upmarket*
voisin(e)	*neighboring (adj.)*
mon copain	*my friend; my boyfriend*
les conseils (*m.*)	*advice*
la faculté	*department (of a school or university)*
rester	*to stay, remain*
faire un stage	*to do an internship*
célèbres (*pl.*)	*famous*
ou bien	*or*
à l'étranger	*overseas, abroad*
ce que	*what*
soutiennent (**soutenir**)	*support*
ils vont me manquer	*I'll miss them*
ainsi que	*as well as*
en revanche	*on the other hand*
nous écrire	*write (to) each other*
vite	*quickly*

Questions

After reading the selection, answer the questions in French.

1. Quel âge a Clarice? Quelles études fait-elle?

   _____.

2. Quelles décisions doit-elle faire cette année?

   _____.

3. Qu'est-ce qu'elle veut faire à l'avenir?

   _____.

4. En ce moment, quelles sont les possibilités de Clarice?

   _____.

5. Si elle va en Amérique du Nord, comment va-t-elle rester en contact avec la famille?

   _____.

8
Irregular Verbs II and Relative Pronouns

Connaître (to know, be acquainted with) Versus savoir (to know [facts])

The irregular verbs **connaître** and **savoir** both mean *to know, to have knowledge of* (*s.th. or s.o.*). However, they are used in different contexts.

Present Tense of *connaître* and *savoir*

connaître (*to know, be acquainted with*)

je **connais**	nous **connaissons**
tu **connais**	vous **connaissez**
il/elle/on **connaît**	ils/elles **connaissent**

savoir (*to know* [*facts*])

je **sais**	nous **savons**
tu **sais**	vous **savez**
il/elle/on **sait**	ils/elles **savent**

Verbs conjugated like **connaître** are spelled with a circumflex accent (^) on the letter **-i-** in forms where **-î-** precedes **-t**, including the infinitive (**connaître**, **elle connaît**). The circumflex is also seen in the future and the conditional forms of **connaître** (Chapter 15).

Connaissez-vous bien la ville de New York?	*Do you **know** New York City well?*
—Eh bien, je **sais** où trouver un bon restaurant français!	*—Well, I **know** where to find a good French restaurant!*
Arthur **sait** parler trois langues.	*Arthur **knows how to** speak three languages.*

161

Other verbs conjugated like **connaître** include:

apparaître (*to appear, come into view*)

disparaître (*to disappear*)

paraître (*to seem, appear*)

reconnaître (*to recognize*)

Reconnais-tu cette dame-là?	***Do** you **recognize** that woman?*
Ses idées me **paraissent** justes.	*Her/His ideas **seem** correct to me.*
Nous savons faire **disparaître** nos amis. On leur demande s'ils savent faire le ménage!	*We know how to make our friends **disappear**. We ask them if they know how to clean house!*

Uses of *connaître* and *savoir*

The model sentences below will help you learn the meanings of **connaître** and **savoir**.

- **Connaître** + noun means *to be acquainted with*. It always takes a direct object noun or pronoun (a person, a place, an idea, or a thing).

Tu **connais Marie-Laure**?	***Do** you **know** Marie-Laure?*
—Non, je ne **la connais** pas.	*—No, I don't **know her**.*
Connaissez-vous **les contes de Balzac**?	*Are you **acquainted with Balzac's short stories**?*
Pierre **connaît** très bien **le métro parisien**.	*Pierre **knows the Paris metro (system)** very well.*

- **Savoir** + subordinate clause means *to know (a fact)*. **Savoir** can be followed by a noun referring to a fact or simple information. But it is very often followed by a subordinate clause starting with **que** (*that*), **qui** (*who*), **quand** (*when*), **pourquoi** (*why*), **si** (*if*), **où** (*where*), or **quel(le)(s)** (*what*).

Je **sais** l'adresse.	*I **know** the address.*
Éloïse a trois ans; elle **sait** déjà l'alphabet.	*Éloïse is three; she already **knows** the alphabet.*
Sais-tu **qui** parle ce soir?	***Do** you **know who** is speaking this evening?*
—Désolée, je **ne sais pas**.	*—Sorry, I **don't know**.*
Nous **ne savons pas pourquoi** le train est en retard.	*We **don't know why** the train is late.*

Followed by an infinitive, **savoir** means *to know how to* (*do s.th.*).

Je sais monter à bicyclette.   *I know **how to ride a bike**.*
Savez-vous **faire la cuisine**?   ***Do you know how to cook**?*

 ## Exercise 8.1

Create sentences in the present tense from the elements provided. Pay attention to verb forms, contractions, and agreement of verbs and adjectives.

1. Françoise/connaître/bien/la ville/de/Dakar

   _____.

2. nous/savoir/jouer de/le trombone

   _____.

3. savoir/vous/qui/arriver/ce/soir?

   _____?

4. ils/connaître/des artistes/italien

   _____.

5. savoir/on/pourquoi/Roland/ne... pas/venir?

   _____?

6. je/reconnaître/toujours/la voix (*voice*) de/mon/ami

   _____.

7. connaître/tu/Adélaïde?

   _____?

8. les étudiantes/paraître/heureux/aujourd'hui

   _____.

Exercise 8.2

*Match the verbs to their possible sentence endings, writing the letters corresponding to **Je connais** or **Nous savons** on the lines provided.*

1. Je connais _____, _____, _____, _____.

2. Nous savons _____, _____, _____, _____.

   a. Paris
   b. faire de la céramique
   c. l'adresse du prof
   d. les romans d'Amélie Nothomb

   e. pourquoi la boutique est fermée
   f. nager
   g. la philosophie de J.-P. Sartre
   h. ton amie

Exercise 8.3

Answer the personal questions in writing.

1. Quelles villes connaissez-vous bien? Quels quartiers préférez-vous?

   _____.

2. Connaissez-vous des villes francophones? Lesquelles? Quels quartiers préférez-vous?

   _____.

3. Connaissez-vous des écrivains ou cinéastes (*filmmakers*) français ou francophones? Qui connaissez-vous?

   _____.

4. Savez-vous où vos grands-parents sont nés? Où sont-ils nés?

   _____.

5. Quels sports savez-vous faire?

   _____.

6. Quelles tâches ménagères savez-vous faire?

   _____.

Voir (to see) and *croire* (to believe)

Voir and **croire** have different infinitive spellings, but their conjugations are alike. The similarities will help you memorize these verbs.

Present Tense of *voir* and *croire*

voir (*to see*)		croire (*to believe*)	
je **vois**	nous **voyons**	je **crois**	nous **croyons**
tu **vois**	vous **voyez**	tu **crois**	vous **croyez**
il/elle/on **voit**	ils/elles **voient**	il/elle/on **croit**	ils/elles **croient**

- **Revoir** (*to see again*) is conjugated like **voir**. **Aller voir** means *to visit, go see a person*.

- **Croire à** means *to believe in a concept* or *an idea*. **Croire en** means *to trust* (*a person*), or *to believe* (*in God*).

- **Je crois que oui** means *I think so*; **je crois que non** means *I don't think so*.

Tu **vois** cet arbre?	***Do** you **see** that tree?*
Voyez-vous ce que je veux dire?	***Do** you **see** what I mean?*
Voyons si je suis libre dimanche. Je **crois** que oui.	***Let's see** if I'm free Sunday. I **think** so.*
Elles **croient** qu'il a raison.	*They **believe** (that) he's right.*
Allons voir Grand-père demain.	***Let's go see** Grandfather tomorrow.*
Je le **revois** chaque fois que je vais à Lyon.	*I **see** him whenever I go to Lyon.*
Je **ne crois pas** en l'existence de Dieu.	*I **don't believe** in the existence of God.*
—Faut pas le dire à mon père.	*—You mustn't tell my father.*
Il **croit**?	*He **is** a **believer**? (He **believes**?)*
—Mon père, oui.	*—My dad, yes. (James Joyce, Ulysses)*

Exercise 8.4

Translate the sentences into French. Use the present tense of **voir** *and* **croire***.*

1. We believe. (We're believers.) _____.

2. Does she see well? _____?

3. Sophie and Bernard believe that we're coming. _____.

4. Do you (*fam.*) see Nicole sometimes? _____?

5. I don't think so. _____.

6. They (*f.*) believe in (**en**) Einstein! _____!

7. They (*m.*) see the sun again in the spring. _____.

8. We don't see Jo very often. _____.

9. He believes that it's true (**c'est vrai**). _____.

10. Whom do you (*fam.*) see? _____?

Courir (to run) and *rire* (to laugh)

The infinitives of **courir** and **rire** are spelled differently, but their conjugations are similar. Learn them together.

Present Tense of courir *(to run)*

je **cours**	nous **courons**
tu **cours**	vous **courez**
il/elle/on **court**	ils/elles **courent**

The present tense forms of **courir** resemble verbs like **partir**. But they differ in the **passé composé** (Chapter 13), the future, and the conditional (Chapter 15). Other verbs conjugated like **courir** include:

accourir	*to rush, rush up*
concourir	*to compete*
parcourir	*to go, travel through*
secourir	*to rescue, come to the aid of*

Patrick et Nelly **courent** tous les matins.	*Patrick and Nelly **run** every morning.*
Je **cours**! Le bus va partir!	*I am running! The bus is leaving!*

Chaque été nous **parcourons** l'Europe.	*Each summer we **travel through** Europe.*
La foule **accourt** à l'arrivée des vedettes.	*The crowd **rushes up** when the movie stars arrive.*

Present Tense of rire (*to laugh*)

je **ris**	nous **rions**
tu **ris**	vous **riez**
il/elle/on **rit**	ils/elles **rient**

The verb **sourire** (*to smile*) is conjugated like **rire**.

Pourquoi **ris**-tu? Ce n'est pas amusant!	*Why **are** you **laughing**? It's not funny!*
Nous **sourions** aux gambades des petits chiens.	*We **smile** at the puppies' antics.*
On **rit** aux éclats aux frères Marx.	*People **laugh** out loud at the Marx Brothers.*

The Group *offrir* (to offer)

The present tense endings of the group **offrir** are the same as the present tense endings of regular **-er** verbs.

Present Tense of offrir (*to offer, give*)

j'**offre**	nous **offrons**
tu **offres**	vous **offrez**
il/elle/on **offre**	ils/elles **offrent**

Other verbs conjugated like **offrir** include:

couvrir	*to cover*
découvrir	*to discover, find out*
ouvrir	*to open*
souffrir	*to suffer; to tolerate*

J'**ouvre** la fenêtre. J'étouffe!	*I **am opening** the window. I'm suffocating!*
À Noël nous **offrons** toujours des cadeaux.	*At Christmas we always **give** gifts.*

Qu'est-ce qu'elle **découvre** dans   *What **is** she **finding out** in that*
   ce document?   *   document?*
Nous **couvrons** la cage avant   *We **cover** the cage before going*
   de sortir.   *   out.*

 ## Exercise 8.5

Translate the sentences into French using the present tense and verbs from the groups **courir**, **rire**, *and* **offrir**.

1. We run on Saturday mornings. _____.

2. Does she laugh a lot? _____?

3. Do dogs smile? _____?

4. They're (*f.*) discovering some important effects (**effets**, *m.*).

   _____.

5. To whom are you (*fam.*) offering the books?

   _____?

6. I have a cold (**un rhume**). . . I'm suffering! _____!

7. Do you (*pol.*) run if (**si**) you're late? _____?

8. Don't they (*m.*) open the windows at night (**la nuit**)?

   _____?

9. Every time that (**Chaque fois que**) he speaks, we laugh.

   _____.

10. I do some exercise, but I don't run. _____.

11. The audience members (**Les spectateurs**) rush up when they see the actor.

    _____.

12. She offers a meal to the homeless (**aux sans-abri**).

    _____.

13. Is he traveling through Europe? _____?

14. It's cold. I'm covering the children. _____.

15. Are you (*pol.*) opening the doors now? _____?

The Group *conduire* (to drive; to lead)

All verbs ending in **-uire** are conjugated like **conduire**.

Present Tense of conduire (*to drive; to lead*)

je **conduis**	nous **conduisons**
tu **conduis**	vous **conduisez**
il/elle/on **conduit**	ils/elles **conduisent**

Other verbs like **conduire** include:

construire	(*to build, construct*)	réduire	(*to reduce*)
détruire	(*to destroy*)	séduire	(*to charm; to seduce*)
produire	(*to produce*)	traduire	(*to translate*)

Vous **conduisez** un bus?	*Do you drive a bus?*
Quand il neige, on **conduit** avec beaucoup de soin.	*When it snows, people drive very carefully.*
C'est quoi cette musique? Elle **séduit** les enfants.	*What's that music? It is captivating the children.*
Roland ne comprend pas; nous **traduisons**.	*Roland doesn't understand; we are translating.*

Suivre (to follow; to take a course) and *vivre* (to live)

The first- and second-person singular forms of the verb **suivre** (**je suis, tu suis**) are identical to the first-person singular form of **être** (**je suis**). Always look at the context to clarify which verb is being used.

Vivre means *to live* in a general sense; it can also refer to the places where one lives. **Habiter** means only *to reside at* or *in*.

Present Tense of *suivre* and *vivre*

suivre (*to follow; to take [a course]*)		**vivre** (*to live*)	
je **suis**	nous **suivons**	je **vis**	nous **vivons**
tu **suis**	vous **suivez**	tu **vis**	vous **vivez**
il/elle/on **suit**	ils/elles **suivent**	il/elle/on **vit**	ils/elles **vivent**

Est-ce que tu **suis** un cours d'italien?	*Are you taking an Italian class?*
Le détective **suit** la suspecte.	*The detective follows the suspect.*
Pourquoi **suivez**-vous ce taxi?	*Why are you following that taxi?*

On **vit** bien sur la Côte d'Azur.	*People (They) **live** well on the Riviera.*
Combien de temps **vivent** ces papillons?	*How long **do** these butterflies **live**?*

Another verb like **suivre** is **poursuivre** (*to pursue; to continue*).

Nous **poursuivons** nos études en Europe.	*We **are continuing** our studies in Europe.*
Poursuit-on cet homme en justice?	*Are proceedings **being brought** against that man?*

Other verbs like **vivre** include:

revivre	*to relive; to come alive*	survivre (à)	*to survive*

Grand-père **revit**-il ses expériences?	***Is** Grandfather **reliving** his experiences?*
Nous **survivons** grâce à nos économies.	*We **are surviving** thanks to our savings.*

The Group *craindre* (to be afraid of)

The spelling of this group of irregular **-ndre** verbs has a distinctive **-gn-** in the plural forms.

Present Tense of craindre (de) (*to fear, be afraid of*)

je **crains**	nous **craignons**
tu **crains**	vous **craignez**
il/elle/on **craint**	ils/elles **craignent**

Les enfants **craignent** le noir.	*The children **are afraid of** the dark.*
Je **ne crains pas de** dire que je n'aime pas ce film.	*I **am not afraid** to say I don't like this movie.*

Other verbs like **craindre** include:

atteindre	*to reach, attain*	peindre	*to paint*
feindre (de)	*to pretend (to)*	plaindre	*to pity*

Le jour, elle est serveuse; le soir, elle **peint**.

Enfin, nous **atteignons** nos objectifs.

*During the day she's a server; evenings she **paints**.*

*Finally, we **are reaching** our goals.*

Exercise 8.6

Create sentences in the present, paying attention to agreement of verbs, articles, and adjectives.

1. les/étudiants/suivre/des/cours/intéressant

   _____.

2. qu'est-ce que/vous/craindre?

   _____?

3. nous/vivre/à/Lausanne

   _____.

4. produire/on/beaucoup de/vin/en/Californie?

   _____?

5. il/atteindre/finalement/la/destination

   _____.

6. nous/conduire/lentement/quand/il/neiger

   _____.

7. le/gendarme/poursuivre/les/suspects

   _____.

8. je/vivre/pour/faire du ski!

   _____!

9. ils/feindre/de/lire/le/livre/de maths

   _____.

10. Jacqueline/ne... pas/conduire/en/hiver

    _____.

11. revivre/elle/les/événements/difficile?

    _____?

12. je/ne... pas/suivre/de/cours/de/physique

_____.

13. traduire/elles/les/documents?

_____?

14. vous/peindre/quand/vous/avoir/le/temps?

_____?

15. tu/ne... pas/conduire/raisonnablement!

_____!

16. généralement/un/orage/ne... pas/détruire/beaucoup de/arbres

_____.

 ## Exercise 8.7

Translate the sentences into French using the present tense and verbs from the groups
conduire, **suivre**, **vivre**, _and_ **craindre**.

1. I'm following Jacques and David. _____.

2. We're not reaching our goals (**nos buts**). _____.

3. Are they (_f._) building a new house? _____?

4. The patrolmen (**Les gendarmes**) are pursuing the red car.

_____.

5. Agnès is taking an English class. _____.

6. Chloé and I (**moi**), we're reducing energy use (**l'utilisation d'énergie**).

_____.

7. Do turtles (**tortues**, _f._) live a long time? _____?

8. You (_fam._) drive fast! _____!

9. He lives to eat; she eats to live. _____.

10. The children are pretending to be sick. _____.

11. Isn't she painting the bedroom? _____?

12. Are you (_fam._) afraid of the cold? _____?

13. In the winter, we pity especially (**surtout**) the homeless (**les sans-abri**).

_____.

14. France produces a lot of cheese. _____.

15. I don't live in the country. _____.

16. What career are you (*pol.*) pursuing?

    _____?

17. What city do the Dubonnets live in? _____?

18. Are you (*pol.*) translating Baudelaire's poems? _____?

19. Uncle Olivier is reliving his youth.

    _____.

20. The chemistry students don't take easy courses. _____.

Relative Pronouns: *qui*, *que*, *où*, *dont*, and *lequel*

A relative pronoun (in English: *who, that, which, whom, whose, where*) links a relative (or dependent) clause to the main clause of a sentence. A dependent clause has a relative pronoun, a subject, and a verb, but it usually cannot stand alone. See the boldface parts of the following sentences:

The movie ***that* she's watching** is a classic.	(*that* = object of the clause)
The man ***who* took the car** was not its owner.	(*who* = subject of the clause)
Is this the restaurant ***where* you ate**?	(*where* = place)
That's the moment ***when* we met**.	(*when* = time)

Notice that the sentences can stand without the boldface clauses.

Que, *qui*, and *où*

Qui is used as the *subject* and **que** is used as the *direct object* of a relative clause. **Où** is a relative pronoun used for *time* or *place*.

Qui or *que* in a Relative Clause?

Qui (*who, that, which*) is the relative pronoun used as the *subject* of a relative clause. It refers to both people and things. **Qui**, the subject of the dependent clause, immediately precedes the conjugated verb of the clause.

Nous avons une voiture. **Elle** ne marche pas.	We have a car. **It** is not running.
Nous avons une voiture *qui* **ne marche pas**.	We have a car **that's not running**.
Nous attendons le dépanneur. **Il** va réparer la voiture.	We're waiting for the mechanic. **He** is going to fix the car.
Nous attendons le dépanneur *qui* **va réparer la voiture**.	We're waiting for the mechanic **who is going to fix the car**.

Que (*who, whom, that, which*) is the relative pronoun used as the *direct object* of a relative clause. It refers to both people and things. **Que/qu'**, the direct object of the dependent clause, is usually followed by a subject + verb construction.

Les fraises viennent du Maroc. J'achète **les fraises**.	The strawberries come from Morocco. I'm buying **the strawberries**.
Les fraises *que* **j'achète** viennent du Maroc.	The strawberries **that I'm buying** come from Morocco.
Marc appelle une copine. Il rencontre souvent **cette copine** à l'université.	Marc is calling a friend. He often meets **that friend** at the university.
Marc appelle une copine *qu'il* **rencontre** souvent à l'université.	Marc is calling a friend **whom he** often **meets** at the university.

The Relative Pronoun *où*

Où, which you already know as the question word *where*, is also a relative pronoun of *time* and *place*. It means *in, on, when, which,* or *where*.

Voici la librairie **où** j'adore bouquiner.	Here's the bookstore **where** I love to browse.
Voilà le gymnase **où** nous faisons du karaté.	There's the gym **where** we do karate.
C'est le mois **où** les cours recommencent.	That's the month **when** classes start.
Pierre décrit les moments **où** il est heureux.	Pierre is describing the times **when** he's happy.

Exercise 8.8

Create a single sentence out of the two sentences provided. Use the suggested relative pronoun for each group. In each of the sentences for nos. 6–15, the words in italics should be dropped.

Use **qui**:

1. Je vais voir un ami. Il attend au café.

   _____.

2. Papa achète une voiture. La voiture a cinq ans.

   _____.

3. Tu veux voir le film? Il décrit la vie en Afrique.

   _____.

4. Nous aimons les étudiants. Ils répondent correctement.

   _____.

5. J'ai un nouveau parapluie. Il marche très bien dans le vent.

   _____.

Use **que**:

6. Thérèse fait un beau tableau. Tu vas aimer *le tableau*.

   _____.

7. Ils rangent la chambre. Vous allez peindre *la chambre*.

   _____.

8. Je jette les vieux catalogues. Nous recevons *les catalogues*.

   _____.

9. Tu choisis le professeur. Elle aime aussi *ce professeur*.

   _____.

10. On appelle les clients. Pierre voit souvent *ces clients*.

   _____.

Use **où**:

11. C'est le moment. Je préfère voyager à *ce moment-là*.

_____.

12. Nous pensons au jour. Marc arrive *ce jour-là*.

_____.

13. Ils achètent l'appartement. Je vais habiter *cet appartement*.

_____.

14. C'est une région chaude. On produit beaucoup d'oranges *dans cette région*.

_____.

15. Vous allez dans un musée. Ils offrent des visites guidées *dans ce musée*.

_____.

Exercise 8.9

Complete each of the sentences with **qui**, **que**, *or* **où**.

1. Tu vois une place _____ on peut laisser la voiture?

2. Margot attend les amis _____ doivent bientôt arriver.

3. On va à pied au café _____ Jeanne-Marie préfère.

4. Aimes-tu les boissons _____ sont gazéifiées (*carbonated*)?

5. C'est une rue _____ ils peuvent faire une belle promenade.

6. Je descends à un hôtel _____ a une bonne réputation.

7. L'hôtel a un restaurant _____ nous aimons dîner.

8. Le serveur, _____ apporte la carte, est toujours aimable.

9. Je n'aime pas vraiment les plats _____ vous choisissez.

10. Je préfère les salades _____ Sylvie recommande.

11. Tu veux une table dans la salle _____ Georges dîne déjà?

12. Nous allons payer l'addition _____ le serveur prépare.

Relative Pronouns with Prepositions; *lequel* and *dont*

Sometimes the relative clause is formed with a preposition (**à**, **de**, **avec**, **dans**, etc.).

Qui as the Object of a Preposition

The relative pronoun **qui** is frequently used in a dependent clause as the object of a preposition referring to *people*.

C'est l'amie **avec qui** Pierre passe du temps.	*This is the friend **with whom** Pierre spends time.*
C'est le collègue **à côté de qui** je travaille.	*That's the colleague **next to whom** I work.*

Lequel as a Relative Pronoun

Lequel (*which*), which you learned as an interrogative (*which one*), can also be a relative pronoun used as the object of a preposition. It refers to specified things, and at times to people. **Lequel** agrees in gender and number with its antecedent.

C'est le portable **avec lequel** tu préfères écrire?	*Is this the laptop **with which** you prefer to write?*
C'est la salle **dans laquelle** on monte la pièce.	*That's the hall **in which** we're staging the play.*
L'auteur **auquel** j'écris souvent est très connu.	*The author I often write **to** (**to whom** I often write) is very well known.*

When the relative pronoun refers to a person, **qui** is more generally used.

L'auteur **à qui** j'écris souvent est très connu.	*The author I often write **to** (**to whom** I often write) is very well known.*

Où is preferred when one refers to a place or location.

Voilà la salle **où** on monte la pièce.	*There's the hall **where** we're staging the play.*

Exercise 8.10

Complete each of the sentences with the French equivalent of the English relative pronoun given. Some items may have more than one correct answer.

1. C'est le copain (*with whom*) _____ j'adore passer du temps.

2. Voici le voisin (*next to whom*) _____ nous habitons.

3. Louis a un nouvel ordinateur (*with which*) _____ il écrit de la poésie.

4. On préfère les arbres (*m.*) (*under which*) _____ on peut faire la sieste.

5. J'ai une table ancienne (*on which*) _____ tu peux mettre le vase.

6. Les politiciens (*to whom*) _____ nous écrivons répondent toujours.

7. Le boulanger (*to whom*) _____ je dois téléphoner fait les gâteaux.

8. Nous organisons une soirée (*during which*) _____ il va raconter des histoires.

9. Je vois des pommes (*f.*) (*with which*) _____ on peut faire une belle tarte.

10. C'est le magasin (*next to which*) _____ tu vas trouver la poste.

11. Jeanne achète un studio (*in which/where*) _____ elle espère vivre.

12. Ce sont des chambres (*f.*) (*in which/where*) _____ vous allez bien dormir.

The Relative Pronoun *dont*

The relative pronoun **dont** (*of whom, of which, whose*) replaces **de** + an object. **Dont** is preferred (to forms with **lequel**) when the preposition or implied preposition is **de**. As a relative pronoun **dont** refers to both people and things.

It is used instead of **de qui**, when referring to *people* in verbal expressions with **de** (**parler de** *to talk about*; **avoir peur de** *to be afraid of*), and also replaces possessive constructions with **de** or the possessive adjective (Chapter 10). In the following examples, notice how **dont** links the two original sentences:

C'est une bonne amie. Odette parle souvent **de cette amie**.
C'est une bonne amie ***dont*** Odette parle souvent.

*She's a good friend. Odette often speaks **about that friend**.*
*She's a good friend **about whom** Odette often speaks.*

J'ai un jeune cousin. Les chiens **de mon cousin** sont adorables.
J'ai un jeune cousin ***dont*** les chiens sont adorables.

*I have a young cousin. **My cousin's** dogs are adorable.*
*I have a young cousin **whose** dogs are adorable.*

Voici une jolie maison. J'aime le jardin **de cette maison**.
Voici une jolie maison ***dont*** j'aime le jardin.

*Here's a pretty house. I love the garden **of that house**.*
*Here's a pretty house **whose** garden I love.*

 ## Exercise 8.11

*Create a single sentence out of the two sentences given. Use **dont** in each sentence. (The words in italics will not appear in the sentences you write.)*

1. Voici la librairie anglaise. Liliane parle *de la librairie*.

   _____.

2. C'est le dictionnaire français. J'ai besoin *d'un dictionnaire français*.

   _____.

3. J'ai une bonne amie. La famille *de mon amie* est très aimable.

   _____.

4. Roger est un jeune avocat. Le travail *de Roger* est difficile.

   _____.

5. Ce sont des examens de maths. Les étudiants ont peur *des examens*.

   _____.

6. Les notes sont mauvaises. J'ai honte *de ces notes*.

   _____.

7. Le travail est impeccable. Catherine est fière *de son* (*her*) *travail*.

   _____.

8. Voilà un collègue. Je connais la femme *de mon collègue*.

   _____.

9. La glace est délicieuse. Nathalie a envie *de glace*.

   _____.

10. J.-P. Melville est un cinéaste classique. Nous apprécions les films *de J.-P. Melville*.

   _____.

Indefinite Relative Pronouns: Statements from Questions

The relative pronouns **ce qui**, **ce que**, and **ce dont** all refer to indefinite things or ideas, *not* to people. (**Ce** stands in for the indefinite antecedent.) These expressions are translated by *what* in English. In these clauses, **ce qui** is the subject, **ce que** the direct object, and **ce dont** replaces an expression with **de**.

J'explique **ce que** je fais au travail.	*I'm explaining **what** I do at work.*
Nous ne savons pas **ce qui** intéresse le public.	*We don't know **what** interests the public.*
Ce dont j'ai besoin, c'est d'un verre d'eau froide!	***What** I need is a glass of cold water!*

The indefinite relative pronouns **ce qui**, **ce que**, and **ce dont** correspond to some of the interrogative pronouns you learned in Chapter 3.

Qu'est-ce qui est près de la porte?	***What** is near the door?*
—Je ne vois pas **ce qui** est près de la porte.	*—I don't see **what** is near the door.*
Qu'est-ce qu'on fait ce soir? (**Que** fait-on ce soir?)	***What** are we doing tonight?*
—Corinne demande **ce qu'**on fait ce soir.	*—Corinne asks **what** we're doing tonight.*

De quoi is the interrogative expression corresponding to **ce dont**. **De quoi** can also be used as an indefinite relative pronoun for expressions with **de**.

De quoi parle-t-il?   ***What*** *is he talking **about**?*
—Je ne sais pas **ce dont/de**   —*I don't know **what** he's talking*
   quoi il parle.   ***about**.*
De quoi as-tu peur?   ***What*** *are you scared **of**?*
—**Ce dont** j'ai peur c'est de la   —***What** I fear is the economic*
   crise économique.   *downturn.*

Exercise 8.12

Complete each of the sentences with **ce que/qu'**, **ce qui**, **ce dont**, *or* **de quoi**.

1. Chez le marchand de vins, il achète _____ n'est pas cher.

2. Je ne sais pas _____ elle veut.

3. _____ parlez-vous en classe?

4. Nous voyons _____ elle a peur.

5. _____ plaît toujours à toute la famille, c'est une promenade à la plage.

6. On ne sait pas toujours _____ va arriver.

7. _____ as-tu besoin, mon enfant?

8. Crois-tu tout _____ tes grands-parents disent?

9. Elles savent _____ nous pouvons faire.

10. _____ j'ai envie, c'est d'une pizza aux champignons.

Exercise 8.13

Write a question in French that calls for each answer below. The questions will vary.

1. Il est midi et demi. _____?

2. Ce dont nous parlons, c'est de nos études. _____?

3. J'invite plusieurs amis samedi. _____?

4. Nous faisons ce que nous voulons faire. _____?

5. Ce que je veux, c'est un week-end à la plage. _____?

6. Elles pensent à plusieurs acteurs. _____?

7. Ce qui arrive, c'est un événement significatif. _____?

8. Ce dont Julie a besoin, c'est d'un nouvel appartement. _____?

9. Il va faire mauvais demain. _____?

10. Nous voyons de nombreux films au festival. _____?

 # Key Vocabulary

In an increasingly global community, workers pursue jobs and professions across national borders. Foreign language skills are becoming more and more important. Note that several professions have only a masculine form in French. You may occasionally see the expressions: **une femme médecin**, **une femme ingénieur**, **une femme sculpteur**, etc.

Les métiers et les professions (Jobs and Professions)

l'acteur (-trice) (*actor*)

l'agent de change (*m.*) (*stockbroker*)

l'agent de police (*m.*) (*police officer*)

l'agent de voyages (*m.*) (*travel agent*)

l'agriculteur (-trice) (*farmer*)

l'archéologue (*m., f.*) (*archeologist*)

l'architecte (*m., f.*) (*architect*)

l'artisan(e) (*artisan*)

l'artiste (*m., f.*) (*artist*)

l'assistant(e) social(e) (*social worker*)

l'astronome (*m., f.*) (*astronomer*)

l'athlète (*m., f.*) (*athlete*)

l'auteur (*m.*) (*author*)

l'avocat(e) (*lawyer*)

le/la banquier (-ière) (*banker*)

le/la biologiste (*biologist*)

le/la boulanger (-ère) (*baker*)

le cadre (*manager*)

le/la chanteur (-euse) (*singer*)

le chauffeur de taxi (*taxi driver*)

le/la chercheur (-euse) (*researcher*)

le/la chimiste (*chemist*)

le/la cinéaste (*filmmaker*)

le/la coiffeur (-euse) (*hairdresser*)

le/la commerçant(e) (*retailer*)

le/la comptable (*accountant*)

le cordonnier (*shoemaker*)

le/la danseur (-euse) (*dancer*)

l'écrivain (*m.*) (*writer*)

l'électricien(ne) (*electrician*)

l'entrepreneur (*m.*) (*entrepreneur*)

l'épicier (-ière) (*grocer*)

la femme politique (*politician*)

le/la fonctionnaire (*civil servant*)

l'historien(ne) (*historian*)

l'homme politique (*politician*)

l'hôtesse de l'air (*f.*) (*flight attendant*)

l'infirmier (-ière) (*nurse*)

l'informaticien(ne)
  (software engineer)
l'ingénieur (m.) (engineer)
l'instituteur (-trice) (school
  teacher)
l'interprète (m., f.) (interpreter)
le/la jardinier (-ière) (gardener)
le/la journaliste (journalist)
le magistrat (judge)
le maire (mayor)
le marin (sailor)
le médecin (physician)
le menuisier (carpenter)
le militaire (serviceman)
le/la musicien(ne) (musician)
l'ouvrier (-ière) (factory worker)
le/la paléontologue
  (paleontologist)
le/la peintre (painter)
le/la philosophe (philosopher)

le/la photographe (photographer)
le/la physicien(ne) (physicist)
le pilote (pilot)
le plombier (plumber)
le pompier (firefighter)
le professeur (lycée/university
  teacher)
le/la psychologue (psychologist)
le/la publicitaire (publicist)
le/la représentant(e) (sales rep)
le/la scientifique (scientist)
le/la serveur (-euse) (server)
le soldat (soldier)
le steward (flight attendant [m.])
le/la technicien(ne) (technician)
le/la traducteur (-trice)
  (translator)
le/la vendeur (-euse) (salesperson)
le/la vétérinaire (veterinarian)

Exercise 8.14

Answer the questions out loud and in writing, using words from the previous vocabulary list.

1. Nommez quelques professions scientifiques:

   _____

2. Nommez quelques professions artistiques:

   _____

3. Nommez quelques professions dans les affaires (*business*):

   _____

4. Nommez des ouvriers qualifiés (*skilled*):

   _____

5. Nommez des personnes qui travaillent dans le gouvernement:

   _____

6. Quelles professions avez-vous faites jusqu'ici (*have you done till now*)?

Jusqu'ici j'ai été (*I have been*)... _____

 ## Reading Comprehension

Une nouvelle carrière

Je m'appelle Claude Carreau. Je suis avocat, ayant travaillé depuis plus de vingt ans comme avocat d'entreprise dans **une grande société** parisienne. J'ai une famille: ma femme Sonia est **enseignante de lettres**; nous avons deux enfants, Alain et Pomme — un garçon et une fille, de jeunes adolescents. La famille voit, **selon** ce que je dis presque tous les jours, que, pour moi, le travail que je fais devient **de moins en moins** intéressant. Alors, je viens de décider que c'est le moment de changer de vie, et ma famille veut bien suivre mon projet.

Heureusement, la famille de ma mère possède une assez grande propriété près de La Rochelle sur la côte ouest atlantique de France. Elle **n'est plus** cultivée depuis des années. Aujourd'hui les agriculteurs représentent moins de trois pour cent de la population **active** française. À une époque où beaucoup de petits agriculteurs ou fermiers français quittent leur terre pour aller travailler dans des commerces ou des bureaux, moi, j'ai l'intention de lancer une ferme **biologique** pour cultiver des légumes, des salades et **des baies**. On sait que le climat là-bas est idéal. Je vais utiliser mes capacités dans les affaires pour bien **gérer** la nouvelle entreprise. De nos jours les produits biologiques sont très demandés par **des particuliers** et aussi par les chefs des bons restaurants des environs. Je suis sûr de pouvoir réussir et aussi d'**améliorer** notre vie de famille.

une grande société (*a large company*)	active (*working*)
enseignante de lettres (*humanities teacher*)	biologique (*organic*)
	des baies (*f.*) (*berries*)
selon (*according to*)	gérer (*to manage*)
de moins en moins (*less and less*)	des particuliers (*m.*) (*individuals*)
n'est plus (*is no longer*)	améliorer (*to improve*)

Questions

After reading the selection, answer the questions in French.

1. Décrivez la vie actuelle de Claude. Est-il satisfait de son travail? Pourquoi?

   _____.

2. Qu'est-ce que Claude a l'intention de faire?

   _____.

3. À votre avis, Claude va-t-il réussir sa nouvelle entreprise? Pourquoi?

   _____.

4. Voulez-vous changer de vie? Si oui, comment?

   _____.

9

Prendre and *boire*, the Partitive Article, and Object Pronouns

The Group *prendre* and the Verb *boire*

The verbs **prendre** (*to take; to have*) and **boire** (*to drink*) are often linked together since they are both used to talk about eating and drinking.

Present Tense of *prendre* and *boire*

prendre (*to take*; *to have*)		boire (*to drink*)	
je **prends**	nous **prenons**	je **bois**	nous **buvons**
tu **prends**	vous **prenez**	tu **bois**	vous **buvez**
il/elle/on **prend**	ils/elles **prennent**	il/elle/on **boit**	ils/elles **boivent**

Take note of the double **n** in the spelling of the third-person plural form of **prendre** (**ils/elles prennent**) and the **-uv-** in the **nous** and **vous** forms of **boire**: **nous buvons, vous buvez**.

Prenez-vous le petit déjeuner à 7h30?	*Do you* ***eat*** *(take) breakfast at 7:30 A.M.?*
Elles **prennent** un taxi quand il pleut.	*They* ***take*** *a taxi when it rains.*
Nous **ne buvons pas** de café après dîner.	*We* ***don't drink*** *coffee after dinner.*
Il fait froid. Tu **prends** une tisane?	*It's cold out.* ***Would*** *you* ***like*** *a cup of herbal tea?*
Je **bois** plus d'un litre d'eau par jour.	*I* ***drink*** *more than a liter of water every day.*

- Some common verbal expressions with **prendre** include:

prendre à gauche (à droite)   *to take a left (a right) turn*
prendre le bus (le train, l'avion, etc.)   *to take the bus (the train, a plane, etc.)*
prendre le petit déjeuner   *to have breakfast*
prendre un repas   *to have a meal*
prendre son temps   *to take one's time*
prendre un verre   *to have a drink*

Vous **prenez à gauche** devant l'école?	*Are you **taking a left turn** in front of the school?*
Nous **prenons notre temps** le dimanche.	*We **take our time** on Sundays.*
On **prend un verre** au café du coin?	***Shall** we **have a drink** at the corner café?*
Demain je **prends le train** pour Marseille.	*Tomorrow I **will take the train** to Marseille.*

- *To have lunch* is usually expressed with the verb **déjeuner**; *to have dinner* is expressed with the verb **dîner**. But one also hears the following said as well.

Elle **prend** son déjeuner.	*She **is having** lunch.*
Tu **prends** ton dîner?	***Are** you **having** dinner?*

Other verbs conjugated in the same way as **prendre** include:

apprendre (à)   *(to learn)*
apprendre à qqun à   *(to teach someone [how] to)*
comprendre   *(to understand)*
surprendre   *(to surprise)*

Comprenez-vous ce qu'il dit?	***Do** you **understand** what he's saying?*
Ce qu'il dit **ne surprend pas**.	*What he says **isn't surprising**.*
Je **comprends** l'espagnol, mais je ne parle pas bien.	*I **understand** Spanish, but I don't speak well.*
Qu'est-ce qu'elles **apprennent** dans ce cours?	*What **are** they **learning** in that course?*

- When an infinitive follows **apprendre**, the preposition **à** must precede it.

J'apprends à conduire.	*I am learning (**how**) to drive.*
Les élèves **apprennent à lire**.	*The pupils **are learning to read**.*

In the following example, **apprendre à** means *to teach*. The person being taught becomes the *indirect object*.

Jacquie **apprend à** son frère **à faire** du ski.	*Jacquie **is teaching** her brother **how to ski**.*

Exercise 9.1

Create complete sentences, paying attention to verb agreement and the use of contractions when necessary.

1. je/boire/une/grand/tasse/de/thé _____.
2. nous/ne... pas/boire/de/alcool/à/le/déjeuner _____.
3. que/prendre/tu/à/le/goûter/de/quatre heures? _____?
4. comprendre/vous/ce que/elle/vouloir/dire? _____?
5. quand/on/être/en retard/on/prendre/le/métro _____.
6. ils/boire/beaucoup de/eau/en été _____.
7. nous/prendre/à/droite/après/la/église? _____?
8. je/apprendre/à/jouer/de/le/banjo _____.

Exercise 9.2

*Translate the sentences into French using **boire** and verbs from the group **prendre**.*

1. Are we having a drink at the café? _____?
2. I understand what he's saying. _____.
3. Alex is taking the bus today. _____.
4. You're (*fam.*) learning to ride a bike. _____.
5. Isn't Gabrielle drinking too much (**trop de**) coffee? _____?
6. The students don't surprise the teacher. _____.

7. I drink a cup of consommé before dinner. _____.

8. Are you (*pol.*) taking a left at the next street (**au prochain carrefour**)?

_____?

The Partitive Article

You've already learned to use the definite articles (**le/la/l'/les**) and the indefinite articles (**un/une/des**). French also has a third article, the partitive: **du/de la/de l'**.

> Vous prenez **du** sucre, Monsieur?   *Do you take **any/some** sugar, sir?*

The partitive article refers to a *part* of a quantity that is *measured*, rather than counted.

Countable objects are used with the indefinite article **un/une/des**. In the plural they may include **des pommes** (*apples*), **des petits pains** (*dinner rolls*), **des bouteilles** (*bottles*), **des œufs** (*eggs*), etc.

Measurable quantities, such as food and drink used with the partitive article, could be **du sucre** ([*some*] *sugar*), **du lait** ([*some*] *milk*), **de la viande** ([*some*] *meat*), **de la glace** ([*some*] *ice cream*), **de l'eau** (*f.*) ([*some*] *water*), or **de la soupe** ([*some*] *soup*), where an amount is measured out of a larger whole or a container.

The partitive article (**du/de la/d'/des**) is always used in French sentences, even when the word *some* is omitted in English.

Je vais chercher **du** pain et **des** oranges.	*I'm going to get (**some**) bread and (**some**) oranges.*
Tu prépares **de la** soupe et **du** poisson ce soir?	*Are you preparing soup and fish tonight?*

Many *abstract* nouns in French are often expressed with the partitive article.

Ce candidat a **de la confiance** et **du courage**.	*This candidate has **confidence** and **courage**.*

Uses of the Partitive Article

As shown above, the partitive is always singular; it corresponds in gender to the noun it precedes. **De l'** can be both feminine and masculine.

Nous allons chercher...	We're going to get . . .
du fromage,	(**some**) cheese,
de la glace,	(**some**) ice cream,
et **de l'**eau (*f.*).	and (**some**) water.

Verbs such as **aller chercher** (*to go get*), **prendre** (*to eat; to drink; to have*), **manger** (*to eat*), **commander** (*to order*), and **acheter** (*to buy*) often take the partitive article, since one goes to get, eats, orders, or buys a *portion* of something.

Verbs of Preference

Verbs of *preference*, such as **aimer** (*to like, love*), **aimer mieux** (*to prefer*), **préférer** (*to prefer*), and **détester** (*to hate*), usually take the definite article (**le/la/l'/les**) rather than the partitive.

J'**adore** *les* fruits de mer.	I **love** seafood.
Les enfants **n'aiment pas** *les* épinards.	Children **don't like** spinach.

Exercise 9.3

Complete the sentences, choosing from the indefinite plural article **des**, *the singular partitive article* (**du/de la/de l'**), *or the definite article* (**le/la/l'/les**). *(See the Key Vocabulary of Chapter 4 for the gender of food items.)*

1. Madame, vous prenez _____ sucre? Préférez-vous _____ crème ou _____ lait?

2. Pour faire une omelette, nous mélangeons _____ œufs, _____ sel, _____ poivre, _____ fines herbes et parfois _____ fromage. Puis, nous mettons _____ beurre dans la poêle (*pan*).

3. Tout le monde adore _____ fromage suisse.

4. Au petit déjeuner on commande _____ café, _____ pain, _____ croissants, _____ beurre et _____ confiture.

5. Ce soir, j'achète _____ poisson et _____ crevettes.

6. Renée mange _____ viande et _____ poulet, mais elle déteste _____ fruits de mer.

7. Martine, si tu vas au supermarché, je veux _____ pommes de terre, _____ olives et _____ eau.

8. Il boit _____ chocolat chaud tous les matins.

The Partitive Article Shortened to *de/d'*

- In the negative, the partitive article reduces from **du/de la/de l'** to **de/d'** before the noun:

Je prends **du** thé.	*I drink tea.*
Je **ne** prends **pas de** thé.	*I don't drink tea.*
Tu manges **de la** viande.	*You eat meat.*
Tu **ne** manges **pas de** viande.	*You don't eat meat.*

The plural indefinite article **des** also becomes **de/d'** after a negative construction.

Serge commande **des** œufs.	*Serge orders eggs.*
Serge **ne** commande **pas d'**œufs.	*Serge doesn't order eggs.*

Ne... ni... ni... is the French equivalent of *neither . . . nor . . . .* This negative expression begins with **ne/n'**, and **ni** precedes each element negated.

Je **n'**aime **ni le** poisson **ni** l'agneau.	*I like **neither** fish **nor** lamb (in general).*

The entire partitive article is omitted after a **ne... ni... ni...** construction.

Je bois **du** thé et **du** café.	*I drink (both) tea and coffee.*
Je **ne** bois **ni** thé **ni** café.	*I drink **neither** tea **nor** coffee.*
Nous **ne** prenons **ni** beurre **ni** confiture.	*We have (eat) **neither** butter **nor** jam.*

- Partitive articles also reduce to **de/d'** after all expressions of *quantity*.

Combien de/d'... ?   *How much, many . . . ?*

assez de	*(enough)*	un kilo de	*(a kilo[gram] of)*
une assiette de	*(a plate of)*	un litre de	*(a liter of)*
beaucoup de	*(a lot, much, many)*	une livre de	*(a pound of)*
une boîte de	*(a can of)*	un peu de	*(a little)*
une bouteille de	*(a bottle of)*	tant de	*(so much, many)*
cent grammes de	*(one hundred grams of)*	une tasse de	*(a cup of)*

une cuillérée de *(a spoonful of)*	trop de *(too much)*
une douzaine de *(a dozen)*	un verre de *(a glass of)*

Combien de café prends-tu le matin?	*How much coffee do you have in the morning?*
Michel a **deux bouteilles d'**eau.	*Michel has two bottles of water.*
Tu veux prendre **un peu de** fromage?	*Do you want to have a little cheese?*
J'achète **beaucoup de** fruit et **de** légumes.	*I buy a lot of fruit and vegetables.*
Ils ne peuvent pas boire **tant de** lait.	*They can't drink so much milk.*

- **De/d'** alone is used with *unmodified* nouns that follow **avoir besoin de** *(to need, require)* and **avoir envie de** *(to wish, want)*.

Maman, a-t-on besoin **de lait**?	*Mom, do we need milk?*
—Non, mais j'ai besoin **d'oignons**.	*—No, but I need onions.*
J'ai envie **de chocolat** et **de vacances**!	*I long for chocolate and a vacation!*

Exercise 9.4

Translate the phrases and sentences into French.

1. a dozen eggs _____

2. too much coffee _____

3. a kilo of oranges _____

4. a liter of milk _____

5. enough vegetables _____

6. a little mustard (**moutarde**) _____

7. a bottle of beer (**bière**) _____

8. lots of pepper _____

9. I don't want any cream. _____.

10. We need olive oil and butter. _____.

11. I'm coming to borrow (**emprunter**) a cup of sugar. _____.

12. How many dinner rolls do they (f.) want? _____?

13. Eugène doesn't take salt. _____.

14. She must not drink so much wine. _____.

15. They (*m.*) eat neither chocolate nor butter. _____.

Direct Objects

Direct objects are nouns that receive the action of a verb. They usually answer the question **quoi?** (*what?*) or **qui?** (*whom?*).

In the English sentence *Jennifer buys a car*, *a car* is the direct object of the verb *buys*. Direct object pronouns replace direct object nouns: *Jennifer buys it*. In French, the direct object pronoun is placed before the conjugated verb form.

Je lis **le mail**.	*I read **the e-mail**.*	Je **le** lis.
Je lis **l'article** (*m.*).	*I read **the article**.*	*I read **it**.*
Je lis **le journal**.	*I read **the paper**.*	

Je regarde **la télé**.	*I watch **television**.*	Je **la** regarde.
Je regarde **l'étoile** (*f.*).	*I look at **the star**.*	*I watch (look at) **it**.*
Je regarde **la lune**.	*I look at **the moon**.*	

French and English sometimes differ in whether the object is direct or indirect. In French, **regarder** (*to look at; to watch*) always takes a direct object. In English, *to look **at*** takes an indirect object, and *to watch* takes a direct object.

Forms and Placement of Direct Object Pronouns

Here are the direct object pronouns used in French:

SINGULAR		PLURAL	
me (m')	*me*	**nous**	*us*
te (t')	*you*	**vous**	*you*
le (l')	*him, it*	**les**	*them*
la (l')	*her, it*	**les**	*them*

- Third-person direct object pronouns agree in gender and number with the nouns they replace.

  le (l') replaces a masculine singular noun

  la (l') replaces a feminine singular noun

  les replaces any plural noun

Vous retrouvez **Luc et Sophie**?	*Are you meeting **Luc and Sophie**?*
—Oui, nous **les** retrouvons à midi.	*—Yes, we're meeting **them** at noon.*
Roger commande **la crème brûlée**?	*Is Roger ordering **the crème brûlée**?*
—Oui, il **la** commande.	*—Yes, he's ordering **it**.*

- **Me**, **te**, **le**, and **la** become **m'**, **t'**, and **l'** before a vowel or a mute **h**. In the case of **l'**, context reveals the *antecedent* (the noun it replaces).

Je **l'**achète.	*I'm buying **it** (this cheese, his car, the house).*
Paul **t'**aime bien.	*Paul likes **you**.*
La science **m'**intéresse beaucoup.	*Science interests **me** a lot.*

- If the direct object pronoun is the object of an infinitive, it precedes the infinitive.

Elles vont prendre **le métro**.	*They are going to take **the metro**.*
Elles vont **le** prendre.	*They're going to take **it**.*

- In the negative, the direct object pronoun precedes the verb form of which it is the object.

Tu ne regardes pas **la télé**.	*You don't watch **TV**.*
Tu ne **la** regardes pas.	*You don't watch **it**.*
Je ne vais pas acheter **le gâteau**.	*I'm not going to buy **the cake**.*
Je ne vais pas **l'**acheter.	*I'm not going to buy **it**.*

- Direct object pronouns also precede **voici** (*here is/are*) and **voilà** (*there is/are*). **Voici** and **voilà** are used to present or point out people or objects.

Le voilà!	*There **he** (**it**) is!*	**Me** voici!	*Here **I** am!*

Exercise 9.5

*Answer each question with a complete sentence, starting with **oui** or **non** as directed. Use a direct object pronoun (**me/m'**, **te/t'**, **le/la/l'**, **nous**, **vous**, **les**) in each answer.*

1. Est-ce que tu m'écoutes? —Oui, _____.

2. Me regardes-tu? —Non, _____.

3. Tu me comprends? —Oui, _____.

4. Tu aimes bien Mélanie? —Oui, _____.

5. Tu appelles les autres étudiants? —Non, _____.

6. Est-ce que tu invites Paul demain? —Oui, _____.

Now, answer each of the questions with a direct object pronoun preceding **voici**
(here is/are) or **voilà** *(there is/are).*

7. Où sont les livres de français? —_____.

8. Je cherche le numéro de téléphone. —_____.

9. Où est la confiture? —_____.

10. Marie et Richard, où êtes-vous? —_____.

11. Nous ne voyons pas les valises. —_____.

12. Tu es là? —_____.

Exercise 9.6

Complete the sentences, translating the expressions (direct object pronoun + verb)
into French. The object pronoun precedes the infinitive if it is the object of the
infinitive.

1. Jean (*waits for me*) _____ jusqu'à six heures
   chaque soir.

2. Il (*knows you* [*fam.*]) _____, mais il ne sait pas
   d'où.

3. Nos amis (*are going to help us*) _____ avec les
   devoirs.

4. Cécile et Suzanne partent en voyage demain. Elles (*are going to call me*)
   _____ des États-Unis.

5. Henri est absent aujourd'hui. Je (*am looking for him*)
   _____, mais je (*am not finding him*)
   _____.

6. Françoise aime son copain Paul; elle (*loves him*) _____
   beaucoup.

7. Qui veut (*to go see her*) _____?

8. Où sont les jeunes filles? (*Do you* [*pol.*] *see*
   them?) _____?

9. Voyez-vous vos amis tous les jours? —Non, nous (*don't see them*)
_____ souvent.

10. Ton copain est sympathique. Je ne comprends pas pourquoi tu (*are leaving him*) _____.

11. Les Boileau veulent une baby-sitter. Ils (*call her*) _____ pour ce soir.

12. Je (*am going to call him*) _____, puis je prépare le dîner.

13. Ça, c'est ma copine Annie. —Oui, nous (*know her*) _____ aussi.

Indirect Objects

Indirect object nouns and pronouns usually answer the questions *to whom?* or *for whom?* Indirect objects refer to persons, sometimes to pets. In English, the word *to* is often omitted: *I give the gift **to Josette**. = I give **Josette** the gift.*

- In French, the preposition **à** (occasionally **pour**) is used before an indirect object noun. If a sentence has an indirect object noun, it usually also has a direct object.

Tu montres les photos **aux voisins**?	*You're showing the photos **to the neighbors**?*
On achète un foulard **pour Tante Simone**?	*Are we buying a scarf **for Aunt Simone**?*

- The following verbs commonly have both direct and indirect objects.

acheter (*to buy*)	envoyer (*to send, ship*)
apporter (*to bring*)	expliquer (*to explain*)
apprendre (*to learn*)	indiquer (*to point out*)
demander (*to ask*)	montrer (*to show*)
dire (*to tell*)	offrir (*to offer*)
donner (*to give*)	poser (une question) (*to ask [question]*)
écrire (*to write*)	prêter (*to lend*)

Patrick **offre** le journal **au professeur**.	*Patrick **gives** the newspaper **to the professor**.*
Vous **envoyez** un cadeau **à Jeanne**?	*You **are sending** a gift **to Jeanne**?*

Je **prête** souvent des livres à mes amis.	*I often **lend** books **to my friends**.*

- A few verbs—**parler à** (*to talk to*), **téléphoner à** (*to call, phone*), and **répondre à** (*to answer*)—take only an indirect object in French.

Je **parle** souvent **à la boulangère**.	*I often **talk to the baker**.*
Tu vas **répondre à Papa**?	*Are you going **to answer Dad**?*

Indirect Object Pronouns

Indirect object pronouns replace indirect object nouns. Like the equivalent nouns, they refer only to persons. Here are the French indirect object pronouns:

Singular		Plural	
me (m')	*(to/for) me*	**nous**	*(to/for) us*
te (t')	*(to/for) you*	**vous**	*(to/for) you*
lui	*(to/for) him/her (m., f.)*	**leur**	*(to/for) them (m., f.)*

- As usual, the letter **-e** is dropped (**m'**, **t'**) before a vowel or a mute **h**.

Dorothée **m'**envoie deux mails par jour.	*Dorothée sends **me** two e-mails a day.*
Je **t'**offre une semaine de vacances.	*I'm offering **you** a week of vacation.*

Indirect object pronouns do not show the gender of the person(s) referred to. Keep track of the context. Who is speaking to whom?

- The indirect object pronoun is placed before the conjugated verb. If the verb is followed by an infinitive, the indirect object pronoun precedes the infinitive.

Je **lui** prépare deux gâteaux délicieux.	*I'm preparing two delicious cakes **for him/her**.*
Tes parents? Marc veut bien **leur** répondre.	*Your parents? Marc is willing to answer **them**.*

- In the negative, the pronoun precedes the verb of which it is the object. The negative construction surrounds the verb being negated.

Elle **ne lui** téléphone **pas**; elle **ne** va **pas lui** écrire.	*She does **not** phone **him**; she's **not** going to write **to him**.*

Exercise 9.7

*Translate the sentences into French using an indirect object pronoun (**me/m'**, **te/t'**, **lui**, **nous**, **vous**, **leur**) for the pronouns in italics.*

1. I phone *him*. _____.

2. We buy *her* gifts. _____.

3. They (*f.*) give *us* some money. _____.

4. He writes *to them*. _____.

5. Chantal offers *me* the dictionary. _____.

6. Are you (*fam.*) sending *me* a letter? _____?

7. Édouard explains the problem *to us*. _____.

8. Do you (*pol.*) say hello *to them*? _____?

9. I'm going to speak *to you* (*fam.*) later. _____.

10. She doesn't answer *me*. _____.

11. Are you (*fam.*) going to bring *me* some cheese? _____?

12. We don't show *them* the answers. _____.

13. Camille lends *her* some money. _____.

Exercise 9.8

Complete the sentences, translating the English expressions into French.

1. Julie (*writes me*) _____ deux cartes postales chaque semaine.

2. Je (*want to sell you* [*fam.*]) _____ mon vieil ordinateur.

3. Les copains (*send us*) _____ des mails d'Abidjan.

4. Charles (*gives me*) _____ les notes d'aujourd'hui.

5. Qui (*can teach them*) _____ la leçon de mercredi?

6. Je (*ask you* [*pol.*]) _____ si mes clés sont chez vous.

7. Vous (*tell her*) _____ que votre cousine vit à Strasbourg.

8. Nous (*must answer him*) _____ immédiatement.

9. (*Are you [fam.] going to bring them*) _____ des boissons?

10. Je (*repeat to you [fam.]*) _____ l'adresse de Véronique?

11. Il (*often asks me*) _____ de ne pas prendre la voiture.

12. Tu (*are buying for us*) _____ trop de cadeaux!

13. (*Can you [pol.] lend me*) _____ la voiture?

The Pronouns *y* and *en*

The pronouns **y** and **en** behave like object pronouns. **Y** refers to places and things; **en** refers to quantities.

The Pronoun *y*

The pronoun **y** can refer to a *location* (a country, city, building, room, etc.) that has already been mentioned in a conversation. Its English equivalent is *there*. **Y** does not refer to people. It replaces a prepositional phrase, such as **à Montréal** (*in/to Montreal*), **à la pharmacie** (*at the drugstore*), **chez Maurice** (*at Maurice's place*), **en Australie** (*in/to Australia*).

- Like direct and indirect object pronouns, **y** precedes the conjugated verb. This is also true for negative and interrogative sentences.

Tu vas **chez Théophile**?	*Are you going **to Théophile's** (**place**)?*
—Oui, j'**y** vais. Mais Gilberte **n'y** va **pas**.	*—Yes, I'm going **there**. But Gilberte is **not** (going **there**).*
Qu'est-ce qu'on achète **à la droguerie**?	*What do we buy **at the hardware store**?*
—On **y** achète des produits ménagers.	*—**There** we buy household products.*
J'achète des vêtements **à la friperie**. **Y** trouves-tu aussi des choses?	*I buy clothes **at the second-hand store**. Do you find things **there**, too?*

- The pronoun **y** can also replace the preposition **à** + a previously mentioned *object* or *idea*.

Nous pensons **aux vacances**.	*We're thinking **about vacation**.*
Nous **y** pensons tout le temps!	*We think **about it** all the time!*
Je tiens **à la vieille voiture** de Maman.	*I'm very attached **to** Mom's **old car**.*
J'**y** tiens.	*I'm very attached **to it**.*

Exercise 9.9

*Rewrite each sentence or question, replacing the phrase in italics with the pronoun **y**.*

1. Je vais *à la banque*. _____.

2. Nous pensons *aux nouveaux cours*. _____.

3. Est-ce que tu vas voyager *en Europe*? _____?

4. Charlotte cherche des lampes *au marché*. _____.

5. Vous retrouvez des copains *au café*. _____.

6. Arielle n'a pas besoin d'aller *en ville*. _____.

7. Elles réfléchissent *à l'avenir* (*the future*). _____.

8. Je n'achète pas les provisions *à l'hypermarché*. _____.

9. Tu réussis géneralement *aux examens*? _____?

10. On sert de bons repas *chez Victor*. _____.

11. Tenez-vous *à nous accompagner*? _____?

12. Les étudiants veulent faire un stage *au Japon*. _____.

The Pronoun *en*

Expressed in English by *some* or *any*, the pronoun **en** replaces nouns preceded by a partitive article (**du/de la/de l'**), by an indefinite article (**un/une/des**), or by **de/d'**, in cases where the rest of the article is omitted.

- The pronoun **en** is placed directly before the verb of which it is the object.

Tu prends **du café** le matin?	*Do you drink **coffee** in the morning?*
—Oui, j'**en** prends le matin.	*—Yes, I have **some** in the morning.*
Y a-t-il **des restaurants élégants** à Lyon?	*Are there **elegant restaurants** in Lyon?*
—Oui, il y **en** a.	*—Yes, there are (**some**).*
Il y a **de bonnes idées** dans l'article?	*Are there **any good ideas** in the article?*
—Non, il **n'y en** a **pas**.	*—No, there are **not** (**any**).*
As-tu **de l'argent**?	*Do you have **any money**?*
—Hélas, je **n'en** ai **pas**.	*—Alas, I do **not** have **any**.*

- When a noun following **un** or **une** is replaced by en, the singular indefinite article **un** or **une** is repeated in an affirmative answer. **Un** or **une** is *not* repeated in a negative answer.

Elle a **une valise convenable**?	*Does she have **an appropriate suitcase**?*
—Oui, elle **en** a **une**.	*—Yes, she has **one**.*
—Non, elle **n'en** a **pas**.	*—No, she does **not** have (**one**).*

En also replaces a noun modified by a *number* or by an *expression of quantity*, such as **un(e)** (*one*), **cinq** (*five*), **plusieurs** (*several, a few*), **beaucoup de** (*a lot of, many*), **un kilo de** (*a kilo[gram] of*), **assez de** (*enough*), **trop de** (*too, too much*), etc.

When **en** is used in an affirmative sentence, **de/d'** + the noun is dropped, and the number or expression of quantity is *repeated*. In this situation, **en** is always expressed in French.

Est-ce que tu as **beaucoup de devoirs**?	*Do you have **a lot of homework**?*
—Oh, oui, j'**en** ai **beaucoup**!	*—Oh yes, I have **a lot** (**of it**)!*
Combien **de trains** voyez-vous?	*How many trains do you see?*
—J'**en** vois **plusieurs**.	*—I see **a few** (**of them**).*
Benoît suit combien **de cours**?	*Benoît is taking how many classes?*
—Il **en** suit **quatre**.	*—He's taking **four** (**of them**).*
Marina va chercher **trois bouteilles de vin**.	*Marina's going to get **three bottles of wine**.*

—Elle va **en** chercher **trois**?

—She's going to get **three** (**of them**)?

—Non, elle ne va pas **en** chercher.
Tu achètes **un kilo d'oranges**?
—Oui, j'**en** achète **un kilo**.

—No, she's not going to get **any**.
You're buying **a kilo of oranges**?
—Yes, I'm buying **a kilo** (**of them**).

- **En** also replaces **de/d'** + a noun referring to a *thing* or an *idea* in sentences with verbal expressions using **de**: **parler de** (*to speak of, about*), **avoir besoin de** (*to need*), **avoir envie de** (*to wish for, want*), **être fier** (**fière**) **de** (*to be proud of*), etc.

Est-ce que François parle **des chiens**?

Is François talking **about the dogs**?

—Oui, il **en** parle.
Avez-vous besoin **d'argent**?
—Oui, nous **en** avons besoin.
Marthe est fière **de la maison**.
Elle **en** est fière.

—Yes, he's talking **about them**.
Do you need **money**?
—Yes, we need **some**.
Marthe is proud **of the house**.
She's proud **of it**.

Exercise 9.10

*Answer the questions affirmatively (**Oui, ...**) with a complete sentence, replacing the phrase in italics with the pronoun **en**.*

EXAMPLE: *Prenez-vous beaucoup de salade?* _____ *Oui, nous en* _____
*prenons beaucoup.* _____

1. Vous allez acheter *des provisions*? _____.

2. Sébastien a-t-il *de l'argent*? _____.

3. Est-ce que tu bois *du lait*? _____.

4. Les étudiants ont-ils beaucoup *de devoirs*? _____.

5. Madonna possède-t-elle trois *maisons*? _____.

6. Nous avons assez *de légumes*? _____.

7. On va chercher une douzaine *d'œufs*? _____.

8. As-tu besoin *de logement*? _____.

9. Claudie prend deux *kilos de pommes de terre*? _____.

10. On utilise trop *d'énergie*? _____.

11. Tu as un *euro à me prêter* (lend)? _____.

*Now, answer the questions in the negative (***Non, ... ***).*

12. Est-ce que les enfants boivent *du café?* _____.

13. Avez-vous assez *de farine (flour)?* _____.

14. Léonard achète-t-il *des chaussures de marche?* _____.

15. Tu as besoin *de quelques centimes?* _____.

16. Benoîte prend-elle *une tasse de thé?* _____.

17. Tes amies mangent-elles beaucoup *de sucreries (sweets)?* _____.

Exercise 9.11

Rewrite the sentences and questions, replacing the element in italics with a direct object pronoun, an indirect object pronoun, **y,** *or* **en**.

1. Nous achetons beaucoup *de fruits.* _____.

2. Elle met de la crème *dans la tasse.* _____.

3. Je vais bientôt *en France.* _____.

4. À Noël, nous offrons *des cadeaux* aux collègues. _____.

5. À Noël, on offre des cadeaux *aux collègues.* _____.

6. Elles lisent toujours *les romans policiers.* _____.

7. Achètes-tu des bonbons *pour les enfants?* _____?

8. N'écris-tu pas *à Monique?* _____?

9. Papa mange trop *de pain.* _____.

10. Je tiens fort *(greatly)* *à ma collection de vieux albums.* _____.

11. Vous appréciez *les comédies classiques.* _____.

12. Montrent-elles *la photo* à Martine? _____?

13. François ne remet pas les devoirs *au professeur.* _____.

14. Ils travaillent *dans un bureau en ville.* _____.

15. Je cherche trois *livres de classe.* _____.

16. Nous voulons passer du temps *au Brésil.* _____.

17. Marc ne voit pas *son amie Nicole* ce week-end. _____.

18. Tu oublies encore *le parapluie?* _____?

Key Vocabulary

Urban and rural dwellers alike have a close connection with their environment.

Les animaux (Animals)

l'agneau (*m.*) (*lamb*)
l'aigrette (*f.*) (*egret*)
l'âne (*m.*) (*donkey*)
le canard (*duck*)
le cerf (*deer*)
le chameau (*camel*)
le chat (*cat*)
le cheval (*horse*)
la chèvre (*goat*)
le chien (*dog*)
le chimpanzé (*chimpanzee*)
le cochon (*pig*)
le colibris (*hummingbird*)
le coq (*rooster*)
le corbeau (*crow*)
le crapaud (*toad*)
le crocodile (*crocodile*)
le dauphin (*dolphin*)
le dindon (*turkey*)
l'écureuil (*m.*) (*squirrel*)
l'éléphant (*m.*) (*elephant*)
le faucon (*falcon*)
la gazelle (*gazelle*)
la girafe (*giraffe*)
le gorille (*gorilla*)
la grenouille (*frog*)

le *hibou (*owl*)
le kangourou (*kangaroo*)
le lapin (*rabbit*)
le lion (*lion*)
le loup (*wolf*)
le moineau (*sparrow*)
le mouton (*sheep*)
l'oie (*f.*) (*goose*)
l'oiseau (*m.*) (*bird*)
l'ours (*m.*) (*bear*)
le perroquet (*parrot*)
le pigeon (*pigeon*)
le pingouin (*penguin*)
la poule (*chicken, hen*)
le rat (*rat*)
le renard (*fox*)
le requin (*shark*)
le serpent (*snake*)
le singe (*monkey*)
la souris (*mouse*)
le taureau (*bull*)
le tigre (*tiger*)
la tortue (*turtle*)
la vache (*cow*)
la volaille (*poultry*)
le zèbre (*zebra*)

Les plantes (Plants)

l'arbre (*m.*) (*tree*)
l'arbuste (*m.*) (*bush*)
le bois (*wood*)
la branche (*branch*)
le cactus (*cactus*)

le champignon (*mushroom*)
le chêne (*oak tree*)
le citronnier (*lemon tree*)
l'écorce (*f.*) (*tree bark*)
la feuille (*leaf*)

la fleur (*flower*)	le pin (*pine tree*)
la forêt (*forest*)	le pommier (*apple tree*)
le gazon (*lawn*)	la racine (*root*)
l'herbe (*f.*) (*grass*)	le rameau (*twig*)
l'iris (*m.*) (*iris*)	la rose (*rose*)
le lilas (*lilac*)	la souche (*tree stump*)
le lys (*lily*)	la tige (*stem*)
la marguerite (*daisy*)	le tronc (*tree trunk*)
l'olivier (*m.*) (*olive tree*)	la tulipe (*tulip*)
l'orchidée (*f.*) (*orchid*)	la vigne (*vine*)
l'orme (*f.*) (*elm tree*)	le vignoble (*vineyard*)
la pétale (*petal*)	

Exercise 9.12

Use the previous vocabulary list to answer the questions.

1. Nommez quelques mammifères qu'on trouve au zoo.

   _____

2. Nommez des oiseaux. Quels oiseaux aimez-vous particulièrement?

   _____

3. Nommez des reptiles et des amphibiens.

   _____

4. Nommez des animaux qu'on trouve dans une ferme.

   _____

5. Quelles plantes mettez-vous dans votre jardin idéal?

   _____

Reading Comprehension

Le jardin zoologique idéal

Qui n'aime pas aller au zoo? Composé de jardins botaniques, d'un Muséum d'Histoire Naturelle et d'une ménagerie d'**un millier** d'animaux, le Jardin des Plantes de Paris, dans le cinquième arrondissement sur **la Rive gauche**, existe depuis 1794. C'est à cette date — **à la suite de** la Révolution Française — qu'**on crée** un parc public qui rassemble les plantes et animaux des collections **des rois** de France. Les premiers animaux viennent de la ménagerie royale de Versailles et de la ménagerie privée du duc d'Orléans. En plus, les nouvelles autorités révolutionnaires y **ajoutent** les animaux **des forains** (les gens présentant des spectacles animaliers de rue, maintenant **interdits**).

Avec son architecture qui date du dix-huitième et du dix-neuvième siècles, la ménagerie est le plus ancien zoo du monde conservé dans son aspect originel. **Comme** elle n'est pas très grande, elle contient **surtout des espèces** de **petite taille** (mammifères, oiseaux, reptiles, amphibiens et même des insectes), qui sont **soignées** par une soixantaine de personnes, **y compris** des vétérinaires. Le zoo **accueille** bien sûr les visiteurs, mais on y **mène** aussi des études **de comportement** et de reproduction d'espèces rares, souvent en collaboration avec des chercheurs d'autres pays. Le zoo participe à de nombreux projets d'**élevage** d'animaux **menacés de disparition** dans leurs milieux naturels. C'est le cas des petits chevaux de Przewalski qui **n'existent plus** à l'état sauvage. Pour certaines espèces, on pense même les réintroduire dans leurs zones d'origine.

un millier (*about a thousand*)	des espèces (*f.*) (*species*)
la Rive gauche (*the Left Bank*)	petite taille (*small size*)
à la suite de (*following*)	soignées (*cared for*)
on crée (*they create*)	y compris (*including*)
des rois (*m.*) (*of the kings*)	accueille (**accueillir**) (*welcomes*)
ajoutent (*add*)	mène (**mener**) (*conduct*)
des forains (*m.*) (*of the street entertainers*)	de comportement (*behavior*)
	l'élevage (*m.*) (*breeding*)
interdits (*prohibited*)	menacés de disparition (*endangered*)
comme (*since, because*)	
surtout (*above all*)	n'existent plus (*no longer exist*)

Questions

After reading the selection, answer the questions in French.

1. Où est le zoo dont on parle ici?

   _____

2. D'où viennent les premiers animaux du Jardin des Plantes? Pourquoi?

   _____

3. Quels animaux y sont exposés (*displayed*)?

   _____.

4. Comment sont les animaux? Pourquoi?

   _____.

5. Quelles activités est-ce qu'on mène dans ce zoo?

   _____.

6. Quels aspects du Jardin des Plantes vous intéressent? Pourquoi?

   _____.

10

Possessives, Demonstratives, Comparatives, and Adverbs

Possessive Adjectives and Pronouns

French possessive adjectives and pronouns agree in number and gender with the nouns they modify or replace.

Possessive Adjectives

Since the possessive adjectives match the *nouns* they modify in number and gender, they don't match the "owner" of the noun. Here are the French possessive adjectives:

Singular

	MASCULINE		FEMININE	
my	**mon**	*père*	**ma**	*mère*
your	**ton**	*père*	**ta**	*mère*
his/her/its/one's	**son**	*père*	**sa**	*mère*
our	**notre**	*père*	**notre**	*mère*
your	**votre**	*père*	**votre**	*mère*
their	**leur**	*père*	**leur**	*mère*

Plural

MASCULINE OR FEMININE

my	**mes**	*cousins (ou) cousines*
your	**tes**	*cousins (ou) cousines*
his/her/its/one's	**ses**	*cousins (ou) cousines*
our	**nos**	*cousins (ou) cousines*
your	**vos**	*cousins (ou) cousines*
their	**leurs**	*cousins (ou) cousines*

Voilà **sa** maison.	*There's **his/her** house.*
Appelles-tu souvent **ton** fiancé et **ses** parents?	*Do you often call **your** fiancé and **his** parents?*
Mes voisines dînent avec **leur** oncle.	***My** neighbors (f.) are having dinner with **their** uncle.*

The possessive adjective **leur** (*their*) has the same spelling as the plural indirect object pronoun **leur** (*to them*). But the possessive adjective has a plural form: **leurs**.

Nos amis prennent **leur** voiture et **leurs** bagages.	***Our** friends are taking **their** car and **their** bags.*

The forms **mon**, **ton**, and **son** must be used before *singular feminine* nouns that begin with a vowel or mute **h**.

adresse (*f.*)	**mon** adresse	***my** address*
amie (*f.*)	**ton** amie	***your** (fam.) friend*
histoire (*f.*)	**son** histoire	***his** (or ***her***) story*

Exercise 10.1

Complete the phrases with the French possessive adjective, given here in English.

1. (*my*) _____ maison
2. (*her*) _____ oncle
3. (*our*) _____ problèmes
4. (*their*) _____ chien
5. (*your* [*fam.*]) _____ jardin
6. (*your* [*pol.*]) _____ grands-parents
7. (*our*) _____ appartement
8. (*my*) _____ voisines
9. (*his*) _____ amis
10. (*your* [*fam.*]) _____ livres

Exercise 10.2

*Complete each sentence using the appropriate French possessive adjective (**mon**, **ma**, **mes**, etc.).*

1. Je suis étudiant; _____ livres sont dans _____ sac à dos (*backpack*).

2. C'est un excellent prof; _____ idées sont intéressantes.

3. Ils sont avocats; _____ clients sont ou coupables ou innocents.

4. Notre frère (*brother*) est architecte, mais _____ parents sont professeurs.

5. Voilà ma grand-mère; _____ maison est en Provence.

6. Le cousin de Cécile est menuisier; _____ employés sont très qualifiés.

7. Vous êtes étudiants; _____ livres sont lourds!

8. Liliane est à Toulouse; _____ sœurs ne sont pas loin. Elles sont à Bordeaux.

Possessive Pronouns

Possessive pronouns replace nouns that are modified by a possessive adjective or other possessive construction or idea. In English, the possessive pronouns are *mine, yours, his, hers, its, ours,* and *theirs: The textbooks? I have **mine** and they have **theirs***. In French, the definite article (**le/la/les**) is always used with a possessive pronoun.

	Singular		Plural	
	MASCULINE	FEMININE	MASCULINE	FEMININE
mine	**le mien**	**la mienne**	**les miens**	**les miennes**
yours	**le tien**	**la tienne**	**les tiens**	**les tiennes**
his/her/its	**le sien**	**la sienne**	**les siens**	**les siennes**
ours	**le nôtre**	**la nôtre**	**les nôtres**	**les nôtres**
yours	**le vôtre**	**la vôtre**	**les vôtres**	**les vôtres**
theirs	**le leur**	**la leur**	**les leurs**	**les leurs**

Le/la/les nôtre(s) and le/la/les vôtre(s)

Note the circumflex accent in the spelling of **le/la/les nôtre(s)** and **le/la/les vôtre(s)**.

- The circumflex requires the pronunciation [oh], long vowel, for the letter **o**. In the possessive pronouns **notre** and **votre**, which do not have the circumflex, the letter **o** is pronounced [uh].

Notre [nuhtR] cours est intéressant.   ***Our*** class is interesting.

—Hélas, **le nôtre** [nohtR] est   —Alas, ***ours*** is very boring!
très ennuyeux!

In the plural possessive pronoun (**leurs**), masculine and feminine forms are the same. Possessive pronouns have the gender and number of the object or person "owned," *not* the "owner."

Où sont **leurs outils**?	*Where are **their tools**?*
—**Les leurs** sont ici, **les miens** sont là-bas.	—***Theirs** are here; **mine** are over there.*
Ça, c'est **ma sœur**. Où est **la tienne**?	*That's **my sister**. Where's **yours**?*
—**La mienne** est encore à la fac.	—***Mine** is still at the university.*
Mes bagages sont là-bas. Où sont **les vôtres**?	***My bags** are over there. Where are **yours**?*
—**Les nôtres** sont déjà dans le taxi.	—***Ours** are already in the taxi.*

The definite article preceding possessive pronouns is contracted with the prepositions **à** and **de**. (**L'** and **la** do not contract.)

Je pense **à mes vacances** et vous pensez **aux vôtres**.	*I'm thinking **about my vacation** and you're thinking **about yours**.*
Florence a **son vélo**; elle n'a pas besoin **du tien**.	*Florence has **her bike**; she doesn't need **yours**.*

Exercise 10.3

Read the sentences, and complete each question by replacing the nouns in italics with the logical French possessive pronoun: **le/la/les mien(ne)(s)**, **le/la/les vôtre(s)**, *etc.*

1. Je fais *mes devoirs* l'après-midi. Quand fais-tu _____?

2. Nous ne prêtons pas *notre voiture*. Prêtez-vous parfois _____?

3. Paulette arrive à terminer *son travail*. Paul arrive-t-il à terminer _____?

4. Jean-Pierre ressemble à *son père*. Que penses-tu? Ressemblons-nous _____?

5. Je téléphone souvent à *mes parents*. Est-ce que Michelle téléphone _____?

6. Nous avons besoin *de notre motocyclette* (f.) aujourd'hui. Avez-vous besoin _____?

Demonstrative Adjectives and Pronouns

Demonstrative adjectives and pronouns point out or specify a particular person, object, or idea.

Demonstrative Adjectives

French demonstrative adjectives, **ce/cette/ces**—the equivalent in English of singular *this/that* and plural *these/those*—always precede a noun and agree with the noun in gender and in number. **Ce** becomes **cet** before masculine singular nouns that start with a vowel or mute **h**. Plural **ces** is the same for masculine and feminine.

	Masculine		Feminine	
Singular	**ce**	livre	**cette**	chaise
	cet	homme	**cette**	adresse
Plural	**ces**	livres	**ces**	chaises
	ces	hommes	**ces**	adresses

Pronunciation Before a Vowel or Mute *h*

Pronounce the **liaison** between the demonstrative adjectives **cet** and **ces** before a vowel or mute **h**.

Cet_appartement est bien équipé.	***This/That*** *apartment is well equipped.*
Ces_œuvres sont très intéressantes.	***These/Those*** *works are very interesting.*

Qui est **cette** dame? Et **cet** homme là-bas?	*Who's **this/that** woman? And **that** man over there?*
Je trouve **ce** manteau très convenable.	*I find **this/that** coat quite suitable.*
On aime bien **ces** hommes d'état.	***Those** statesmen are much appreciated.*

-Ci (*this* [*here*]) or **-là** (*that* [*there*]) is sometimes attached to nouns that are preceded by a demonstrative adjective. **-Ci** and **-là** may indicate relative distance and are also used to make a simple distinction between persons or objects.

Amélie parle de **cette maison-ci**.   *Amélie is talking about **this house**.*
   Cette maison-là n'est pas   ***That one** isn't for rent.*
   à louer.

Exercise 10.4

*Complete the phrases with the correct demonstrative adjective (**ce**, **cet**, **cette**, or **ces**).*

1. _____ belles fleurs
2. _____ nouvel appartement
3. _____ gentil chat
4. _____ repas délicieux

5. _____ arbre ancien
6. _____ grosse valise
7. _____ soldats courageux
8. _____ article important

Exercise 10.5

*Complete the sentences using **ce**, **cet**, **cette**, or **ces**. Add **-ci** or **-là** when appropriate; otherwise leave the second space blank.*

1. Qui est _____ homme _____ qui sort avec Julie? (*that*)

2. _____ magazine _____ est intéressant, mais _____ article _____ contient plus d'information. (*this/that*)

3. Tu aimes _____ chemises _____, ou bien tu préfères _____ chemises _____? (*these/those*)

4. Où voulez-vous manger, dans _____ restaurant _____ ou dans _____ cafétéria (f.) _____? (*this/that*)

5. _____ dames _____ vont courir dans le marathon. (*those*)

Demonstrative Pronouns

Demonstrative pronouns (in English: *this one, that one, those*) refer to a person, thing, or idea mentioned previously in a conversation. In French, they agree in gender and number with the nouns they replace. Demonstrative pronouns must be followed by **-ci** or **-là**, a preposition, or a relative pronoun.

	Masculine	Feminine
Singular	**celui...**	**celle...**
Plural	**ceux...**	**celles...**

Un **dictionnaire**? J'aime **celui qui** a de bonnes définitions.

A **dictionary**? I like **the one that** has good definitions.

La **maison**? **Celle que** j'achète a un prix raisonnable.

The **house**? **The one** I'm buying has a reasonable price.

Ces **étudiants**? **Ceux qui** sont des Verts sont plutôt militants.

Those **students**? **Those who** are Greens are rather militant.

Des **idéologies**? Les gens choisissent **celles qu'**ils peuvent comprendre.

Ideologies? People choose **the ones** (**those**) they can understand.

Demonstrative pronouns do not stand alone. They are always used in one of these contexts:

- **With the suffixes -ci or -là to make a distinction between objects or persons**

  Voici plusieurs **magazines**. Tu veux **celui-ci** ou **celui-là**?

  Here are a few **magazines**. Do you want **this one** or **that one**?

- **Followed by a preposition (often de/d' or a compound preposition with de/d')**

  Quelle **littérature** aimes-tu mieux? **Celle d'**Amérique latine ou **celle de** France?

  Which **literature** do you prefer? Latin American or French? (Literally: **That of** Latin America or of France?)

  De quel **restaurant** parle-t-il? **Celui à côté de** la banque ou **celui au coin de** la rue?

  Which **restaurant** is he talking about? **The one next to** the bank or **the one at** the corner?

- **Followed by a clause introduced by a relative pronoun (qui, que, or dont)**

  Cet auteur a une douzaine de **romans policiers**. **Celui que** je lis est formidable!

  That author has a dozen **mystery novels**. **The one** I'm reading is terrific!

  Mireille veut suivre trois **cours**, mais on n'offre pas **ceux dont** elle a besoin.

  Mireille wants to take three **classes**, but they're not offering **the ones** she needs.

Indefinite Demonstrative Pronouns

Ceci (*this*), **cela** (*that*), and **ça** (*that*, informal) are *indefinite* demonstrative pronouns. They refer to an idea or object (not a person) with no definite antecedent. The indefinite demonstrative pronouns do not show gender or number. They sometimes precede the indefinite subject **ce/c'**.

Cela (**Ça**) m'est égal.	*It is all the same to me.*
Tu vois **ceci**?	*Do you see **this**?*
Ça, c'est tout ce dont nous avons besoin.	***That** is all we need.*

Exercise 10.6

*Translate the sentences into French using demonstrative pronouns (**celui...** , **celle...** , **ceux...** , **celles...**) or indefinite demonstratives (**cela**, **ça**, **ceci**) for the words in italics.*

1. I love reading novels. *Those that* I prefer are full of adventures (**pleins d'aventures**).

   _____.

2. Marc's courses are interesting, especially *those* in the history department (**la faculté d'histoire**).

   _____.

3. Which car do you (*fam.*) want to rent (**louer**)? *This one* or *that one?*

   _____?

4. These are good computers. *Those that* run (**marcher**) well aren't very expensive.

   _____.

5. Here are a few movies. *The one that* you (*fam.*) want to see is available (**disponible**).

   _____.

6. The books are on the table. I'm reading *this one*. Do you want *that one?*

   _____?

7. I need to borrow (**emprunter**) some notes (**notes** [*f.*]). *Anne's* are always easy to read.

   _____.

8. We're going to see a play on Saturday. *The one that* we're going to see is a comedy.

   _____.

Comparatives and Superlatives

It is natural to make comparisons among people and things, and, at times, we are called upon to make evaluations. French has simple patterns for comparing adjectives, nouns, verbs, and adverbs.

The Comparative with Adjectives

Terms that indicate *greater*, *equal*, and *lesser* are: **plus** (*more*), **aussi** (*as*), and **moins** (*less*).

Que/qu' always precedes the element being compared. When a pronoun is needed, a stressed pronoun (see Chapter 11) follows **que**.

Nous sommes [*We are*] { **plus** grands **que** [*taller than*] / **aussi** grands **que** [*as tall as*] / **moins** grands **que** [*shorter than*] } lui. [*he (is).*]

Je suis **plus pauvre que** M. Buffett.	*I am **poorer than** Mr. Buffett.*
Adam est **moins fort que** toi.	*Adam is **less strong** (**weaker**) **than** you (are).*
Elles sont **aussi intelligentes que** vous.	*They are **as intelligent as** you (all) (are).*

The Comparative with Nouns

When nouns are compared, **de/d'** always precedes the noun. The expression of equality, **autant de**, is used instead of **aussi**.

J'ai [*I have*] { **plus de** [*more*] / **autant de** [*as many*] / **moins de** [*fewer*] } cousins **qu'**elle. [*cousins **than** she (has).*] / [*cousins **as** she (has).*] / [*cousins **than** she (has).*]

Maurice a **plus de** temps libre **que** moi.	*Maurice has **more** free time **than** I (do).*
Je n'ai pas **autant d'**argent **que** mon frère.	*I don't have **as much** money **as** my brother.*
Mon père fait **moins de** courses **que** ma mère.	*My father does **fewer** errands **than** my mother.*

Comparing Verbs

When you compare action verbs, use **plus que** (*more than*), **autant que** (*as much as*), and **moins que** (*less than*) after the verb. **Que/qu'** is followed by a noun, a stressed pronoun, an adverb of time, or another verb.

Khaled **travaille plus que** Fatima.	*Khaled **works more than** Fatima.*
Jeanne **étudie autant que** moi.	*Jeanne **studies as much as** I (do).*
Ma grand-mère **lit moins qu'**avant.	*My grandmother **reads less than** before.*
Nous **skiions autant que** nous travaillons!	*We **ski as much as** we work!*

Exercise 10.7

Complete the sentences with the French equivalent of the phrases given in English. Pay attention to the agreement (gender and number) of adjectives.

1. Sa voiture est chère, mais elle n'est pas _____ la mienne. (*as expensive as*)

2. Notre cours de mathématiques est _____ le cours d'économie politique. (*more interesting than*)

3. Vous avez _____ examens _____ nous. (*as many . . . as*)

4. Ta maison est _____ mon appartement. (*smaller than*)

5. Ces films sont _____ les émissions de télévision. (*more exciting* [**passionnants**] *than*)

6. Ma sœur cadette (*younger*) est _____ mon frère aîné (*older*). (*happier than*)

7. Les rues sont _____ les avenues. (*less wide* [**larges**] *than*)

8. Tu crois que les chevaux sont _____ les chiens? (*as intelligent as*)

9. Cette maison rouge est _____ la maison jaune. (*older than*)

10. Je lis _____ toi. (*more than*)

11. Il en sait _____ nous. (*less than*)

12. Je pense que Monique est _____ Martine. (*older*)

13. La cuisine indienne est _____ la cuisine chinoise. (*spicier* [**épicée**] *than*)

14. Notre salle de bains est _____ la salle à manger. (*cleaner* [**propre**] *than*)

15. Nous sommes _____ les voisins. (*nicer* [**sympathiques**] *than*)

16. Je n'ai pas _____ argent _____ mes parents. (*as much . . . as*)

17. Je suis actuellement _____ mes amis. (*less sad than*)

18. Les parents sont _____ leurs enfants. (*more tired than*)

19. Isabelle pense que le soleil est _____ la lune; Raymond pense que la lune est _____. (*more important than/more important*)

20. Les filles jouent à _____ sports _____ les garçons. (*as many . . . as*)

21. À la confiserie, je vends _____ bonbons _____ je ne mange! (*fewer . . . than*)

22. Ils gagnent _____ argent _____ Pierre. (*more . . . than*)

The Superlative of Adjectives and Nouns

The definite article **le/la/les** is always used in French superlative constructions. It matches the noun in gender and number.

Superlative of Adjectives

In the superlative, adjectives, preceded by **le/la/les**, keep their position before or after the noun. When the adjective follows the noun, the definite article is repeated after the noun. The preposition **de/d'** expresses *in* or *of* (a place or a group).

Jean est	intelligent.
Micheline est	**plus** intelligente **que** Jean.
Claire est	(l'étudiante) **la plus** intelligente **des** trois.

Josée est **la moins travailleuse**.	*Josée is **the least hardworking**.*
Voici **le plus jeune membre de** ma famille.	*Here's **the youngest member of** my family.*
Quelle est **la plus belle île du** monde?	*Which is **the most beautiful island in the** world?*

Superlative of Nouns

In the superlative, nouns are preceded by **le moins de** (*the least*) or **le plus de** (*the most*). Use **de/d'** (*of* or *in*) before the name of the place or the group.

Marc fait **le moins de devoirs de** la classe!	*Marc does **the least homework in** the class!*
M. Gates a **le plus d'argent de** tous.	*Mr. Gates has **the most money of** everyone.*

Superlative of Verbs

To express the superlative of verbs, simply use **le plus** (*the most*) or **le moins** (*the least*) after the verb, always with the impersonal singular **le**:

Moi, je **travaille le moins**.	*Me, I **work the least**.*
C'est l'émission qu'elle **regarde le plus**.	*That's the program she **watches (the) most**.*
Voilà ce qui leur **plaît le plus**.	*That's what they **like best** (what **pleases them most**).*

Irregular Comparative and Superlative Adjectives

It's important to know the difference between the *adjectives* **bon** (*good*) and **mauvais** (*bad*) and the *adverbs* **bien** (*good*) and **mal** (*bad*). For adverbs, see the section later in this chapter called "Comparatives and Superlatives of Adverbs."

Two comparative and superlative adjectives have irregular forms:

Comparative

bon(ne)(s)	*good*	**meilleur(e)(s)**	*better*
mauvais(e)(s)	*bad*	**plus mauvais(e)(s)**; **pire(s)**	*worse*
petit(e)(s)	*small*	**plus petit(e)(s)**	*smaller*

Superlative

le/la/les meilleur(e)(s)	*the best*
le/la/les plus mauvais(e)(s);	*the worst*
le/la/les pire(s)	
le/la/les moindre(s)	*the least*

La cuisine française est **bonne**; mais Paola dit que la cuisine italienne est **meilleure**.	*French cuisine is **good**, but Paola says Italian cuisine is **better**.*
Mme Lemoine? C'est mon **meilleur** professeur!	*Mme Lemoine? She's my **best** teacher!*
Ce restaurant-ci est **mauvais**, mais celui-là est **pire**!	*This restaurant is **bad**, but that one is **worse**!*
Ça, c'est **le plus mauvais** film (**le pire** film) **de** l'année.	*That's **the worst** movie **of** the year.*
Cet examen? C'est **la moindre de** mes difficultés.	*That exam? It's **the least of** my problems.*

 ## Exercise 10.8

Complete the sentences with the French equivalent of the phrases given in English. Pay attention to the agreement (gender and number) with adjectives.

1. Ce film est bon; c'est même _____ de tous. (*the best*)

2. L'appartement de Nicole est _____ de l'immeuble (*building*). (*the biggest*)

3. Elle est _____ David, mais elle n'est pas _____ étudiant de la classe. (*taller/tallest*)

4. Ils vivent dans _____ région du pays. (*the most beautiful*)

5. Ce restaurant sert _____ repas de la ville. (*the best* [*pl.*])

6. La petite Annie a deux ans. Elle est _____ de sa famille. (*the youngest*)

7. Qui est _____ politicien ou _____ politicienne des États-Unis? Qui est _____ politicien ou _____ politicienne? (*the best/the worst*)

8. La date de la guerre de Crimée? Je n'en ai pas _____ idée. (*the least*)

9. C'est _____ roman de l'année. (*the worst*)

10. Cette émission (*program*) est celle qu'on regarde _____. (*the least*)

11. Voici _____ plat de ce restaurant. (*the best*)

12. Nous avons _____ d'animaux domestiques de tous nos amis. (*the most*)

13. Je gagne _____ salaire (*m.*) de mon groupe. (*the smallest*)

14. Mon appartement a _____ de pièces de tout l'immeuble; je n'en ai qu'une! (*the fewest*)

Adverbs

Adverbs include any word or expression that modifies a verb, another adverb, or an adjective. Here are some English examples:

*They walk **quickly**.*
*The pupil reads **quite easily**.*
*She's **very** hardworking.*

Common Adverbs and Their Placement

You have already been using adverbs in French, including the following words:

beaucoup   (*much, a lot*)   souvent   (*often*)
bien   (*well*)   très   (*very*)
mal   (*badly*)   trop   (*too, too much*)
peu   (*little, not very*)   vite   (*fast, quickly*)

Jeannette mange **trop vite**!	*Jeannette eats **too fast**!*
Mon voisin est **assez** vieux;	*My neighbor is **rather** old; he*
il travaille **peu**.	* works **very little**.*
Moi, je ne vais pas au bal;	*Me, I'm not going to the dance;*
je danse **mal**!	* I dance **badly**!*

- Adverbs usually follow verbs, coming after **pas** in negative constructions.

Claude **n'est pas très** actif, et	*Claude is **not very** active, and*
il mange **beaucoup**.	* he eats **a lot**.*

- When adverbs modify adjectives, they usually precede them.

Il est **trop** gros.	*He is **too** fat.*

- Adverbs that modify an entire sentence may be placed at the beginning of the sentence. In verb + verb constructions, the French adverb usually follows the verb that it modifies.

Heureusement, Claude va	***Luckily**, Claude is **soon** going to*
bientôt commencer à suivre	* start a diet.*
un régime.	

- Adverbs of time and place are usually placed at the beginning or end of a sentence.

Ils vont passer nous voir **demain**.	*They're going to come by to see us **tomorrow**.*
Demain, ils vont passer nous voir.	***Tomorrow**, they're going to come by to see us.*

Formation of Adverbs with *-ment*

A number of adverbs are formed from adjectives by adding the ending **-ment**, often corresponding to *-ly* in English.

- If the masculine form of the adjective ends in a *vowel*, **-ment** is usually added to the masculine form of the adjective to make the adverb.

Masculine Adjectives	Masculine Adverbs
absolu (*absolute*)	absolument (*absolutely*)
admirable (*admirable*)	admirablement (*admirably*)
vrai (*true*)	vraiment (*truly, really*)

Fait-elle **vraiment** la cuisine tous les soirs?	*Does she **really** do the cooking every evening?*

- If the masculine form of the adjective ends in a *consonant*, **-ment** is usually added to the feminine form to make the adverb.

French MASC. ADJ.	French FEM. ADJ.	English MEANING	French ADVERB
actif	active	*active*	activement *(actively)*
doux	douce	*soft, gentle*	doucement *(softly, gently)*
faux	fausse	*false*	faussement *(falsely)*
franc	franche	*frank*	franchement *(frankly)*
heureux	heureuse	*happy*	heureusement *(fortunately, happily)*
lent	lente	*slow*	lentement *(slowly)*

Heureusement, il ne neige pas aujourd'hui.	***Fortunately**, it's not snowing today.*
Renée parle toujours **doucement**.	*Renée always speaks **softly**.*

Note that the adverbs **brièvement** (*briefly*) and **gentiment** (*nicely*) do not follow this rule. They are based on **bref** (**brève**) (*brief*) and **gentil**(**le**) (*nice, polite*).

- If the masculine form of the adjective ends in **-ent** or **-ant**, the corresponding adverbs have the endings **-emment** (for **-ent**) and **-amment** (for **-ant**).

Masculine Adjectives		Masculine Adverbs	
constant	*(constant)*	constamment	*(constantly)*
différent	*(different)*	différemment	*(differently)*
évident	*(evident)*	évidemment	*(evidently, obviously)*

Sylvie répond **intelligemment**.	*Sylvie is answering **intelligently**.*
Parles-tu **couramment** le russe?	*Do you speak Russian **fluently**?*

Exercise 10.9

Write the adverb that corresponds to each adjective. Make sure you know the meaning of both the adjective and the adverb.

1. amical _____

2. vrai _____

3. faux _____

4. gentil _____

5. évident _____

6. vif _____

7. franc _____

8. différent _____

9. bref _____

10. terrible _____

11. lent _____

12. intelligent _____

13. cruel _____

14. constant _____

15. doux _____

Comparatives and Superlatives of Adverbs

Comparatives of adverbs are formed with **plus/aussi/moins... que** (*more . . . than/as . . . as/less . . . than*), as they are with adjectives.

Fait-elle la cuisine **plus** souvent **que** toi?	*Does she do the cooking **more** often **than** you?*
Tu joues au golf **aussi** bien **que** Richard.	*You play golf **as** well **as** Richard.*
Le politicien parle **moins** bien **que** mon prof.	*The politician speaks **less** well **than** my teacher.*
Je cours **moins** vite **qu'**eux.	*I run slower (**less fast**) **than** they (do).*

In the superlative form of an adverb, **le plus** or **le moins** precedes the adverb. The article is always **le**.

Ce cheval-là court **le plus** lentement!	*That horse is running **the slowest**!*
Moi, je vais au cinéma **le moins** souvent.	*I go to the movies **the least often**.*

Mieux (*better*) and **le mieux** (*best*) are irregular comparatives of the adverb **bien** (*well*).

	Comparative		Superlative	
bien (*well*)	**mieux**	(*better*)	**le mieux**	(*the best*)
mal (*bad[ly]*)	**plus mal**	(*worse*)	**le plus mal**	(*the worst*)

Tu ne danses pas très **bien**, et
    moi, je danse **plus mal** (**moins**
    bien) **que** toi!

*You don't dance very **well**, and*
    *I dance **worse than** you!*

Arthur danse **mieux que** moi,
    et Mireille danse **le mieux**.

*Arthur dances **better than** I do,*
    *and Mireille dances **the best**.*

 ### Exercise 10.10

Translate the sentences into French, using the comparative or superlative of adverbs.

1. He sings badly, but I sing worse.

    _____.

2. Does she cook more often than you (*pol.*)?

    _____?

3. In the marathon, Sami runs the slowest.

    _____.

4. Do you (*fam.*) play the violin better than me?

    _____?

5. I write well, but my friend writes better. _____.

6. Colette writes the best. _____.

7. Frédéric works faster than Jeanne. _____.

8. Isabelle works the fastest. _____.

9. Does Paul arrive earlier than you (*pol.*)? _____?

10. Claudine speaks Italian worse than I do (**moi**); Émilie speaks it the worst!

    _____!

11. They (*f.*) sing better than their brothers. _____.

12. Marcel dances worse than his wife. _____.

Key Vocabulary

Here is a list of common adverbs. Some of them will be familiar to you.

Adverbes (**Adverbs**)

à droite (*to the right*)	mieux (*better*)
à gauche (*to the left*)	moins (*less*)
à l'arrière (*in back, behind*)	ne... plus (*no longer*)
à l'extérieur (*outside*)	parfois (*sometimes*)
à l'intérieur (*inside*)	plus (*more*)
au fond (*at the back, bottom*)	plus mal (*worse*)
de bonne heure (*early [morning]*)	presque (*almost*)
dehors (*outside*)	quelquefois (*sometimes*)
déjà (*already*)	souvent (*often*)
en avant (*in front, forward*)	tant (*so much*)
en bas (*downstairs, down*)	tard (*late*)
en ce moment (*right now*)	tôt (*early*)
en haut (*upstairs, up*)	toujours (*always*)
encore (*still, yet*)	tout à l'heure (*in a while;*
ici (*here*)	*a while ago*)
là, là-bas (*there, over there*)	tout de suite (*immediately*)
là-haut (*up there*)	tout droit (*straight ahead*)
loin (*far*)	tout près (*nearby*)
maintenant (*now*)	

Exercise 10.11

Complete the sentences with the French equivalent of the adverbs given in English.

1. J'arrive _____. (*immediately*)

2. Il faut tourner _____ au coin. (*to the left*)

3. Elle danse _____ moi. (*worse than*)

4. Robert dort assez peu, mais je dors même _____.
   (*less*)

5. Tu vas trouver la poste _____. (*close by*)

6. En voiture, je mets _____ les enfants _____.
   (*always/in the back*)

7. Est-ce que tu vois _____ avec tes nouvelles lunettes? (*far*)

8. Même si nous regardons _____ nous ne voyons pas Minou. (*up there*)

9. Le matin, devez-vous partir _____? (*early*)

10. On va arriver _____. (*in a little while*)

11. Oui, je vois _____ les tours de l'église. (*already*)

12. Mais, il fait noir _____ de cette armoire! (*inside*)

13. Si tu marches _____, tu vas pouvoir nous dire où nous allons. (*up ahead*)

14. Les enfants jouent-ils _____ le soir en été? (*outside*)

15. Dînent-elles _____ _____ pendant le week-end? (*sometimes/very late*)

 ## Key Vocabulary

Les membres de la famille (Family Members)

In conversation, it's helpful to be able to describe your family members. **Les parents** means both *parents* and *relatives* in general.

les parents (*m. pl.*)	*parents*
le père	*father*
la mère	*mother*
le beau-père	*stepfather or father-in-law*
la belle-mère	*stepmother or mother-in-law*
les grands-parents (*m. pl.*)	*grandparents*
le grand-père	*grandfather*
la grand-mère	*grandmother*
les arrière-grands-parents (*m. pl.*)	*great-grandparents*
l'arrière-grand-père (*m.*)	*great-grandfather*
l'arrière-grand-mère (*f.*)	*great-grandmother*
l'époux *ou* le mari	*husband*
l'épouse *ou* la femme	*wife*
le fils; la fille	*son; daughter*
le beau-fils	*stepson or son-in-law*

la belle-fille	*stepdaughter or daughter-in-law*
le petit-fils	*grandson*
la petite-fille	*granddaughter*
les parents (*m. pl.*)	*relatives, relations*
le parent	*(male) relative*
la parente	*(female) relative*
le frère; la sœur	*brother; sister*
aîné(e); cadet(te)	*older; younger*
le beau-frère	*brother-in-law or stepbrother*
la belle-sœur	*sister-in-law or stepsister*
l'oncle; la tante	*uncle; aunt*
le neveu; la nièce	*nephew; niece*
le cousin; la cousine	*(male) cousin; (female) cousin*
le parrain; la marraine	*godfather; godmother*
le filleul; la filleule	*godson; goddaughter*

Exercise 10.12

Gérard is describing his family. Complete the sentences with members of the family, using possessive pronouns and the preceding vocabulary list.

1. Le frère de ma mère est _____.

2. Le fils de ma tante est _____.

3. Le frère de ma femme est _____.

4. Le garçon dont je suis responsable de l'éducation morale
   est _____.

5. La fille de ma fille est _____.

6. La fille de ma femme (ce n'est pas ma fille à moi)
   est _____.

7. La femme responsable de mon éducation morale
   est _____.

8. Le fils de ma sœur est _____ et sa petite sœur
   est _____.

9. La femme que j'épouse est _____

   ou _____.

10. La mère de ma femme est _____.

 Reading Comprehension

La famille française moderne

Il y a récemment une **légère hausse** du nombre de mariages en France; mais en général, les mariages continuent à diminuer. Les nouveaux mariés français ont **en moyenne** cinq ans de plus qu'il y a vingt ans. Il y a plusieurs raisons de cela: l'**union libre**, déjà très fréquente, n'est plus aujourd'hui une simple **période d'essai**, mais **un mode de vie**. Pour ceux qui préparent une carrière, les études sont prolongées. Et finalement, il y a **le chômage**, un problème qui touche à toute l'Europe. Il devient de plus en plus difficile aux jeunes d'entrer dans le monde du travail et de trouver un emploi **convenable**.

La famille française d'aujourd'hui est plus petite. En général, les mères ont leur premier enfant (et leur dernier) plus tard. Près de **la moitié** des enfants naissent hors mariage (les parents non mariés **bénéficient** d'une partie des **allocations** familiales). Dans le cas du premier enfant, la proportion est même de cinquante-cinq pour cent hors mariage. Le mariage est aussi plus fréquemment **dissous** par le divorce (un mariage sur trois), ce qui explique le doublement du nombre de familles monoparentales. C'est le plus souvent la mère qui élève **quasi** seule un ou plusieurs enfants. Il y a **par conséquent** une **nette** augmentation de familles « recomposées », formées par le remariage d'un ou des deux parents.

On continue pourtant à **garder** une grande nostalgie de la famille d'hier: dîners du dimanche chez les grands-parents, grandes vacances passées en famille à la campagne, etc. Selon **les enquêtes**, la famille reste toujours **la valeur** première de tous les Français. **Ce ne sont que** les pratiques de la vie familiale qui sont en train d'**évoluer**.

légère hausse (*slight rise*)	convenable (*suitable*)
en moyenne (*on average*)	la moitié (*half*)
l'union libre (*f.*) (*living together*)	bénéficient (*benefit*)
une période d'essai (*trial period*)	allocations (*f.*) (*government subsidies*)
un mode de vie (*lifestyle*)	
le chômage (*unemployment*)	dissous (*dissolved*)

quasi *(almost)*
par conséquent *(consequently)*
net(te) *(clear, net)*
garder *(to keep, retain)*

les enquêtes *(f.)* *(surveys)*
la valeur *(value)*
ce ne sont que... *(it's only . . .)*
évoluer *(to evolve)*

Questions

After reading the selection, answer the questions in French.

1. Décrivez quelques changements récents dans la famille française.

   _____.

2. Pourquoi les mariages diminuent-ils?

   _____.

3. Donnez une définition des deux expressions suivantes: *l'union libre, la famille recomposée.*

   _____.

4. Cette description ressemble-t-elle à votre vie de famille? Comment?

   _____.

5. Qui sont les membres de votre famille?

   _____.

6. Décrivez les membres de votre famille étendue (*extended*) ou recomposée.

   _____.

II

Affirmative and Negative Expressions, Forming the Imperative, and Using Pronominal Verbs

11

Affirmatives Versus Negatives, Stressed Pronouns, and the Imperative

More Ways to Say Yes and No

Most affirmative expressions have a corresponding negative expression (in English, *always* vs. *never*, *something* vs. *nothing*). In French, they are easy to memorize in pairs or groups.

Most French negative expressions resemble the **ne... pas** construction. They omit **pas** and combine **ne/n'...** with another word (**jamais**, **plus**, **rien**, etc.) instead.

As with **ne... pas**, the indefinite article (**un/une/des**) and the partitive article (**du/de la/de l'**) become **de/d'** before a noun. Definite articles (**le/la/les**) do not change.

Affirmative	≠	Negative
parfois (*sometimes*) **quelquefois** (*sometimes*) **souvent** (*often*) **toujours** (*always*)	≠	**ne... jamais** (*never*)

Prend-il **toujours du** café le matin?	*Does he **always** have coffee in the morning?*
—Non, il **ne** prend **jamais de** café le matin.	*—No, he **never** has coffee in the morning.*
(—Non, il **n'**en prend **jamais** le matin.)	*(—No, he **never** has any in the morning.)*
Tu travailles **quelquefois** le samedi?	*Do you **sometimes** work on Saturdays?*
—Non, je **ne** travaille **jamais** le samedi.	*—No, I **never** work on Saturdays.*

232

In the negative, *object pronouns* follow **ne/n'** and precede the verb, as they do with the **ne... pas** construction.

Faites-vous **souvent** la cuisine?   Do you **often** do the cooking?
—En réalité, je **ne la** fais **jamais**!   —Actually, I **never** do **it**!

Affirmative	≠	Negative
déjà (*already*)	≠	**ne... pas encore** (*not yet*)
encore (*still*)	≠	**ne... plus** (*no longer*, not anymore)

Vas-tu **encore** à ce gymnase?   Do you **still** go to that gym?
—Non, je **ne** vais **plus** à ce   —No, I **no longer** go to that gym.
  gymnase.
(—Non, je **n'y** vais **plus**.)   (—No, I do **not** go **there**
                                             anymore.)

Tu manges **déjà** le dessert?   You're eating dessert **already**?
—Non, je **ne** mange **pas encore**   —No, I'm **not** eating dessert **yet**.
  le dessert.
(—Non, je **ne le** mange **pas encore**.) (—No, I'm **not** eating **it yet**.)

Affirmative	≠	Negative
quelque chose (*something*)	≠	**ne... rien** (*nothing, not anything*)
tout (*everything*)		
quelqu'un (*someone*)	≠	**ne... personne** (*no one, not anyone*)
tout le monde (*everyone*)		

Tu vois **quelque chose**?   Do you see **anything**?
—Non, je **ne** vois **rien**.   —No, I do **not** see **anything**.
Ils entendent **quelqu'un**?   Do they hear **someone**?
—Non, ils **n'**entendent **personne**.   —No, they do **not** hear **anyone**.

 ## Exercise 11.1

Here is a description of your friend Guy. Counter each statement with a description of his friend Suzy, following the model. Note the affirmative expressions in italics.

EXAMPLE: *Guy a toujours des dettes (debts).*   <u>Suzy n'a jamais de</u>
          <u>dettes.</u>

1. Guy fait *encore* ses études.

   Suzy _____.

2. Guy a *encore* des examens à passer.

   Suzy _____.

3. Guy dépense (*spends*) *toujours* son argent.

   Suzy _____.

4. Guy est *déjà* fatigué à sept heures du soir.

   Suzy _____.

5. Guy emprunte (*borrows*) *parfois* de l'argent.

   Suzy _____.

6. Guy passe *souvent* le soir à regarder la télé.

   Suzy _____.

7. Guy achète *quelque chose* à la friperie (*secondhand store*).

   Suzy _____.

8. Guy mange *quelque chose* au bar.

   Suzy _____.

Exercise 11.2

Read the questions and answer each one with a complete sentence in the negative.
Use **ne... pas** *or another logical negative expression.*

1. Entend-elle tout?

   Non, _____.

2. Apprenez-vous quelque chose dans ce cours?

   Non, _____.

3. Est-ce que tu invites quelqu'un ce soir?

   Non, _____.

4. Regardes-tu toujours les actualités (*news*)?

   —Non, _____.

5. Est-ce qu'elles ont beaucoup d'ennemis?

—Non, _____.

6. Es-tu déjà libre de voyager?

—Non, _____.

7. Trouvent-ils quelque chose au marché aux puces (*flea market*)?

—Non, _____.

8. Tu sors parfois danser?

—Non, _____.

9. Allez-vous encore à la plage chaque été?

—Non, _____.

10. Est-ce qu'il y a quelqu'un au téléphone?

—Non, _____.

Quelque chose, **quelqu'un**, **rien**, and **personne**, when required, are objects of a preposition following **à** or **de/d'**. In these instances, the position of **ne/n'** does not change.

De quoi Laurent a-t-il peur?	**What** is Laurent scared **of**?
—Il **n'**a peur **de rien**!	—He's **not** scared **of anything**!
Tu penses **à quelqu'un**?	Are you thinking **about someone**?
—Non, Je **ne** pense **à personne**.	—No, I'm **not** thinking **about anyone**.

Jamais, **rien**, **personne**, **pas encore**, and **pas toujours** can be simple answers by themselves, without using **ne/n'**.

Qui t'appelle souvent?	*Who calls you often?*
—**Personne**.	—**No one**.
Tu reçois un salaire pour ton travail?	*Do you get a salary for your work?*
—**Pas encore**.	—**Not yet**.
Alors, qu'est-ce qu'ils font?	*So, what are they doing?*
—**Rien**.	—**Nothing**.
Est-ce que vous mangez du porc?	*Do you eat pork?*
—**Jamais**.	—**Never**.

Rien and **personne** can also be used as *subjects* of a sentence. In this construction **rien** and **personne** precede **ne/n'**.

Tu as l'air triste, Aimée...	*You look sad, Aimée . . .*
—C'est vrai. **Rien ne** m'intéresse.	*—That's true. **Nothing** interests me.*
Vous leur téléphonez?	*Are you calling them?*
—Oui, mais **personne ne** répond.	*—Yes, but **no one** is answering.*

Expressing Limits with *ne... que...*

Ne... que (*only*), is not a negative expression, but a limiting one. Its synonym is **seulement**.

In expressions using **ne... que**, the element **que** is placed before the noun (i.e., the amount that is "limited").

Je **n'**ai **que** cinq euros. (J'ai **seulement** cinq euros.)	*I have **only** five euros.*
Il **ne** fait **que** deux sports.	*He does **only** two sports.*
Nous **ne** pouvons lire **que** trois livres par an.	*We can read **only** three books a year.*

Exercise 11.3

Answer each question with a single word sentence in the negative.

1. Ta mère lit-elle parfois de la science fiction? —Non, _____.

2. Qui veut sortir avec nous samedi soir? —_____.

3. Que fais-tu cet après-midi? —_____.

4. Vous mangez quelquefois des fruits de mer? —Non, _____.

5. Thomas réussit-il toujours aux examens? —Non, _____.

6. Quelqu'un nous appelle? —Non, _____.

7. Qui veut bien nous aider à la cuisine? —_____.

8. Elle t'emprunte parfois de l'argent? —Non, _____.

Exercise 11.4

Answer the personal questions with a complete sentence in the negative.

1. As-tu peur de quelque chose?

   —Non, _____.

2. Prépare-t-il quelque chose de délicieux?

   —Non, _____.

3. Est-ce que quelqu'un arrive bientôt?

   —Non, _____.

4. Téléphones-tu à quelqu'un?

   —Non, _____.

5. Lisez-vous quelque chose d'original?

   —Non, _____.

6. Nous écrivons à quelqu'un?

   —Non, _____.

7. Dorothée réfléchit-elle à quelque chose?

   —Non, _____.

8. Connais-tu quelqu'un de drôle?

   —Non, _____.

Exercise 11.5

*Answer each personal question with **ne/n'... que** (only). Then, if possible, repeat your answer using the object pronoun **en**, following the model.*

EXAMPLE: *Combien de voitures avez-vous?*   —Je n'ai qu'une voiture.
        Je n'en ai qu'une.

1. Combien de cours suivez-vous?

   _____.

2. Aujourd'hui avez-vous du temps libre?

   _____.

3. Combien d'heures dormez-vous chaque nuit?

   _____ .

4. Avez-vous beaucoup de DVD?

   _____ .

5. Combien de litres de lait achetez-vous par semaine?

   _____ .

6. Combien d'animaux domestiques avez-vous?

   _____ .

Stressed Pronouns

Stressed pronouns, also called tonic pronouns, are used after prepositions, in compound subjects, and for emphasis. They can be placed at the beginning or at the end of a sentence. Several stressed pronouns are identical in form to subject pronouns.

moi	_I, me_	**nous**	_we, us_
toi	_you_	**vous**	_you_
lui	_he, him, it_	**eux**	_they, them (m. pl.)_
elle	_she, her, it_	**elles**	_they, them (f. pl.)_
soi	_oneself_		

Uses of Stressed Pronouns

Stressed pronouns are used in several ways:

- **_As objects of prepositions_**

  On va passer **chez lui** ce soir.   _We'll stop by **his place** this evening._

  Après vous!   **_After you!_**
  Qui veut venir **avec nous**?   _Who wants to come **with us**?_
  On doit avoir confiance **en soi**.   _One must trust **oneself**._

- **_In compound objects and subjects_**

  Je préfère dîner avec **Thomas et toi**.   _I prefer to eat dinner with **Thomas and you**._
  Valérie et moi, nous allons gagner!   **_Valérie and I, we_** _are going to win!_

The subject pronoun (**nous**, in the previous example) can be omitted or retained for emphasis.

- ***To emphasize the subject of the verb, when it is a subject pronoun***

Lui, il adore cuisiner; **elle**, elle préfère le bricolage.	*He loves to cook; she prefers doing household projects.*
Ils ont beaucoup de chance, **eux**!	*They are very lucky!*

- ***After c'est/ce sont, either standing alone or preceding a relative clause***

C'est vous, Roger et Michelle?	*Is it you, Roger and Michelle?*
—Oui, **c'est nous**.	*—Yes, it's us.*
C'est moi qui gagne!	*I am winning!* (***It is I*** *who is winning!*)
Ce sont eux avec qui je parle.	*They're the ones with whom I'm speaking.*

- ***With être à to indicate possession***

C'est la voiture de Caroline?	*Is that Caroline's car?*
—Non, elle **est à moi**. La vieille voiture **est à elle**.	*—No, it **is mine**. The old car **is hers**.*
Ces skis-là **sont à nous**.	*Those skis **are ours**.*

Être + stressed pronoun is an alternative to using a possessive pronoun (**le/la/les mien[ne][s]**, etc.).

Ces enfants sont **à vous**? Ce sont **les vôtres**?	*Are those children **yours**? Are they **yours**?*

- ***To replace nouns referring to* persons *after certain verbs + a preposition***

These verbs include the following expressions:

penser à/songer à   *(to think about, reflect on)*
penser de   *(to think of, have an opinion of)*
renoncer à   *(to renounce, give up on)*
tenir à   *(to cherish, hold dear)*

Tu penses souvent **à ton frère**?	*Do you often think **about your brother**?*
—Oui, je pense souvent **à lui**.	*—Yes, I often think **about him**.*
Que penses-tu **d'elle**?	*What do you think **of her**?*
—Je pense **qu'elle** est formidable!	*—I think (**that**) **she** is great!*
Tu tiens **à tes amis**?	*Do you value **your friends**?*
—Oui, je tiens beaucoup **à eux**.	*—Yes, I value **them** a great deal.*
Je n'aime plus ce type. Je renonce **à lui**.	*I no longer like that guy. I'm giving up **on him**.*

- ***In combination with -même(s) for emphasis (in English: -self, -selves)***

Tu conduis **toi-même**?	***You** are driving **yourself**?*
Font-**ils** le ménage **eux-mêmes**?	*Are **they** doing the housework **themselves**?*
Dans la vie, **on** peut faire beaucoup **soi-même**.	*In life, **one** can do a great deal **oneself**.*

- ***Following que/qu' in a comparison (Chapter 10)***

Tu écris mieux **que moi**?	*You write better **than me (I do)**.*

Exercise 11.6

*Create complete sentences from the following elements, using a stressed pronoun and **être** in each sentence, following the model.*

EXAMPLES: *nous/contents* Nous, nous sommes contents.

   Richard/anxieux Richard, lui, est anxieux.

1. je/très occupé _____.

2. Alice/courageuse _____.

3. Léon/heureux _____.

4. les étudiantes/intelligentes _____.

5. les voisins/tranquilles _____.

6. André et nous/drôles _____.

Exercise 11.7

*Complete each line of the dialogue with stressed pronouns (**moi, toi, lui,** etc.). These two friends use the form **tu** with each other, but note carefully the places where they are talking about or addressing others.*

1. CAMILLE: Cécile et _____, nous allons bientôt partir au match de football (*soccer*). Et _____?

2. ROBERT: _____ aussi, je pars bientôt. Et Cécile et _____, vous allez prendre la voiture?

3. CAMILLE: _____? Oui, nous sommes en retard. On tient à voir Zidane. Et _____, qu'est-ce que tu penses de _____?

4. ROBERT: Ah! _____, je le trouve formidable. C'est _____ la vedette (*star*) de l'équipe (*team*).

5. CAMILLE: Alors, c'est _____ qui allons l'applaudir.

Exercise 11.8

Translate the sentences into French.

1. We work harder (**dur**) than they (*m.*) (do).

   _____.

2. Am I richer than you (*fam.*) (are)?

   _____?

3. He's not taller than I (am).

   _____.

4. Are you (*pol., f.*) happier than she (is)?

   _____?

5. I walk as fast as they (*f.*) (do).

   _____.

6. She writes better than he (does).

   _____.

7. They (*f.*) don't sing louder (**fort**) than I (do).

   _____.

Exercise 11.9

*Substitute a stressed pronoun (**moi, toi, lui,** etc.) for each of the suggested alternatives or use the pronoun provided. Change the subjects and verb forms when necessary.*

1. Ces raquettes de tennis sont *à moi.* (Éloïse, Jacques, mes amies, Maurice et son collègue)

   _____

2. Qui doit réserver le court? —C'est *elle* qui *doit* le faire. (moi, Mireille et Chantal, nos voisins, vous)

   _____

3. Vous cherchez les balles vous-mêmes? —Oui, *je* le *fais moi-même.* (Mathilde, nous, tu, ton amie et toi, Max)

   _____

The Imperative and Its Forms

The imperative (or command) form of a verb is used to give instructions, to make requests, to make suggestions, or to give orders.

The regular imperative forms are easy to learn, since they are based on the present tense. French has three imperative forms, corresponding to the person or persons being addressed.

tu   (second-person familiar, singular)

vous (second-person polite, both singular and plural, and familiar plural)

nous (first-person plural, includes the group the speaker belongs to)

Imperative forms do not use subject pronouns.

The Imperative of *-er* Verbs

The letter **-s** in the **tu** form of **-er** verbs is dropped in the spelling of the imperative. Pronunciation remains the same.

parler *(to speak)*		
tu parles	**Parle!**	*Speak!*
vous parlez	**Parlez!**	*Speak!*
nous parlons	**Parlons!**	*Let's speak!*

écouter (*to listen to*)

tu écoutes	**Écoute!**	*Listen!*
vous écoutez	**Écoutez!**	*Listen!*
nous écoutons	**Écoutons!**	*Let's listen!*

Regarde cet oiseau-là!	***Look*** *at that bird!*
S'il vous plaît, **parlez** plus lentement.	*Please* ***speak*** *more slowly.*
Nous avons le temps; **écoutons** cette chanson.	*We have time;* ***let's listen*** *to this song.*

The Imperative of *-ir* Verbs

The letter combination **-iss-** occurs in the **nous** and **vous** endings of regular **-ir** imperatives, just as it does in the present tense conjugation.

choisir (*to choose*)

tu choisis	**Choisis!**	*Choose!*
vous choisissez	**Choisissez!**	*Choose!*
nous choisissons	**Choisissons!**	*Let's choose!*

finir (*to finish*)

tu finis	**Finis!**	*Finish!*
vous finissez	**Finissez!**	*Finish!*
nous finissons	**Finissons!**	*Let's finish!*

Choisissons un film pour ce soir.	***Let's choose*** *a movie for this evening.*
Réfléchissez bien **à** vos choix.	***Consider*** *your choices well.*
Finis tes légumes!	***Finish*** *your vegetables!*

The Imperative of *-re* Verbs

Note that the final **-s** in the **tu** form of the present tense also appears in the imperative of regular **-re** verbs.

attendre (*to wait for*)

tu attends	**Attends!**	*Wait!*
vous attendez	**Attendez!**	*Wait!*
nous attendons	**Attendons!**	*Let's wait!*

descendre (*to go down; to get off*)

tu descends	**Descends!**	*Come down!/Go down!/Get off!*
vous descendez	**Descendez!**	*Come down!/Go down!/Get off!*
nous descendons	**Descendons!**	*Let's go down!/Let's get off!*

Attends! J'arrive!	*Wait! I'm coming!*
Descendons à Odéon, d'accord?	*Let's get off at Odéon, O.K.?*
Vendez la bicyclette bleue; elle est trop petite.	*Sell the blue bike; it's too small.*

Imperative Forms of Irregular Verbs

The imperative forms of irregular verbs are usually identical to their present tense forms. However, note in the following chart that the letter **-s** in the **tu** form of **aller** (**tu vas**) is *omitted* in the imperative. Pronunciation remains the same.

faire (*to make; to do*)	**aller** (*to go*)
Fais... !	**Va... !**
Faites... !	**Allez... !**
Faisons... !	**Allons... !**

A verb in the imperative can also precede an infinitive.

Faisons du jogging demain matin.	*Let's go jogging tomorrow morning.*
Allez chercher deux baguettes.	*Go get two baguettes.*
On sonne; **va** ouvrir!	*Someone's ringing; **go** open the door!*
Fais le ménage. Moi, je fais la cuisine.	*(You) **Clean up** and I'll cook.*

Être and **avoir** have irregular imperative forms that differ from their present tense forms.

être (*to be*)		**avoir** (*to have*)	
tu es	**Sois... !**	tu as	**Aie... !**
vous êtes	**Soyez... !**	vous avez	**Ayez... !**
nous sommes	**Soyons... !**	nous avons	**Ayons... !**

Sois calme, il n'y a pas de danger.   *Stay calm, there's no danger.*
Soyez sages, les enfants!   *Be good, children!*
Ayez confiance en vos amis.   *Trust your friends.*

Negative Commands

In negative commands, **ne/n'** comes before the imperative verb form and **pas** follows it.

N'achetez pas de tabac.   *Don't buy (any) tobacco.*
N'aie pas honte.   *Don't be ashamed.*
Ne faisons pas de bruit.   *Let's not make (any) noise.*
Ne parlez pas de ces difficultés.   *Don't talk about these problems.*
N'ayez pas peur.   *Don't be afraid.*

The Imperative in Sentences

As you have seen, the imperative (like other verbs), can be followed by adjectives, adverbs, direct object/indirect object nouns, prepositional phrases, and verb infinitives.

Adjective:	Sois **calme**.	*Be (Stay) calm.*
Adverb:	Réfléchissez **bien**.	*Think carefully.*
	Ne descends pas **ici**!	*Don't get off here!*
Direct object noun:	Achète **du beurre**.	*Buy (some) butter.*
Indirect object noun:	Répondons **au professeur**.	*Let's answer the teacher.*
Prepositional phrase:	Allons **au cinéma**!	*Let's go to the movies!*
Verb infinitive:	Va **faire** le marché.	*Go do the shopping.*

There are more conversational or polite ways to express commands. They use verbs in the imperfect (Chapter 14), the future (Chapter 15), the conditional (Chapter 15), and the subjunctive (Chapter 16). For example:

Pourriez-vous me faire une réservation?   *Could you make me a reservation?*

Si **tu téléphonais** à maman?   *How about calling Mom?*

Exercise 11.10

*Change the instructions and advice to the **vous** imperative form. See the example.*

EXAMPLE: *Il faut manger moins.* __Mangez moins.__

1. Il faut faire de l'exercice. _____.

2. Il faut boire assez d'eau. _____.

3. Il faut essayer de rester (*stay*) calme. _____.

4. Il ne faut pas fumer (*smoke*). _____.

5. Il faut réfléchir à la vie. _____.

6. Il faut être sociable. _____.

7. Il ne faut pas manger trop de viande. _____.

8. Il ne faut pas prendre l'ascenseur (*elevator*). _____.

Exercise 11.11

*Change these instructions and advice to the **tu** imperative form.*

EXAMPLE: *Tu ne dois pas jouer dans la rue.* __Ne joue pas dans la rue!__

1. Tu dois finir tes devoirs. _____!

2. Tu ne dois pas manger de bonbons. _____!

3. Tu dois mettre tes lunettes quand tu lis. _____!

4. Il faut aller au lit à dix heures. _____!

5. Il ne faut pas regarder la télé le soir. _____!

6. Tu ne dois pas trop parler au téléphone. _____!

7. Tu dois écrire à ta grand-mère. _____!

8. Tu ne dois pas perdre ton parapluie. _____!

The Imperative with an Object Pronoun

Direct object pronouns, indirect object pronouns, and the pronouns **en** and **y** are attached to *affirmative* commands by a hyphen. This is also true for reflexive pronouns (Chapter 12). However, in negative commands, the object pronouns *precede* the verb.

Achète **ces pommes**! Achète-**les**!	*Buy those apples! Buy them!*
Ne les achète **pas**!	***Don't** buy them!*
Buvez **de l'eau**! Buvez-**en**!	*Drink **some** water! Drink **some**!*
N'en buvez **pas**!	***Don't** drink **any**!*
Allons **au match**! Allons-**y**!	*Let's go **to the game**! Let's go **there**!*
N'y allons **pas**!	*Let's **not** go **there**!*

- **Me** and **te** become **moi** and **toi** when they follow an affirmative command.

Passe-**moi** le pain, s'il te plaît.	*Pass **me** the bread, please.*
Non, **ne me** passe **pas** le pain.	*No, do **not** pass **me** the bread.*

- The letter **s** (pronounced [z]) reappears when **en** or **y** is added to the imperative **tu** form of **-er** verbs or **aller**.

Parle! (Ne parle pas!)	*Speak! (Don't speak!)*
Parle**s-en**! (**N'en** parle **pas**!)	*Talk **about it**! (Do **not** talk **about it**!)*
Va au marché! (Ne va pas au marché!)	*Go to the market! (Don't go to the market!)*
Va**s-y**! (**N'y** va **pas**!)	*Go **there**! (Do **not** go **there**!)*

Exercise 11.12

Change each affirmative command to a negative command, following the model. Pay attention to the placement of object pronouns.

EXAMPLE: Prends-le! _Ne le prends pas!_____

1. Mangez-en! _____!

2. Rends-les! _____!

3. Passe-moi le sel! _____!

4. Réfléchissez-y! _____!

5. Finis-la! _____!

6. Répète-le! _____!

7. Vas-y! _____!

8. Achètes-en! _____!

9. Donnez-lui le cahier! _____!

10. Dis-leur bonjour! _____!

Exercise 11.13

Rewrite each command, replacing the object noun in italics by an object pronoun.

1. Achète *des fruits*! _____!

2. Passez les crayons *aux élèves*! _____!

3. N'écoutez pas *la radio*! _____!

4. Bois *de l'eau*! _____!

5. Allez *au supermarché*! _____!

6. Range *ta chambre*! _____!

7. Ne donnez pas *le livre* à Georges! _____!

8. Ne donnez pas le livre à *Georges*! _____!

9. Faites *de l'exercice*! _____!

10. Écris à *ta mère*! _____!

 Exercise 11.14

Read these situations in English and create commands in French for that person.

1. There are dishes in the sink (and it's not your turn).

   _____.

2. Your spouse brought work home again.

   _____.

3. Your colleague lives close, but always drives.

   _____.

4. Your young neighbor is playing with a pair of scissors (**les ciseaux**).

   _____!

5. Your dog looks thirsty.

   _____.

6. Your friend seems ill and tired today.

   _____.

Key Vocabulary

L'entretien de la maison et du jardin (House and Garden Maintenance)

You may find yourself keeping house in a French-speaking area, shopping at the hardware store, doing fix-it tasks, or talking to workers, tradespeople, or your landlord.

Use constructions with the verb **faire** for household activities: **faire le ménage**, **faire le lit**, **faire la vaisselle**, **faire la lessive**, etc. To explain that something doesn't work, say **Le/La/L'... ne marche pas**. The verbs **laver** (_to wash_), **nettoyer** (_to clean_), **repasser** (_to iron_), and **ranger** (_to straighten, organize_) are also useful.

l'ampoule (_f._)   (_lightbulb_)
l'arrosoir (_m._)   (_watering can_)
l'aspirateur (_m._)   (_vacuum_)
la baignoire   (_bathtub_)
le balai   (_broom_)
la bouilloire   (_kettle_)
le micro-ondes   (_microwave_)
la brosse   (_brush_)
la brouette   (_wheelbarrow_)
la cafetière   (_coffeepot_)
le carrelage   (_tile floor_)
la cave   (_cellar_)
le chiffon   (_rag_)
les couverts (_m._)   (_silverware_)
la couverture   (_blanket_)
la cuisinière   (_stove_)
le déplantoir   (_trowel_)
les draps (_m._)   (_sheets_)
l'éponge (_f._)   (_sponge_)
l'escabeau (_m._)   (_stepstool_)
l'escalier (_m._)   (_stairs_)
l'évier (_m._)   (_sink_)
le fer à repasser   (_clothes iron_)
le four   (_oven_)
la fourche   (_digging fork_)
le frigo   (_refrigerator_)
le garde-robe   (_clothes closet_)
le grenier   (_attic_)

le grille-pain   (_toaster_)
la houe   (_hoe_)
le lavabo   (_washbasin_)
le lave-vaisselle   (_dishwasher_)
la lessive   (_laundry_)
la literie   (_bedding_)
la machine à coudre   (_sewing machine_)
la machine à laver   (_washing machine_)
le mixer   (_blender_)
l'ouvre-boîtes (_m._)   (_can opener_)
le parquet   (_wood floor_)
la pelle   (_spade; dustpan_)
les persiennes (_f._)   (_blinds_)
le placard   (_cupboard_)
la planche à repasser   (_ironing board_)
le plumeau   (_feather duster_)
le pot de fleurs   (_flowerpot_)
la poubelle   (_garbage, trash can_)
le râteau   (_rake_)
le seau   (_pail, bucket_)
le sécateur   (_pruning shears_)
le sèche-linge   (_clothes dryer_)
la serviette   (_towel; napkin_)
le sous-sol   (_basement_)
le store   (_window shade_)

le tablier   (*apron*)
la tignasse   (*floor mop*)
la tondeuse   (*lawn mower*)
le tuyau   (*hose; pipe*)

la vaisselle   (*dishes/plates*)
la ventouse   (*toilet plunger*)
le W.C.   (*toilet*)

Le bricolage (Do-It-Yourself Projects)

l'atelier (*m.*)   (*workshop*)
la caisse à outils   (*toolbox*)
le chauffage   (*heating*)
le chauffe-eau   (*water heater*)
les ciseaux (*m.*)   (*scissors*)
la clé   (*key; wrench*)
la climatisation   (*air-conditioning*)
les clous (*m.*)   (*nails*)
l'échelle (*f.*)   (*ladder*)
l'étau (*m.*)   (*vise*)
la fiche   (*electric plug*)
la hache   (*ax*)
l'interrupteur (*m.*)   (*switch*)
la lampe de poche   (*flashlight*)
le marteau   (*hammer*)
le moteur   (*motor*)
la peinture   (*paint*)

la perceuse   (*drill*)
la pince   (*pliers*)
le pinceau   (*paintbrush*)
la plomberie   (*plumbing*)
la prise de courant   (*electric outlet*)
le rabot   (*plane [tool]*)
le robinet   (*faucet*)
le rouleau   (*paint roller*)
la salopette   (*overalls*)
la scie   (*saw*)
le scotch   (*tape*)
la serrure   (*lock*)
le tourne-vis   (*screwdriver*)
le ventilateur   (*fan*)
les vis (*f.*)   (*screws*)

Exercise 11.15

Imagine the following everyday activities and list the tools and supplies that will help you accomplish them. Refer to the previous vocabulary lists.

1. Vous voulez repeindre la cuisine. Vous allez chercher:

   _____

2. C'est le printemps. Vous allez refaire votre jardin. Vous prenez:

   _____

3. Votre appartement est un désastre! Quels termes associez-vous avec cette situation?

   _____

Reading Comprehension

Un week-end de bricolage

Qu'est-ce que le bricolage? C'est l'activité qui consiste à faire des travaux manuels chez soi, **en tant qu'**amateur, **surtout** si on a sa propre maison et son jardin. C'est la décoration, la réparation, **l'aménagement**, la construction, etc., des pièces et des **appareils** de sa maison.

On dit que soixante-dix pour cent des Français bricolent de temps en temps et trente-sept pour cent déclarent le faire souvent ou très souvent. Cette activité continue à connaître **une croissance** spectaculaire. Hommes et femmes, la plupart mariés, sont **les pratiquants** les plus passionnés. Les personnes plus âgées ou **à la retraite** refont leur logement ou aident leurs enfants dans leur installation. On pose, par exemple, un carrelage ou **une moquette**; on installe ou modifie les systèmes électriques ou la plomberie; on construit des murs ou **cloisons**; on répare **le toit**; ou bien on construit **une pièce supplémentaire**. Ces **ménages** possèdent parfois aussi **une résidence secondaire en province** où ils passent souvent le week-end à ne faire que du bricolage!

Pourquoi le faire soi-même si on peut engager **des gens du métier**? Le bricolage est un moyen de retrouver des activités manuelles, de combattre la tendance générale de l'abstraction qu'on trouve dans tant de professions. Il donne de la satisfaction — surtout aux personnes des **professions libérales** — de développer des capacités dans de nouveaux domaines. Et cela économise aussi en aidant le budget!

en tant que   (*as*)
surtout   (*above all*)
l'aménagement (*m.*)   (*setting up*)
les appareils (*m.*)   (*appliances*)
une croissance   (*growth*)
les pratiquants (*m.*)   (*practitioners*)
à la retraite   (*retired*)
une moquette   (*wall-to-wall carpet*)
les cloisons (*f.*)   (*partitions*)
le toit   (*roof*)

une pièce supplémentaire
   (*room addition*)
les ménages (*m.*)   (*households*)
une résidence secondaire
   (*second home*)
en province   (*in the country*)
des gens (*m.*) du métier
   (*contractors*)
les professions libérales (*f.*)
   (*the professions*)

Questions

After reading the selection, answer the questions in French.

1. Qui aime bricoler en France?

   _____.

2. Quelles sortes d'activités sont les plus populaires?

   _____.

3. Quels sont les avantages du bricolage? Y a-t-il des inconvénients?

   _____.

4. Pourquoi, à votre avis, les Français aiment-ils tant faire du bricolage?

   _____.

5. Le bricolage vous intéresse-t-il? Qu'est-ce que vous aimez faire?

   _____.

6. Pourquoi faites-vous du bricolage? L'économie? le plaisir? la satisfaction? l'apprentissage (*learning*)? l'esthétique?

   _____.

12

Reflexive Pronouns with Pronominal Verbs and the Present Participle

What Is a Pronominal Verb?

A pronominal verb is always accompanied by an object pronoun, called a *reflexive pronoun*, which is identical to the subject. In English, they are the *-self/-selves* pronouns.

> **The child** dressed **himself**.
> Did **you** hurt **yourself**?
> **We** talk to **ourselves**.
> **I** bought **myself** a new computer.

French has three types of pronominal verbs: the *reflexive, reciprocal,* and *idiomatic* pronominals. In reflexive constructions, the action of the verb reflects back upon the subject.

> **Je me réveille** à sept heures.   *I wake up (I wake myself) at seven A.M.*
>
> **Ces enfants s'endorment** trop tard.   *Those children fall asleep too late.*

The reflexive pronouns correspond to the six verb forms.

me (m')	*myself*	**nous**	*ourselves*
te (t')	*yourself*	**vous**	*yourself/yourselves*
se (s')	*him-/her-/oneself*	**se (s')**	*themselves*

The infinitive of a reflexive or pronominal verb is written with the pronoun **se/s'**: **se réveiller** (*to wake up*), **s'endormir** (*to fall asleep*). The reflexive pronoun always precedes the conjugated verb form (**Je me reveille**, *I wake up*), except in the affirmative imperative, where it follows. See the later section: "Imperatives of Pronominal Verbs."

Reflexive Verbs

In French, the action of true reflexive verbs always reflects back upon the subject.

Present Tense of se lever (*to get up*, *to stand up*)

je **me lève**	*I get up*	nous **nous levons**	*we get up*
tu **te lèves**	*you get up*	vous **vous levez**	*you get up*
il/elle/on **se lève**	*he/she/one gets up*	ils/elles **se lèvent**	*they get up*

Present Tense of s'endormir (*to fall asleep*)

je **m'endors**	*I fall asleep*	nous **nous endormons**	*we fall asleep*
tu **t'endors**	*you fall asleep*	vous **vous endormez**	*you fall asleep*
il/elle/on **s'endort**	*he/she/one falls asleep*	ils/elles **s'endorment**	*they fall asleep*

Nous nous levons toujours pendant la pause.

We always **get up** during the break.

Est-ce que **vous vous endormez** tard le week-end?

Do you go to sleep late on the weekend?

—Oui, je **m'endors** après minuit.

—Yes, *I **fall asleep*** after midnight.

 ## Key Vocabulary

Here's a list of reflexive verbs dealing with everyday routines and activities:

La vie quotidienne (Everyday Routines)

s'amuser   *to have a good time, have fun*
se baigner   *to take a bath*; *to go swimming*
se brosser (les dents, les cheveux)   *to brush (one's teeth, hair)*
se coucher   *to go to bed*

se déshabiller   *to get undressed*
se doucher   *to take a shower*
s'endormir   *to fall asleep*
s'ennuyer   *to become bored*
s'entraîner   *to work out; to train*
s'habiller   *to get dressed*
s'installer   *to sit down, get settled*
se laver (les mains, le visage)   *to wash oneself (one's hands, face)*
se lever (je me lève)   *to stand up, get up*
se maquiller   *to put on makeup*
se peigner   *to comb (one's hair)*
se préparer (à)   *to get ready, to prepare (for, to)*
se promener (je me promène)   *to take a walk, a drive, etc.*
se raser   *to shave (oneself)*
se regarder   *to look at (oneself)*
se reposer   *to rest*
se réveiller   *to wake up*

Tu te réveilles à quelle heure?	*What time **do you wake up**?*
—**Je me réveille** vers sept heures.	—*I **wake up** around seven A.M.*
Je me rase avant le petit déjeuner.	*I **shave** before breakfast.*
Tu ne t'habilles pas pour sortir?	***Aren't you getting dressed** to go out?*
Georges se promène dans le parc.	***Georges takes a walk** in the park.*
Elles s'entraînent pour le marathon.	***They're training** for the marathon.*

Pronominal Verbs in Infinitive Constructions

In verb + verb constructions, the reflexive pronoun precedes its infinitive.

Nous allons **nous préparer** avant de partir.	*We're going **to get ready** before leaving.*
Elle ne veut pas **se promener** avec nous?	*Doesn't she want **to take a walk** with us?*
Les jeunes élèves doivent **se coucher** assez tôt.	*Schoolchildren have **to go to bed** rather early.*
Je peux **me laver les cheveux** le soir.	*I can **wash my hair** in the evening.*

Exercise 12.1

Create complete sentences from the following elements. Make sure the reflexive pronoun and the verb match the subject and that you understand the meaning of the sentence.

1. je/se réveiller/tard/le week-end _____.

2. ma sœur/se regarder/longtemps/dans/la glace _____.

3. nous/se lever/de bonne heure/lundi matin _____.

4. André et Paul/s'habiller/en jean _____.

5. Maman/se maquiller/rapidement _____.

6. Papa/se raser/tous les jours _____.

7. je/s'ennuyer/dans/le bus _____.

8. les enfants/s'amuser/après/les cours _____.

Exercise 12.2

Translate each sentence into French, using a reflexive verb.

1. I take a shower at seven o'clock. _____.

2. My sister puts on makeup. _____.

3. We go to bed quite (**assez**) late. _____.

4. You (*pol.*) get ready quickly. _____.

5. They (*f.*) wake up at dawn (**à l'aube**). _____.

6. They (*m.*) get up when Mom calls them. _____.

7. You (*fam.*) take a walk in the evening. _____.

Exercise 12.3

Complete the sentences with the correct forms of the verbs listed. Use each verb only once. Don't forget to include the reflexive pronoun.

se brosser, s'entraîner, s'installer, se laver, se lever, se raser

1. Après le petit déjeuner, je _____ les dents.

2. Les garçons commencent à _____ vers quatorze ou quinze ans.

3. Les serveurs au restaurant _____ les mains très souvent.

4. Nous _____ pendant la pause chercher un verre d'eau.

5. Tu _____ pendant six semaines avant de courir dans le marathon.

6. Les Boisvert déménagent; la semaine prochaine ils vont _____ dans leur nouvelle maison.

Pronominal Verbs: Negative, Interrogative, and Imperative Forms

Negatives and interrogatives of pronominal verbs resemble their non-pronominal forms, except for the use of the reflexive pronoun. Imperative forms are different in the affirmative and negative.

Negatives of Pronominal Verbs

In the negative, **ne** precedes the reflexive pronoun, and **pas** follows the verb.

Tu **ne te reposes pas** suffisamment.	*You **don't get enough rest** (**don't rest** enough).*
Elle **ne se maquille pas** le week-end?	***Doesn't** she **put on makeup** on the weekend?*
Les enfants **ne se couchent pas encore**.	*The children **aren't going to bed yet**.*

Interrogatives of Pronominal Verbs

Question forms of pronominal verbs can be made with intonation, **est-ce que**, or inversion.

Tu **t'habilles** déjà?	***Getting dressed*** *already?*
Les étudiants **se baignent** le samedi?	***Do*** *the students* ***go swimming*** *on Saturdays?*
Est-ce que vous vous brossez les dents souvent?	***Do you brush*** *your teeth often?*

In the inverted question form of a pronominal verb, the *subject* pronoun is inverted and follows the verb, attached by a hyphen. The *reflexive* pronoun precedes the inverted verb + subject pronoun.

Vous endormez-vous tard le week-end?	***Do you fall asleep*** *late on the weekend?*
Ne te lèves-tu pas quand le réveil sonne?	***Don't you get up*** *when the alarm rings?*

When there is a *subject noun*, it precedes the verb and is repeated by the attached subject pronoun, as for non-pronominal verbs.

Rachelle se lève-t-elle à midi?	***Does Rachelle get up*** *at noon?*
Les professeurs s'installent-ils tôt à leur bureau?	***Do the teachers sit down*** *at their desks early?*

Imperatives of Pronominal Verbs

In the affirmative imperative, the reflexive pronoun follows the verb and is attached to it by a hyphen. **Te/t'** becomes **toi** after the verb. However, in the negative imperative, the reflexive pronoun *precedes* the verb.

se lever *(to get up, to stand up)*

IMPERATIVE	NEGATIVE IMPERATIVE
Lève-toi!	Ne te lève pas!
Levez-vous!	Ne vous levez pas!
Levons-nous!	Ne nous levons pas!

s'endormir *(to fall asleep)*

IMPERATIVE	NEGATIVE IMPERATIVE
Endors-toi!	Ne t'endors pas!
Endormez-vous!	Ne vous endormez pas!
Endormons-nous!	Ne nous endormons pas!

Lève-toi, il est déjà tard!	***Get up***, *it's already late!*
Promenez-vous après le dîner.	***Take a walk*** *after dinner.*
Ne vous endormez pas devant la télé!	***Don't fall asleep*** *in front of the TV!*
Installons-nous là-bas, d'accord?	***Let's sit down*** *over there, O.K.?*
Ne t'entraîne pas juste avant de te coucher.	***Don't work out*** *just before going to bed.*

Exercise 12.4

Rewrite each of the sentences as a question with inversion, using the subject given. Then write the answer to each question in the negative.

1. Nous nous levons à huit heures.

   (vous) _____?

   _____.

2. Le matin, je m'entraîne tôt.

   (tu) _____?

   _____.

3. Margot se réveille difficilement.

   (Margot) _____?

   _____.

4. Elles s'habillent bien.

   (elles) _____?

   _____.

5. Je m'endors devant la télé.

   (tu) _____?

   _____.

Exercise 12.5

Translate the commands into French.

Use the polite (pl.) form.

1. Don't get up. _____.
2. Wake up! _____!
3. Brush your teeth. _____.
4. Don't sit down here. _____.

Now use the familiar form.

5. Go to bed. _____.
6. Get dressed. _____.
7. Don't go swimming now. _____.
8. Have a good time! _____!

Exercise 12.6

Read the situations and create a command in French.

1. Your sister is sleeping too late. _____!
2. Your two friends ask you to help keep them awake. _____!
3. Your little nephew has very muddy hands. _____!
4. Your little sister wears too much makeup. _____.
5. She's going to a party and is getting dressed very early. _____.
6. Your mother looks tired. _____.

Review: à and *pour* in Sentences with Indirect Object Nouns

In French *indirect object nouns* are normally preceded by the preposition **à**, sometimes by **pour**.

Je téléphone **à mes amis**.   *I phone **my friends**.*

Nous offrons un cadeau **à Annie**.   *We give **Annie** a gift.*

Verbs of communication (**parler à**, **écrire à**, **téléphoner à**) generally require an indirect object. When an indirect object pronoun replaces the noun, **à** is understood:

Je téléphone **à mes parents**.	*I phone **my parents**.*
Je **leur** téléphone.	*I phone **them**.*
Nous offrons un cadeau **à Laure**.	*We give **Laure** a gift.*
Nous **lui** offrons un cadeau.	*We give **her** a gift.*

Reflexive Verbs with Parts of the Body

Reflexive and other pronominal verbs can have both an indirect and a direct object. Note the use of the *definite article* with parts of the body.

On **se** peigne **les cheveux** avant l'interview.	*One combs **one's** (We comb **our**) hair before the interview.*

In the preceding sentence, **les cheveux** is the *direct* object of **se peigne**, while **se** is the *indirect* object. The indirect object preposition **à** is understood.

Find the direct object and the indirect object in the following sentences.

Nous **nous** lavons **les mains**.	*We wash **our hands**.*
Elle **se** brosse **les dents** après manger.	*She brushes **her teeth** after eating.*
Les garçons doivent-ils **se** raser **la barbe**?	*Do the boys have to shave (**their beard**)?*

 ## Exercise 12.7

Give a personal answer to each of the questions.

1. Quand vous brossez-vous les dents?

   _____.

2. Si on a un rhume (*a cold*) combien de fois par jour faut-il se laver les mains?

   _____.

3. Vous lavez-vous les cheveux tous les jours? Pourquoi ou pourquoi pas?

_____.

4. Les petits enfants se peignent-ils les cheveux eux-mêmes?

_____.

Reciprocal Reflexive Verbs

Some verbs can be used in the plural as *reciprocal* verbs. Reciprocal verbs show that an action is mutual, involving two or more people. Thus, they are usually plural verb forms.

Reciprocal constructions take either a direct or indirect object, depending on the verb used. The reflexive pronouns **nous**, **vous**, and **se/s'** are used as both direct and indirect object pronouns.

Nous nous parlons. (**nous**: *indirect object*, **parler à**)	*We speak **to each other**.*
Vous vous envoyez des mails? (**vous**: *indirect object*, **envoyer à**)	*Do **you** e-mail **each other**?*
Ils se voient souvent. (**se**: *direct object*, **voir** qqun/qqch)	*They see **each other** often.*
Elles s'écrivent. (**se**: *indirect object*, **écrire à qqun**)	*They write (**to**) **each other**.*
Nous nous téléphonons et **nous nous écrivons** aussi.	*We call **each other**, and **we write**, too.*
Ils se regardent longuement.	*They look at **each other** for a long time.*
Vous ne vous quittez pas?	*You aren't separating?*
Quand **les Français se rencontrent**, on s'embrasse ou **on se serre la main**.	*When **the French meet, they kiss** or **they shake hands**.*

- With reciprocals in a verb + verb construction, the reflexive pronoun precedes the infinitive.

Nous **devons nous quitter**.   *We **must leave each other**.*
Ils **vont se revoir**.   *They **are going to see each other again**.*

Vous **préférez vous écrire**?   ***Do** you **prefer writing to each other**?*

- **On**, the third-person singular subject pronoun, is used conversationally to express a reciprocal action, replacing the **nous** form. It is used with **se/s'** and the verb remains singular.

Nous nous revoyons (**On se revoit**) au Nouvel An.   *We **will see each other again** at New Year's.*
On s'écrit plus tard, d'accord?   *We'**ll write (to) each other** later, O.K.?*

- The following verbs and expressions are often used with a reciprocal meaning. In the list, the indication [**à**] shows that the reflexive pronoun is an *indirect* object.

s'aider   *to help each other*
se comprendre   *to understand each other*
se connaître   *to get acquainted with, know each other*
se disputer   *to argue*
se donner rendez-vous [à]   *to make an appointment with each other*
s'écrire [à]   *to write each other*
s'entendre (bien, mal)   *to get along (well, badly) with each other*
s'envoyer (des mails) [à]   *to send (e-mails) to each other*
se faire des cadeaux [à]   *to give gifts to each other*
se parler [à]   *to speak to each other*
se regarder   *to look at each other*
se rencontrer   *to come across each other*
se ressembler [à]   *to resemble each other*
se retrouver   *to meet each other (planned)*
se revoir   *to see each other again*
se serrer la main [à]   *to shake hands*
se téléphoner [à]   *to phone each other*
se voir   *to see each other*

Yves et Simone **se font des cadeaux**.	*Yves and Simone **give each other gifts***.
Ton frère et toi, **vous ressemblez-vous**?	***Do** you and your brother **resemble each other**?*
Nous nous retrouvons tous les jours à midi.	***We get together** every day at noon.*
Alors, **on se revoit** samedi soir?	*So, **we'll see each other** Saturday night?*

Exercise 12.8

Complete the sentences in the following story with a verb chosen from the suggested list. Pay attention to verb forms and the reflexive pronoun.

s'aimer, se connaître, se disputer, s'écrire, s'entendre, se parler, se retrouver, se revoir, se voir

1. Guillaume Dumont et moi, nous _____ depuis trois ans.

2. Nous sommes voisins. Donc, nous _____ presque tous les jours et nous _____ de tout.

3. Des fois, nous _____ à midi en ville pour déjeuner.

4. Quand nous partons en vacances, nos familles _____ des cartes et des mails.

5. Nos femmes et nos enfants _____ aussi très bien.

6. Les enfants n'ont pas le même âge, mais ça ne fait rien (*that's not a problem*). Ils _____ le week-end pour les jeux vidéo.

7. Ils _____ parfois quand ils ne sont pas d'accord.

8. Mais en général ils _____ bien.

Exercise 12.9

Give a personal answer to each question.

1. Vos amis et vous, où vous retrouvez-vous le week-end?

   _____.

2. Dans votre famille, vous écrivez-vous, ou bien préférez-vous vous téléphoner?

   _____.

3. Dans votre famille, est-ce qu'on se voit souvent? Est-ce qu'on se donne rendez-vous?

   _____.

4. Au travail ou à l'école, vos collègues/camarades s'entendent-ils généralement bien?

   _____.

5. Vous dites-vous bonjour le matin? Est-ce que vous vous serrez la main? De quoi vous parlez-vous?

   _____.

Idiomatic Pronominal Verbs

French has many idiomatic pronominal verbs. The reflexive form is used for a specific meaning of the verb. The same verb may have different meanings in a non-pronominal form.

s'en aller   *to leave, depart*
s'apercevoir de (qqch, qqun)   *to notice (s.th., s.o.)*
s'appeler   *to be named, called*
se décider à + *inf.*   *to decide to (do s.th.)*
se demander   *to wonder; to ask oneself*
se dépêcher de + *inf.*   *to hurry to (do s.th.)*
se disputer avec (qqun)   *to argue with (s.o.)*
s'ennuyer de + *inf.*   *to get bored (doing s.th.)*
s'entendre avec (qqun)   *to get along with (s.o.)*
se fâcher avec (qqun)   *to get angry with (s.o.)*
se faire à   *to get accustomed to*
s'habituer à   *to get accustomed to*
se marier avec (qqun)   *to marry, get married to (s.o.)*

se mettre à + *inf.*   *to begin to (do s.th.)*
s'occuper de (qqch, qqun)   *to take care of, busy oneself with (s.th., s.o.)*
se passer de (qqun, qqch)   *to manage, do without (s.o., s.th.)*
se rappeler (qqch, qqun)   *to remember, recall (s.th., s.o.)*
se rendre compte de/que (qqch)   *to realize (s.th.)*
se souvenir de/que (qqch, qqun)   *to remember, recall (s.th., s.o.)*
se tromper de (qqch)   *to make a mistake (in s.th.)*

Nous allons **nous mettre à** travailler.	*We are going **to start** working.*
Que **je m'ennuie de** ces exercices!	*How **bored I am with** these exercises!*
Samuel ne peut pas **se passer de** déjeuner.	*Samuel can't **go without** lunch.*
Ils se souviennent de leur pays natal.	*They **remember** their home country.*
Roger se marie avec Sylvie dimanche.	*Roger **is marrying** Sylvie on Sunday.*

- When they are not pronominal, the verbs in the previous list (with the exception of **souvenir**) have different meanings from those given.

Comment est-ce que **tu t'appelles**?	*What **is your name**?*
J'appelle le patron pour m'excuser.	*I'm calling the boss to excuse myself.*

- **S'apercevoir de** (*to notice*) and **apercevoir** (*to glimpse*) are conjugated like the irregular verb **recevoir** (*to receive*).

s'apercevoir de (*to notice*)

je m'aperçois	nous nous apercevons
tu t'aperçois	vous vous apercevez
il/elle/on s'aperçoit	ils/elles s'aperçoivent

Tu **t'aperçois de** sa mauvaise humeur?	*Do **you notice** his/her bad mood?*
Elles **s'aperçoivent que** nous nous trompons.	*They **notice that** we're making a mistake.*

- When they refer to a person, pronominal verbs are followed by a *stressed pronoun* (**moi**, **toi**, etc.); they don't use a preceding indirect object pronoun.

Nous nous fions **à nos amis**.   *We trust **our friends**.*
   Nous nous fions **à eux**.   *We trust **them**.*
Il s'occupe **de sa sœur**. Il   *He takes care **of his sister**.*
   s'occupe **d'elle**.   *He takes care **of her**.*

 Exercise 12.10

Translate the sentences into French, using the suggested verbs. Pay attention to the prepositions.

se dépêcher de, s'entendre avec, se fier à, s'habituer à, s'intéresser à, se marier avec, se mettre à, s'occuper de, se passer de, se rappeler, se rendre compte de/que, se souvenir de/que, se tromper de

1. I'm getting used to this city. _____.

2. We're hurrying to arrive there on time. _____.

3. Mathilde is marrying him. _____.

4. She takes care of me. _____.

5. Do you (*pol.*) realize that it's snowing?

   _____?

6. I trust my teacher. _____.

7. We remember our former school. _____.

8. Michel gets along well with Charles. _____.

9. Laure is not interested in soccer (**au football**).

   _____.

10. They (*m.*) don't often make a mistake in the address.

    _____.

11. The children begin to play. _____.

12. You (*fam.*) can't do without your computer, right?

    _____?

Exercise 12.11

Complete each sentence with the correct form of an idiomatic pronominal verb. Choose among the verbs from the list in Exercise 12.10, and pay attention to the prepositions.

1. J'ai bonne mémoire; je _____ nos premiers jours à l'école.

2. Olivier aime la viande. Mais sa femme est végétarienne, alors ces jours-ci Olivier _____ très bien _____ bifteck.

3. Mais, Robert, il est tard! Tu dois _____.

4. Si vous _____ travailler maintenant, nous allons être en retard!

5. Tu _____ qu'il est deux heures passées?

6. C'est un ami fidèle. Nous _____ lui.

Non-Pronominal Forms of Pronominal Verbs

Many pronominal verbs are also used in their simple (non-pronominal) form, often with an object noun or pronoun. In the simple (non-pronominal) form, the subject of the verb acts upon another object.

Je me réveille facilement.	*I wake up easily.*
(**me** = reflexive, direct object)	
Plus tard, **je réveille ma femme**.	*Later, I wake my wife.*
(**ma femme** = direct object)	
Je la réveille.	*I wake her.*
(**la** = direct object pronoun)	

As a Pronominal	**As a Non-Pronominal**
s'amuser *to have a good time, have fun*	amuser *to amuse (s.o.)*
s'arrêter de *to stop (oneself)*	arrêter *to stop (s.th., s.o.)*
s'ennuyer *to get bored, annoyed*	ennuyer *to bore, annoy (s.o.)*
se fâcher *to become angry, annoyed*	fâcher *to anger, annoy (s.o.)*
se parler *to talk to oneself, each other*	parler (à) *to speak, talk (to s.o.)*
se regarder *to look at oneself, each other*	regarder *to look at (s.th., s.o.)*

Amusez-vous!	***Have a good time**!*
Parfois, **je me parle** à haute voix.	*Sometimes **I talk to myself** out loud.*
Regarde-toi de près, que vois-tu?	***Look at yourself** closely, what do you see?*
Nous nous ennuyons quand il pleut.	***We're bored** when it rains.*
Ce politicien **m'ennuie**.	*That politician **bores me**.*
Agnès, **arrête** ce taxi, s'il te plaît.	*Agnès, please **stop** that taxi.*

Exercise 12.12

Translate the sentences into French.

1. We stop working at six o'clock. _____.

2. She stops the car in front of my house. _____.

3. Are you (*fam.*) going to walk the dogs? _____?

4. We're going for a walk. _____.

5. He bores us. _____.

6. I get bored sometimes in class. _____.

7. Don't get angry! (*fam.*) _____!

8. That idea (**idée**, *f.*) angers me. _____.

Se with Impersonal Expressions

Many verbs are commonly used with the third-person reflexive pronoun **se** to convey a truism or other generality. The pronoun to express generalities is always **se/s'**; the third-person verb form is singular or plural, depending on the subject.

Le vin blanc **se boit** frais.	*White wine **is drunk** cold/cool.*
Les maillots de bain **se vendent** bien en été.	*Bathing suits **sell** well in the summer.*
Cela **ne se fait pas** ici.	*That **isn't done** here.*
Ici, les omelettes **ne se mangent pas** le matin.	*Here, omelets **are not eaten** in the morning.*
Le bruit **s'entend** d'ici.	***You can hear** the noise from here.*

Exercise 12.13

Read the generalities expressed with **on**, *and rewrite each sentence using the new subjects (in italics) according to the model.*

EXAMPLE: On oublie vite *les bonnes idées.* <u>Les bonnes idées s'oublient vite.</u>

1. On parle *français* au Québec. _____.

2. On vend *les skis* en automne. _____.

3. On mange *beaucoup de fromage* en France. _____.

4. On fait rarement du *jogging* sous la pluie. _____.

5. On apprend facilement *les nouveaux mots.* _____.

6. On ne boit pas de *boissons froides* avec la fondue. _____.

The Present Participle

In English, the present participle ends in *-ing: While* **living** *abroad, Christine gained a better understanding of her own country.*

Formation of the Present Participle

The French present participle is formed by dropping the **-ons** ending from the **nous** form of the present tense and adding **-ant**.

boire (*to drink*)	nous **buv**ons	**buvant** (*drinking*)
donner (*to give*)	nous **donn**ons	**donnant** (*giving*)
faire (*to do; to make*)	nous **fais**ons	**faisant** (*doing; making*)
finir (*to finish*)	nous **finiss**ons	**finissant** (*finishing*)
perdre (*to lose*)	nous **perd**ons	**perdant** (*losing*)
vouloir (*to wish, want to*)	nous **voul**ons	**voulant** (*wanting*)

Three verbs have irregular present participles:

avoir (*to have*)	**ayant** (*having*)
être (*to be*)	**étant** (*being*)
savoir (*to know*)	**sachant** (*knowing*)

Uses of the Present Participle

The present participle is often preceded by the preposition **en** (*while, upon*) to express an action taking place *at the same time* as the main verb. Both actions are performed by the same subject.

J'écoute la radio **en faisant** mes devoirs.	*I listen to the radio **while doing** my homework.*
Ne parle pas au téléphone **en conduisant**!	*Don't talk on the phone **while driving**!*
En rentrant, il allume les lampes.	***Upon arriving home**, he turns on the lights.*

The present participle with **en** can also indicate a relationship of *cause and effect*. With this meaning, **en** corresponds to the English prepositions *in* or *by*. An object pronoun, if needed, follows **en** and precedes the present participle.

C'est **en voyageant** qu'on devient voyageur.	*It's **by traveling** that you become a traveler.*
Nous apprenons le français **en étudiant**.	*We learn French **by studying**.*
Je fais la connaissance d'un ami **en lui parlant**.	*I get to know a friend **by speaking to him**.*

Exercise 12.14

Jacques loves his MP3 player. Use the model to describe Jacques' day.

EXAMPLE: se lever *Il l'écoute en se levant.*

Il l'écoute...

1. se brosser les dents _____.

2. prendre sa douche _____.

3. conduire la voiture _____.

4. monter l'escalier _____.

5. s'installer au travail _____.

6. faire du jogging _____.

7. manger _____.

8. s'endormir _____ .

9. prononcer le français _____ .

10. boire son café _____ .

 Exercise 12.15

Respond to each question with a personal answer, using **en** + *a present participle.*

1. Comment apprenez-vous les verbes français? _____ .

2. Quand écoutez-vous la radio? _____ .

3. Comment vous amusez-vous? _____ .

4. Quand vous ennuyez-vous? _____ .

5. Comment passez-vous de bonnes vacances? _____ .

6. Comment fait-on la connaissance d'un nouveau pays? _____ .

 Describing People

Describe physical characteristics, such as hair and eye color, with **avoir** + definite article (**le/la/les/**) + part of the body.

Ma mère a **les** yeux bleus.	*My mother has blue eyes.*
Ginette a **les** cheveux noirs.	*Ginette has black hair.*
Lui, il a **le** front large.	*He has a broad forehead.*

Say that *something hurts* by using **avoir mal à** + **le/la/l'** + part of the body. Use **un mal de…** to mean *a pain* or *ache.*

J'ai **mal à la tête**.	*I **have a headache**.*
Il **a mal à l'estomac**? Ce sont les bonbons...	*He **has a stomachache**? It's the candy. . . .*
Après une journée au clavier, elle **a mal aux mains**.	*After a day at the keyboard, her **hands hurt**.*
Je souffre de **maux de tête** fréquents.	*I suffer from frequent **headaches**.*

Key Vocabulary

You may need this vocabulary to explain something at a doctor's or dentist's office, or at the pharmacy. Let's hope this doesn't happen often!

Les parties du corps (Parts of the Body)

la bouche (*mouth*)	la joue (*cheek*)
le bras (*arm*	la langue (*tongue*)
les cheveux (*m.*) (*hair*)	les lèvres (*f.*) (*lips*)
la cheville (*ankle*)	la main (*hand*)
le cœur (*heart*)	le menton (*chin*)
les côtes (*f.*) (*ribs*)	le nez (*nose*)
le cou (*neck*)	le nombril (*navel*)
le coude (*elbow*)	l'œil/les yeux (*m.*) (*eye/eyes*)
le crâne (*skull*)	l'ongle (*m.*) (*nail*)
la cuisse (*thigh*)	l'oreille (*f.*) (*ear*)
les dents (*f.*) (*teeth*)	l'orteil (*m.*) (*toe*)
le doigt (*finger*)	le pied (*foot*)
le dos (*back*)	le poignet (*wrist*)
l'épaule (*f.*) (*shoulder*)	la poitrine (*chest, breast*)
l'estomac (*m.*) (*stomach*)	le pouce (*thumb*)
la figure (*face*)	les seins (*m.*) (*breasts*)
le front (*forehead*)	le sourcil (*eyebrow*)
les genoux (*m.*) (*knees*)	la taille (*waist; size*)
la gorge (*throat*)	le talon (*heel*)
la hanche (*hip*)	la tête (*head*)
la jambe (*leg*)	le ventre (*abdomen*)

Exercise 12.16

Où avez-vous mal? (Where does it hurt?) For each of these people, explain what hurts, using the expression **avoir mal à** *+ definite article + part of the body. Change the subject as necessary.*

1. Votre sac à dos, plein de livres, est très lourd. _____.

2. Cyrille doit aller chez le dentiste. _____.

3. Agnès fait de l'alpinisme à la montagne. _____.

4. Il fait très froid et vous n'avez pas de chapeau. _____.

5. La cravate de Simon est trop serrée (*tight*). _____.

6. Il fait du soleil... et il y a beaucoup de neige. _____.

7. Le chien mange du chocolat! _____.

8. Albertine chante tout l'après-midi. _____.

9. Les bottes de Madeleine sont trop petites. _____.

10. Tu apprends à jouer de la harpe. _____.

 # Reading Comprehension

Un accueil chaleureux?

Tous les pays de l'Union Européenne accueillent des immigrés. Sa géographie, **son statut** d'ancien **pouvoir** colonial et son **taux de naissance** assez **faible** font de la France un grand pays de migration. Un immigré est « une personne **née étrangère à l'étranger** et entrée en France... en vue de s'établir sur le territoire français de façon durable. » Un immigré peut **acquérir** la nationalité française par naturalisation, par mariage ou par **filiation**. Comme aux États-Unis, l'enfant de parents étrangers, né en France, est **accordé** la nationalité française. (Les habitants ayant la nationalité française ne sont plus comptés dans la population d'immigrés.)

Les pays sources de migration **restent** les anciennes colonies ou territoires français du **Maghreb** (l'Algérie, le Maroc, la Tunisie), ainsi que les anciennes colonies françaises d'Afrique sub-saharienne. Certains immigrants viennent des pays de l'Union Européenne et d'autres régions, **telles que** l'Asie (**y compris** la Turquie). On **se déplace** pour chercher du travail ou pour **se réunir avec** des parents **proches**. Pourtant, le chômage, l'éducation et d'autres facteurs d'ordre économique, religieux ou culturel marginalisent certains groupes dans des ghettos urbains — comme c'est souvent le cas des nouvelles populations. Ceci peut mener à des manifestations de xénophobie et même de racisme.

L'intégration est peut-être lente, mais avec le temps, elle tend à réussir. Un quart de la population française **actuelle** a un parent ou un grand-parent immigré. Le niveau éducatif des nouveaux immigrés est **en hausse**. Et la France est le pays qui enregistre le plus grand nombre de **demandes d'asile**, politique ou humanitaire.

un accueil (*a welcome*)
chaleureux (*warm*)
son statut (*its status*)
le pouvoir (*power*)
taux de naissance (*birth rate*)
faible (*weak, low*)
née étrangère (*foreign born*)
à l'étranger (*in/to a foreign country*)
acquérir (*to acquire, obtain*)
la filiation (*family relation*)
accordé (*given, granted*))
restent (*remain [**rester**]*)

le Maghreb (*Maghreb [North Africa]*)
tel(le) que (*such as*)
y compris (*including*)
se déplacer (*to move, change place*)
se réunir avec (*to reunite with*)
proches (*close*)
l'intégration (*f.*) (*assimilation*)
actuel(le) (*current, present-day*)
en hausse (*rising*)
demandes (*f.*) d'asile (*applications for asylum*)

Questions

After reading the selection, answer the questions in French.

1. Pourquoi la France est-il un grand pays de migration?

   _____

2. Comment peut-on obtenir la nationalité française?

   _____

3. D'où viennent les immigrés en France?

   _____

4. Quels problèmes sociaux sont liés (*linked*) à l'immigration?

   _____

5. Venez-vous d'une famille d'immigrés? Donnez des détails.

   _____

6. Êtes-vous tenté(e) (*tempted*) d'aller vivre à l'étranger? Où voulez-vous aller? Pourquoi?

   _____

III

The Past and Future Tenses, the Conditional, and the Subjunctive Mood

13

Forms and Uses
of the *passé composé*

What Is the *passé composé?*

Like English, French has more than one past tense. The two most common are the **passé composé** (the *present perfect* in English) and the **imparfait** (the *imperfect*).

The **passé composé** indicates completed action or actions in the past. It is the usual tense that recounts events and incidents, used far more often than the English present perfect ("*I **have seen** that movie*"). The French **passé composé** is also a compound tense. It is formed with the present tense of the auxiliary verbs **avoir** or **être** + the past participle of the verb showing the action.

Verbs conjugated with the auxiliary **être** are presented later in this chapter. The **imparfait**, with its uses, is presented in Chapter 14.

Formation of the *passé composé* with *avoir*

The **passé composé** of *most* French verbs is formed with the present tense of the auxiliary verb **avoir** + the past participle of the verb.

Passé composé of parler *(to speak, talk)*

j'**ai parlé**	nous **avons parlé**
tu **as parlé**	vous **avez parlé**
il/elle/on **a parlé**	ils/elles **ont parlé**

The **passé composé** has several equivalents in English: **J'ai parlé** can mean *I spoke, I have spoken,* or *I did speak.*

Est-ce que **tu as parlé** avec le prof?	***Did you speak*** *with the professor?*
Marie et Blanche ont parlé de l'étude.	***Marie and Blanche spoke*** *about the study.*

Regular and Irregular Past Participles

The forms of French past participles (the equivalent of *acted, spoken, gone, seen, written,* etc.) are regular for regular verbs and generally irregular for irregular verbs.

Regular Past Participles

To form regular past participles of **-er** and **-ir** verbs, the final **-r** is dropped from the infinitive. For **-er** verbs, an accent aigu (´) is added to the final **-e** (**-é**).

achet**er**	achet**é**
commenc**er**	commenc**é**

J'**ai acheté** un DVD.	***I bought** a DVD.*
Le film **a commencé**?	***Did** the movie **start**?*

Regular **-ir** verbs simply drop the final **-r** of the infinitive to form the past participle.

chois**ir**	chois**i**
fin**ir**	fin**i**

Jean **a choisi** un appartement.	*Jean **chose** an apartment.*
Nous **avons fini** de manger.	*We **finished** eating.*

To form regular past participles of **-re** verbs, drop the **-re** from the infinitive, and add the letter **-u**.

attend**re**	attend**u**
perd**re**	perd**u**

Tu **as attendu** longtemps?	***Did** you **wait** long?*
Elles **ont perdu** leurs clés.	*They **lost** their keys.*
Mon cousin **a fini** par faire son droit.	*My cousin **ended up** studying law.*

Alors, tu **as vendu** ton appartement?	So, **did** you **sell** your apartment?
On **a dîné** et on **a discuté** longtemps.	We **had dinner** and we **chatted** a long time.
Samedi, nous **avons rendu visite** à Maman.	On Saturday, we **visited** Mom.

Exercise 13.1

Change the verbs from the present to the **passé composé***.*

1. nous écoutons _____
2. tu réfléchis _____
3. on attend _____
4. vous choisissez _____
5. elles parlent _____
6. nous commençons _____
7. ils entendent _____
8. tu achètes _____
9. nous mangeons _____
10. j'envoie _____

Exercise 13.2

Translate the sentences into French. Use the **passé composé** *in each one.*

1. I finished my work. _____.
2. We ate dinner at eight o'clock. _____.
3. She lost her keys. _____.
4. My brother waited at the café. _____.
5. They (*f.*) chose their courses. _____.
6. You (*pol.*) began to run. _____.
7. I bought a cake. _____.
8. You (*fam.*) sold the car. _____.

Irregular Past Participles

Most irregular verbs have irregular past participles. Make sure to review the meaning of the following verbs.

- **Irregular verbs with past participles ending in -u**

apercevoir (*to glimpse*): **aperçu**	pleuvoir (*to rain*): **plu**
avoir (*to have*): **eu**	pouvoir (*to be able to*): **pu**
boire (*to drink*): **bu**	recevoir (*to receive*): **reçu**
connaître (*to know*): **connu**	revoir (*to see again*): **revu**
croire (*to believe*): **cru**	savoir (*to know*): **su**
devoir (*to have to*): **dû**	tenir (*to hold*): **tenu**
lire (*to read*): **lu**	vivre (*to live*): **vécu**
obtenir (*to obtain*): **obtenu**	voir (*to see*): **vu**
paraître (*to appear, seem*): **paru**	vouloir (*to wish, want to*): **voulu**
plaire (*to please*): **plu**	

A Word About the Verb *plaire à* (to please)

Here is the present tense of the irregular verb **plaire à** (*to please, be pleasing to; to like*): je **plais**, tu **plais**, il/elle/on **plaît**, nous **plaisons**, vous **plaisez**, ils/elles **plaisent**; past participle: **plu**.

The subject of **plaire** is always the thing or person that pleases; the person *who is pleased* is the indirect object of the verb:

Georges **plaît à** Sylvie.	*Sylvie **likes** Georges. (Georges **is pleasing to** Sylvie.)*
Tu **me plais**.	*I **like** (**love**) you. (You **please me**.)*
Ce restaurant **m'a plu**.	*I **liked** that restaurant. (That restaurant **pleased me**.)*

- **Irregular verbs with past participles ending in -s**

apprendre (*to learn*): **appris**	prendre (*to take*): **pris**
comprendre (*to understand*): **compris**	promettre (*to promise*): **promis**
mettre (*to put*): **mis**	remettre (*to postpone; to submit*): **remis**
permettre (*to allow, permit*): **permis**	

- **Irregular verbs with past participles ending in -t**

conduire (*to drive*): **conduit**
couvrir (*to cover*): **couvert**
découvrir (*to discover*): **découvert**
dire (*to say*): **dit**
écrire (*to write*): **écrit**
faire (*to do; to make*): **fait**
feindre de (*to pretend to*): **feint**

offrir (*to offer*): **offert**
ouvrir (*to open*): **ouvert**
produire (*to produce*): **produit**
réduire (*to reduce*): **réduit**
souffrir (*to suffer*): **souffert**
traduire (*to translate*): **traduit**

- **Irregular verbs with past participles ending in -i**

dormir (*to sleep*): **dormi**
mentir (*to lie*): **menti**
poursuivre (*to pursue, continue*): **poursuivi**
rire (*to laugh*): **ri**

sentir (*to feel; to smell*): **senti**
servir (*to serve*): **servi**
sourire (*to smile*): **souri**

suivre (*to follow*): **suivi**

Vous **avez lu** le journal aujourd'hui?	*Did you read the paper today?*
Khaled **a bu** trois tasses de café.	*Khaled drank three cups of coffee.*
J'**ai mis** mon imperméable ce matin.	*I put on my raincoat this morning.*
Tu **as appris** la nouvelle?	*Did you learn the news?*
Le marchand m'**a offert** un rabais.	*The storekeeper offered me a discount.*
Nous **avons écrit** beaucoup de mails.	*We wrote many e-mails.*
As-tu **fait** le ménage?	*Did you clean house?*
Danielle **a feint** de comprendre.	*Danielle pretended to understand.*
Les enfants **ont souri**.	*The children smiled.*
Roseanne **a poursuivi** ses études.	*Roseanne continued her studies.*

- **The past participle of être (to be) is été**

Être in the **passé composé** always uses the auxiliary verb **avoir**. It can have the meaning of *to go, to travel (to)*.

Ont-ils **été** en Angleterre au printemps?	*Did they go to England in the spring?*
Je **n'ai jamais été** au Canada.	*I have never been to Canada.*

Exercise 13.3

Create a complete sentence in the **passé composé** *with the elements provided.*

1. nous/faire/le ménage _____.

2. Isabelle/écrire/une lettre _____.

3. ils/apprendre/la nouvelle _____.

4. je/suivre/trois cours _____.

5. tu/boire/un thé _____.

6. je/mettre/une cravate _____.

7. vous/offrir/un cadeau _____.

8. on/être/en Afrique _____.

Exercise 13.4

Complete the sentences with a verb in the **passé composé** *chosen from the list of verbs provided.*

devoir, dormir, obtenir, poursuivre, prendre, rire, servir, vivre

1. Les enfants _____ tard ce matin.

2. Tu _____ de bonnes notes?

3. On _____ devant le spectacle comique.

4. Vous _____ le train pour venir en ville, n'est-ce pas?

5. Je/J' _____ le dessert après le dîner.

6. Nous _____ trois ans au Québec.

7. Hier soir, je/j' _____ téléphoner à mes grands-parents.

8. Les agents de police _____ le suspect.

Negatives, Interrogatives, and Adverbs with the *passé composé*

Negatives and questions in the **passé composé** parallel their present tense equivalents. The placement of adverbs can vary.

The *passé composé* in the Negative

In negative sentences in the **passé composé**, **ne/n'... pas** and other negative expressions surround the auxiliary verb. In this type of sentence, **rien** (*nothing*) and **personne** (*no one, anyone*) can follow a preposition.

Nous **n'avons pas fait** ce devoir.	We **didn't do** (**haven't done**) that assignment.
Elle **n'a pas dit** bonjour.	She **didn't say** (**hasn't said**) hello.
Je **n'ai jamais voyagé** en Asie.	I **have never traveled** in Asia.
Ils **n'**ont écrit **à personne**.	They did **not write to anyone**.

The Interrogative of the *passé composé*

Questions in the **passé composé** can be made with intonation, **est-ce que**, and inversion. In questions using inversion, invert the auxiliary verb only and attach the subject pronoun. Noun subjects are repeated by an inverted subject pronoun.

Vous avez lu les romans de Camus?	**Have you read** Camus's novels?
Est-ce que Michel a choisi une voiture?	**Did Michel choose** a car?
As-tu vu Hélène?	**Did you see** Hélène?
Où a-t-il acheté sa voiture?	**Where did he buy** his car?
Jean-Luc a-t-il pris son vélo?	**Did Jean-Luc take** his bike?
N'ont-ils pas voyagé en Europe?	**Didn't they travel** in Europe?

Adverbs with the *passé composé*

Short adverbs such as **déjà** (*already*), **souvent** (*often*), and **toujours** (*always*) are usually placed between the auxiliary verb and the past participle in the **passé composé**. In a negative sentence, they follow **pas**.

Tu as **déjà** visité Chartres?	*Have you **already** visited Chartres?*
Nous avons **souvent** pris du cidre.	*We've **often** had cider.*
J'ai **toujours** conduit une Renault.	*I've **always** driven a Renault.*
On **n'**a **pas beaucoup** mangé au déjeuner.	*We did **not** eat **much** at lunch.*

Key Vocabulary

Transition words help relate events in chronological order in the present, past, or future.

Expressions de transition (Transition Words)

d'abord   *first (of all)*

D'abord, ils ont quitté la maison.	***First**, they left the house.*

puis   *next*

Puis, ils ont pris leur voiture.	***Next**, they took their car.*

ensuite...   *and then . . .*

Ensuite, ils ont conduit jusqu'au centre-ville.	***And then**, they drove all the way downtown.*

après...   *after that . . .*

Après, ils ont déjeuné dans un bistro.	***After that**, they had lunch in a bistro.*

enfin/finalement   *finally*

Enfin (**Finalement**), ils ont retrouvé leurs copains.	***Finally**, they met their friends.*

Puis and **ensuite** can be used interchangeably, as can **enfin** and **finalement**.

The following adverbs describe the recent past.

hier   *yesterday*

Hier, j'ai eu un rendez-vous avec le prof.	***Yesterday**, I had an appointment with the teacher.*

---

avant-hier   *day before yesterday*

Nous avons passé un examen **avant-hier**.	*We took an exam (the) **day before yesterday**.*

hier matin   *yesterday morning*

Hier matin, j'ai quitté la maison assez tôt.	*Yesterday morning, I left the house rather early.*

hier après-midi, hier soir   *yesterday afternoon; yesterday evening/ last night*

Hier soir, j'ai retrouvé mes copains en ville.	*Yesterday evening, I met my friends in town.*

The following expressions also signal the use of the **passé composé**.

à ce moment-là   *at that moment*
l'année (la semaine) passée   *last year (week)*
ce jour-là   *(on) that day*
hier   *yesterday*
lundi (mardi, ...)   *Monday (Tuesday, . . .)*
pendant   *for, during + period of time*
(Pendant) Combien de temps... ?   *(For) How long . . . ?*
soudain   *suddenly*
tout à coup   *suddenly*
un jour   *one day*
une (deux...), une fois   *once (twice . . .), one time*

When expressing a span of time, or what was done during a time period, use the feminine nouns **journée** (*day*), **matinée** (*morning*), and **soirée** (*evening*), rather than **jour**, **matin**, **soir**. These terms are used with **toute** (*all, the whole*).

toute la matinée (journée, soirée)   *the whole morning (day, evening)*

J'ai passé **toute la soirée** à terminer ce devoir!	*I spent **the entire evening** finishing that assignment!*

Exercise 13.5

*Ask a question in the **passé composé** using inversion, based on each statement. Then answer the new question in the negative.*

1. Tu lis un roman de Balzac. _____?

   _____.

2. Je vois mes amis samedi soir. _____?

   _____.

3. Émilie conduit un petit camion. _____?

   _____.

4. Je fais la lessive. _____?

   _____.

5. Les étudiants ont des devoirs à faire. _____?

   _____.

6. Nous mettons des chaussures de marche. _____?

   _____.

7. Ils vivent trois ans à Lyon. _____?

   _____.

Exercise 13.6

*Translate the sentences from English to French. Use the **passé composé** and an expression of time or a transition word.*

1. First, you (*pol.*) had lunch. _____.

2. Then, we did the dishes. _____.

3. Finally, I left the house. _____.

4. Last year, you (*fam.*) took an Italian course. _____.

5. Have you (*pol.*) already been to France? _____?

6. He ate a lot at breakfast. _____.

7. Yesterday evening, she saw a beautiful sunset. _____.

8. I've always loved French cooking. _____.

The *passé composé* with *être*

The **passé composé** of a limited group of verbs is formed with the auxiliary **être**; many of these verbs express change of position or state.

In the **passé composé** with **être**, the past participle always *agrees with the subject* in gender and number. As with adjectives, add an **-e** for the feminine and an **-s** for the plural forms.

Passé composé of aller *(to go)*

je **suis allé(e)**	nous **sommes allé(e)s**
tu **es allé(e)**	vous **êtes allé(e)(s)**
il/on **est allé**	ils **sont allés**
elle **est allée**	elles **sont allées**

The verbs in the following list are conjugated with **être** in the **passé composé**. Most indicate a change of position like **monter** (*to climb*) and **tomber** (*to fall*) or a state of being like **devenir** (*to become*) and **rester** (*to remain*). It helps to learn the **être** verbs as pairs or groupings. Several have irregular past participles.

aller: **allé(e)(s)**	*to go*
partir: **parti(e)(s)**	*to leave*
rester: **resté(e)(s)**	*to stay, remain*
sortir: **sorti(e)(s)**	*to go out*
venir: **venu(e)(s)**	*to come*
descendre: **descendu(e)(s)**	*to go, get down*
monter: **monté(e)(s)**	*to go up, climb up*
tomber: **tombé(e)(s)**	*to fall (down)*
arriver: **arrivé(e)(s)**	*to arrive*
entrer: **entré(e)(s)**	*to enter, go in*
rentrer: **rentré(e)(s)**	*to return, go home*
retourner: **retourné(e)(s)**	*to return, come back*
revenir: **revenu(e)(s)**	*to come back*
devenir: **devenu(e)(s)**	*to become*
mourir: **mort(e)(s)**	*to die*
naître: **né(e)(s)**	*to be born*

Naître and *mourir*

The present tense conjugation of **naître** (*to be born*) is: je **nais**, tu **nais**, il/elle/on **naît**, nous **naissons**, vous **naissez**, ils/elles **naissent**; past participle: **né(e)**.

The present tense conjugation of **mourir** (*to die*) is: je **meurs**, tu **meurs**, il/elle/on **meurt**, nous **mourons**, vous **mourez**, ils/elles **meurent**; past participle: **mort(e)**.

Mme Curie est née à Varsovie, en Pologne, en 1867. En 1891 **elle est allée** à Paris poursuivre ses études à la Sorbonne. **Elle est devenue** chef du laboratoire et a reçu le Prix Nobel de Physique en 1903, à côté de son mari, Pierre Curie. **Son mari** Pierre **est mort** tragiquement en 1906. **Mme Curie est restée** en France toute sa vie; **elle est retournée** à Varsovie pour y fonder un laboratoire de radioactivité. **Morte** en 1934, elle reste la seule femme à avoir reçu deux Prix Nobel (Physique, 1903, et Chimie, 1911).

*Madame Curie **was born** in Warsaw, Poland, in 1867. In 1891 **she went** to Paris to continue her studies at the Sorbonne. **She became** head of the laboratory and received the Nobel Prize in Physics in 1903, along with her husband, Pierre Curie. **Her husband** Pierre **died** tragically in 1906. **Madame Curie remained** in France her entire life; **she returned** to Warsaw to establish a radioactivity lab there. **She died** in 1934 and remains the only woman to have received two Nobel Prizes (Physics, 1903, and Chemistry, 1911).*

Exercise 13.7

Create complete sentences in the **passé composé** *with the elements provided. Begin each sentence with* **Il y a** *(ago) + the period of time.*

1. trois jours/je (*f.*)/sortir/avec Sylvain

   _____.

2. une semaine/tu (*m.*)/aller/au théâtre

   _____.

3. six mois/nous (*f.*)/partir/en France

   _____.

4. quelques jours/ils/rentrer/chez eux

_____.

5. une heure/nous (*m.*)/descendre/faire le marché

_____.

6. un instant/le vase/tomber/dans l'escalier

_____.

 ## Exercise 13.8

Complete the story in the **passé composé**, *choosing from the verb list provided. Some items have more than one possible answer.*

aller, arriver, descendre, monter, partir, rentrer, rester, retourner, sortir, tomber, venir

Hier, mes deux sœurs _____ (1) à l'université à la fin des

vacances. Martine _____ (2) de notre maison avec deux

grosses valises. Elle _____ (3) deux ou trois fois dans la

maison pour chercher quelque chose. Tout à coup, les valises d'Arlette

_____ (4) de la voiture. Je/J' (*m.*) _____

(5) de la maison les ramasser. Puis, les voisins _____ (6) leur

dire au revoir. Ensuite, Daniel et moi, nous _____ (7) dans

la voiture avec elles, et nous _____ (8). La voiture est petite,

donc, Maman n'y _____ pas _____ (9); elle

_____ (10) à la maison. Enfin, nous _____

(11) ensemble à Montpellier.

 Conjugating the Verbs *être* and *avoir* in the *passé composé*

Remember that the verbs **être** (past participle: **été**) and **avoir** (past participle: **eu**) are both always conjugated with the auxiliary **avoir**.

Tu **as été** au supermarché?   ***Did* you *go* to the supermarket?**

Bruno **a eu** une excellente idée.   *Bruno **got** a great idea.*

The *passé composé* with Object Pronouns

Direct and indirect object pronouns are placed before the auxiliary in the **passé composé**.

J'ai lu **cet article**. Je l'ai lu.	*I read **that article**. I read **it**.*
Tu aimes **ce film-là**?	*Do you like **that movie**?*
L'avez-vous vu?	*Did you see **it**?*
Tu as vu **Anny**? On ne **lui** a	*Did you see **Anny**? We didn't*
pas parlé.	*speak **to her**.*

Agreement of Object Pronouns with the Past Participle

In the **passé composé** with **avoir**, a *direct object preceding* the conjugated verb agrees in gender and number with the past participle of that verb. Add **-e** or **-s** to the past participle as needed. (This agreement is always seen in spelling but is often not heard.)

Tu as acheté **ces livres**?	*You bought **those books**?*
Tu **les** a achetés?	*You bought **them**?*
J'ai pris **tes chaussures**.	*I took **your shoes**. I took **them**.*
Je **les** ai pris**es**.	
Marielle a choisi **cette école**.	*Marielle chose **this school**.*
Elle **l'**a choisi**e**.	*She chose **it**.*

- However, the past participle does *not* agree with a preceding *indirect* object pronoun, and there is no agreement with the *partitive* pronoun **en**.

On n'a pas écrit **aux parents**.	*We didn't write **to our parents**.*
On ne **leur** a pas **écrit**.	*We didn't **write to them**.*
J'ai mangé **des légumes**.	*I ate **some vegetables**.*
J'**en** ai **mangé**.	*I ate **some**.*

- Past participles of verbs conjugated with **être** always agree with the *subject* of the verb; this includes sentences with the pronoun **y**.

Suzanne et sa sœur sont	***Suzanne and her sister***
part**ies** ce matin.	*left this morning.*
Non, **nous** ne sommes pas né**es**	*No, **we** weren't born in Brussels.*
à Bruxelles. **Nous** n'**y** sommes	*We weren't born **there**.*
pas né**es**.	
Nos amis sont entrés dans le	***Our friends** entered the theater.*
théâtre. **Ils y** sont entré**s**.	***They** entered **it**.*

- The rules of agreement also apply within *relative clauses* in the **passé composé**.

Les spectateurs **qui sont arrivés** tôt attendent dans le foyer. (**qui** + **être** verb)	*The audience members **who arrived** early are waiting in the lobby.*
Les personnes **que j'ai invitées** apportent du vin. (**que**, replacing **les personnes**, as preceding direct object)	*The people **(whom) I invited** are bringing wine.*

Exercise 13.9

*Rewrite the sentences, replacing the noun object in italics by an object pronoun, **y**, or **en**. Pay attention to the agreement of the past participle.*

1. J'ai vu *mes neveux* hier. _____.

2. Catherine a écrit à *Marc*. _____.

3. Nous avons bu *de l'eau minérale*. _____.

4. Laure et Sami sont allés à *EuroDisney*. _____.

5. Tu as acheté *des meubles (furniture)*? _____?

6. Avez-vous reçu *les lettres (f.) de Raoul*? _____?

7. Ils ont fait *la vaisselle*. _____.

8. J'ai mis *ma veste noire*. _____.

The *passé composé* of Pronominal Verbs

All pronominal verbs are conjugated with **être** in the **passé composé**. In general, the past participle of a pronominal verb agrees in gender and number with its reflexive pronoun, and therefore with the subject of the verb.

Note the use of **avoir** (non-pronominal) or **être** (pronominal) as the auxiliary verbs in the following examples:

Elle a levé les rideaux.	***She raised*** *the curtains.*
Hier, **elle s'est levée** vers six heures.	*Yesterday, **she got up** at about six A.M.*

Nous avons rencontré Éric ce matin.	*We **met** Éric this morning.*
Nous nous sommes rencontrés à Paris.	*We **ran into each other** in Paris.*
Tu as déjà **vu** Sylvain?	***Did you** already **see** Sylvain?*
—Oui, **on s'est vu(s)** hier.	*—Yes, **we saw each other** yesterday.*
Yvonne s'est regardée dans la glace.	***Yvonne looked at herself** in the mirror.*

When the Past Participle Does Not Agree

There are exceptions to the past participle agreement with a reflexive pronoun:

- The past participle does *not* agree if the verb takes an *indirect* object. The following verbs (**téléphoner**, **parler**, **poser des questions**) always take **à** + an indirect object.

Ils se sont **téléphoné**.	*They **phone** each other.*
Elles se sont **parlé**.	*They **spoke to** each other.*
Nous nous sommes **posé des questions**.	*We **asked** each other **some questions**.*

- In addition, the past participle does *not* agree when the verb is *followed by a direct object noun*, usually a part of the body.

  In the following first example, the reflexive pronoun **s'** (referring to **Hélène**) is the direct object of the verb **laver**, and there *is* agreement. In the second example, **les mains** (following **laver**) is the direct object of the verb, while the pronoun **s'** serves as the indirect object (**à Hélène**). Thus there is *no* agreement.

Hélène **s'est lavée**.	*Hélène **washed up** (**washed herself**).*
Hélène **s'est lavé les mains**.	*Hélène **washed her hands**.*
Nous **nous sommes brossé les dents**.	*We **brushed our teeth**.*
Anne et Marie **se sont lavé les cheveux**.	*Anne and Marie **washed their hair**.*

Exercise 13.10

*Translate the sentences into French. Use the **passé composé** and the suggested verbs. Pay attention to the agreement—or not—of the past participle.*

se brosser les cheveux, se connaître, s'écrire, s'endormir, se faire connaissance, s'occuper de, se réveiller, se tromper de, se voir

1. We (*f.*) saw each other yesterday. _____.

2. Mireille and Claude wrote to each other. _____.

3. I (*m.*) woke up at noon. _____.

4. My daughters brushed their hair. _____.

5. What time did the children (*m.*) fall asleep? _____?

6. Did you (*fam., f.*) take care of the laundry? _____?

7. I (*f.*) made a mistake in the address. _____.

8. They (*m.*) got acquainted a year ago. _____.

Key Vocabulary

Le sport (Sports)

Sports are truly international. Notice how many French sports are cognate words.

> assister à (un match)   *to attend (a match, game, show)*
> être fana de...   *to be crazy about . . .*
> être passionné(e) de...   *to be passionate about . . .*
> faire du/de la/de l'...   *to do . . .*
> jouer au...   *to play . . .*

l'alpinisme (*m.*) (*mountain climbing*)	le basket(-ball) (*basketball*)
les arts martiaux (*m.*) (*martial arts*)	le bateau (*boating*)
le jujitsu (*jujitsu*)	le canoë-kayak (*kayaking*)
le karaté (*karate*)	la course (*race*)
le tai-chi chuan (*tai chi*)	le cyclisme (le vélo) (*biking*)
le base-ball (*baseball*)	le deltaplane (*hang gliding*)
	l'équitation (*f.*) (*horseback riding*)
	l'escrime (*f.*) (*fencing*)

le foot(ball)   *(soccer)*

le football américain   *(football)*

le footing   *(jogging)*

le golf   *(golf)*

la gymnastique   *(gymnastics)*

le hockey   *(hockey)*

le jogging   *(jogging)*

le marathon   *(marathon)*

la natation   *(swimming)*

le patinage   *(skating)*

le ping-pong   *(Ping-Pong)*

la planche à roulettes   *(skateboarding)*

la planche à voile   *(windsurfing)*

la randonnée   *(hiking)*

le roller   *(rollerblading)*

le rugby   *(rugby)*

le saut   *(high jump)*

le ski   *(skiing)*

le snowboard   *(snowboarding)*

le surf   *(surfing)*

le tennis   *(tennis)*

la voile   *(sailing)*

le volley(-ball)   *(volleyball)*

le yoga   *(yoga)*

Les distractions (Leisure and Entertainment)

Hobbies and interests enrich everyone's life and are always good topics of conversation.

l'art (*m.*)   *(art)*

l'aquarelle (*f.*)   *(watercolors)*

le dessin   *(drawing)*

la peinture à l'huile   *(oil painting)*

la sculpture   *(sculpture)*

l'artisanat (*m.*)   *(crafts)*

la céramique   *(ceramics)*

la menuiserie   *(woodworking)*

la poterie   *(pottery)*

le vitrail   *(stained glass)*

le bricolage   *(do-it-yourself)*

les cartes (*f.*)   *(cards)*

le bridge   *(bridge)*

le poker   *(poker)*

le cirque   *(circus)*

la danse   *(dance)*

le ballet   *(ballet)*

le drame   *(drama)*

le film d'amour   *(love story)*

le film d'aventures   *(adventure film)*

le film d'horreur   *(horror film)*

la séance   *(showing)*

la cassette   *(cassette)*

la chanson   *(song)*

le chœur   *(choir)*

le concert   *(concert)*

le lecteur de DVD/CD   *(DVD/CD player)*

le lecteur MP3   *(MP3 player)*

la musique classique   *(classical music)*

la musique de chambre   *(chamber music)*

l'opéra (*m.*)   *(opera)*

l'orchestre (*m.*)   *(orchestra; band)*

le pop/rap/rock/jazz   *(pop/rap/rock/jazz)*

le quatuor   *(string quartet)*

la danse de salon   *(ballroom)*

la danse folklorique   *(folk dance)*

le tango   *(tango)*

la danse moderne   *(modern dance)*

le jardinage   *(gardening)*

les jeux de hasard (*m.*) (*gaming*)
les jeux de société (*board games*)
les échecs (*m.*) (*chess*)
les dames (*f.*) (*checkers*)
les jeux électroniques
     (*electronic games*)
la lecture (*reading*)
la bande dessinée (*comics*)
la biographie (*biography*)
l'essai (*m.*) (*nonfiction*)
les magazines (*m.*) (*magazines*)
le roman (*novel*)
le roman d'amour (*romance novel*)
le roman d'aventures (*adventure
     novel*)
le roman illustré (*graphic novel*)
le roman policier (*mystery*)
les mots croisés (*m.*) (*crossword*)
le musée (*museum*)
l'exposition (*f.*) (*exhibition*)
le spectacle (*show*)
le cinéma (*film, movies*)
le billet (*ticket*)
le dessin animé (*animated film*)
le documentaire (*documentary*)
la symphonie (*symphony*)
l'observation (*f.*) des oiseaux
     (*bird-watching*)

la photographie (*photography*)
un appareil-photo ([*still*] *camera*)
un caméra (*movie camera*)
un caméscope (*video camera*)
la télévision (*television*)
le podcast (*podcast*)
la radio (*radio*)
la chaîne (*channel*)
l'émission (*f.*) (*program*)
le théâtre (*theater*)
les spectateurs (*m.*) (*audience
     members*)
la salle de théâtre (*theater*)
la pièce (*play*)
le drame (*drama*)
la comédie (musicale) ([*musical*]
     comedy)
la tragédie (*tragedy*)
le sudoku (*sudoku*)
les travaux (*m.*) d'aiguille
     (*needlework*)
la broderie (*embroidery*)
la couture (*sewing*)
le crochet (*crocheting*)
la tapisserie (*needlepoint*)
le tissage (*weaving*)
le tricot (*knitting*)

 ## Exercise 13.11

Answer the questions using the previous vocabulary lists.

1. Nommez les sports que vous aimez regarder.

   _____.

2. Nommez les sports que vous avez déjà faits ou que vous faites
   actuellement.

   _____.

3. Quelles sont vos distractions préférées? en été? en hiver?

_____.

4. Expliquez pourquoi vous vous intéressez à ces activités.

_____.

5. Qu'avez-vous fait le week-end passé?

_____.

6. Quel sport ou quelle activité voulez-vous apprendre? Pourquoi?

_____.

 # Reading Comprehension

Une soirée mouvementée

Nous nous sommes aperçus pour la première fois dans un cours de danse folklorique africaine. Je suis arrivée un peu en retard ce soir-là. Les autres danseurs m'ont regardé entrer avec beaucoup d'intérêt, puisqu'ici, on arrive en général avant l'heure pour se préparer. J'assiste à ce cours depuis plusieurs années déjà, et je trouve que **je m'y connais** déjà assez **bien** en danse africaine. Je ne me trompe presque plus de **pas** ni de rythme. Dans le cours, **il s'agit de** la danse des pays d'Afrique de l'Ouest. Nous invitons des musiciens qui jouent des instruments traditionnels — tels le kora (une sorte de guitare) et des tambours, dont le *djembé*. **Nous nous consacrons** aux danses de plusieurs pays: le Sénégal, le Mali, la Côte d'Ivoire et la Guinée.

Alors, ce jour-là, j'ai dû traverser la salle pour rejoindre mon groupe. **En m'y dirigeant**, j'ai regardé de côté où j'ai aperçu le nouveau joueur de djembé. Lui aussi, il a levé la tête pour m'observer. Qu'est-ce que je peux dire? C'est **le coup de foudre**! Il est grand et beau, au visage tranquille mais intelligent. À ce moment-là, j'ai fait un faux pas, **j'ai trébuché** et je suis tombée! J'ai rougi, **j'ai balbutié**. Lui, **il a laissé tomber** son tambour et m'a aidée à me relever. Heureusement, je ne me suis pas fait mal. J'ai rejoint le groupe, il a repris son djembé. Je me suis mise à suivre les pas des autres danseurs.

mouvementé(e)   (*eventful*)
je m'y connais... bien   (*I'm very familiar*)
le pas   (*step*)
il s'agit de   (*it concerns*)
nous nous consacrons   (*we devote ourselves*)
en m'y dirigeant   (*on my way there*)
le coup de foudre   (*love at first sight*)
j'ai trébuché   (*I tripped*)
j'ai balbutié   (*I stuttered*)
il a laissé tomber   (*he dropped*)

Questions

After reading the selection, answer the questions in French.

1. À quoi s'intéresse la narratrice? Depuis combien de temps s'y consacre-t-elle?

   _____

2. Qu'est-ce qui s'est passé (*happened*) ce soir-là, à son arrivée?

   _____

3. Imaginez la rencontre de ces personnes après le cours. Employez le passé composé.

   _____

4. Racontez un incident tiré (*taken from*) de votre vie.

   _____

14

The *imparfait*, Past Narration, and More About Object Pronouns

Summary of the *passé composé*

In Chapter 13 you learned the **passé composé**, which recounts completed actions or a series of actions in the past. The **passé composé** is formed with an auxiliary verb (the present tense of **avoir** or **être**) + the past participle. It has three types of conjugations:

- *Most verbs are conjugated with* avoir.

  Pour passer l'été en France, **j'ai dû** faire des préparatifs. D'abord, en février, **j'ai réservé** mon vol. Ensuite, **j'ai fini** un tas de projets. Finalement, **j'ai attendu** le jour du départ avec impatience. **J'ai fait** mes valises bien en avance.
  *To spend the summer in France, **I had to** get ready. First, in February **I reserved** my flight. Then, **I finished** a lot of projects. Finally, **I waited** impatiently for my departure date. **I packed** my bags well in advance.*

- *Some verbs are conjugated with* être.
  Verbs conjugated with **être** are *intransitive*. They have no direct or indirect object (though they may be followed by a preposition). The past participle always agrees with the subject, in gender and number.

  Enfin, **le 15 juin est arrivé**. **Je suis partie** pour l'aéroport en disant au revoir à la famille. **Nous sommes passés** par la sécurité et **sommes montés** dans l'avion. Un passager a oublié un petit sac dans la salle d'attente, mais évidemment, **il n'est pas descendu** le reprendre.

299

*Finally, **June 15 arrived**. **I left** for the airport bidding good-bye to my family. **We went** through security and **boarded** the plane. One passenger forgot a small bag in the waiting room, but obviously, **he didn't get off** to retrieve it.*

- *Pronominal (reflexive, reciprocal, and idiomatic) verbs (Chapter 12) are also conjugated with être.*

Pronominal verbs always keep their reflexive pronoun, which refers back to the subject. In general, the past participle of pronominal verbs agrees with the subject.

Enfin, tous **les passagers se sont installés**. Vers dix heures vingt, **l'avion s'est mis** à rouler. À ce moment-là, moi aussi, **je me suis souvenue de** quelque chose: mon guide de France, oublié chez moi… Une fois l'avion atterri à Paris, **je me suis dépêchée d'**en acheter un autre, en français.

*At last, all **the passengers took their seats**. Around ten twenty, **the plane started** to taxi. At that moment, **I remembered** something, too: my guidebook to France, forgotten at home. As soon as the plane landed in Paris, **I hurried** to buy another one, in French.*

Exercise 14.1

*Complete the sentences in the **passé composé** with the verbs provided.*

1. Samedi nous _____ de faire un pique-nique à la montagne. (décider)

2. On _____ des tas de bonnes choses à manger. (préparer)

3. Antoine _____; il _____ même _____ des serviettes et une nappe dans le panier. (ne rien oublier, mettre)

4. Nous _____ la maison et nous _____ à dix heures. (quitter, partir)

5. Dans la voiture nous _____ chanter, mais Papa nous _____ de regarder le paysage. (se mettre à, dire)

6. Nous _____ près d'un village où nous _____. (arriver, s'arrêter)

7. Je/J' _____ nos paniers, et nous _____.
   (prendre, s'y installer)

8. Après déjeuner, je/j' _____ une randonnée avec Antoine, et on _____ par visiter le village. (faire, finir)

The *imparfait* (Imperfect Tense)

The *imperfect* (**l'imparfait**) is a past tense used to describe continuous or habitual past actions or states. It is also used for descriptions in the past.

Forms of the *imparfait*

To form the **imparfait**, drop the **-ons** ending from the **nous** form of the present tense (regular and irregular verbs), and add the endings **-ais**, **-ais**, **-ait**, **-ions**, **-iez**, **-aient**.

Present Tense	Imparfait	
nous dans**ons**	nous dans**ions**	(*we were dancing*)
nous fais**ons**	ils/elles fais**aient**	(*they used to do, make*)
nous choisiss**ons**	tu choisiss**ais**	(*you were choosing*)
nous répond**ons**	je répond**ais**	(*I answered*)
nous pouv**ons**	vous pouv**iez**	(*you were able to*)

For verbs ending in **-ger**, insert an **-e-** before the ending when the ending starts with the letter **-a** or **-o**. For verbs ending in **-cer**, change **-c-** to **-ç-** before **-a** or **-o**. Four **imparfait** endings start with **-a**.

Present Tense	Imparfait		
nous mang**e**ons	nous mangions	ils/elles mang**e**aient	*we/they were eating*
nous commen**ç**ons	nous commencions	ils/elles commen**ç**aient	*we/they were starting*

The **imparfait** is easy to learn: all conjugations, except for the verb **être**, are formed in the same way. Reflexive and object pronouns are placed as they are in the present tense; negatives and interrogatives also follow present tense patterns.

Here are the imperfect forms for **parler** (*to speak*), **finir** (*to finish*), **attendre** (*to wait for*), and **être** (*to be*). The irregular imperfect stem of **être** is **ét-**.

parler (*to speak*)	**finir** (*to finish*)
je parl**ais**	je fin**issais**
tu parl**ais**	tu fin**issais**
il/elle/on parl**ait**	il/elle/on fin**issait**
nous parl**ions**	nous fin**issions**
vous parl**iez**	vous fin**issiez**
ils/elles parl**aient**	ils/elles fin**issaient**

attendre (*to wait for*)	**être** (*to be*)
j'attend**ais**	j'ét**ais**
tu attend**ais**	tu ét**ais**
il/elle/on attend**ait**	il/elle/on ét**ait**
nous attend**ions**	nous ét**ions**
vous attend**iez**	vous ét**iez**
ils/elles attend**aient**	ils/elles ét**aient**

Meanings and Uses of the *imparfait*

The **imparfait** has several equivalents in English. **Je parlais** can mean *I talked, I was talking, I used to talk,* or *I would (= used to) talk.* **Nous étions** can mean *we were* or *we used to be.*

À dix heures, **je** t'**attendais** au coin.	At ten o'clock, **I was waiting** for you at the corner.
Autrefois, **nous** ne **nous écrivions** pas.	In the past, **we** didn't **write to each other**.
Où **habitiez-vous** en 1995?	Where **were you living** in 1995?
—En 1995, **j'avais** un petit appartement à Paris.	—In 1995, **I had** a small flat in Paris.
Il était rue du Terrage.	**It was** on rue du Terrage.
J'allais chez ma tante le dimanche.	**I used to go** to my aunt's on Sunday.
Nous faisions la cuisine ensemble.	**We'd** cook together.

The **imparfait** expresses unbroken or continuous actions or situations existing for an indefinite period of time in the past. There is usually no mention of the beginning or end of the event. The **imparfait** is used in a number of ways:

- ### *In descriptions, to set a scene*

  C'était une soirée tranquille. Dehors, **il neigeait** et **il faisait** froid.
  Mme Dupont lisait un roman; **M. Dupont regardait** un DVD.
  Fido se reposait devant le feu.
  *It was a peaceful evening. Outside, **it was snowing** and **it was** cold.
  Mme Dupont was reading a novel; **M. Dupont was watching** a
  DVD. **Fido was resting** in front of the fire.*

- ### *For habitual or customary past actions*

  Quand **j'étais** jeune **j'allais** chez mes grands-parents en été. **Nous
  nous amusions** toujours très bien. Tous les soirs **on faisait** de belles
  promenades sur la plage.
  *When **I was** young **I used to** (**would**) **go** to my grandparents' place in
  the summer. **We** always **had a** very **good time**. Every evening **we
  used to** (**would**) **take** lovely walks on the beach.*

- ### *To describe feelings and mental or emotional states in the past*

  Jean-Charles était mécontent;　　**Jean-Charles was** unhappy;
  　il avait envie de laisser　　　　　*he wanted to drop his studies.*
  tomber ses études.

- ### *To tell time of day or to express age in the past*

  Il était sept heures et demie.　　*It was seven-thirty* A.M.
  C'était l'anniversaire d'Iris; **elle**　*It was Iris's birthday; **she was**
  　avait dix-huit ans.　　　　　　*eighteen years old.*

- ### *To describe an action or situation that was happening when another event (usually in the* passé composé) *interrupted it*

  Il **prenait sa douche** quand　　*He **was showering** when I **rang**
  　j'**ai sonné**.　　　　　　　　**the bell**.

Exercise 14.2

Create complete sentences in the **imparfait** *using the elements given.*

Cette nuit, à une heure du matin...

1. vous/s'amuser à la disco _____.
2. tu/s'endormir _____.
3. Michaël/faire de beaux rêves _____.
4. je/commencer/à lire _____.
5. Papa/prendre un bain _____.
6. les chats/se disputer _____.
7. nous/être à la cuisine _____.
8. Suzanne et sa sœur/manger _____.

Exercise 14.3

Complete the paragraph in the **imparfait** *choosing from the list of verbs given. Several verbs will be used more than once.*

aller, avoir, discuter, être, falloir, se mettre, s'occuper, se parler, se réunir, travailler

Quand j' _____ (1) quinze ans je/j' _____ (2)
à une école assez particulière. Il n'y _____ (3) pas de vrais
cours ni de profs. Nous _____ (4) tous les matins sous les
arbres du jardin. Puis, nous _____ (5) avec les adultes, qui
_____ (6) en réalité nos profs, mais qui, dans cette école,
_____ (7) à côté de nous. Alors, nous
_____ (8) d'accord sur ce qu'il _____ (9)
faire ce jour-là: travaux d'agriculture ou de construction, ou bien on
_____ (10) des animaux (poules, chèvres, lapins). Tout
en travaillant, nous _____ (11) de choses pratiques, de
l'environnement, de nos lectures et de comment réussir notre vie.
C' _____ (12) vraiment une école spéciale.

Key Vocabulary

Expressions de temps au passé **(Expressions of Time in the Past)**

Sentences in the **imparfait** are often marked by adverbs and expressions of time. Using them in past tense sentences makes the meaning of the **imparfait** clearer.

à ce moment-là *(at that time)*	le lundi *(on Mondays)*
à cette époque-là *(at that time)*	le week-end *(every weekend)*
auparavant *(previously)*	ne… jamais *(never)*
autrefois *(in the past)*	normalement *(normally)*
désormais *(from then on)*	parfois *(sometimes)*
de temps à autre *(from time to time)*	par moments *(occasionally)*
de temps en temps *(from time to time)*	pendant que *(while)*
	quelquefois *(sometimes)*
d'habitude *(usually)*	souvent *(often)*
	toujours *(always)*
il y a *(a span of time + ago)*	tous les jours *(every day)*

Except for **auparavant** *(previously)* and **autrefois** *(in the past)*, these expressions are also used with other verb tenses.

D'habitude, **les enfants avaient** faim à midi.	*The children were usually hungry at noon.*
On dormait *pendant que* **Corinne travaillait**.	*We were sleeping while Corinne worked.*
Il y a trois mois, **il travaillait** à l'étranger.	*Three months **ago**, **he was working** abroad.*
Autrefois, **je** ne **tenais** pas compte de lui.	**In the past**, *I **did** not **take** him into account.*

Exercise 14.4

Give a personal answer in the **imparfait** *to each of the questions.*

1. Que faisiez-vous tous les jours quand vous aviez quinze ans?

   _____.

2. Où habitiez-vous autrefois? Aimiez-vous cet endroit (*place*)? Pourquoi?

   _____.

3. Décrivez l'été à l'endroit où vous habitiez à quinze ans. Que faisait-on en été?

   _____.

Narration: The *passé composé* and the *imparfait* Used Together

To recount past events in French, you will need to use both the **passé composé** and the **imparfait**, often in the same sentence.

- In English, when we refer to past events, we choose among several forms of past tenses.

  She worked.   She did work.   She has worked.
  She was working.   She used to work.   She would work . . . on Fridays.

  Similarly in French, your choice of the **passé composé**: **Elle** *a travaillé* **hier** (*She* **worked** *yesterday*) or the **imparfait**: **À cinq heures, elle** *travaillait* **encore** (*At five o'clock she* **was** *still* **working**) depends on your perception of the past event.

- The **passé composé** expresses a completed past action or a sequence of actions. It gives the idea that the action ended in the past or was repeated a *countable* number of times.

  L'année passée **je suis allée** deux   *Last year* ***I went to*** *France twice.*
      fois en France.

- In contrast, the **imparfait** indicates ongoing, habitual, and background actions, descriptions, and mental or physical states in the past. It does not focus on the completion of the action. The **imparfait** sets the scene in the past. The past actions are assumed to be repeated an *undetermined* number of times.

Quand **j'étais** jeune, **j'allais** chez ma tante en été.	*When **I was** young, **I used to go** to my aunt's place in the summer.*

- An action, a feeling, or a situation in the **imparfait** may be "interrupted" by an action in the **passé composé**. Compare the first and second verbs in the next three examples:

J'avais faim quand **je me suis réveillé**.	*I was (**felt**) hungry when I woke up.*
Georges était malade quand **tu es venu**.	*Georges was ill when **you got here**.*
Nous jouions aux cartes quand **il y a eu** une panne d'électricité.	*We were playing cards when there was a power outage (a power outage occurred).*

- The **passé composé** in the following sentences recounts a sudden change at a specific moment. The **imparfait** in the second sentence of each set describes the subject's state or situation prior to this change.

J'ai eu faim vers midi.	*I got (**became**) hungry around noon.*
Avant midi **je n'avais** pas faim.	*Before noon, **I was** not hungry.*
Georges **est tombé malade** hier soir.	*Georges **fell ill** last night.*
Avant sept heures il **était** en bonne forme.	*Before seven o'clock he **was** fine.*

- Read the following account of Claire's day. Remain aware of all the French verbs, paying close attention to the use of the **passé composé** and the **imparfait**.

Hier, quand je me suis levée, il faisait beau. Dehors, le soleil brillait et les oiseaux chantaient. Je me sentais contente et pleine de courage. Mais, tout à coup, le ciel s'est couvert. Il a commencé à pleuvoir. À ce moment-là, j'ai perdu courage, et je me suis recouchée. La situation me semblait bien triste. J'ai fini par rester au lit tout l'après-midi... Enfin, la pluie s'est arrêtée. Puis, Micheline a téléphoné parce que les copains m'attendaient. On allait faire du bateau sur le lac. Soudain, je me suis sentie beaucoup plus optimiste.

*Yesterday, when I got up, the weather was beautiful. Outside, the
sun was shining and the birds were singing. I felt happy and
full of energy. But, suddenly, the sky got dark. It started to rain.
At that moment, I got depressed and went back to bed. The
situation seemed quite sad. I ended up staying in bed the whole
afternoon. . . . Finally, the rain stopped. Then, Micheline phoned
because our friends were waiting for me. We were going to go
boating on the lake. Suddenly, I felt much more optimistic.*

Exercise 14.5

Translate the sentences into French using the **passé composé** *and the* **imparfait**.

1. When I (*f.*) arrived in Paris, the weather was beautiful.

   _____.

2. We were resting when Éric called.

   _____.

3. He was leaving the house when he remembered the books.

   _____.

4. I was still wearing my raincoat when, suddenly, the rain stopped.

   _____.

5. She wasn't feeling well last night, but she went out anyway (**quand
   même**).

   _____.

6. Yesterday, you (*fam.*) found the café where they (**on**) used to serve that
   good soup.

   _____.

Exercise 14.6

Write a personal ending to each sentence in the **passé composé** *or* **imparfait** *according to the context.*

1. Quand je me suis réveillé(e) ce matin, _____.

2. Hier soir, il pleuvait. Alors, mon ami et moi, _____.

3. Nous voulions nous retrouver au café, mais _____.

4. J'ai fait la connaissance de mon/ma meilleur(e) ami(e) il y a
   _____ quand _____.

5. Ce matin je devais _____, mais
   _____.

6. Qu'est-ce que vous alliez faire l'année passée que vous n'avez pas fait?
   _____.

More About Object Pronouns

French can use object pronouns, **y**, **en**, and reflexive pronouns by twos. In English: *I give **the book** to **Liliane**. I give **it** (= direct object) **to her** (= indirect object).* In French, both object pronouns precede the verb.

For a review of object pronouns and reflexive pronouns see Chapters 9, 11, and 12.

Double Object Pronouns

When two object pronouns are used in a sentence or question (and also in the negative imperative), they always appear in the following order:

Object Pronouns

me (m')	le	lui	y/en + verb
te (t')	la	leur	
se	les		
nous			
vous			

The first column in this chart includes direct object, indirect object, and reflexive pronouns. The second column has only *direct* object pronouns and the third column has only *indirect* object pronouns. **Y** and **en** come last and follow each other in that order. In negative sentences, **ne** precedes the double object pronoun.

Declarative Sentences and Questions

Joseph envoyait **des mails à Corinne**. Il **lui en** envoyait.

*Joseph used to send **e-mails to Corinne**. He used to send **her some**.*

Tu **me** donnes **cette écharpe**?	*Are you giving **me that scarf**?*
Tu **me la** donnes?	*Are you giving **it to me**?*
Non, je ne **t'**offre pas **d'argent**.	*No, I'm not offering **you any***
Je ne **t'en** offre pas.	***money**. I'm not offering **you**
	***any**.*
Elle **vous** a retrouvés **à la gare**?	*Did she meet **you** (pl.) **at the**
Elle **vous y** a retrouvés?	***station**? Did she meet **you**
	***there**?*

Pronominal Verbs

Je **me** lave **les mains**. Je **me les** lave.	*I wash **my hands**. I wash **them**.*
Sonja **s'**est brossé **les cheveux**. Elle **se les** est brossés.	*Sonja brushed **her hair**. She brushed **it**.*

In the previous example, **brossés** *agrees* with the preceding direct object **les** = **les cheveux**.

Negative Imperatives

Ces cahiers? Non, ne **me les** donnez pas.	*Those notebooks? No, don't give them to me.*
Ce film? Ne **nous en** parle pas! (**parler de**)	*That movie? Don't talk to us about it!*

Double Object Pronouns with Affirmative Imperatives

All object pronouns precede *negative* imperatives, as you see in the previous examples. However, in an affirmative imperative, object pronouns *follow* the verb. When there are two object pronouns in an affirmative imperative, they occur in this order:

Affirmative Commands

le	moi (m')	nous	y	en
la	toi (t')	vous		
les	lui	leur		

The first column in the chart is made up of *direct* objects; the six pronouns in the second and third columns are all *indirect* objects; **y** and **en** follow.

Vous voulez mon billet?	*Do you want my ticket?*
—Oui, donnez-**le-moi**.	*—Yes, give **it to me**.*

Je t'apporte des gâteaux?	*Shall I bring you some cookies?*
—Oui, apporte-**m'en**.	*—Yes, bring **me some**.*
On achète ces cadeaux pour les enfants?	*Shall we buy these gifts for the children?*
—Oui, achetons-**les-leur**.	*—Yes, let's buy **them for them**.*

Exercise 14.7

Rewrite the sentences, replacing the object nouns in italics with object pronouns and using the existing object pronouns. There will be two pronouns in each sentence. Use **y** *or* **en** *when needed.*

1. Je donne *la pomme au professeur.* _____.

2. Tu *m'*offres *dix euros.* _____.

3. Nous parlions *du film à nos amis.* _____.

4. Mathieu n'a pas retrouvé *ses copains au bar.* _____.

5. Je *me* suis brossé *les dents* (f. pl.). _____.

Exercise 14.8

Translate the commands into French using the antecedent provided. Give both the familiar and the polite forms.

1. Ces cahiers? (*Give them to me.*)

   _____.

   _____.

2. De l'argent? (*Offer him some.*)

   _____.

   _____.

3. Des fruits? (*Don't eat any.*)

   _____.

   _____.

4. La voiture? (*Don't sell it to her.*)

_____.

_____.

5. Ce restaurant? (*Go there.*)

_____.

_____.

 Key Vocabulary

Les voyages et le logement (**Travel and Lodgings**)

Many travelers plan another trip as soon as they return from one. Though English is spoken in many tourist locations, you should plan to use your French when traveling in Francophone countries.

- **En voyage** *(On a Trip)*

  l'aéroport (*m.*)   (*airport*)

  aller-retour   (*round-trip*)

  l'arrêt d'autobus (*m.*)   (*bus stop*)

  l'autocar (*m.*)/le car   (*inter-city bus*)

  l'avion (*m.*)   (*plane*)

  le billet   (*ticket*)

  la carte d'embarquement
      (*boarding pass*)

  la carte d'identité   (*I.D. card*)

  une carte routière   (*road map*)

  la ceinture de sécurité   (*seat belt*)

  un chariot (à bagages)   (*[luggage]
      cart*)

  un charter   (*charter flight*)

  le compartiment   (*compartment*)

  composter le billet   (*to punch
      the ticket*)

  la consigne   (*checkroom, lockers*)

  la douane   (*customs*)

  un horaire   (*schedule*)

  la location de voitures
      (*car rental*)

  le passeport   (*passport*)

  un plan   (*city map*)

  première/deuxième classe   (*first/
      second class*)

  la porte   (*gate [airport]*)

  le quai   (*train platform*)

  la salle d'attente   (*waiting room*)

  le siège   (*seat [plane, train]*)

  le syndicat d'initiative   (*tourist
      office*)

  le tarif   (*price, fare*)

  le TGV   (*high-speed train*)

  le train   (*train*)

  un voyage d'affaires   (*business
      trip*)

- **À l'hôtel (At the Hotel)**

l'addition (f.) (bill)
l'ampoule (f.) (lightbulb)
l'annuaire (m.) (phone book)
l'ascenseur (m.) (elevator)
une auberge de jeunesse
    (youth hostel)
une chambre (room)
à un (deux) lit(s) (with one
    [two] bed[s])
un grand lit (double bed)
qui donne sur... (that looks
    out on . . .)
un chasseur (bellboy)
le chauffage (heat)
... ne marche pas.
    (. . . doesn't work.)
des cintres (m.) (coat hangers)
les clés (f.) (keys)
le coffre-fort (safe)
le couloir (hallway)
une couverture (blanket)
l'escalier (m.) (stairs)
des draps (m.) (sheets)
l'étage (m.) (floor [building])

la femme de chambre
    (chambermaid)
la climatisation (air-conditioning)
la lampe (lamp)
le loyer (rent)
un oreiller (pillow)
la note/l'addition (f.) (the bill)
la demi-pension (half-pension
    [with dinner])
tout compris (all included)
le petit déjeuner compris
    (breakfast included)
la pension complète (full pension
    [three meals])
une lumière (pour lire) (reading
    lamp)
le/la réceptionniste (desk clerk)
une salle de bain privée
    (private bath)
avec une baignoire (with a tub)
avec douche (with a shower)
du savon (soap)
le ventilateur (fan)
un verre (drinking glass)

Exercise 14.9

Review the previous vocabulary words and answer the questions.

1. Vous téléphonez à un hôtel pour réserver une chambre. Qu'est-ce que vous demandez au réceptionniste? Dites-lui ce dont vous avez besoin.

   _____.

2. Y a-t-il du vocabulaire concernant les voyages dont vous avez besoin, mais qui ne se trouve pas ici? Comment allez-vous l'apprendre?

   _____.

3. Racontez un incident qui vous est arrivé en voyage. (Utilisez le passé composé et l'imparfait.)

   _____.

Reading Comprehension

Un voyage mémorable

Moi, je n'ai pas eu une enfance très **aisée**. Ma mère était **veuve**, ayant perdu mon père assez jeune. Donc, elle nous a élevés seule, mes deux frères et moi. Évidemment nous étions pauvres. Bien sûr qu'on travaillait dur. Mon frère a même dû quitter l'école pour aider à **nous soutenir**. (Heureusement, plus tard il a réussi dans la vie et est devenu entrepreneur **à son propre compte**.) Nous ne voyagions presque jamais, sauf de rares visites chez des cousins qui avaient **une villa** en Auvergne.

Pourtant, j'allais à une bonne école où il y avait des programmes de voyage pour les élèves pendant les vacances de Pâques, au printemps. L'été où j'avais quatorze ans j'ai pu partir au Maroc, en voyage organisé. Quelle expérience et quelle révélation! J'ai voyagé bien sûr en **car** avec mes camarades de classe et nos profs. Mais les villages et les paysages marocains que nous avons vus **m'ont éblouie**, et les gens étaient vraiment formidables. Je ne vais jamais oublier notre traversée du désert, la visite à Marrakech et des villages **berbères**. Je sais qu'en rentrant je n'étais plus la même personne. Ce voyage m'a changée profondément. Mes nouveaux intérêts et cette nouvelle perspective m'ont permis de me construire une vie satisfaisante.

aisé(e) (*comfortable [financially]*)
veuve (*widow*)
nous soutenir (*to support us*)
à son propre compte (*self-employed*)

une villa (*vacation house*)
un car (*chartered bus*)
m'ont éblouie (*astonished me*)
berbère(s) (*Berber [native North African people]*)

Questions

After reading the selection, answer the questions in French.

1. Décrivez la vie d'enfance de la narratrice (à l'imparfait).

   _____.

2. Qu'est-ce qu'elle a pu faire quand elle avait quatorze ans?

   _____.

3. Qu'est-ce qui l'a impressionnée le plus?

   _____.

4. Avez-vous eu une expérience qui vous a changé(e)? Racontez-la.

   _____.

15

The Future Tense, the Conditional, and Indefinite Adjectives and Pronouns

The Future Tense

In French, the future (**le futur**) is a simple (one-word) form. The stem of the future tense is the *entire* verb infinitive. The final **-e** of the infinitive of **-re** verbs is dropped before endings are added, however. Add the following future endings to the infinitive: **-ai**, **-as**, **-a**, **-ons**, **-ez**, **-ont**.

If you think of the present tense forms of **avoir** (**j'ai**, **tu as**, **il/elle a**, **nous avons**, **vous avez**, **ils/elles ont**), the endings of the future tense are easy to learn, since they are nearly the same. Interrogatives, negatives, and object pronouns are treated as they are in the other simple conjugations, the present tense and the **imparfait**.

The Future

parler	*(to speak)*	**finir**	*(to finish)*
je	parler**ai**	je	finir**ai**
tu	parler**as**	tu	finir**as**
il/elle/on	parler**a**	il/elle/on	finir**a**
nous	parler**ons**	nous	finir**ons**
vous	parler**ez**	vous	finir**ez**
ils/elles	parler**ont**	ils/elles	finir**ont**

vendre	*(to sell)*		
je	vendr**ai**	nous	vendr**ons**
tu	vendr**as**	vous	vendr**ez**
il/elle/on	vendr**a**	ils/elles	vendr**ont**

Parleras-tu au congrès le mois prochain?	*Will you speak at the conference next month?*
Elles **finiront** leur projet ce soir.	*They will finish their project this evening.*
Non, je ne **vendrai** jamais cette vieille voiture!	*No, I will never sell this old car!*

Irregular Forms of the Future Tense

In the future tense, verb endings are the same for all French verbs. However, some verbs have *irregular stems*.

- ### *Verbs with spelling changes*

With one exception, verbs with spelling changes (Chapter 5) in the present tense have the same spelling change in the stem of *all* persons of the future. The exception: the stem of verbs like **espérer** and **préférer** is *regular* in the future (no spelling change).

On te **rappellera** ce soir, d'accord?	*We will call you again this evening, OK?*
Achèteront-ils leurs skis samedi?	*Will they buy their skis Saturday?*
J'**essaierai** ce beau manteau.	*I will try on this beautiful coat.*
Je pense que tu **préféreras** ce restaurant-là.	*I think you will prefer that restaurant.*

- ### *Verbs with irregular stems*

These irregular verbs in the future tense don't follow a specific pattern and must simply be memorized. Remember that the future verb endings are the same for all verbs:

aller (*to go*): **ir-**
avoir (*to have*): **aur-**
courir (*to run*): **courr-**
devoir (*to have to*): **devr-**
envoyer (*to send*): **enverr-**
être (*to be*): **ser-**
faire (*to make; to do*): **fer-**
falloir (*to be necessary*): **il faudra**
mourir (*to die*): **mourr-**
pleuvoir (*to rain*): **il pleuvra**
pouvoir (*to be able to*): **pourr-**

savoir (*to know*): **saur-**
venir (*to come*): **viendr-**
voir (*to see*): **verr-**
vouloir (*to want*): **voudr-**

NOTE: **Il pleuvra** (*it will rain*) and **il faudra** (*it will be necessary to*) are used
only in the singular impersonal form (**il**).

Qu'est-ce que tu **feras** pendant le week-end?	*What **will** you **do** on the weekend?*
Nous **devrons** chercher une vidéo.	*We **will have** to look for a video.*
Quels cours **voudra**-t-il suivre?	*What classes **will** he **want** to take?*
La météo dit qu'il **pleuvra** demain.	*The weather report says it **will rain** tomorrow.*
Il y aura dix invités demain soir.	*There **will be** ten guests tomorrow night.*

Exercise 15.1

Create complete sentences in the future tense using the elements provided.

Après-demain,

1. Renée/partir _____.

2. Olivier/acheter/ses/billets _____.

3. nous/prendre/le/ train _____.

4. mon amie/venir/me/voir _____.

5. vous/être/déjà/à Boston _____.

6. il/falloir/remettre/ce/devoir _____.

7. ils/avoir/besoin de/faire le marché _____.

8. tu/pouvoir/me prêter/la/voiture _____.

Uses of the Future Tense

The future tense in French is used very nearly like the English future (*will*, *shall*). It can replace the "near" future construction **aller** + infinitive (*to be going to*) and is also seen in more formal contexts. It may express a more distant future than **aller** + infinitive.

- In if-clause sentences in French, the verb after **si** (*if*) is *always* in the *present tense* when the main clause verb is in the future. **Si** elides to **s'** only before **il/ils** (**s'il vient**), and *not* before **elle/elles** (**si elle**).

Si tu le **veux**, je **prendrai** le métro.   ***If* you *want*, I *will take* the metro.**
Si elle **est** libre, nous **irons** à Paris.   ***If* she *is* free, we *will go* to Paris.**
S'ils peuvent, ils nous **aideront**.   ***If* they *can*, they *will help* us.**

- In sentences with **quand** (*when*), **lorsque** (*when*), **dès que** (*as soon as*), and **aussitôt que** (*as soon as*), the future tense is used in *both* clauses if both actions are in the future.

Je **partirai** *dès que* j'**aurai** mon diplôme.   *I **will leave** as soon as I **get** my diploma.*
Quand Marthe **arrivera**, nous **déjeunerons**.   ***When*** Marthe **gets here**, we **will have lunch**.*

 ## Exercise 15.2

Translate the sentences into French using the present tense after **si**. *In sentences with* **quand/lorsque** *(when) or* **dès que/aussitôt que** *(as soon as), remember to use the future for both clauses.*

1. If I leave, will you (*fam.*) follow me?

   _____?

2. She will come, if we invite her.

   _____.

3. As soon as it starts to snow, we (**on**) will go home.

   _____.

4. When I arrive at your (*fam.*) place, I'll wait for you.

   _____.

5. If I have the money, I'll go to Quebec (City) this summer.

   _____.

6. He'll call us as soon as he's arrived.

   _____.

Exercise 15.3

Tell about your future plans by answering these personal questions.

1. Que ferez-vous le week-end prochain? et cet été?

   _____

2. Si vous ne travaillez pas demain, que ferez-vous?

   _____

3. Où serez-vous l'année prochaine?

   _____

The Conditional

In English, the conditional is a compound verb: *would* + the infinitive. *He* ***would travel***; *we* ***would go***. It describes an action that depends on a condition: *He **would travel** if he had the time.*

In French, the conditional (**le conditionnel**), like the future tense, is a simple (one-word) verb form. The endings **-ais**, **-ais**, **-ait**, **-ions**, **-iez**, and **-aient** are added to the infinitive. Also like the future, the final **-e** of **-re** verbs is dropped before the endings are added. The conditional endings are easy to learn, as they parallel the endings of the **imparfait**.

The Conditional

parler *(to speak)*		**finir** *(to finish)*	
je	parler**ais**	je	finir**ais**
tu	parler**ais**	tu	finir**ais**
il/elle/on	parler**ait**	il/elle/on	finir**ait**
nous	parler**ions**	nous	finir**ions**
vous	parler**iez**	vous	finir**iez**
ils/elles	parler**aient**	ils/elles	finir**aient**

vendre   *(to sell)*

je	vend**rais**
tu	vend**rais**
il/elle/on	vend**rait**
nous	vend**rions**
vous	vend**riez**
ils/elles	vend**raient**

J'aimerais faire un peu plus d'exercice.	*I **would like** to do a bit more exercise.*
Nous te **vendrions** volontiers ce canapé.	*We **would** gladly **sell** you this sofa.*

Verbs with spelling changes and verbs with irregular stems in the future (see the section, "Irregular Forms of the Future Tense," earlier in the chapter) have the same irregular stems in the conditional.

Il **voudrait** des conseils sur les vols.	*He **would like** some advice on the flights.*
Nous **serions** heureux de vous inviter.	*We **would be** happy to invite you.*
J'achèterais cet ordinateur si possible.	*I **would buy** this computer if possible.*
Marc m'a dit qu'il **irait** bientôt en Europe.	*Marc told me he **would** soon **go** to Europe.*

Exercise 15.4

Create complete sentences in the conditional using the elements given.

1. je/aimer/sortir _____.

2. ils/vouloir/voyager _____.

3. Mathieu/aller/en Europe/si possible _____.

4. nous/venir/volontiers *(gladly)* _____.

5. je/prendre/deux verres d'eau _____.

6. elles/être/heureuses de/nous accompagner _____.

7. faire/tu/aussi/ce/voyage? _____?

8. est-ce que/vous/revoir/ce film/avec nous? _____?

Uses of the Conditional

The present conditional is used in French much as it is in English.

- It expresses wishes or requests politely, and is in fact used far more often than the French imperative (command) forms.

Je **voudrais** deux cafés, s'il vous plaît.	*I **would like** (May I have) two coffees, please.*
Pourriez-vous me dire où se trouve la pharmacie?	***Could** you tell me where the pharmacy is located?*

- The present conditional of **devoir** (*to have to, must*) + infinitive gives advice and recommendations.

Vous **devriez voir** le nouveau film de Michel Gondry.	*You **should see** Michel Gondry's new movie.*

- The conditional also expresses a future action as seen from a point in the past.

Je savais qu'elle y **réussirait**.	*I knew she **would pass** it (the test).*
Les Dubois m'ont dit qu'ils **seraient** en retard.	*The Dubois told me they **would be** late.*

- As in English, the conditional in French is used in the main clause of sentences with **si** (*if*) clauses. Use the **imparfait** after **si** to express a hypothetical situation: **Si j'avais le temps...** (*If I had time, . . .*). Then, use the present conditional in the main clause to say what would happen if the condition of the **si** clause were met: **... je lirais le journal tous les matins** (*. . . I would read the paper every morning*).

Si Marthe **avait** le temps, elle **voyagerait** plus.	*If Marthe **had** time, she **would travel** more.*
Si je **pouvais**, je **ferais** la cuisine régulièrement.	*If I **could**, I **would** cook regularly.*

Exercise 15.5

*Translate the sentences into French, remembering that the **imparfait** directly follows* **si** *(if) in a* **si**-*clause sentence. The conditional is then used in the main clause.*

1. If I were free, I would be with you (*fam.*).

   _____.

2. We knew Armand would come.

   _____.

3. If he came to the party, she would be happy.

   _____.

4. If you (*fam.*) had enough money, would you travel?

   _____?

5. You (*fam.*) should do some exercise.

   _____.

6. If you (*pol.*) wanted it (**le**), I would buy it.

   _____.

7. We'd like to order three cups of coffee.

   _____.

8. Léon told us that he would do the errands.

   _____.

Exercise 15.6

Answer the personal questions with a **si**-*clause sentence and the present conditional.*

1. Si vous étiez libre aujourd'hui, que feriez-vous?

   _____.

2. Si des parents ou amis proches venaient vous voir, où iriez-vous?

   _____.

3. Si vous aviez assez d'argent pour aider les pauvres, à qui ou à quoi en offririez-vous?

   _____.

The Pluperfect and the Past Conditional

Another kind of **si**-clause sentence, describing an event that *did not* occur because conditions were not met, is expressed with the *pluperfect* (**le plus-que-parfait**) and the *past conditional* (**le passé du conditionnel**). These two past compound tenses are easy to learn since they are made up of elements you already know.

The Pluperfect

The pluperfect is a compound (two-word) tense. It conveys the English *had done (something)*. It indicates a past action that occurred *before* another past action that may be either stated or implied.

The pluperfect is made up of the **imparfait** of the auxiliary verbs **avoir** or **être** + the past participle of the main verb.

J'avais terminé ce travail avant mon départ.	*I **had finished** that job before my departure.*
Gilles **était** déjà **parti** (quand je suis arrivée).	*Gilles **had** already **left** (when I arrived).*

The pluperfect is often used with **quand** and **lorsque** (both meaning *when*) and the adverb **déjà** (*already*); the more recent action is expressed in the **passé composé** or the **imparfait**.

Lorsque nous avons appelé, Marie **s'était** déjà **couchée**.	***When** we phoned, Marie **had** already **gone to bed**.*

Exercise 15.7

What had already happened when Charles got home? Complete the sentences in the pluperfect, translating the elements into French.

Quand je suis rentré,

1. Marc had gone to bed. _____.

2. the neighbor (f.) had paid a visit. _____.

3. the children had taken a bath. _____.

4. the dogs had fallen asleep. _____.

5. they (**on**) had served dinner. _____.

6. Simone had left for the airport. _____.

7. we had both (**tous les deux**) worked late. _____.

8. no one had washed the dishes. _____.

The Past Conditional

The past conditional (**le passé du conditionnel**) expresses an action or event that would have occurred if some set of conditions had been present: *We **would have come*** (*if we had known*).

The past conditional is a compound tense, formed with the conditional of the auxiliary (**avoir** or **être**) + the past participle of the main verb.

> j'aurais parlé   (*I would have spoken*)
> nous serions sortis   (*we would have gone out*)
> elles se seraient inquiétées   (*they would have worried*)

In **si**-clause sentences of "regret," the pluperfect follows the **si** clause and the past conditional is used in the main clause. The regret reflects what did not happen.

Si Mathilde **était partie** plus tôt, elle n'**aurait** pas **raté** son train.	*If Mathilde **had left** earlier, she **would** not **have missed** her train.*
Si tu en **avais goûté**, tu l'**aurais aimé**.	*If you **had tasted** some, you **would have liked** it.*

If the consequences are still going on, the *present conditional* (**le conditionnel**) may be used after the pluperfect.

Si je ne **m'étais** pas **couchée** si tard, je ne **serais** pas fatiguée aujourd'hui.	*If I **had** not **gone to bed** so late, I **would** not **be** tired today.*

Exercise 15.8

Translate each sentence ending into French, using the past conditional.

Si je n'avais pas raté (missed) *mon train,*

1. I would have been on time. _____.

2. I would have seen the movie. _____.

3. we would have come home earlier. _____.

4. you (*fam.*) would not have lost the keys. _____.

5. the children would have gone to bed. _____.

6. Cathy would have finished her homework. _____.

7. the neighbor (*f.*) would have found us. _____.

8. we would not have gotten up so late today. _____.

Advice and Regret

You have already used the verb **devoir** in the present conditional to give advice.

Tu **ne devrais pas manger** tant de sucre.	You **shouldn't eat** so much sugar.
Les étudiants **devraient faire** plus d'exercice.	Students **should exercise** more.

In the past conditional, **devoir** expresses reproach or regret, for oneself or for others.

Tu **aurais dû travailler** plus.	You **should have worked** (**studied**) more.
Mes parents **auraient dû vendre** la ferme.	My parents **should have sold** the farm.
Je **n'aurais jamais dû conduire** si vite!	I **should never have driven** so fast!

Exercise 15.9

Read about your friends' situations and give each one personal advice, using the verb **devoir**.

1. Your friend is working madly to finish a project he started months ago.

   _____.

2. Your sister has been exercising too much.

   _____.

3. Your colleague (use **vous**) brings very unwholesome-looking lunches to work.

   _____.

4. Et vous? Y a-t-il quelque chose que vous regrettez? Qu'est-ce que vous auriez dû faire?

   _____.

Tout and Other Indefinite Adjectives and Pronouns

Forms of **tout** (*all, any; everything; every one; very*) are used as adjectives, pronouns, and even adverbs. Other common indefinite adjectives and pronouns (such as **d'autres**, **quelques**, **quelqu'un**, etc.) are also used in several forms. It's best to learn them in context.

Forms and Uses of *tout*

Tout is used as an adjective, a plural pronoun, a neutral pronoun, or an adverb.

- As an adjective, **tout** (**toute/tous/toutes**) can be followed by an article (**le**, **une**, etc.), a possessive adjective (**mon**, **ses**, etc.), or a demonstrative adjective (**ce**, **cette**, etc.).

Nous avons roulé **tout** l'après-midi.	*We drove **all** afternoon.*
Voilà. Je t'ai expliqué **toutes** mes difficultés.	*There. I explained **all my** problems to you.*
Ils ont mangé **tous ces** gâteaux?	*They ate **all those** cookies?*

- The plural pronouns **tous** and **toutes** mean *everyone, every one (of them),* *all of them.* When the masculine plural **tous** is a *pronoun,* its final **-s** is pronounced: [toos]. However, the **-s** of the plural *adjective* form **tous** is silent: **tous** [too] **les gâteaux**.

Voici la liste de lectures. **Toutes** sont intéressantes.	*Here's the list of readings.* **All** *are interesting.*
Ces clients veulent **tous** [toos] acheter le même costume!	*Those customers* **all** *want to buy the same suit!*
J'ai à lire quelques études. Dans **toutes**, on parle du taux de criminalité.	*I have to read several studies. In* **all of them,** *they talk about the crime rate.*

- The neutral (masculine singular) pronoun **tout** means *all, everything.* It is used as a subject or an object.

Est-ce que **tout** va bien?	*Is* **everything** *going well?*
Vous avez **tout** compris?	*Did you understand* **everything**?
Calme-toi. Tu ne peux pas **tout** faire.	*Relax. You can't do* **everything.**

Exercise 15.10

Look at these activities and describe Aimée's trip to Tunisia using the adjective **tout,** **tous, toute**(*s*) *where possible.*

EXAMPLE: goûter aux gâteaux tunisiens *J'ai goûté à tous les*
gâteaux tunisiens.

1. voir le musée _____.

2. visiter la collection d'amphores (*amphoras*) _____.

3. marchander (*to bargain*) avec les vendeurs (*m.*) _____.

4. parcourir la vieille ville _____.

5. acheter des tapis (*m.*) _____.

6. faire le tour des mosquées (*f.*) _____.

Other Indefinite Adjectives and Pronouns

Other words and expressions in French can be used as both adjectives and pronouns.

- The following expressions have the same forms whether they precede a noun (as adjectives) or replace a noun (as pronouns).

un(e) autre *(another)*	certain(e)s *(certain [ones], some*
d'autres *(m., f. pl.)* *(others)*	*[of them])*
les autres *(m., f. pl.)* *(the others)*	le/la/les même(s) *(the same [ones])*
	plusieurs (de) *(several [of])*

Adjectives

Mes autres projets sont terminés.	***My other** projects are finished.*
Plusieurs tableaux n'étaient pas encore accrochés.	***Several** paintings were not yet hung.*
Certains invités n'ont pas pu venir.	***Certain** guests could not come.*

Pronouns

Ces films sont passionnants. **D'autres** sont moins intéressants.	*These movies are fascinating. **Others** are less interesting.*
—Oui, j'en ai vu **certains**.	*—Yes, I've seen **certain** (**ones**).*
—Nous avons peut-être regardé **les mêmes**.	*—Maybe we watched **the same ones**?*

- The following indefinite expressions have *separate* adjective and pronoun forms:

Adjectives

quelques *(pl., invariable)* (+ *noun*)	some, several
chaque *(sing., invariable)* (+ *noun*)	each, every

Pronouns

quelqu'un *(invariable)*	someone, anyone
quelqu'un de (+ *masc. adj.*)	someone, anyone (+ *adj.*)
quelque chose	something, anything
quelque chose de (+ *masc. adj.*)	something, anything (+ *adj.*)
quelques-uns/quelques-unes *(pl.)*	some, a few
chacun/chacune	each (one)

Le public a offert **quelques** idées.	*The audience came up with **some** ideas.*
Chaque élève apporte son propre goûter.	*Every pupil brings his/her own snack.*
Il y a **quelqu'un**?	*Is **anyone** there (here)?*
Je cherche **quelqu'un de** libre.	*I'm looking for **someone** (who's) free.*
Elle n'a rien à offrir. Tu as **quelque chose**?	*She has nothing to give. Do you have **anything**?*
Didier veut **quelque chose de** moins cher.	*Didier wants **something** less expensive.*
Quelques-unes de mes amies viendront plus tard.	*Several of my friends will come later.*
Nous avons vingt membres. J'ai envoyé un mail à **chacun**.	*We have twenty members. I sent an e-mail to **each one**.*

No, No One, None

Ne... aucun(e) or **aucun(e)... ne...** (*no, no one, none*) is used as a negative adjective or pronoun. It is singular and agrees in gender with the noun being used. As a pronoun, it is the subject of the sentence.

Où est le patron?	*Where's the boss?*
—Je **n'**en ai **aucune** idée.	*—I've **no** idea.*
Mes employés? **Aucun ne** pose de problèmes.	*My employees? **None** presents any problems.*

Exercise 15.11

Read these lines out loud, making the necessary substitutions and changes to the sentences orally.

1. *Plusieurs* amis ont appelé. (Quelques, Les mêmes, Tous ses, Chaque)

2. *Certains* voulaient emprunter de l'argent. (Tous, Plusieurs, Chacun)

3. *D'autres* vous ont invité. (Quelqu'un, Chacun, Les mêmes, Quelques-unes, Plusieurs)

Key Vocabulary

À la banque (Business and Banking)

Money matters go along with travel. In Europe, many transactions can be done at a post office. Currency is often exchanged at a **bureau de change**, and ATMs (**un DAB**) are widely available.

un acompte	*down payment*
la banque	*bank*
le/la banquier (-ière)	*banker*
des billets (de 10€) (*m.*)	*(10€) bills*
un bureau de change	*currency exchange*
la caisse	*cashier's desk*
le carnet de chèques	*checkbook*
la carte de crédit	*credit card*
la carte de paiement	*ATM/debit card*
le/la cassier (-ière)	*teller, cashier*
changer de l'argent	*to exchange currency*
le chèque	*check*
le chèque sans provision	*bad check*
les chèques de voyage	*traveler's checks*
le coffre-fort	*safe*
le coffre de sureté	*safe-deposit box*
le compte en banque	*bank account*
le compte courant	*checking account*
le compte d'épargne	*savings account*
le cours/le taux du change	*rate of exchange*
déposer/verser de l'argent	*to deposit money*
un dépôt en banque	*bank deposit*
le dépôt de garantie	*security deposit*
le distributeur (de billets) (DAB)	*ATM*
emprunter ≠ prêter	*to borrow ≠ to lend*
endosser un chèque	*to sign a check*
des espèces (*f.*)	*cash*
faire de la monnaie	*to make change*
la fiche/le bordereau	*deposit slip*
les frais (*m.*)	*costs*
les grosses coupures (*f.*)	*large bills*
le guichet	*(teller's) window*

les heures d'ouverture (*f.*)	*opening hours*
l'hypothèque (*f.*)	*mortgage*
les impôts (*m.*)	*taxes*
un livret	*bankbook*
le mandat	*money order*
la monnaie	*currency; change*
la petite monnaie	*small change*
le montant	*sum, total*
ouvrir un compte	*to open an account*
le paiement	*payment*
payer les factures	*to pay the bills*
la poste (la PTT)	*post office*
retirer de l'argent	*to withdraw money*
le retrait	*withdrawal*
le taux d'intérêt	*interest rate*
toucher un chèque	*to cash a check*
transférer	*to transfer*
le transfert de fonds	*funds transfer*

Exercise 15.12

Answer the questions using vocabulary from the previous list.

1. Vous venez d'arriver dans un pays francophone. Trouvez les termes ci-dessus (*above*) qui correspondent à ce que vous devez faire le premier jour.

   _____

2. Si vous alliez rester un an dans le pays, qu'est-ce que vous auriez besoin de faire?

   _____

3. Qu'avez-vous fait la dernière fois que vous êtes allé(e) à la banque? Quelles transactions avez-vous faites? Avec qui avez-vous parlé?

   _____.

Reading Comprehension

Rêves d'avenir

Je ne suis ni **avare** ni particulièrement ambitieux. Au début, je voudrais avoir une vie assez aventureuse (je ne crains pas le risque) mais aussi **saine** et productrice. On m'a parlé de certaines professions où on gagne **un tas d'argent**, mais qui **à la longue** se révèlent **décevantes**, sur le plan intellectuel ou de la satisfaction. Je sais que les Français se voient depuis longtemps hostiles à l'idée de l'argent **en soi**. Quelles en sont les raisons? On dit que ça s'explique par l'excellente sécurité sociale dont bénéficient tous les citoyens: **assurances** médicales, vacances annuelles, allocations familiales, **assurance chômage**, pension de retraite, etc. Est-ce qu'on travaille moins en France parce que ces systèmes fonctionnent bien? Peut-être. Mais, moi, je sais que cette attitude culturelle date depuis **des siècles** (« l'argent ne fait pas **le bonheur** »). Même aujourd'hui, face aux grands entrepreneurs et au matérialisme contemporain auquel presque tout le monde **se plaît**, le Français se dit que gagner l'argent pour l'argent est **méprisable**. Les vraies **valeurs** se trouvent **ailleurs**.

Qu'est-ce que je ferai dans dix ans? J'aurai assez pour vivre, **un boulot** qui me plaira (dans le domaine de la sociologie peut-être), une vie de famille solide et une maison confortable avec un jardin. Je lirai beaucoup, je jouerai au tennis et nous ferons des voyages à l'étranger. Mais pour le moment, il me faut trouver un job d'été...

> rêves d'avenir (m.) *future dreams*
> avare *greedy*
> sain(e) *healthy*
> un tas de/d' *a pile of, whole lot of (fam.)*
> à la longue *in the long run*
> décevant(e)(s) *disappointing*
> en soi *in and of itself*
> des assurances (f.) *insurance*
> l'assurance chômage (f.) *unemployment insurance*
> des siècles (m.) *centuries*
> le bonheur *happiness*
> se plaît (**se plaire à**) *enjoys*
> méprisable *contemptible*
> les valeurs (f.) *values*
> ailleurs *elsewhere*
> un boulot *a job (fam.)*

Questions

After reading the selection, answer the questions in French.

1. Que pensez-vous de l'attitude que décrit ce narrateur? À votre avis, est-ce logique?

    _____.

2. L'attitude envers (*toward*) l'argent est-elle différente dans votre pays? En quoi diffère-t-elle?

    _____.

3. À votre avis, est-ce que les diverses classes sociales ont des idées différentes à cet égard? Pourquoi?

    _____.

4. Et vous? Où serez-vous dans dix ans? Que ferez-vous?

    _____.

16

The Subjunctive

The Subjunctive Mood

We talk about the *tense* (past, present, future) of a verb; but we can also talk about its *mood*. You have used the *indicative* mood all along; it states facts and asks questions. The *conditional* (Chapter 15) is a mood expressing an action that depends on other conditions.

The *subjunctive* mood expresses the speaker's feelings about an action or state of being. It often concerns necessity, importance, or a request. In English, for example:

Indicative	Subjunctive
She goes to work at eight.	It's necessary *that she go* to work at eight.
We are on time.	They ask *that we be* on time.

In English, choosing the subjunctive creates a formal impression. But, in French, for certain well-defined grammatical contexts, the subjunctive must be used.

The French subjunctive most often appears in the second clause of a two-clause sentence. It is linked to the first clause by **que/qu'** (*that*).

The verb in the main clause can be in the present, past, or future, while the verb in the second clause remains in the *present* subjunctive.

Principal Clause (Indicative)	+ que/qu' +	Dependent Clause (Subjunctive)
Il faut	**que**	tu **fasses** la vaisselle.
It's necessary	*that*	*you **do** the dishes.*
Il fallait	**que**	tu **fasses** la vaisselle.
It was necessary	*that*	*you **do** the dishes.*

334

Il est nécessaire	**qu'**	il **sorte** plus.
It's necessary	*that*	*he **go out** more.*
Il sera nécessaire	**qu'**	il **sorte** plus.
It will be necessary	*that*	*he **go out** more.*

Forms of the Present Subjunctive

For all but two verbs (**être** and **avoir**), drop the final **-ent** from the third-person plural form of the present indicative (**ils/elles finissent**), and add the subjunctive endings: **-e**, **-es**, **-e**, **-ions**, **-iez**, and **-ent**.

Irregular verbs (see the upcoming section, "Irregular Subjunctives") use the same endings, but may have irregular *stems* in the present subjunctive. It is best to learn their forms individually or as small groups.

The Present Subjunctive

	parler	**finir**	**vendre**	**dormir**
	(TO SPEAK)	*(TO FINISH)*	*(TO SELL)*	*(TO SLEEP)*
que je	parl**e**	finiss**e**	vend**e**	dorm**e**
que tu	parl**es**	finiss**es**	vend**es**	dorm**es**
qu'il/elle/on	parl**e**	finiss**e**	vend**e**	dorm**e**
que nous	parl**ions**	finiss**ions**	vend**ions**	dorm**ions**
que vous	parl**iez**	finiss**iez**	vend**iez**	dorm**iez**
qu'ils/elles	parl**ent**	finiss**ent**	vend**ent**	dorm**ent**

Il est important **que tu choisisses** tes amis.	*It's important **that you choose** your friends.*
Il ne faut pas **que tu t'endormes** trop tôt.	*You mustn't **fall asleep** too early.*

Some subjunctive forms resemble the present indicative and the **imparfait**. Context will show if the verb is in the subjunctive. For example, look for a clause starting with **que/qu'**.

Exercise 16.1

Change these subjunctive verb forms from singular to plural, or from plural to singular (**que je** *becomes* **que nous**; **que tu** *becomes* **que vous**; **qu'il/qu'elle** *becomes* **qu'ils/qu'elles**).

1. que je choisisse _____
2. que tu achètes _____
3. que vous dormiez _____
4. que nous parlions _____
5. qu'il finisse _____
6. qu'elles vendent _____
7. que j'entende _____
8. que tu partes _____

Irregular Subjunctives

As previously mentioned, all French verbs except **être** and **avoir** use the subjunctive endings **-e**, **-es**, **-e**, **-ions**, **-iez**, and **-ent**. The following verbs show irregularities in their *stems*.

Verbs with a Second Subjunctive Stem

Like regular verbs, some irregular verbs derive their subjunctive stem from the **ils/elles** form of the present indicative. Others use a *second stem* in the **nous** and **vous** forms of the subjunctive, derived from the stem of the **nous** form of the present indicative: **nous prenons: que nous prenions** and **que vous preniez**.

		Indicative	Subjunctive
boire	(*to drink*)	ils/elles boivent	que je **boive**
		nous buvons	que nous **buvions**
croire	(*to believe*)	ils/elles croient	que je **croie**
		nous croyons	que vous **croyiez**
devoir	(*to have to*)	ils/elles doivent	que je **doive**
		nous devons	que nous **devions**
prendre	(*to take*)	ils/elles prennent	que je **prenne**
		nous prenons	que vous **preniez**
recevoir	(*to receive*)	ils/elles reçoivent	que je **reçoive**
		nous recevons	que nous **recevions**
venir	(*to come*)	ils/elles viennent	que je **vienne**
		nous venons	que vous **veniez**
voir	(*to see*)	ils/elles voient	que je **voie**
		nous voyons	que nous **voyions**

Il faut que Robert **boive** moins!   *It's necessary that Robert **drink** less!*

Il est important que vous **voyiez** le patron.   *It's important that you (go) **see** the boss.*

Seven More Irregular Subjunctive Forms

Several irregular verbs have completely irregular subjunctive stems. In addition, the **nous** and **vous** forms of **être**, **avoir**, **aller**, and **vouloir** have unique stems within their conjugation.

	faire	**pouvoir**	**savoir**
	(TO DO; TO MAKE)	*(TO BE ABLE TO)*	*(TO KNOW)*
que je	**fasse**	**puisse**	**sache**
que tu	**fasses**	**puisses**	**saches**
qu'il/elle/on	**fasse**	**puisse**	**sache**
que nous	**fassions**	**puissions**	**sachions**
que vous	**fassiez**	**puissiez**	**sachiez**
qu'ils/elles	**fassent**	**puissent**	**sachent**

	être	**avoir**	**aller**	**vouloir**
	(TO BE)	*(TO HAVE)*	*(TO GO)*	*(TO WANT)*
que je	**sois**	**aie**	**aille**	**veuille**
que tu	**sois**	**aies**	**ailles**	**veuilles**
qu'il/elle/on	**soit**	**ait**	**aille**	**veuille**
que nous	*soyons*	*ayons*	*allions*	*voulions*
que vous	*soyez*	*ayez*	*alliez*	*vouliez*
qu'ils/elles	**soient**	**aient**	**aillent**	**veuillent**

Pour réussir au travail, il faut que vous **soyez** à l'heure, que vous **fassiez** de votre mieux, que vous **ayez** de la patience et que vous **sachiez** vous entendre avec vos collègues.

*To succeed at work, it's necessary that you **be** on time, that you **do** your best, that you **be** patient and that you **know how** to get along with your colleagues.*

Pronouncing *avoir* and *aller* in the Subjunctive

Practice pronouncing these forms of **avoir** (*to have*) and **aller** (*to go*).

que j'**aie**	[eh]	que j'**aille**	[ahy]
qu'elles_**aient**	[eh]	qu'ils_**aillent**	[ahy]

Exercise 16.2

Complete the sentences with the present subjunctive using the verbs in parentheses.

1. Il faut que tu _____ à l'heure. (être)

2. Il est essentiel qu'il _____ de son mieux. (faire)

3. Il est important que nous _____ au bureau. (aller)

4. Il ne faut pas que vous y _____ trop tard. (rester)

5. Il n'est pas essentiel que je _____ tout aujourd'hui. (faire)

6. Il faut que nous _____ contents. (être)

7. Il est nécessaire qu'elle _____ réussir. (vouloir)

8. Il n'est pas important qu'ils _____ toujours raison. (avoir)

9. Il est important que tu _____ l'adresse. (savoir)

10. Il faut que vous _____ me comprendre. (pouvoir)

Exercise 16.3

*Read your friend's remark and give him personal advice, using **il faut que tu...** or another expression of necessity.*

1. Je veux trouver de nouveaux amis. _____.

2. Je veux parler mieux le français. _____.

3. Il y a trop de stress dans ma vie. _____.

4. Comment passer le week-end? _____.

Uses of the Subjunctive

The subjunctive occurs in dependent clauses after specific types of main clauses: expressions of *necessity*, *opinion*, *emotion*, *possibility*, and *doubt*, both impersonal and personal. The two clauses must have different subjects, with the impersonal **il** or a specific person in the first clause.

The Subjunctive with Expressions of Necessity

Impersonal expressions of necessity include these main clauses:

il est essentiel de/que   (*it's essential to/that*)
il est important de/que   (*it's important to/that*)
il est indispensable de/que   (*it's indispensable/crucial to/that*)
il est nécessaire de/que   (*it's necessary to/that*)
il est temps de/que   (*it's time to/that*)
il faut (que)   (*it's necessary to/that, one/you must*)
il ne faut pas (que)   (*you/one must not*)
il vaut mieux (que)   (*it's better to/that*)

Il était temps **que** tu **fasses** ce voyage.	*It was time **that** you **make** (**made**) that trip.*
Il vaut mieux **que** je **m'en aille**.	*I had **better go**.*
Il faudra **que** les électeurs **prennent** la décision.	*It will be necessary that the voters **make** the decision. (Voters will have to **make** the decision.)*

Before an infinitive, impersonal expressions of necessity (**il faut**, **il est nécessaire de**, etc.) express a *general* obligation. Except for the verbs **falloir** and **valoir**, they all use the preposition **de/d'** before an infinitive.

Il fallait arriver au bureau avant neuf heures.	*We **had to arrive** at the office before nine o'clock.*
Il est important de bien **faire attention**.	*It's very important to pay close **attention**.*

A Word About *falloir* and *valoir*

Falloir (il faut) and **valoir (il vaut mieux)**, followed by an infinitive or by a subjunctive clause with **que**, are conjugated in the impersonal form only (with **il**). Note that the following chart also reviews all the verb conjugations you have learned. See the Table of Contents or the Index in this book for the chapters that introduce these conjugations.

	falloir	**valoir mieux**	
	(TO BE NECESSARY)	*(IT'S BETTER [THAT])*	
present	**il faut**	**il vaut mieux**	(que je parte)
passé composé	**il a fallu**	**il a mieux valu**	(que je parte)
imparfait	**il fallait**	**il valait mieux**	(que je parte)
near future	**il va falloir**	**il va mieux valoir**	(que je parte)
future	**il faudra**	**il vaudra mieux**	(que je parte)
conditional	**il faudrait**	**il vaudrait mieux**	(que je parte)
past conditional	**il aurait fallu**	**il aurait mieux valu**	(que je parte)
pluperfect	**il avait fallu**	**il avait mieux valu**	(que je parte)

Il va falloir **que nous partions** tôt.

*It's going to be necessary **that we leave** early.*

Il va falloir **partir** tôt.

*It's going to be necessary **to leave** early.*

Il valait mieux **que tu fasses** ton jogging.

*It was better **that you go** for your run.*

Il valait mieux **faire** ton jogging.

*It was better **to go** for your run.*

The Subjunctive with Other Impersonal Expressions

Other impersonal expressions may express *opinion, emotion, possibility,* or *doubt.* As with **il faut**, etc., use of the infinitive in the dependent clause creates a generalization; use of the subjunctive makes it personal.

Opinion and Emotion

il est bizarre de/que   *(it's bizarre [strange] to/that)*
il est bon de/que   *(it's good to/that)*
il est dommage de/que   *(it's a pity to/that)*
il est étrange de/que   *(it's strange to/that)*
il est injuste de/que   *(it's unfair [unjust] to/that)*
il est inutile de/que   *(it's useless to/that)*
il est juste de/que   *(it's fair [just] to/that)*
il est préférable de/que   *(it's preferable to/that)*
il est regrettable de/que   *(it's regrettable to/that)*
il est utile de/que   *(it's useful to/that)*

Il est dommage qu'Hélène soit *It's too bad Hélène is late.*
en retard.

Il serait utile que tu lises *It would be useful for you to*
les dossiers.   *read the files.*

Il est préférable de manger *It's preferable to eat more*
plus de légumes.   *vegetables.*

Il est injuste de ne pas **pouvoir** *It's unfair not to be able to sue.*
porter plainte.

Possibility and Doubt

il est douteux que   *(it's doubtful that)*
il est impossible de/que   *(it's impossible to/that)*
il est peu probable que   *(it's improbable that)*
il est possible de/que   *(it's possible to/that)*
il semble que   *(it seems that)*
il se peut que   *(it's possible that)*

Some of these expressions (**il est douteux**, **il est peu probable**, **il se peut**, and **il semble**) *cannot* be used with the infinitive; they are always followed by **que/qu'** + subjunctive.

Il est douteux que cette loi   *It's doubtful that this law will*
soit approuvée.   *be approved.*

Il se peut que nos amis **s'en** *It's possible that our friends*
aillent tôt.   *will leave early.*

 ## Exercise 16.4

Giving advice to a friend, match elements in the two columns to create six sentences in the affirmative or negative. Use an impersonal expression + **que tu...** *.*

1. il est dommage   faire de ton mieux

2. il est bon   choisir bien ta carrière

3. il est douteux   pouvoir avoir un bon salaire

4. il se peut   aller dans une autre ville

5. il est bizarre   s'ennuyer

6. il est utile   savoir t'avancer

_____

_____

_____

_____

_____

Impersonal Expressions with the Indicative

When impersonal expressions imply *certainty* or *probability*, they are followed by the *indicative* in the dependent clause.

il est certain que   (*it's certain that*)
il est clair que   (*it's clear that*)
il est évident que   (*it's obvious that*)
il est probable que   (*it's probable [likely] that*)
il est sûr que   (*it's certain that*)
il est vrai que   (*it's true that*)

Il est probable qu'ils sont chez eux aujourd'hui.	***It's likely that they're** at home today.*
Il est évident qu'il y a assez de place.	***It's obvious that there is** enough room.*

But in *negative* or *interrogative* sentences with these expressions, the subjunctive is used in the second clause to express uncertainty, doubt, or conjecture.

Il n'est pas certain que je puisse vous rejoindre.	***It isn't certain that I can** join you.*
Est-il vrai qu'elle fasse toujours du violon?	***Is it true that she still plays** the violin?*

Exercise 16.5

*Create sentences in the affirmative (**que** followed by the future tense) or in the negative (**que** followed by the subjunctive) starting each sentence with an impersonal expression like **Il (n')est (pas) vrai que...** .*

1. je/devenir/célèbre _____.

2. nous/pouvoir/retourner/dans la lune _____.

3. les artistes/être/appréciés _____.

4. les gens/cesser d'avoir/des enfants _____.

5. je/faire/une découverte importante _____.

6. mon copain/écrire/un best-seller _____.

The Subjunctive with Personal Expressions of Volition, Emotion, and Doubt

Personal expressions of will, preference, emotion, and doubt require the subjunctive in the dependent clause *if there is a change of subject.* If there is no change of subject, use an infinitive.

Je **préfère que tu** le **fasses**.	*I prefer that you do it.* (two subjects)
Je **préfère** le **faire** moi-même.	*I prefer to do it myself.* (one subject)

- *Personal expressions of will and preference*
  aimer mieux que   *(to prefer, like better that)*
  aimer que   *(to like, love that)*
  demander que   *(to ask that)*
  désirer que   *(to desire, want that)*
  exiger que   *(to demand, require that)*
  préférer que   *(to prefer that)*
  souhaiter que   *(to wish, hope that)*
  vouloir bien que   *(to be willing that)*
  vouloir que   *(to want, to wish that)*

The verb **espérer** (*to hope*) is always followed by the *indicative*, never the subjunctive. When it is followed by the future indicative tense, **espérer** is often used instead of **souhaiter** (*to wish, hope*) and so avoids use of the subjunctive (which always follows **souhaiter que**).

Papa **espère que** tu **seras** heureux.	*Dad **hopes** you **will be** happy.*
Papa **souhaite que** tu **sois** heureux.	*Dad **wants** you to **be** happy.*
Je **voudrais partir** assez tôt.	*I **would like to leave** rather early.*
Nos amis **exigent que** nous **soyons** à l'heure.	*Our friends **demand that** we **be** on time.*

- *Personal expressions of emotion*
  avoir peur que/de   (*to fear, be afraid that/of*)
  être content(e) que/de   (*to be happy that/to*)
  être désolé(e) que/de   (*to be sorry that/to*)
  être furieux (furieuse) que   (*to be angry that*)
  être heureux (heureuse) que/de   (*to be happy that/to*)
  être ravi(e) que/de   (*to be delighted that/to*)
  regretter que/de   (*to regret, be sorry that/to*)
  être surpris(e) que/de   (*to be surprised that/to*)

Je **regrette que** tu ne **puisses** pas me rejoindre.	*I **am sorry that** you **can't** come with me (join me).*
Mes parents **sont ravis que** nous y **allions**.	*My parents **are delighted that** we **are going** there.*
Avez-vous **peur qu**'il **neige**?	*Are you **afraid** it **will** (**may**) snow?*
Elle **serait heureuse de dîner** avec nous.	*She **would be happy to have dinner** with us.*

- *Personal expressions of doubt and uncertainty*
  je doute que   (*I doubt that*)
  je ne suis pas sûr(e) que/de   (*I'm not sure that*)
  je ne suis pas certain(e) que/de   (*I'm not certain that*)

Les jeunes **doutent que** leurs parents **aient** raison.	*Young people **doubt that** their parents **are** right.*
Ariane **n'est pas sûre de pouvoir** venir ce soir.	*Ariane **isn't sure she can** come this evening.*
Vous **n'êtes pas certains qu**'ils **sachent** l'adresse?	*You **aren't sure** they **know** the address?*

The verbs **penser** (*to think*) and **croire** (*to believe*) can (optionally) be followed by the subjunctive, but only when they are used in a *negative* or *interrogative* sentence.

Tu ne penses pas que le patron **ait** de bonnes idées?	***You don't think*** *the boss* ***has*** *good ideas?*
Croyez-vous que le bus **soit** à l'heure?	***Do you think*** *the bus* ***is*** (***will be***) *on time?*

Exercise 16.6

Create complete sentences from the elements provided. In the second clause, use the present subjunctive (if there are two subjects in the sentence) or an infinitive (if there is just one subject).

1. je/douter que/on/savoir/quoi faire _____.

2. nous/préférer/se mettre d'accord _____.

3. les profs/exiger que/nous/apprendre _____.

4. nous/avoir peur que/le train/être en retard _____.

5. mon père/regrette de/quitter son emploi _____.

6. elle/espérer/voyager/en été _____.

7. vous/ne pas être sûrs que/je/réussir _____.

8. le patron/vouloir que/tu/revenir _____.

Exercise 16.7

Complete the sentences with a personal statement.

1. Je regrette que/de _____.

2. Ma sœur est ravie que/de _____.

3. Je suis furieux (-euse) que _____.

4. Les électeurs sont surpris que _____.

5. Mon meilleur ami doute que _____.

The Past Subjunctive with *avoir* or *être*

The *past subjunctive*, formed with the subjunctive of **avoir** or **être** + the past participle, is used in specific situations.

It indicates the opinion or feeling of the first subject about something *that has already occurred*. The verb in the past subjunctive follows **que** and always introduces a second subject.

Elle est mécontente que **nous ne soyons pas venus**.
She is unhappy that **we did not come**.

Je suis ravie que **tu aies réussi**!
I am delighted that **you passed** (the exam)!

Il est dommage qu'**Annie soit tombée malade**.
It is a shame that **Annie got sick**.

Subjunctive Versus Infinitive

Spoken French often avoids the subjunctive by substituting an infinitive for a subjunctive clause, or by choosing the prepositional form of certain conjunctions. Compare the following sets of sentences:

Je demande **que tu fasses** le lit.
I ask **that you make** the bed.

Je **te** demande **de faire** le lit.
I ask **you to make** the bed.

Il faut **que nous nous entraînions**.
It is necessary **that we work out**.

Il faut **nous entraîner**.
It's necessary **for us to work out**.

Nous devons **nous entraîner**.
We must **work out**.

The conjunctions in the left-hand column below take the subjunctive. However, they have corresponding simple or compound *prepositions*, which are easier to use. The prepositions (in the middle column) precede an infinitive. Such sentences have a single subject.

à condition que	**à condition de**	*provided that*
afin que	**afin de**	*in order to*
à moins que	**à moins de**	*unless*
avant que	**avant de**	*before*
pour que	**pour**	*in order to*
sans que	**sans**	*without*

On mange bien **pour rester** en bonne santé.	*We eat well (**in order**) **to stay** in good health.*
Simon retrouve son sac à dos **avant de sortir**.	*Simon finds his backpack **before going out**.*
Je serai avec vous, **à moins d'avoir** à travailler.	*I'll be with you, **unless I have to work**.*

Exercise 16.8

*Give a personal answer (affirmative or negative) to each question, using the preposition given in parentheses. Each answer will have a single subject (**je**).*

1. Pourquoi étudiez-vous le français? (pour) _____.

2. Allez-vous déménager? (à condition de) _____.

3. Changerez-vous d'emploi? (à moins de) _____.

4. Partirez-vous en voyage? (avant de) _____.

5. Pouvez-vous travailler la nuit? (sans) _____.

Key Vocabulary

Liens d'amitié (Friendship Ties)

Skills in your new language are most valuable when meeting new friends and associates. You already know most of the vocabulary and constructions you'll need. Review the Greetings at the beginning of this book.

Je voudrais vous (te) présenter...	*I'd like to present . . .*
Voici mon ami(e)...	*This is my friend . . .*
Je m'appelle...	*My name is . . .*
Enchanté(e) (d'avoir fait votre connaissance).	*Delighted to meet (have met) you.*
Moi de même.	*Likewise.*
D'où venez-vous? (D'où êtes-vous?)	*Where are you from?*
Depuis quand êtes-vous à... ?	*How long have you been in . . . ?*
Combien de temps allez-vous rester ici?	*How long are you going to stay here?*

Où habitez-vous?	*Where do you live (are you staying)?*
Que faites-vous dans la vie?	*What do you do?*
Vous avez une famille? des enfants?	*Do you have a family? Children?*
À quoi vous intéressez-vous?	*What are your interests?*
Vous aimez les sports (l'art, le cinéma...)?	*Do you like sports (art, movies . . .)?*
Êtes-vous libre de... ? (Tu es libre de... ?)	*Are you free to . . . ?*
Voudriez-vous (Veux-tu) y aller ensemble?	*Would you like to go there together?*
Oui, d'accord. Avec plaisir.	*Yes, fine. With pleasure.*
Volontiers.	*Gladly.*
Oui, j'aimerais bien. (Oui, je voudrais bien.)	*Yes, I'd like to.*
Désolé(e), je suis occupé(e).	*Sorry, I'm busy.*
C'est dommage. Je suis pris(e) ce soir-là.	*What a shame. I'm busy that evening.*
Pourriez-vous venir nous (me) voir... ?	*Can you come see us (me) . . . ?*
Je pourrais venir vous chercher, si vous voulez.	*I can come pick you up, if you wish.*
Je peux (Nous pouvons) vous téléphoner?	*May I (we) call you?*
Quel est votre numéro de téléphone?	*What's your phone number?*
Quelle est votre adresse? votre adresse courrielle?	*What's your address? Your e-mail?*
Nous vous attendrons (Je vous attendrai) à...	*We'll (I'll) wait for you at . . .*

Exercise 16.9

Use the vocabulary list and your own experience to answer these questions.

1. Vous faites la connaissance d'un(e) collègue, d'un(e) camarade de classe ou d'un(e) voisin(e). Posez-lui plusieurs questions.

   _____.

2. On vous invite à sortir, mais vous devez refuser. Comment refuser poliment?

   _____.

3. Vous avez un ami assez timide. Donnez-lui des conseils pour faire la connaissance de quelqu'un.

   _____.

Reading Comprehension

Créer des liens

Comment créer des liens avec **autrui**? On dit que de nos jours, il devient de plus en plus difficile de faire connaissance avec les autres et de se faire de véritables amis. Les circonstances de la vie moderne **ne se prêtent pas** bien à la création de liens: les longues heures de travail et de transport urbain et de **banlieue**, les **grands immeubles pleins d'**appartements où les voisins **ne se voient guère**, la disparition graduelle des petits commerces et des cafés du quartier. Même le mauvais temps peut y contribuer, si on ne sort pas de chez soi. Enfin, nous disposons d'un vaste monde virtuel: la télévision, Internet, les blogs et les jeux électroniques, même les lecteurs MP3. Tous servent à nous rendre isolés tout en nous donnant l'illusion de ne pas l'être. On peut même être seul **au sein de** la famille. Si on le leur demandait, les **internautes** et les téléspectateurs **nieraient** être isolés.

Et pourtant nous avons besoin les uns des autres. Il est clair qu'entre amis la vie et la conversation s'améliorent, **la santé** physique et mentale aussi. Des études scientifiques l'ont prouvé. Quoi faire alors? Il faut d'abord comprendre qu'on a besoin de l'autre. Il est indispensable que les communautés se mettent à créer des opportunités de se réunir et qu'elles sachent attirer des personnes de diverses générations et de divers intérêts: le sport, la politique, l'artisanat, le volontarisme, la musique, le jardinage, les livres... Ce ne sera pas facile au début, mais il faudra le faire.

créer des liens   (*making ties*)
autrui   (*other people*)
ne se prêtent pas   (*don't lend themselves to*)
de banlieue   (*suburban*)
de grands immeubles (*m.*)   (*large apartment buildings*)
plein(e)(s) de   (*full of, filled with*)
ne se voient guère   (*hardly see each other*)
au sein de   (*in the heart of*)
internautes (*m., f.*)   (*Web surfers*)
nieraient   (*would deny*)
la santé   (*health*)

Questions

After reading the selection, answer the questions in French.

1. Donnez un résumé du passage, en une ou deux phrases, si possible.

   _____

   _____.

2. Êtes-vous d'accord avec cet auteur? Avez-vous eu cette expérience?

   _____

   _____.

3. À votre avis, quelle en est la solution?

   _____

   _____.

4. Et vous, comment créez-vous des liens?

   _____

   _____.

Answer Key

Answers in the form of questions are generally shown with inversion. Sample answers to personal questions are labeled: (*Answers will vary.*).

Chapter 1
Nouns, Articles, and Descriptive Adjectives

1.1　1. l'　2. l'　3. la　4. la　5. l'　6. le　7. l'　8. la　9. la　10. la
11. le　12. la　13. la　14. le

1.2　1. des artistes　2. des hors-d'œuvre　3. les milieux　4. les étudiantes
5. des Français　6. des cafés　7. les chapeaux　8. les eaux　9. les fenêtres
10. des choix　11. des préférences　12. les travaux　13. les nez　14. des cours

1.3　1. (the) window　2. cycling　3. (the) hospitals *m.*　4. a guard/watchman
5. (the) writers *m.*　6. (the) friends　7. (some) hats *m.*　8. (the) work　9. (some)
choices *m.*　10. a course/class　11. (some) hors d'œuvres *m.*　12. (some) men *m.*
13. (the) skin　14. the German woman　15. (the) books *m.*　16. a place　17. (some)
stories/histories *f.*　18. a clock　19. (some) cakes/cookies *m.*　20. the woman

1.4　1. intéressante　2. naïve　3. agréable　4. sérieuse　5. jaune　6. marron
7. bleue　8. costaude　9. fière　10. chic　11. chère　12. conservatrice
13. belle　14. grosse　15. active　16. gentille　17. travailleuse　18. drôle
19. vieille　20. heureuse

1.5　1. vieil　2. difficile　3. belle　4. gentille　5. jaunes　6. sincères
7. grand　8. ancienne　9. anciens　10. bon marché/pas chers　11. drôle
12. intéressant

1.6　1. des lampes bleues　2. des amis sérieux　3. les chats gris　4. des Suisses
sympathiques　5. des personnes costaudes　6. les beaux appartements　7. de jeunes
garçons　8. des examens difficiles　9. les derniers trains　10. les quartiers anciens

1.7　1. les hommes bruns　2. la femme gentille/sympathique　3. des chaussures
rouges　4. les vieux hôtels　5. les beaux appartements　6. les cours intéressants
7. les héros courageux　8. les hors-d'œuvre riches　9. des voitures chères　10. des

351

Américains idéalistes   11. les grandes universités   12. de nouveaux livres   13. les chapeaux orange   14. des tragédies tristes   15. les professeurs travailleurs   16. des personnes fières

Chapter 2
The Verbs *être* and *avoir*, Subject Pronouns, and Negation

2.1   1. Vous   2. Je   3. Elles   4. Nous   5. Tu   6. Je   7. Ils   8. Ils
9. Georges et Marilyn, vous   10. Il

2.2   1. est   2. sont; est   3. sont   4. sont   5. est   6. sommes   7. sont
8. sont   9. suis; êtes   10. est

2.3   1. Je suis dans le jardin.   2. Les fleurs rouges sont belles.   3. Elles sont sur la table.   4. Nous sommes devant la bibliothèque.   5. Charles est professeur. Il est jeune et intelligent.   6. Tu es triste et fatigué? Je suis désolée!   7. Marie-Laure est en voiture. Elle est en retard!   8. Vous êtes du Canada?   9. On est sympathique dans ce quartier.
10. Sara et Patrick sont en voyage. Ils sont à Montréal.

2.4   1. Elle est   2. Ce sont   3. Il est   4. C'est   5. C'est   6. Il est

2.5   1. sommes; sont, es; ce sont   2. es; suis   3. êtes; nous sommes, est   4. est; C'est; sommes   5. vous êtes; Je suis, est; Ce sont   6. Non, il est généralement en retard.
7. Non, elle est martiniquaise.   8. Non, ils sont italiens.   4. Non, il est ingénieur.
10. Non, ils sont coptes.

2.6   1. sommes en vacances   2. sont en train de   3. est de retour   4. est d'accord
5. est en coton   6. es prêt; sommes sur le point de

2.7   1. quelquefois/parfois, très   2. ici, aujourd'hui   3. maintenant
4. Aujourd'hui, un peu   5. assez/plutôt   6. souvent   7. toujours   8. mais, très
9. très   10. beaucoup, trop   11. un peu   12. là-bas

2.8   1. elle n'est pas vieille.   2. Non, je ne suis pas acteur/actrice.   3. Non, nous ne sommes pas en retard.   4. Non, je ne suis pas à la maison.   5. Non, ils ne sont pas de retard.   6. Non, elles ne sont pas d'accord.   7. Non, Georges n'est pas en train de danser.
8. Non, tu n'es pas/vous n'êtes pas trop fière.

2.9   1. J'ai un vélo rouge.   2. Arthur a une nouvelle amie.   3. Tu as beaucoup de devoirs?   4. Elles n'ont pas de jardin.   5. Je n'ai pas d'amis ici.   6. Simon et Annie ont une vieille voiture/une voiture ancienne.   7. Nous n'avons pas de bicyclettes.   8. Il y a trop de touristes en ville.   9. Il y a un problème difficile en classe.   10. Il n'y a pas assez de restaurants à l'université.

2.10   1. Il n'y a pas beaucoup de devoirs ce soir.   2. Nous avons un rendez-vous aujourd'hui.   3. Il n'y a pas de voiture devant la maison.   4. J'ai un dictionnaire.   5. Ils ne sont pas en classe ce matin.   6. Mes parents n'ont pas de nouvel appartement.   7. Je ne suis pas souvent à la montagne le week-end.   8. Elles ont des idées concrètes.   9. Tu a des copains ici?   10. Il y a assez de livres pour les étudiants.

2.11   1. J'ai froid et j'ai sommeil.   2. Il a vingt-cinq ans.   3. Nous avons besoin d'un nouvel appartement.   4. Elle a de la chance à Las Vegas!   5. Nous avons faim! Nous avons envie de déjeuner.   6. Tu as honte de tes mauvaises notes?   7. Les enfants ont soif. 8. La réunion a lieu ce soir.   9. Elle n'a pas mal à la tête aujourd'hui.   10. Ils n'ont pas l'habitude de dîner tard.

2.12   (*Answers will vary.*)   1. J'ai dix-neuf (19) ans.   2. Oui, j'ai froid en hiver ici. 3. J'ai toujours raison dans les discussions politiques!   4. Non, les fêtes n'ont pas lieu ce week-end.   5. Oui, j'ai mal à la tête quand j'ai faim.   6. Non, il n'a pas l'air intelligent. 7. Ah oui, j'ai envie de danser ce soir.   8. Quelquefois, les étudiants ont sommeil en classe. Le professeur a rarement sommeil en classe.   9. Non, le professeur n'a pas toujours raison. 10. Oui, les petits enfants ont souvent peur des clowns.

2.13   1. une cuisine moderne   2. un appartement agréable   3. des placards spacieux 4. un fauteuil bleu marine   5. devant la grande fenêtre   6. une vieille glace   7. un four propre   8. un nouvel ordinateur   9. une salle de bains privée   10. de longs rideaux   11. les murs intérieurs   12. un grand salon/un salon spacieux   13. un très beau piano   14. une table avec six chaises   15. un frigo blanc

QUESTIONS: (*Answers will vary.*)   1. La maison (Elle) est vieille.   2. La cuisine (Elle) est grande/spacieuse.   3. Le piano (Il) est dans le salon.   4. Non, Jean-Pierre (Il) n'a pas de salle de bains privée.   5. Non, il a une chambre ensoleillée.   6. L'ordinateur de Jean-Pierre (Il) est dans la bibliothèque.

Chapter 3
Days and Months, Regular *-er* Verbs in the Present Tense, and Interrogatives

3.1   (*Answers will vary.*)   1. lundi, mardi, mercredi, jeudi et vendredi   2. samedi et dimanche   3. le lundi, le mercredi et le vendredi après-midi; quelquefois, le soir   4. Nous sommes lundi. Nous sommes en mars.   5. (Je préfère) le printemps.   6. décembre, janvier, février (mars); (juin) juillet, août, septembre   7. *Action de grâces*: novembre (U.S.), octobre (Canada); *Noël*: décembre; *Pâques*: mars ou avril; *Fête nationale*: juillet (le 4 juillet); *Canada Day*: juillet (le 1 juillet); *le jour de la Bastille*: juillet (le 14 juillet); *Ramadan*: août, septembre, octobre; *Hanoukka*: décembre; *Fête de la Reine*: mai; *jour du Souvenir*: novembre

3.2   1. nous parlons   2. elle écoute   3. j'aime   4. elles louent   5. vous utilisez 6. nous habitons   7. j'arrive   8. il déteste   9. tu rêves   10. elle trouve

3.3   1. nous adorons   2. je danse   3. tu regardes   4. vous expliquez   5. ils cherchent   6. elle ferme   7. tu parles   8. j'explique   9. elles utilisent   10. vous détestez

3.4   (*Answers will vary.*)   1. ne chante pas bien   2. ne travaille pas à la banque 3. n'écoute pas souvent la radio   4. ne rêvons pas en classe   5. n'aime pas mieux le jogging   6. ne cherchent pas de nouvelle maison

3.5   1. J'écoute   2. étudions   3. n'aime pas   4. utilisez   5. parles 6. refusent   7. adorent regarder   8. ne danses pas   9. aimons mieux   10. trouve

3.6   1. déteste travailler   2. cherche un emploi   3. n'aime pas voyager   4. parle au professeur après le cours   5. n'étudions pas beaucoup

3.7   1. écoute   2. étudie, sont   3. arrivons   4. chantent, jouent   5. parle 6. parlent, ont   7. sommes, regarder   8. n'ai, louer, j'habite

3.8   (*Answers will vary.*)   1. Tu es/Vous êtes étudiante, n'est-ce pas?   2. Est-ce que Léonard et Claudine/Est-ce qu'ils aiment le cinéma?   3. Les voisins/Ils ont un petit chien, n'est-ce pas?   4. Est-ce que vous avez des opinions politiques?   5. Micheline/Elle aime mieux jouer au golf, n'est-ce pas?   6. Est-ce que tu travailles/vous travaillez dans une librairie?   7. Raoul/Il joue de la guitare, n'est-ce pas?   8. Est-ce que vous écoutez la radio vendredi soir?

3.9   1. As-tu un chat?   2. Sylvie joue-t-elle du piano?   3. Êtes-vous américain? 4. Aimes-tu mieux le tennis ou le golf?   5. Jouons-nous au Scrabble ce soir?   6. Les enfants ont-ils faim?   7. Jacques n'est-il pas professeur?   8. Ne travailles-tu pas dans une librairie?

3.10   (*Answers will vary.*)   1. Habitez-vous Boston?   2. Êtes-vous professeur? 3. Travaillez-vous en ville?   4. Aimez-vous la musique?   5. Aimez-vous mieux le cinéma? 6. Jouez-vous d'un instrument de musique?   7. Avez-vous des enfants?   un chien ou un chat?   8. Êtes-vous marié(e)?, etc.

3.11   1. Who is arriving on Saturday?   2. What are the children looking for? 3. Whom are you inviting?   4. What is she looking/does she look at? *or* What is she watching?   5. What do you like/love?   6. Qui est-ce?   7. Qu'est-ce qui arrive? 8. Qu'est-ce que tu as?/Qu'as-tu?   9. Qui écoute-t-elle?/Qui est-ce qu'elle écoute? 10. Que regardez-vous?/Qu'est-ce que vous regardez?

3.12   1. What restaurant do you like?   2. When are we arriving at the movies? 3. Why is Marie-Laure happy?   4. How are you?   5. What's the math teacher like? 6. Comment allez-vous?   7. Pourquoi les étudiants aiment-ils la musique?   8. Où est la librairie?   9. Quels sont les meilleurs cours?   10. Quand étudies-tu?/Quand est-ce que tu étudies?

3.13   (*Answers will vary.*)   1. Je vais bien, merci.   2. Ma famille est à San Francisco. 3. Je suis de (la ville de) Québec.   4. Oui, j'ai une voiture; j'ai une petite Smart Car. 5. Elle/Il est en ville. J'habite dans la rue...   6. Elle est grande/Il est grand et moderne.

3.14   1. un anniversaire spécial   2. un voyage dangereux   3. une fête élégante 4. un bruit curieux/étrange   5. des rêves passionnants   6. une amie fidèle   7. un enfant aveugle   8. un escalier étroit   9. des phrases difficiles   10. des clés lourdes

QUESTIONS: (*Answers will vary.*) 1. Elle est dans une petite ville de Normandie, en France. 2. Non, elle n'est pas seule; elle est avec des amis canadiens.   3. L'école offre des cours de langue, d'art, d'histoire et de musique.   4. Elles étudient le français.   5. Elle est archéologue et il y a des villages très anciens dans les environs.   6. Non, il ne travaille pas; ce sont des vacances tranquilles.

Chapter 4
Numbers, Dates, and Time and Regular *-ir* Verbs in the Present Tense

4.1   1. quatre, cinq, six   2. huit, dix, douze   3. cinquante, soixante, soixante-dix
4. vingt-huit, trente-cinq, quarante-deux   5. soixante-dix, soixante et onze, soixante-douze
6. cinquante-cinq, quarante-quatre, trente-trois

4.2   1. vingt   2. quatre-vingt-dix   3. soixante-trois   4. quarante-cinq
5. cinquante-quatre   6. quatre-vingt-seize

4.3   1. deux euros cinquante centimes   2. quatre euros soixante-quinze centimes
3. quarante-quatre euros   4. cent dix euros   5. cent quatre-vingt-huit euros   6. neuf
mille quatre cent cinquante euros

4.4   1. À Paris, le seizième arrondissement est très élégant.   2. La Sorbonne est dans le
cinquième arrondissement.   3. L'appartement d'Alain est au quatrième étage.   4. C'est
la première fois que je visite Paris.   5. C'est la vingtième fois qu'il regarde le premier *Harry
Potter*!

4.5   1. Le dix-huit juin dix-neuf cent (mille neuf cent) quarante, c'est l'appel du général
de Gaulle vers la France libre.   2. Le vingt-quatre octobre dix-neuf cent (mille neuf cent)
vingt-neuf, c'est le Krach de Wall Street.   3. Le sept décembre dix-neuf cent (mille neuf
cent) quarante et un, c'est l'attaque japonaise de Pearl Harbor.   4. Le vingt-neuf mars dix-
neuf cent (mille neuf cent) soixante-treize, c'est la fin de la guerre du Viêt-Nam.   5. Le
onze septembre deux mille un, ce sont les attentats contre le World Trade Center.   6. Le
dix novembre dix-neuf cent (mille neuf cent) quatre-vingt-neuf, c'est la destruction du mur
de Berlin.   7. Le premier janvier dix-huit cent (mille huit cent) soixante-trois, c'est la
proclamation de l'émancipation des esclaves américains.   8. Le vingt-deux novembre dix-
neuf cent (mille neuf cent) soixante-trois, c'est l'assassinat de John F. Kennedy.

4.6   (*Answers will vary*.)   1. Aujourd'hui, c'est le vingt-cinq mars deux mille huit.
2. a. le premier janvier b. le quatre juillet c. le quatorze juillet d. le premier juillet e. le vingt-
cinq décembre f. le trente et un octobre g. le premier avril   3. Mon anniversaire, c'est le
dix-neuf août.   4. ... dix-neuf cent soixante-quatorze./ ... dix-neuf cent soixante et onze.
5. L'anniversaire de notre mariage, c'est le vingt et un juin; l'anniversaire du mariage de mes
parents est le trente septembre.

4.7   1. Il est six heures moins le quart.   2. Il est neuf heures moins vingt.   3. Il est
midi et demi.   4. Il est deux heures.   5. Il est trois heures et quart/trois heures quinze.
6. Il est dix heures moins dix.

4.8   (*Answers will vary*.)   1. Il est midi et demi.   2. Il est dix heures du matin.
3. Il est six heures du soir.   4. Il est huit heures du soir.   5. Il est neuf heures et demie
du soir.

4.9   1. Nous choisissons.   2. Tu agis bien.   3. Elles rougissent.   4. Je réussis.
5. Les enfants grandissent.   6. On élargit la rue.   7. Vous maigrissez.   8. Je ralentis la
nuit.   9. Les feuilles jaunissent.   10. Nous finissons de travailler.

4.10   1. blanchissez pâlissez   2. remplissons   3. choisis   4. grandissent
5. finissent   6. Réussissez   7. grossir   8. rougit

4.11   1. au magasin de fruits et légumes   2. à la confiserie   3. à la librairie   4. à la papeterie   5. chez le fleuriste   6. à l'agence de voyages   7. à la pharmacie   8. chez l'opticien

4.12   (*Answers will vary.*)   1. œufs, beurre, sel, herbes, poivre   2. farine, beurre, chocolat, sucre, œufs, vanille   3. ananas, oranges, melons, cerises, fraises, bananes, pommes, etc.   4. eau, pommes de terre, tomates, carottes, champignons, haricots verts, céleri, petits pois, herbes, huile d'olive, sel, poivre, etc.

4.13   (*Answers will vary.*)   1. les assiettes, les fourchettes, les couteaux, les cuillères, les verres, les serviettes   2. la carte   3. le café au lait, le pain, les croissants, le beurre, la confiture   4. lait, sucre   5. une salade, une tartine ou un sandwich   6. la viande, les légumes

QUESTIONS: (*Answers will vary.*)   1. Ils déjeunent à une heure.   2. Ils déjeunent dans une brasserie du quartier.   3. Non, le restaurant est plein.   4. Il est plein parce que c'est un jour de fête.   5. Ils choisissent le premier étage pour avoir le menu complet.   6. Il prend le menu du jour: une soupe, du saumon poché, des pommes de terre, des légumes, de la salade, un dessert et une boisson.

Chapter 5
Regular *-re* Verbs in the Present Tense and *-er* Verbs with Spelling Changes

5.1   1. Tu descends?   2. Je perds.   3. Nous répondons.   4. Xavier vend un camion.   5. Elles rendent visite à Grand-père.   6. Vous ne répondez pas.   7. Nous attendons Charles.   8. Ils défendent leurs clients.   9. L'étudiant ne perd pas de temps.   10. Entendez-vous?   11. Rend-elle le livre?   12. Je réponds au téléphone.

5.2   1. perd souvent   2. défends rarement   3. réponds actuellement   4. rendent toujours   5. En ce moment, j'attends   6. Entendez, maintenant   7. vendons bientôt   8. prochaine, répond   9. rend quelquefois/parfois   10. descends plus tard   11. perdent très peu

5.3   (*Answers will vary.*)   1. J'étudie le français depuis six mois.   2. Je suis étudiant depuis 1990 (dix-neuf cent quatre-vingt-dix).   3. Oui, je parle espagnol depuis 1995 (dix-neuf cent quatre-vingt-quinze).   4. J'habite mon appartement depuis 2005 (deux mille cinq).   5. Je travaille depuis cinq ans. Je suis dans la compagnie depuis janvier 2003 (deux mille trois).   6. Je passe du temps avec elle depuis mars 2006 (deux mille six).

5.4   1. Nous partageons le sandwich.   2. Ils mangent bien.   3. Quand commençons-nous à parler?   4. Tu prononces la phrase.   5. Les voisins logent deux étudiants.   6. Lancez-vous la nouvelle entreprise?   7. Charlotte mélange les ingrédients.   8. Annonçons-nous la fête?   9. Échangez-vous des livres?   10. Ne songes-tu pas aux vacances?   11. Le professeur exige les devoirs.   12. Nous obligeons les enfants à manger des légumes.   13. Traces-tu le projet?   14. Le patron n'engage pas de nouveaux employés.   15. Les pronoms remplacent les noms.

5.5   1. Nous achevons le travail.   2. Marthe pèse les oignons.   3. Promènes-tu le chien?   4. Ils emmènent le cheval.   5. Léon enlève les livres.   6. Je n'amène pas Christine ce soir.   7. Nicolas et Lise élèvent bien les enfants.   8. Qu'achètes-tu?   9. Pierre soulève les gros cartons.   10. Le guide mène les touristes à l'hôtel. 11. N'achetez-vous pas d'œufs?   12. Nous levons la main en classe.   13. Émile élève-t-il des lapins?   14. Elles achèvent de parler.   15. Je n'achète pas les provisions.

5.6   1. Nous espérons réussir.   2. Célèbrent-elles l'anniversaire?   3. J'espère voyager en été.   4. Le professeur répète la question.   5. Elle ne possède pas de voiture.   6. Il exagère.   7. L'article révèle la vérité.   8. Considères-tu les faits?   9. Ne répétez-vous pas le cours?   10. Tu inquiètes tes parents!   11. Nous suggérons un bon film.   12. Ne complètes-tu pas le devoir?   13. Préférez-vous le café ou le thé?   14. Elle cède la voie à l'autre voiture.   15. Christophe préfère les haricots verts.

5.7   1. Comment vous appelez-vous?   2. Je m'appelle Rachelle.   3. Appelles-tu Marc?   4. Je ne jette pas les magazines/les revues.   5. Comment épelle-t-on le nom? 6. Nous projetons des vacances.   7. J'appelle Maman le samedi.   8. Elle rappelle Zoé ce soir.   9. Il ne jette pas le ballon.   10. Nous renouvelons la salle de bains.   11. Elle rejette l'idée.   12. Jetez-vous les vieux journaux?   13. Je renouvelle le passeport. 14. Quand projette-t-on le film?   15. Que projettent-ils?

5.8   1. J'envoie des cartes postales.   2. Tu n'essaies pas de réussir.   3. Le petit chien aboie.   4. Elle essaie d'être patiente.   5. Il appuie ma demande.   6. N'employez-vous pas d'ordinateur?   7. Nous employons des dictionnaires.   8. J'essuie la cuisinière. 9. Tu paies le déjeuner.   10. Évelyne nettoie la cuisine.   11. Ennuie-t-elle les étudiants? 12. J'appuie sur les touches.   13. Nous payons leur salaire.   14. Employez-vous bien l'argent?   15. Ils envoient les livres.

5.9   1. Achètes   2. préfèrent   3. projette   4. envoie   5. partageons 6. j'essaie   7. commençons   8. prononçons   9. je jette   10. annonce   11. lève 12. manger   13. voyagent   14. paies   15. appelez   16. répète

5.10   1. un rouge à lèvres   2. un/des caleçon(s)   3. des lames de rasoir   4. des boucles d'oreilles   5. une ceinture   6. une montre   7. un jean   8. un maillot de bain   9. un sac (à main)   10. des mouchoirs   11. un sèche-cheveux   12. une veste   13. des lunettes de soleil   14. un parapluie   15. un portefeuille   16. une jupe   17. (de) la crème solaire   18. un peigne   19. des pantoufles   20. du dentifrice

5.11   (*Answers will vary.*)   1. J'ai besoin d'une brosse à cheveux (d'un peigne, d'une brosse à dents, de dentifrice, de démêlant, de shampooing, de crème solaire, de déodorant, de fil et d'une aiguille, etc.).   2. Dans la valise je place un chapeau (un foulard, un jean, une jupe, des lunettes de soleil, un appareil-photo, un maillot de bain, un pyjama, des sandales, des shorts, des T-shirts, des sous-vêtements [des slips et des soutiens-gorges], etc.).   3. J'achète du dentifrice (des mouchoirs, des lunettes de soleil et des sandales, etc.).

QUESTIONS: (*Answers will vary.*)   1. Elles descendent au centre-ville pour visiter les commerces. Elles visitent l'agence de voyages; elles achètent des provisions et des cadeaux; elles déjeunent.   2. Elles préfèrent les petits commerces (la boulangerie, la boucherie, la papeterie, etc.).   3. Elles feuillettent les brochures de voyage, parce qu'elles projettent des vacances.   4. Elles commandent une bisque de homard, une salade verte et une bombe glacée.

Chapter 6

Expressing the Future with *aller*, Prepositions, and the Verb *faire*

6.1   1. vas   2. va   3. allons   4. va   5. allez   6. vont

6.2   (*Answers will vary.*)   1. Où allez-vous étudier cet après-midi? —Je vais/Nous allons étudier au café (à la bibliothèque, à la maison, etc.).   2. Quand les étudiants vont-ils quitter le campus? —Ils vont quitter le campus vers cinq heures de l'après-midi.   3. Combien d'argent allez-vous gagner cet été? —Je vais/Nous allons gagner deux mille dollars, peut-être.   4. Quels aliments va-t-elle acheter? —Elle va acheter des provisions et des boissons. 5. Que vas-tu nettoyer ce week-end? —Je vais nettoyer la cuisine et la salle de bains...

6.3   1. vais arriver cet après-midi   2. vont visiter le musée la semaine prochaine 3. allons voyager l'année prochaine   4. Vas-tu travailler ce week-end?   5. Où allez-vous (aller)?

6.4   1. sans Nicolas   2. pour réussir   3. en classe/en cours   4. sans attendre 5. pour payer   6. en été

6.5   1. Non, elle répond aux élèves (au serveur, à la femme du prof).   2. Non, nous parlons du livre de sociologie (de la musique des Beatles, des sports américains).   3. Non, il va arriver de la librairie (du cours d'anglais, de Paris).

6.6   1. la classe/le cours de Michelle   2. la carte du restaurant   3. le sac du professeur   4. la maison de Monsieur Dupont   5. les livres des enfants   6. la facture de la pharmacie   7. la veste du voisin   8. la brosse à dents de l'enfant

6.7   Sketches or simple drawings of: 1. a book next to a pencil   2. an apple in between a banana and a sandwich   3. a wallet (with a part showing out) in a handbag   4. a window to the left of a teacher's desk

6.8   1. est hors de la maison.   2. travaille loin de chez elle.   3. passons à droite de l'église.   4. est derrière le cinéma.   5. est à l'est de la France.   6. sont sur la table.

6.9   1. Après le petit déjeuner on va/nous allons attendre Marceline.   2. Je pense/ crois qu'elle va être prête dans deux heures.   3. Je finis le devoir en une heure et demie. 4. On va/Nous allons à pied au supermarché?   5. Joseph et Christine vont en Suisse pour trois semaines.

6.10   1. Je téléphone au professeur.   2. Je jette les vieux journaux.   3. Je pense aux vacances d'été.   4. Je parle des vedettes de cinéma.   5. J'ai besoin d'un verre de limonade.   6. Lesquelles   7. Dans laquelle   8. Desquels   9. Auxquels 10. Lequel

6.11   (*Answers will vary.*)   1. La Belgique, l'Allemagne, la France, la Pologne, l'Angleterre, l'Autriche, la Grèce, l'Espagne, etc.   2. La Tunisie, le Maroc, l'Algérie 3. La Jordanie, la Syrie, Israël, le Liban, la Libye, etc.   4. La Chine, le Japon, le Viêt-Nam, l'Indonésie, la Thaïlande, etc.

6.12   1. en; à   2. en, en   3. à   4. au   5. en   6. Au   7. en Thaïlande 8. en Afghanistan   9. du   10. de   11. d'   12. d'   13. des   14. de

6.13   1. J'adore faire de la photographie.   2. Aujourd'hui, il fait beau, mais il fait frais.
3. Marguerite fait la cuisine et les enfants font la vaisselle.   4. Je fais le plein le vendredi.
5. Les clowns font peur aux enfants.   6. Il fait la connaissance du professeur.   7. Avant
de faire un voyage, quand faites-vous les valises?   8. À l'école, je fais de mon mieux.
9. Marie-Christine fait de la médecine.   10. Nous faisons partie d'une association sportive.

6.14   (*Answers will vary.*)   1. Je préfère faire les devoirs le soir, mais pas trop tard.
2. Oui, je fais de la musique. Je joue de la clarinette depuis dix ans (depuis 2000). (Non, je ne
fais pas de musique.)   3. Aujourd'hui, il fait beau et frais; il fait un peu de vent. Plus tard il
va peut-être pleuvoir.   4. Quand il fait chaud, je porte un T-shirt, un short et des sandales.
5. Chez moi, je fais le ménage. Mais en réalité, nous faisons le ménage ensemble.   6. Je fais
la lessive et la vaisselle. Je fais aussi le lit.

6.15   (*Answers will vary.*)   1. la pluie: la tempête, l'orage, les nuages, le vent, le tonnerre,
la foudre, etc.   2. la lune: l'étoile, le soleil, la comète, le ciel, la terre, la roche, etc.   3. la
montagne: la falaise, la colline, la roche, le canyon, le volcan, la grotte, etc.   4. l'océan:
la mer, la vague, la plage, la dune, la baie, la côte, le marais, etc.   5. une catastrophe: un
tremblement de terre, le réchauffement de la planète, l'ouragan, l'inondation, l'incendie, etc.

QUESTIONS: (*Answers will vary.*)   1. Ils ont l'intention de voyager pour une semaine/de faire
un voyage d'une semaine. Ils préfèrent faire du cyclisme (de la bicyclette).   2. Il fait froid
et il pleut en Bretagne. Chez moi, il fait assez froid en hiver, mais il ne neige pas.   3. Une
copine, Mireille, va accompagner les deux amis, pour la compagnie et pour partager les frais.
Moi, j'aime voyager avec un ou deux amis.   4. Ce week-end, je fais le ménage, les courses
et les devoirs. Je fais aussi une randonnée à bicyclette et je fais la cuisine pour les amis. En
vacances, je fais des voyages; je fais aussi de la voile et du canoë-kayak.

Chapter 7
Irregular Verbs I and Verb + Verb Constructions

7.1   1. Je sers le café.   2. Les chats dorment beaucoup.   3. Vous ne partez pas
bientôt?/Ne partez-vous pas bientôt?   4. Éliane part pour New York.   5. Dors-tu?
6. Nous sortons/On sort vendredi.   7. Papa sert le dîner.   8. Le témoin ment-il?   9. Je
sens des difficultés ici.   10. Sentez-vous la soupe?

7.2   1. Il revient à deux heures.   2. Nous tenons les colis.   3. Elles viennent
plus tard.   4. Je viens de déjeuner.   5. Viens-tu d'arriver?   6. Renée et Yves ne
viennent pas maintenant.   7. Je tiens beaucoup à mes amis.   8. Devenons-nous riches?
9. Tiens-tu compte des autres?   10. J'obtiens les livres pour toi.

7.3   1. Je lis le soir.   2. Écrivez-vous le devoir?   3. Nous ne disons pas toujours au
revoir.   4. Quand écrivent-ils des mails?   5. Vous dites toujours la vérité.   6. Que dit-
il?   7. Elle écrit une lettre.   8. Le professeur décrit-il le problème?   9. Les étudiants
ne lisent pas assez.   10. À qui dis-tu bonjour?

7.4   1. Je mets l'assiette sur la table.   2. La table est libre? Vous permettez?
3. Bats-tu le tapis?   4. Que mettez-vous quand il pleut?   5. Le joueur bat les records.
6. On ne met pas la voiture dans la rue.   7. Promettez-vous d'arriver à l'heure?   8. Nous

ne mettons pas/On ne met pas de chaussures dans la maison.   9. Elle remet le rendez-vous.
10. Je remets mon devoir.

7.5   1. Je dois   2. pouvons   3. veux   4. peuvent   5. J'aperçois   6. déçoivent
7. doivent   8. peut   9. Dois   10. Voulez

7.6   1. Pouvez-vous lire ceci?   2. Je ne veux pas dire au revoir.   3. Il doit deux cents
euros à Claudine.   4. Tu ne dois pas mentir.   5. Quel beau tableau! Il doit être très
vieux/ancien.   6. Nous ne pouvons pas/On ne peut pas venir ce soir.   7. Anne n'est pas
ici; elle doit être malade.   8. Nous voulons/On veut élire un bon président.   9. Reçois-tu
des mails d'Yvonne?   10. Ils veulent acheter une maison.   11. Puis-je/Est-ce que je peux
avoir deux tasses de café?   12. Nous devons/On doit faire les devoirs.   13. Elle ne peut
pas partir à l'heure.   14. Elles doivent dîner avant de partir.   15. Ne voulez-vous pas
regarder le film?   16. J'aperçois deux voitures au loin.

7.7   (*Answers will vary.*)   1. Je veux lire des romans, je veux sortir avec mes amis et
aller à la montagne ou à la plage, mais je dois faire les devoirs et le ménage.   2. Ce week-
end? Je peux choisir: je peux dormir tard, je peux promener le chien et je peux faire la cuisine
pour les copains. Mais avant de préparer le repas, je dois faire le marché.   3. Je dois
téléphoner à mes parents, payer les factures et ranger l'appartement.   4. En semaine, il faut
donner à manger au chien, aller au travail, aller à des réunions le soir ou à ma leçon de piano.
Il faut aussi faire de l'exercice, manger bien et dormir assez.   5. D'habitude, chaque jour je
reçois trois ou quatre coups de téléphone, vingt ou trente mails et une lettre.

7.8   1. à   2. à   3. —   4. à   5. à   6. d'   7. —   8. à   9. de   10. à
11. de   12. de   13. —   14. à   15. de   16. —   17. de   18. de

7.9   1. J'aime danser.   2. Nous préférons/On préfère aller à pied.   3. Elles peuvent
jouer au golf aujourd'hui.   4. Dois-tu partir?   5. Il ne veut pas déjeuner.   6. Nous
venons/On vient aider Guy.   7. Espérez-vous faire votre droit?   8. J'aide mon ami à
finir/à terminer ses devoirs.   9. Nous réussissons/On réussit à gagner.   10. Invites-tu
Madeleine à manger avec nous?   11. Est-ce que je commence à travailler à dix heures?
12. J'enseigne à l'élève à écrire.   13. Nous refusons/On refuse de répondre.   14. Ils
permettent au voisin d'utiliser/d'employer la tondeuse.   15. Tu oublies d'acheter le pain.
16. Elle promet à Maman de faire les courses.   17. J'empêche les étudiants de faire des
fautes.   18. Il regrette de venir/d'arriver si tard.

7.10   (*Answers will vary.*)   1. un roman, un roman policier, des contes, des magazines,
le journal, même des essais et des biographies, etc.   2. des logiciels, une imprimante, un
moteur de recherche, une souris, le clavier, l'écran, Internet, un programme de traitement
de texte, etc.   3. cartes postales, feuilles de papier, un stylo, un timbre, enveloppes, etc.
4. (de l')édition, (de l')éditeur, (du) rédacteur, (de) la publicité, (des) librairies, (des) lecteurs,
(des) critiques, (des) comptes rendus, etc.

QUESTIONS: (*Answers will vary.*)   1. Elle a vingt-quatre ans et elle fait des études
d'hôtellerie.   2. Elle doit choisir une carrière, un emploi ou un stage.   3. À l'avenir elle
veut tenir une auberge dans un village voisin avec son copain.   4. Elle peut rester à Lyon
travailler dans un restaurant ou bien elle peut aller à l'étranger faire un stage, peut-être en
Amérique du Nord.   5. Elle va pouvoir téléphoner, écrire ou envoyer des mails à sa famille.

Chapter 8
Irregular Verbs II and Relative Pronouns

8.1 1. Françoise connaît bien la ville de Dakar. 2. Nous savons jouer du trombone.
3. Savez-vous qui arrive ce soir? 4. Ils connaissent des artistes italiens. 5. Sait-on
pourquoi Roland ne vient pas? 6. Je reconnais toujours la voix de mon ami. 7. Connais-
tu Adélaïde? 8. Les étudiantes paraissent heureuses aujourd'hui.

8.2 1. a, d, g, h 2. b, c, e, f

8.3 (*Answers will vary.*) 1. Je connais bien Chicago et San Francisco; j'aime les
quartiers près du lac et de la baie. 2. Oui, je connais Paris et Genève; à Paris je préfère le
septième arrondissement, et à Genève, le centre-ville. 3. Je connais les romans d'Alexandre
Dumas et de Colette; je connais les films de François Truffaut, d'Agnès Varda et de Michel
Gondry. 4. Oui, je sais qu'ils sont nés en Russie, mais je ne sais pas dans quelle ville.
5. Je sais nager et faire de l'équitation. 6. Je sais faire la lessive et la cuisine; je sais aussi
faire un peu de couture.

8.4 1. Nous croyons. 2. Voit-elle bien? 3. Sophie et Bernard croient que nous
venons. 4. Vois-tu Nicole quelquefois? 5. Je crois que non. 6. Elles croient en
Einstein! 7. Ils revoient le soleil au printemps. 8. Nous ne voyons pas/On ne voit pas Jo
très souvent. 9. Il croit que c'est vrai. 10. Qui vois-tu?/Qui est-ce que tu vois?

8.5 1. Nous courons le samedi matin. 2. Rit-elle beaucoup? 3. Les chiens
sourient-ils? 4. Elles découvrent des effets importants. 5. À qui offres-tu les livres?
6. J'ai un rhume... Je souffre! 7. Courez-vous si vous êtes en retard? 8. N'ouvrent-ils
pas les fenêtres la nuit? 9. Chaque fois qu'il parle, nous rions. 10. Je fais de l'exercice,
mais je ne cours pas. 11. Les spectateurs accourent quand ils voient l'acteur. 12. Elle
offre un repas aux sans-abri. 13. Parcourt-il l'Europe? 14. Il fait froid. Je couvre les
enfants. 15. Ouvrez-vous les portes maintenant?

8.6 1. Les étudiants suivent des cours intéressants. 2. Qu'est-ce que vous craignez?
3. Nous vivons à Lausanne. 4. Produit-on beaucoup de vin en Californie? 5. Il
atteint finalement la destination. 6. Nous conduisons lentement quand il neige. 7. Le
gendarme poursuit les suspects. 8. Je vis pour faire du ski! 9. Ils feignent de lire le
livre de maths. 10. Jacqueline ne conduit pas en hiver. 11. Revit-elle les événements
difficiles? 12. Je ne suis pas de cours de physique. 13. Traduisent-elles les documents?
14. Vous peignez quand vous avez le temps? 15. Tu ne conduis pas raisonnablement!
16. Généralement un orage ne détruit pas beaucoup d'arbres.

8.7 1. Je suis Jacques et David. 2. Nous n'atteignons pas nos buts.
3. Construisent-elles une nouvelle maison? 4. Les gendarmes poursuivent la voiture
rouge. 5. Agnès suit un cours d'anglais. 6. Chloé et moi, nous réduisons l'utilisation
d'énergie. 7. Les tortues vivent-elles longtemps? 8. Tu conduis vite! 9. Il vit
pour manger; elle mange pour vivre. 10. Les enfants feignent d'être malades. 11. Ne
peint-elle pas la chambre? 12. Crains-tu le froid? 13. En hiver, nous plaignons
surtout les sans-abri. 14. La France produit beaucoup de fromage. 15. Je ne vis pas
à la campagne. 16. Quelle carrière poursuivez-vous? 17. Dans quelle ville vivent les
Dubonnet? 18. Traduisez-vous les poèmes de Baudelaire? 19. Oncle Olivier revit sa
jeunesse. 20. Les étudiants de chimie ne suivent pas de cours faciles.

8.8   1. Je vais voir un ami qui attend au café.   2. Papa achète une voiture qui a cinq ans.   3. Tu veux voir le film qui décrit la vie en Afrique?   4. Nous aimons les étudiants qui répondent correctement.   5. J'ai un nouveau parapluie qui marche très bien dans le vent.   6. Thérèse fait un beau tableau que tu vas aimer.   7. Ils rangent la chambre que vous allez peindre.   8. Je jette les vieux catalogues que nous recevons.   9. Tu choisis le professeur qu'elle aime aussi.   10. On appelle les clients que Pierre voit souvent. 11. C'est le moment où je préfère voyager.   12. Nous pensons au jour où Marc arrive. 13. Ils achètent l'appartement où je vais habiter.   14. C'est une région chaude où on produit beaucoup d'oranges.   15. Vous allez dans un musée où ils offrent des visites guidées.

8.9   1. où   2. qui   3. que   4. qui   5. où   6. qui   7. où   8. qui 9. que   10. que   11. où   12. que

8.10   1. avec qui/avec lequel   2. à côté de qui/à côté duquel   3. avec lequel 4. sous lesquels   5. sur laquelle   6. à qui/auxquels   7. à qui/auquel   8. pendant laquelle (où)   9. avec lesquelles   10. à côté duquel   11. dans lequel/où   12. dans lesquelles/où

8.11   1. Voici la librairie anglaise dont Liliane parle.   2. C'est le dictionnaire français dont j'ai besoin.   3. J'ai une bonne amie dont la famille est très aimable.   4. Roger est un jeune avocat dont le travail est difficile.   5. Ce sont des examens de maths dont les étudiants ont peur.   6. Les notes dont j'ai honte sont mauvaises.   7. Le travail dont Catherine est fière est impeccable.   8. Voilà un collègue dont je connais la femme.   9. La glace dont Nathalie a envie est délicieuse.   10. J.-P. Melville est un cinéaste classique dont nous apprécions les films.

8.12   1. ce qui   2. ce qu'   3. De quoi   4. ce dont/de quoi   5. Ce qui   6. ce qui   7. De quoi   8. ce que   9. ce que   10. Ce dont

8.13   (*Answers will vary*.)1. Quelle heure est-il?   2. De quoi parlez-vous?/De quoi est-ce que vous parlez?   3. Qui invites-tu samedi?/Qui est-ce que tu invites samedi?   4. Que faites-vous?/Qu'est-ce que vous faites?   5. Que veux-tu? (Que voulez-vous)/Qu'est-ce que tu veux? (Qu'est-ce que vous voulez?)   6. Auxquels pensent-elles?/À qui pensent-elles?/ Auxquels est-ce qu'elles pensent?   7. Qu'est-ce qui arrive?   8. De quoi Julie a-t-elle besoin?/De quoi est-ce que Julie a besoin?   9. Quel temps va-t-il faire demain?/Quel temps est-ce qu'il va faire demain?   10. Que voyez-vous au festival?/Qu'est-ce que vous voyez au festival?/Où voyez-vous de nombreux films?

8.14   (*Answers will vary*; *most also have a feminine form.*) 1. le technicien, le physicien, le chimiste, l'informaticien, le médecin, le vétérinaire, le biologiste, l'astronome, le chercheur, le paléontologue, l'archéologue, etc.   2. l'artiste, le peintre, le sculpteur, le poète, l'écrivain, le danseur, le musicien, l'acteur, le chanteur, le cinéaste, l'architecte, le photographe, etc. 3. le commerçant, l'entrepreneur, le cadre, l'agent commercial, le banquier, l'agent de change, l'expert-comptable, le publicitaire, le vendeur, etc.   4. l'artisan, l'électricien, le plombier, le menuisier, le jardinier, le cordonnier, etc.   5. l'homme politique, l'assistant social, le maire, le militaire, le magistrat, le fonctionnaire, l'agent de police, etc.   6. professeur, chercheur, rédacteur, écrivain, traducteur et interprète.

QUESTIONS: (*Answers will vary.*)   1. Claude est avocat dans une grande société; il habite à Paris avec sa femme et ses deux enfants. Non, il n'est pas satisfait parce que le travail devient moins intéressant.   2. Il a l'intention de lancer une ferme biologique près de La Rochelle.

3. Je crois qu'il va réussir l'entreprise parce qu'il aime beaucoup l'idée et il connaît bien les affaires.   4. Oui, je veux changer de vie: je veux devenir romancier.

Chapter 9
Prendre and *boire*, the Partitive Article, and Object Pronouns

9.1   1. Je bois une grande tasse de thé.   2. Nous ne buvons pas d'alcool au déjeuner.
3. Que prends-tu au goûter de quatre heures?   4. Comprenez-vous ce qu'elle veut dire?
5. Quand on est en retard on prend le métro.   6. Ils boivent beaucoup d'eau en été.
7. Nous prenons à droite après l'église?   8. J'apprends à jouer du banjo.

9.2   1. Nous prenons/On prend un verre au café?   2. Je comprends ce qu'il
dit.   3. Alex prend le bus aujourd'hui.   4. Tu apprends à faire de la bicyclette/du
vélo.   5. Gabrielle ne boit-elle pas trop de café?   6. Les étudiants ne surprennent pas le
professeur.   7. Je bois une tasse de consommé avant le dîner.   8. Prenez-vous à gauche
au prochain carrefour?

9.3   1. du; la, le   2. des, du, du, des, du; du   3. le   4. du, du, des, du, de la
5. du, des   6. de la, du, les   7. des, des, de l'   8. du

9.4   1. une douzaine d'œufs   2. trop de café   3. un kilo d'oranges   4. un litre
de lait   5. assez de légumes   6. un peu de moutarde   7. une bouteille de bière
8. beaucoup de poivre   9. Je ne veux pas de crème.   10. Nous avons besoin/On a besoin
d'huile d'olive et de beurre.   11. Je viens emprunter une tasse de sucre.   12. Combien de
petits pains veulent-elles?   13. Eugène ne prend pas de sel.   14. Elle ne doit pas boire
tant de vin.   15. Ils ne mangent ni chocolat ni beurre.

9.5   1. Oui, je t'écoute.   2. Non, je ne te regarde pas.   3. Oui, je te comprends.
4. Oui, je l'aime bien.   5. Non, je ne les appelle pas.   6. Oui, je l'invite demain.
7. Les voici/voilà!   8. Le voici/voilà!   9. La voici/voilà!   10. Nous voici/voilà!
11. Les voici/voilà!   12. Me voici/voilà!

9.6   1. m'attend   2. te connaît   3. vont nous aider   4. vont m'appeler   5. le
cherche, ne le trouve pas   6. l'aime   7. aller la voir   8. Les voyez-vous?   9. ne les
voyons pas   10. le quittes   11. l'appellent   12. vais l'appeler   13. la connaissons

9.7   1. Je lui téléphone.   2. Nous lui achetons des cadeaux.   3. Elles nous donnent
de l'argent.   4. Il leur écrit.   5. Chantal m'offre le dictionnaire.   6. M'envoies-tu une
lettre?   7. Édouard nous explique le problème.   8. Leur dites-vous bonjour?   9. Je
vais te parler plus tard.   10. Elle ne me répond pas.   11. Vas-tu m'apporter du fromage?
12. Nous ne leur montrons pas les réponses.   13. Camille lui prête de l'argent.

9.8   1. m'écrit   2. veux te vendre   3. nous envoient   4. me donne   5. peut leur
apprendre   6. vous demande   7. lui dites   8. devons lui répondre   9. Vas-tu leur
apporter   10. te répète   11. me demande souvent   12. nous achètes   13. Pouvez-
vous me prêter

9.9   1. J'y vais.   2. Nous y pensons.   3. Est-ce que tu vas y voyager?   4. Charlotte
y cherche des lampes.   5. Vous y retrouvez des copains.   6. Arielle n'a pas besoin d'y
aller.   7. Elles y réfléchissent.   8. Je n'y achète pas les provisions.   9. Tu y réussis

généralement?   10. On y sert de bons repas.   11. Y tenez-vous?   12. Les étudiants veulent y faire un stage.

9.10   1. Oui, nous allons/je vais en acheter.   2. Oui, il en a.   3. Oui, j'en bois. 4. Oui, ils en ont beaucoup.   5. Oui, elle en possède trois.   6. Oui, nous en avons/on en a assez.   7. Oui, on va en chercher une douzaine.   8. Oui, j'en ai besoin.   9. Oui, elle en prend deux.   10. Oui, on en utilise trop.   11. Oui, j'en ai un.   12. Non, ils n'en boivent pas.   13. Non, je n'en ai pas/nous n'en avons pas assez.   14. Non, il n'en achète pas.   15. Non, je n'en ai pas besoin.   16. Non, elle n'en prend pas.   17. Non, elles n'en mangent pas beaucoup.

9.11   1. Nous en achetons beaucoup.   2. Elle y met de la crème.   3. J'y vais bientôt. 4. À Noël, nous en offrons aux collègues.   5. À Noël, nous leur offrons des cadeaux. 6. Elles les lisent toujours.   7. Leur achètes-tu des bonbons?   8. Ne lui écris-tu pas?   9. Papa en mange trop.   10. J'y tiens fort.   11. Vous les appréciez.   12. La montrent-elles à Martine?   13. François ne lui remet pas les devoirs.   14. Ils y travaillent. 15. J'en cherche trois.   16. Nous voulons y passer du temps.   17. Marc ne la voit pas ce week-end.   18. Tu l'oublies encore?

9.12   (*Answers will vary*.)   1. le lion, le tigre, l'éléphant, la girafe, la gazelle, le loup, le singe, le gorille, etc.   2. le faucon, le perroquet, le hibou, le corbeau, le moineau, le colibris, etc. J'adore les perroquets et les faucons.   3. la grenouille, le crapaud, la tortue, le crocodile, etc.   4. la vache, la chèvre, le cheval, le mouton, les poules, les canards, le lapin, le chat, le chien, etc.   5. Pour moi, le jardin idéal est un vignoble. Je vais avoir beaucoup de vignes et je vais produire du bon vin.

QUESTIONS: (*Answers will vary*.)   1. Il est à Paris, sur la Rive Gauche.   2. Ils viennent principalement des collections royales au moment de la Révolution Française. On crée un parc pour le public.   3. On expose des mammifères, des oiseaux, des reptiles, des amphibiens et même des insectes.   4. Ils sont de petite taille, parce que le zoo n'est pas grand.   5. Il y a des visiteurs, et on mène aussi des études de comportement et de reproduction.   6. Les projets d'élevage des animaux menacés de disparition m'intéressent, parce que la disparition est un très grand problème.

Chapter 10
Possessives, Demonstratives, Comparatives, and Adverbs

10.1   1. ma   2. son   3. nos   4. leur   5. ton   6. vos   7. notre   8. mes 9. ses   10. tes

10.2   1. mes, mon   2. ses   3. leurs   4. nos   5. sa   6. ses   7. vos   8. ses

10.3   1. les tiens   2. la vôtre   3. le sien   4. au nôtre   5. aux siens   6. de la vôtre

10.4   1. ces   2. ce   3. ce   4. ce *or* ces   5. cet   6. cette   7. ces   8. cet

10.5   1. cet, —   2. Ce magazine-ci, cet article-là   3. ces chemises-ci, ces chemises-là 4. ce restaurant-ci, cette cafétéria-là   5. Ces dames, — (Ces dames-là)

10.6   1. J'aime lire les romans. Ceux que je préfère sont pleins d'aventures.   2. Les cours de Marc sont intéressants, surtout ceux dans la faculté d'histoire.   3. Quelle voiture veux-tu louer? Celle-ci ou celle-là?   4. Ce sont de bons ordinateurs. Ceux qui marchent bien ne sont pas très chers.   5. Voici plusieurs films. Celui que tu veux voir est disponible.   6. Les livres sont sur la table. Je lis celui-ci. Veux-tu celui-là?   7. J'ai besoin d'emprunter des notes. Celles d'Anne sont toujours faciles à lire.   8. Nous allons voir une pièce samedi. Celle que nous allons voir est une comédie.

10.7   1. aussi chère que   2. plus intéressant que   3. autant d'... que   4. plus petite que   5. plus passionnants que   6. plus heureuse/contente que   7. moins larges que   8. aussi intelligents que   9. plus vieille que   10. plus que   11. moins que   12. plus vieille/âgée que   13. plus épicée que   14. plus propre que   15. plus sympathiques que   16. autant d'... que   17. moins triste que   18. plus fatigués que   19. plus important que, plus importante   20. autant de ... que   21. moins de ... que   22. plus d'... que

10.8   1. le meilleur   2. le plus grand   3. plus grande que, le plus grand   4. la plus belle   5. les meilleurs   6. la plus jeune   7. le meilleur, la meilleure; le plus mauvais/le pire, la plus mauvaise/la pire   8. la moindre   9. le plus mauvais/le pire   10. le moins   11. le meilleur   12. le plus   13. le plus petit   14. le moins

10.9   1. amicalement   2. vraiment   3. faussement   4. gentiment   5. évidemment   6. vivement   7. franchement   8. différemment   9. brièvement   10. terriblement   11. lentement   12. intelligemment   13. cruellement   14. constamment   15. doucement

10.10   1. Il chante mal, mais je chante plus mal/moins bien.   2. Fait-elle la cuisine plus souvent que vous?   3. Dans le marathon, Sami court le plus lentement.   4. Joues-tu au violon mieux que moi?   5. J'écris bien, mais mon ami(e) écrit mieux.   6. Colette écrit le mieux.   7. Frédéric travaille plus vite que Jeanne.   8. Isabelle travaille le plus vite.   9. Paul arrive-t-il plus tôt que vous?   10. Claudine parle italien plus mal que moi; Émilie le parle le plus mal!   11. Elles chantent mieux que leurs frères.   12. Marcel danse plus mal que/moins bien que sa femme.

10.11   1. immédiatement/tout de suite   2. à gauche   3. plus mal que   4. moins   5. tout près   6. toujours, à l'arrière   7. loin   8. là-haut   9. de bonne heure/tôt   10. tout à l'heure   11. déjà   12. à l'intérieur (de)   13. en avant   14. dehors   15. parfois/quelquefois, très tard

10.12   1. mon oncle   2. mon cousin   3. mon beau-frère   4. mon filleul   5. ma petite-fille   6. ma belle-fille   7. ma marraine   8. mon neveu, ma nièce   9. ma femme, mon épouse   10. ma belle-mère

QUESTIONS: (*Answers will vary.*)   1. Les mariages diminuent; le couple est plus âgé au moment du mariage; on a moins d'enfants; beaucoup d'enfants naissent hors du mariage; il y a plus de divorces et de familles recomposées.   2. Le nombre d'unions libres augmente; les études sont prolongées; il est difficile de trouver un bon emploi.   3. L'union libre: habiter ensemble, partager la vie sans être mariés. La famille recomposée: la famille formée après le remariage de la mère ou du père des enfants.   4. Non, je vis dans une famille plus traditionnelle. Mais nous connaissons déjà plusieurs divorces et des remariages.   5. Dans ma famille, il y a ma femme, nos deux fils; ma belle-mère et mon beau-père. Ma femme et moi, nous avons chacun un frère avec sa famille.   6. Nous avons des nièces et des neveux, des cousins, deux tantes, et aussi le nouveau mari de ma nièce avec ses quatre enfants.

Chapter 11
Affirmatives Versus Negatives, Stressed Pronouns, and the Imperative

11.1   1. ne fait plus ses études/d'études   2. n'a plus d'examens à passer   3. ne dépense jamais son argent   4. n'est pas encore fatiguée à sept heures du soir 5. n'emprunte jamais d'argent   6. ne passe jamais le soir à regarder la télé   7. n'achète rien à la friperie   8. ne mange rien au bar

11.2   1. elle n'entend rien   2. je n'apprends rien dans ce cours/je n'y apprends rien 3. je n'invite personne ce soir   4. je ne regarde jamais les actualités/je ne les regarde jamais 5. elles n'ont pas beaucoup d'ennemis/elles n'en ont pas beaucoup   6. je ne suis pas encore libre de voyager   7. ils ne trouvent rien au marché aux puces/ils n'y trouvent rien   8. je ne sors jamais danser   9. nous n'allons plus à la plage chaque été/nous n'y allons plus chaque été   10. il n'y a personne au téléphone/il n'y a personne

11.3   1. jamais   2. Personne   3. Rien   4. jamais   5. jamais   6. personne 7. Personne   8. jamais

11.4   1. je n'ai peur de rien   2. il ne prépare rien de délicieux   3. personne n'arrive bientôt   4. je ne téléphone à personne   5. je ne lis rien d'original/nous ne lisons rien d'original   6. nous n'écrivons à personne   7. elle ne réfléchit à rien   8. je ne connais personne de drôle

11.5   (*Answers will vary.*)   1. Je ne suis que deux cours/Je n'en suis que deux 2. Aujourd'hui, je n'ai qu'une heure de libre/Je n'en ai qu'une   3. Je ne dors que cinq heures chaque nuit   4. Je n'ai que dix DVD/Je n'en ai que dix   5. Je n'achète que deux litres de lait chaque semaine/Je n'en achète que deux chaque semaine   6. Je n'ai que trois animaux domestiques: deux chats et un chien/Je n'en ai que trois: deux chats et un chien

11.6   1. Moi, je suis très occupé.   2. Alice, elle, est courageuse.   3. Léon, lui, est heureux.   4. Les étudiantes, elles, sont intelligentes.   5. Les voisins, eux, sont tranquilles. 6. André et nous, nous, sommes drôles.

11.7   1. moi; toi   2. Moi; toi   3. Nous; toi, lui   4. Moi; lui   5. nous

11.8   1. Nous travaillons plus dur qu'eux.   2. Est-ce que je suis plus riche que toi? 3. Il n'est pas plus grand que moi.   4. Êtes-vous plus heureuse qu'elle?   5. Je marche aussi vite qu'elles.   6. Elle écrit mieux que lui.   7. Elles ne chantent pas plus fort que moi.

11.9   1. à elle, à lui, à elles, à eux   2. C'est moi qui dois, Ce sont elles qui doivent, Ce sont eux qui doivent, C'est vous qui devez   3. elle le fait elle-même, nous le faisons nous-mêmes, tu le fais toi-même, vous le faites vous-mêmes, il le fait lui-même

11.10   1. Faites de l'exercice.   2. Buvez assez d'eau.   3. Essayez de rester calme. 4. Ne fumez pas.   5. Réfléchissez à la vie.   6. Soyez sociable(s).   7. Ne mangez pas trop de viande.   8. Ne prenez pas l'ascenseur.

11.11 1. Finis tes devoirs! 2. Ne mange pas de bonbons! 3. Mets tes lunettes quand tu lis! 4. Va au lit à dix heures! 5. Ne regarde pas la télé le soir! 6. Ne parle pas trop au téléphone! 7. Écris à ta grand-mère! 8. Ne perds pas ton parapluie!

11.12 1. N'en mangez pas! 2. Ne les rends pas! 3. Ne me passe pas le sel! 4. N'y réfléchissez pas! 5. Ne la finis pas! 6. Ne le répète pas! 7. N'y va pas! 8. N'en achète pas! 9. Ne lui donnez pas le cahier! 10. Ne leur dis pas bonjour!

11.13 1. Achètes-en! 2. Passez-leur les crayons! 3. Ne l'écoutez pas! 4. Bois-en! 5. Allez-y! 6. Range-la! 7. Ne le donnez pas à Georges! 8. Ne lui donnez pas le livre! 9. Faites-en! 10. Écris-lui!

11.14 (*Answers will vary.*) 1. Fais la vaisselle, s'il te plaît. 2. Travaille bien!/Finis ton travail./Ne travaille pas trop tard. 3. Ne conduis pas./Prends ton vélo./Viens au bureau à pied. 4. Laisse tomber les ciseaux!/Ne joue pas avec les ciseaux!/Mets les ciseaux sur la table, s'il te plaît. 5. Viens ici! Bois-en!/Donne à boire au chien, s'il te plaît. 6. Va chez le médecin./Appelle le médecin./Ne va pas au travail./Retourne au lit.

11.15 (*Answers will vary.*) 1. de la peinture, des pinceaux, des rouleaux, une échelle, des chiffons, du scotch, etc. 2. l'arrosoir, le tuyau, le râteau, la houe, la pelle, le sécateur, la tondeuse, la fourche, le déplantoir, la brouette, etc. 3. l'aspirateur, le balai, la tignasse, les chiffons, le carrelage, la vaisselle, l'évier, la lessive, le lavabo, le seau, le plumeau, la poubelle, l'éponge, etc.

QUESTIONS: (*Answers will vary.*) 1. En général, les Français qui ont une maison aiment bricoler. 2. La réparation, la décoration, la construction, la pose du carrelage ou d'une moquette, même l'électricité et la plomberie, sont toutes populaires. 3. Pour les professionnels, le bricolage offre la possibilité d'un travail manuel et il économise de l'argent. Mais ça prend beaucoup de temps et parfois les résultats ne sont pas bons. 4. Ils veulent oublier leur travail au bureau, et ils pensent à leur budget. En plus, ils sont fiers de leur maison. 5. Oui, le bricolage m'intéresse: j'aime peindre les murs et je fais du jardinage. 6. Je le fais pour la satisfaction et pour apprendre quelque chose de nouveau.

Chapter 12
Reflexive Pronouns with Pronominal Verbs and the Present Participle

12.1 1. Je me réveille tard le week-end. 2. Ma sœur se regarde longtemps dans la glace. 3. Nous nous levons de bonne heure lundi matin. 4. André et Paul s'habillent en jean. 5. Maman se maquille rapidement. 6. Papa se rase tous les jours. 7. Je m'ennuie dans le bus. 8. Les enfants s'amusent après les cours.

12.2 1. Je me douche à sept heures (du matin). 2. Ma sœur se maquille. 3. Nous nous couchons assez tard. 4. Vous vous préparez rapidement/vite. 5. Elles se réveillent à l'aube. 6. Ils se réveillent quand Maman les appelle. 7. Tu te promènes le soir.

12.3 1. me brosse 2. se raser 3. se lavent 4. nous levons 5. t'entraînes 6. s'installer

12.4 1. Vous levez-vous à huit heures? Non, nous ne nous levons pas à huit heures. 2. T'entraînes-tu tôt le matin? Non, le matin je ne m'entraîne pas tôt. 3. Margot se réveille-t-elle difficilement? Non, Margot/elle ne se réveille pas difficilement.   4. S'habillent-elles bien? Non, elles ne s'habillent pas bien.   5. T'endors-tu devant la télé? Non, je ne m'endors pas devant la télé.

12.5   1. Ne vous levez pas.   2. Réveillez-vous!   3. Brossez-vous les dents.   4. Ne vous installez pas ici.   5. Couche-toi./Va au lit.   6. Habille-toi.   7. Ne te baigne pas maintenant.   8. Amuse-toi!

12.6   (*Answers will vary.*)   1. Réveille-toi!/Lève-toi!/Ne te couche pas si tard!/Va au lit plus tôt!   2. Ne vous endormez pas!/Ne vous couchez pas!/N'allez pas au lit!/Prenez du café!/Étudiez bien!   3. Lave-toi les mains!/Va te laver les mains!/Ne touche pas aux rideaux! 4. Ne te maquille pas!/Ne mets pas tant de maquillage!/Lave-toi le visage!/Arrête de te maquiller!   5. Ne t'habille pas encore./Ne te prépare pas encore./Mets tes vieux vêtements. 6. Repose-toi pendant le week-end./N'oublie pas de te reposer./Couche-toi tôt./Ne te couche pas tard pendant le week-end./Ne travaille pas trop.

12.7   (*Answers will vary.*)   1. Je me brosse les dents le matin et le soir.   2. Il faut se laver les mains très souvent (dix fois par jour) si on a un rhume.   3. Oui, je me lave les cheveux tous les jours parce que j'ai les cheveux courts.   4. Non, les petits enfants ne se peignent pas les cheveux eux-mêmes.

12.8   1. nous connaissons   2. nous voyons, nous parlons   3. nous retrouvons 4. s'écrivent   5. s'entendent   6. se retrouvent/se voient/se revoient   7. se disputent 8. s'aiment/s'entend

12.9   (*Answers will vary.*)   1. Mes amis et moi, nous nous retrouvons/on se retrouve au café ou au cinéma le week-end.   2. Dans ma famille, nous nous écrivons/on s'écrit parfois, mais nous préférons nous téléphoner/on préfère se téléphoner.   3. Oui, nous nous voyons/on se voit assez souvent et nous nous donnons/on se donne toujours rendez-vous.   4. Oui, mes collègues/mes camarades/ils s'entendent généralement très bien.   5. Oui, nous nous disons (on se dit) bonjour presque toujours et nous nous serrons (on se serre) la main. Nous nous parlons (On se parle) de tout: de la famille, du travail, des vacances.

12.10   1. Je m'habitue à cette ville.   2. Nous nous dépêchons d'y arriver à l'heure. 3. Mathilde se marie avec lui.   4. Elle s'occupe de moi.   5. Vous rendez-vous compte qu'il neige?   6. Je me fie à mon professeur.   7. Nous nous souvenons de/Nous nous rappelons notre ancienne école.   8. Michel s'entend bien avec Charles.   9. Laure ne s'intéresse pas au football.   10. Ils ne se trompent pas souvent d'adresse.   11. Les enfants se mettent à jouer.   12. Tu ne peux pas te passer de ton ordinateur, n'est-ce pas?

12.11   1. je me souviens de/je me rappelle   2. se passe, de   3. te dépêcher   4. vous mettez à   5. te rends compte   6. nous fions à

12.12   1. Nous nous arrêtons de travailler à six heures.   2. Elle arrête la voiture devant ma maison.   3. Vas-tu promener les chiens?   4. Nous allons nous promener.   5. Il nous ennuie.   6. Je m'ennuie parfois en classe.   7. Ne te fâche pas!   8. Cette idée-là me fâche.

12.13   1. Le français se parle au Québec.   2. Les skis se vendent en automne. 3. Beaucoup de fromage se mange en France.   4. Le jogging se fait rarement sous la pluie. 5. Les nouveaux mots s'apprennent facilement.   6. Les boissons froides ne se boivent pas avec la fondue.

12.14 1. en se brossant les dents   2. en prenant sa douche   3. en conduisant la voiture
4. en montant l'escalier   5. en s'installant au travail   6. en faisant du jogging   7. en
mangeant   8. en s'endormant   9. en prononçant le français   10. en buvant son café

12.15 (*Answers will vary.*)   1. J'apprends/Nous apprenons/On apprend les verbes
français en les répétant/en les écrivant/en les lisant/en faisant les exercices.   2. J'écoute la
radio en me préparant/en faisant le ménage/en conduisant.   3. Je m'amuse en lisant/en me
promenant/en regardant un film/en discutant avec mes amis.   4. Je m'ennuie en faisant le
ménage/en écoutant une conférence ennuyeuse/en faisant la queue à la poste.   5. Je passe
de bonnes vacances en voyageant/en faisant du sport/en faisant du bricolage/en me promenant.
6. On fait la connaissance d'un nouveau pays en y voyageant/en parlant avec ses habitants/en
mangeant sa cuisine/en lisant son histoire/en apprenant sa langue.

12.16 (*Answers will vary.*)   1. J'ai/Nous avons mal au dos/au bras/au cou/aux épaules.
2. Il a mal aux dents.   3. Elle a mal aux jambes/aux pieds/à la cheville/au dos/aux genoux/aux
épaules.   4. J'ai/Nous avons mal à la tête/aux oreilles/au nez/aux yeux/aux joues.   5. Il a
mal au cou/à la gorge.   6. J'ai/Nous avons mal aux yeux.   7. Il a mal à l'estomac/au ventre.
8. Elle a mal à la gorge/à la tête.   9. Elle a mal aux pieds/aux orteils/au talon/à la cheville.
10. J'ai mal aux doigts/aux mains/aux bras/aux coudes/aux épaules.

QUESTIONS: (*Answers will vary.*)   1. C'est un ancien pouvoir colonial; elle a une situation
géographique centrale; son taux de naissance est faible.   2. On obtient la nationalité
française en étant né en France, par naturalisation, par filiation ou par mariage.   3. Les
immigrés viennent du Maghreb, d'Afrique sub-saharienne (des anciennes colonies), d'Europe
et d'Asie.   4. Le chômage, l'éducation, les difficultés économiques, les ghettos urbains, la
xénophobie et le racisme sont tous des problèmes.   5. Oui, je viens d'une famille d'immigrés
d'Europe de l'est. Nous sommes ici depuis deux générations. Nous ne parlons plus le russe ni
l'allemand.   6. J'aime mon pays, mais je veux vivre à l'étranger pendant quelque temps, en
France peut-être.

Chapter 13
Forms and Uses of the *passé composé*

13.1 1. nous avons écouté   2. tu as réfléchi   3. on a attendu   4. vous avez choisi
5. elles ont parlé   6. nous avons commencé   7. ils ont entendu   8. tu as acheté
9. nous avons mangé   10. j'ai envoyé

13.2 1. J'ai fini/terminé mon travail.   2. Nous avons/On a dîné à huit heures.   3. Elle
a perdu ses clés.   4. Mon frère a attendu au café.   5. Elles ont choisi leurs cours.
6. Vous avez commencé à courir.   7. J'ai acheté un gâteau.   8. Tu as vendu la voiture.

13.3 1. Nous avons fait le ménage.   2. Isabelle a écrit une lettre.   3. Ils ont appris
la nouvelle.   4. J'ai suivi trois cours.   5. Tu as bu un thé.   6. J'ai mis une cravate.
7. Vous avez offert un cadeau.   8. On a été en Afrique.

13.4 1. ont dormi   2. as obtenu   3. a ri/a souri   4. avez pris   5. J'ai servi
6. avons vécu   7. j'ai dû   8. ont poursuivi

13.5 (*Answers will vary.*)   1. As-tu lu un roman de Balzac? Non, je n'ai pas lu de roman./
Non, je n'en ai pas lu.   2. Avez-vous/As-tu vu vos/tes amis samedi soir? Non, je n'ai pas vu

mes amis./Non, je ne les ai pas vus.   3. Émilie a-t-elle conduit un petit camion? Non, elle n'a pas conduit de camion./Non, elle n'en a pas conduit.   4. Avez-vous/As-tu fait la lessive? Non, je n'ai pas/nous n'avons pas fait la lessive./je ne l'ai pas faite./nous ne l'avons pas faite.
5. Les étudiants ont-ils des devoirs à faire? Non, ils n'ont pas de devoirs./Non, ils n'en ont pas.
6. Avez-vous mis des chaussures de marche? Non, je n'ai pas mis de chaussures de marche./nous n'avons pas mis de chaussures de marche./Non, je n'en ai pas mis./nous n'en avons pas mis.   7. Ont-ils vécu trois ans à Lyon? Non, ils n'ont pas vécu trois ans à Lyon./Non, ils n'y ont pas vécu trois ans.

13.6   1. D'abord, vous avez déjeuné.   2. Puis/Ensuite, nous avons fait/on a fait la vaisselle.   3. Finalement/Enfin, j'ai quitté la maison.   4. L'année passée tu as suivi un cours d'italien.   5. Avez-vous déjà été en France?   6. Il a beaucoup mangé au petit déjeuner.   7. Hier soir, elle a vu un beau coucher de soleil.   8. J'ai toujours aimé la cuisine française.

13.7   1. Il y a trois jours je suis sortie avec Sylvain.   2. Il y a une semaine tu es allé au théâtre.   3. Il y a six mois nous sommes parties en France.   4. Il y a quelques jours ils sont rentrés chez eux.   5. Il y a une heure nous sommes descendus faire le marché.   6. Il y a un instant le vase est tombé dans l'escalier.

13.8   1. sont allées/parties/rentrées/retournées   2. est descendue/sortie   3. est allée/rentrée/retournée   4. sont tombées   5. Je suis sorti/descendu   6. sont arrivés/venus
7. sommes montés   8. sommes partis   9. est, allée   10. est restée   11. sommes arrivés

13.9   1. Je les ai vus hier.   2. Catherine lui a écrit.   3. Nous en avons bu.   4. Laure et Sami/Ils y sont allés.   5. Tu en as acheté?   6. Les avez-vous reçues?   7. Ils l'ont faite.   8. Je l'ai mise.

13.10   1. Nous nous sommes vues hier.   2. Mireille et Claude/Ils se sont écrit.   3. Je me suis réveillé à midi.   4. Mes filles/Elles se sont brossé les cheveux.   5. À quelle heure (les enfants) se sont-ils endormis?   6. T'es-tu occupée de la lessive?   7. Je me suis trompée d'adresse.   8. Ils se sont connus/fait connaissance il y a un an.

13.11   (*Answers will vary.*)   1. J'aime regarder le football et le patinage.   2. J'ai fait du basket, de la natation, du patinage et du tennis.   3. En été, j'aime les randonnées, le jardinage et l'observation des oiseaux. En hiver, je préfère la lecture, les concerts, les DVD et les pièces de théâtre. Je fais aussi un peu de bricolage.   4. C'est parce que je ne suis pas très sportive!   5. Je suis allée à une pièce et aussi un concert (où j'ai travaillé comme ouvreuse [*usher*]). J'ai fait le marché et aussi une longue promenade.   6. Je veux apprendre à faire de la couture et du yoga.

QUESTIONS: (*Answers will vary.*)   1. Elle s'intéresse à la danse africaine depuis plusieurs années.   2. Ce soir-là, à son arrivée, elle est tombée amoureuse du joueur de djembé et elle est tombée par terre en réalité.   3. La danseuse et le joueur de djembé se sont parlé; ils sont sortis prendre un café; ils ont discuté pendant des heures. Ils se sont revus le jour suivant.
4. Il y a quelques années, j'ai vu un canard mère et cinq ou six petits dans une rue en ville. Je les ai suivis jusqu'à un petit fleuve.

Chapter 14

The *imparfait*, Past Narration, and More About Object Pronouns

14.1   1. avons décidé   2. a préparé   3. n'a rien oublié, a, mis   4. avons quitté, sommes partis   5. nous sommes mis à, a dit   6. sommes arrivés, nous sommes arrêtés   7. J'ai pris, nous y sommes installés   8. j'ai fait, a fini

14.2   1. vous vous amusiez à la disco   2. tu t'endormais   3. Michaël faisait de beaux rêves   4. je commençais à lire   5. Papa prenait un bain   6. les chats se disputaient   7. nous étions à la cuisine   8. Suzanne et sa sœur mangeaient

14.3   1. avais   2. j'allais   3. avait   4. nous réunissions   5. discutions   6. étaient   7. travaillaient   8. nous mettions   9. fallait   10. s'occupait   11. nous parlions   12. était

14.4   (*Answers will vary.*)   1. Je me levais, je prenais le petit déjeuner et j'allais à l'école. Je travaillais l'après-midi à la pharmacie, et je faisais mes devoirs.   2. J'habitais à Los Angeles que j'aimais beaucoup, parce que j'avais beaucoup d'amis et il y avait un tas de choses à faire.   3. En été, il faisait beau et chaud. Je ne suivais pas de cours. Donc, avec mes amis, nous allions à la plage ou nous faisions du sport.

14.5   (*Answers will vary.*)   1. Quand je suis arrivée à Paris, il faisait beau.   2. Nous nous reposions quand Éric a appelé/a téléphoné.   3. Il quittait la maison quand il s'est souvenu des livres/s'est rappelé les livres.   4. Je portais toujours mon imperméable, quand soudain/tout à coup la pluie s'est arrêtée/a cessé.   5. Elle ne se sentait pas bien hier soir, mais elle est sortie quand même.   6. Hier, tu as trouvé le café où on servait cette bonne soupe.

14.6   (*Answers will vary.*)   1. il faisait mauvais et il pleuvait, mais j'ai dû aller au travail   2. nous sommes restés à la maison/nous ne sommes pas allés au concert   3. le café était fermé. Donc, nous sommes allés/on est allé(s) au cinéma.   4. cinq ans, nous nous sommes parlé en classe   5. écrire une lettre, je me suis entraînée.   6. J'allais ranger les placards et mon bureau, mais je ne l'ai pas fait.

14.7   1. Je la lui donne.   2. Tu m'en offres dix.   3. Nous leur en parlions.   4. Mathieu ne les y a pas retrouvés.   5. Je me les suis brossées.

14.8   1. Donne-les-moi./Donnez-les-moi.   2. Offre-lui-en./Offrez-lui-en.   3. N'en mange pas./N'en mangez pas.   4. Ne la lui vends pas./Ne la lui vendez pas.   5. Vas-y./Allez-y.

14.9   (*These are all personal answers. No suggestions are included here.*)

QUESTIONS: (*Answers will vary.*)   1. Elle avait une vie difficile; sa mère était veuve.   2. À quatorze ans, elle a pu faire un voyage au Maroc avec sa classe.   3. Les paysages, le désert, les villages berbères et les gens l'ont impressionnée beaucoup.   4. Moi, à cet âge-là, j'ai fait du camping dans le désert près de Los Angeles. C'était formidable!

Chapter 15
The Future Tense, the Conditional, and Indefinite Adjectives and Pronouns

15.1   1. Renée partira.   2. Olivier achètera ses billets.   3. nous prendrons le train.
4. mon amie viendra me voir.   5. vous serez déjà à Boston.   6. il faudra remettre ce
devoir.   7. ils auront besoin de faire le marché.   8. tu pourras me prêter la voiture.

15.2   1. Si je pars, me suivras-tu?   2. Elle viendra, si nous l'invitons.   3. Aussitôt
qu'il/Dès qu'il commencera à neiger, nous rentrerons.   4. Lorsque/Quand j'arriverai chez
toi, je t'attendrai.   5. Si j'ai l'argent, j'irai à Québec cet été.   6. Il nous appellera dès qu'il/
aussitôt qu'il y arrivera.

15.3   (*Answers will vary.*)   1. Je ferai des courses le week-end prochain; je ferai du canoë
cet été.   2. Si je ne travaille pas demain, je dormirai tard.   3. Je serai à l'université de
Montréal.

15.4   1. J'aimerais sortir.   2. Ils voudraient voyager.   3. Mathieu irait en Europe si
possible.   4. Nous viendrions volontiers.   5. Je prendrais deux verres d'eau.   6. Elles
seraient heureuses de nous accompagner.   7. Ferais-tu aussi ce voyage?   8. Est-ce que
vous reverriez ce film avec nous?

15.5   1. Si j'étais libre, je serais avec toi.   2. Nous savions qu'Armand viendrait.
3. S'il venait à la fête, elle serait heureuse.   4. Si tu avais assez d'argent, voyagerais-tu?
5. Tu devrais faire de l'exercice.   6. Si vous le vouliez, je l'achèterais.   7. Nous voudrions/
aimerions commander trois tasses de café.   8. Léon nous a dit qu'il ferait les courses.

15.6   (*Answers will vary.*)   1. Si j'étais libre, j'irais en ville.   2. S'ils venaient me
voir, nous irions à la montagne.   3. Si j'avais assez d'argent, j'en offrirais aux associations
combattant la faim.

15.7   1. Marc s'était couché   2. la voisine avait rendu visite   3. les enfants s'étaient
baignés/avaient pris un bain   4. les chiens s'étaient endormis   5. on avait servi le
dîner   6. Simone était partie pour l'aéroport   7. nous avions tous les deux travaillé tard
8. personne n'avait fait la vaisselle

15.8   1. j'aurais été à l'heure   2. j'aurais vu le film   3. nous serions rentrés plus
tôt   4. tu n'aurais pas perdu les clés   5. les enfants se seraient couchés   6. Cathy aurait
terminé/fini ses devoirs   7. la voisine nous aurait trouvés   8. nous ne serions pas levés si
tard aujourd'hui

15.9   (*Answers will vary.*)   1. Tu aurais dû terminer/finir plus tôt/Tu aurais dû. dormir
plus cette nuit/Tu n'aurais jamais dû accepter de le faire.   2. Tu aurais dû te reposer un peu/
Tu n'aurais pas dû courir dans le marathon.   3. Vous devriez manger mieux/Vous n'auriez
pas dû prendre de bonbons.   4. J'aurais dû apprendre le français plus jeune/Je n'aurais pas
dû m'installer à Miami.

15.10   1. J'ai vu tout le musée.   2. J'ai visité toute la collection d'amphores.   3. J'ai
marchandé avec tous les vendeurs.   4. J'ai parcouru toute la vieille ville.   5. J'ai acheté
tous les tapis.   6. J'ai fait le tour de toutes les mosquées.

15.11 1. Quelques amis/Les mêmes amis/Tous ses amis ont appelé. Chaque ami a appelé.
2. Tous/Plusieurs voulaient emprunter de l'argent. Chacun voulait emprunter de l'argent.
3. Quelqu'un/Chacun vous a invité. Les mêmes/Quelques-unes/Plusieurs vous ont invité.

15.12 (*Answers will vary.*)   1. le distributeur, la carte de paiement, le bureau de change, changer de l'argent, retirer de l'argent, des billets de 20€, etc.   2. ouvrir un compte en banque, demander une carte de crédit, payer un dépôt de garantie, payer les factures, etc.
3. J'ai parlé avec la caissière parce que j'ai versé de l'argent dans mon compte et j'ai fait un transfert de fonds.

QUESTIONS: (*Answers will vary.*)   1. Cette attitude est logique pour un Français. Cela ne s'accorde pas avec l'attitude dans mon pays.   2. Ici, c'est souvent pour l'argent qu'on doit travailler; la sécurité sociale n'est pas aussi évoluée qu'en France.   3. Bien sûr, si on n'a rien ou si on n'a que très peu, on s'inquiète beaucoup au sujet de l'argent.   4. Dans dix ans, mes études seront terminées, je travaillerai probablement comme professeur de lycée et je serais à La Nouvelle-Orléans.

Chapter 16
The Subjunctive

16.1 1. que nous choisissions   2. que vous achetiez   3. que tu dormes
4. que je parle   5. qu'ils finissent   6. qu'elle vende   7. que nous entendions
8. que vous partiez

16.2 1. sois   2. fasse   3. allions   4. restiez   5. fasse   6. soyons
7. veuille   8. aient   9. saches   10. puissiez

16.3 (*Answers will vary.*)   1. Il faut que tu connaisses les amis de ta sœur et que tu trouves une association intéressante.   2. Il est essentiel que tu ailles en France ou au Québec.   3. Il est important que tu te reposes un peu plus.   4. Il faut qu'on se repose, qu'on prenne l'air un peu et qu'on finisse de faire le ménage.

16.4 (*Answers will vary.*)   1. Il est dommage que tu ne fasses pas de ton mieux.   2. Il est bon que tu saches t'avancer.   3. Il est douteux que tu puisses avoir un bon salaire.
4. Il se peut que tu t'ennuies.   5. Il est bizarre que tu n'ailles pas dans une autre ville.
6. Il est utile que tu choisisses bien ta carrière.

16.5 (*Answers will vary.*)   1. Il n'est pas vrai que je devienne célèbre.   2. Il n'est pas certain que nous puissions retourner dans la lune.   3. Il n'est pas sûr que les artistes soient appréciés.   4. Il est peu probable que les gens cessent d'avoir des enfants.   5. Il est certain que je ferai une découverte importante!   6. Il est probable que mon copain écrira un best-seller.

16.6 1. Je doute qu'on sache quoi faire.   2. Nous préférons nous mettre d'accord.
3. Les profs exigent que nous apprenions.   4. Nous avons peur que le train soit en retard.
5. Mon père regrette de quitter son emploi.   6. Elle espère voyager en été.   7. Vous n'êtes pas sûrs que je réussisse.   8. Le patron veut que tu reviennes.

16.7   (*Answers will vary.*)   1. que ma famille vive loin de chez moi   2. que je lui rende bientôt visite   3. le gouvernement déclare la guerre   4. les mêmes personnes soient élues   5. nous puissions nous voir samedi

16.8   (*Answers will vary.*)   1. J'étudie le français pour pouvoir travailler en Afrique. 2. Je vais déménager à condition de trouver un nouvel appartement.   3. Je ne changerai pas d'emploi à moins d'en trouver un autre.   4. Je ne partirai pas en voyage avant d'économiser assez d'argent.   5. Je ne peux pas travailler la nuit sans pouvoir dormir pendant la journée.

16.9   (*Answers will vary.*)   1. Comment vous appelez-vous? Où habitez-vous? Pourquoi êtes-vous venu(e) ici? etc.   2. Je suis désolé(e), mais je suis pris(e) ce soir-là. Pourrons-nous nous revoir bientôt?   3. Il faut que tu t'approches des gens, que tu leur dises bonjour, que tu leur poses des questions sur leur vie, enfin, que tu aies l'air de t'intéresser à eux.

QUESTIONS: (*Answers will vary.*)   1. Il dit qu'on a oublié comment créer des liens avec les autres. C'est à cause de la vie moderne, Internet, etc.   2. Oui, je suis d'accord parce que je sais que je sors moins et je téléphone moins aux personnes que je connais.   3. La solution est de sortir, de faire partie des associations, de suivre des cours, de prendre rendez-vous avec de nouvelles personnes et surtout de parler avec elles.   4. (personal answer)

Index

Put Your French Language into Practice!

At busuu, you can practice your French skills through graded courses and a broad range of engaging activities. And as you study, busuu encourages direct interaction with native speakers through video and audio chat.

With busuu, you can:

- Practice with exercises that hone all four skills (reading, writing, speaking, listening).
- Enjoy flexible language learning—anytime, anywhere—to fit into your busy schedule.
- Receive personalized feedback on your exercises, talk with native speakers via an integrated chat, and get to know people from all over the world.

With over 55 million registered users, busuu is the largest social network for language learning in the world!

Special Offer: 30% off Premium membership

McGraw-Hill Education has partnered with busuu to provide an exclusive discount on busuu's award-winning Premium service.

Discount: 30% off any plan
Access code: BUSUUFRE30
Code expiry date: June 30, 2018

Or Try A New Language!

busuu offers courses in eleven other languages, specially designed by educational experts. With programs ranging from Beginning to Upper Intermediate, you'll quickly find the level that works for you!

Sign up or log in on **www.busuu.com** and enter your discount code on the payment page to get your exclusive discount!